# NICHOLSON

# NICHOLSON

## HOW AN ANGRY IRISHMAN BECAME THE HERO OF DELHI

## DONAL P. McCRACKEN

The
History
Press
Ireland

This book is dedicated to my brother
Dermot McCracken

First published 2018

The History Press
The Mill, Brimscombe Port
Stroud, Gloucestershire, GL5 2QG
www.thehistorypress.co.uk

British Library Cataloguing in Publication Data.
A catalogue record for this book is available from the British Library.

ISBN ISBN 978 0 7509 8810 0

Typesetting and origination by The History Press
Printed and bound in Great Britain by TJ International Ltd

# Contents

# Acknowledgements

In writing this biography, I am grateful to the following people: Sean Barden, David Blake, Peter Chantler, Ben Fellows, Elaine Flanigan, Emeritus Professor Tadhg Foley, William Forgrave, Pam Hamilton, Roger Hamilton, Dr Csaba Lévai, Brian Mackey, Tony McClenaghan, Patricia McCracken, Sean McCracken, Roy Reed, Timothy Smyth, Roberta Thompson, Nicki von der Heyde and Carol Weichman. My thanks also go to Jeffery Bates of Bates and Hindmarch, who provided me with several important documents and original illustrations. And to my publisher, Ronan Colgan, special thanks for his work.

Any biographer of Nicholson should be grateful to Evelyn Werge Thomas (1891–1975) for ensuring the Nicholson papers and her own notes on Nicholson are available to the public in the British Library.

I should like to thank the staff of the following institutions for their help in researching this subject: the Armagh County Museum; the British Library and especially the Asian and African Studies section; the Irish Linen Centre and Linen Museum, Lisburn; the Moravian Settlement in Gracehill, County Antrim; The National Archives at Kew, London; the National Army Museum at Chelsea, London; the National Library of Ireland; the Public Record Office of Northern Ireland; the Representative Church Body Library, Dublin; and the Waterford Museum, Ireland.

This work is in part based upon research sponsored by the National Research Foundation of South Africa and the University of KwaZulu-Natal. Any opinion, findings and conclusions or recommendations expressed in this material are those of the author and therefore the National Research Foundation does not accept any liability in respect thereto.

# Preface

You may rely upon this – that if ever there is a desperate deed to be done in India, John Nicholson is the man to do it.

(Herbert Edwardes to Viceroy Lord Canning, 1857)

Let us never forget the intrepid Nicholson.

(Benjamin Disraeli, House of Commons, 3 December 1857)

Nicholson was an army in himself.

(Unknown source quoted in Kaye, *Lives of Indian Officers*, 1867)

Nothing more redounds to the credit of John Lawrence than the way in which he kept his temper with the fiery Nicholson, who was constitutionally ill-fitted to serve under a leader.

(Forrest, *Field Marshal Sir Neville Chamberlain*, 1909)

You could hear the ring of his horse's hoofs from Attock to the Khaibar.

(Unknown, Punjab, late 1850s)

This great imperial psychopath.

(William Dalrymple, *The Last Mughal*, 2006)

## HERO OR VILLAIN?

These quotations say much about the awe and ultimately the anger that the name of John Nicholson evoked. Born in Dublin, he was sent out to India as a boy soldier at the age of 16. He was involved in the first Anglo-Afghan war, the two Anglo-Sikh wars and the Great Rebellion or Mutiny, dying in the thick of battle as the British army he was leading stormed into the ancient city of Delhi in September 1857. This is a young man's story: he was only 34 years of age when he died.

Nicholson's tale is undoubtedly an epic, even when the more fanciful stories of his life are discarded. In stature, he was at least 6ft 2in (1.9m) tall, with broad shoulders, a great beard and a deep Anglo-Irish accent. Holding his head high as he walked gave the impression of aloofness, a characteristic reinforced in many people's minds by his reserve, which in turn was the product of shyness but also of a distrust of strangers. His manner tended to be unsocial, one of dark foreboding, and there was a certainty and forcefulness about him that brooked no opposition. He gave the impression of one whose destiny was set. As a soldier, he was a terrifying and impressive figure on his grey charger. In the three set-piece battles that he fought as commander, though, he ended up fighting on foot among his troops. He led his men from the front, fighting with a long curved sword and showing neither fear nor mercy on the battlefield. He was described by one contemporary as 'the bravest of the brave'.

There is an interesting and telling passage in Sieveking's partial biography of Nicholson that is worth quoting:

> For most men have their weak times – times when they break away from their moorings … Yes, but there comes sooner or later a turn in the tide, a time when the wind drops and the sails flap idly, and the buoyancy of swinging freely before the wind of a brilliant wit, on the tide of a wonderful charm of personality, is exchanged for a sudden stagnation when conditions alter, and then – *then* it is that the value of an absolute unchanging strength and consistency of character is felt most absolutely. John Nicholson was like a rock against which tides had no effect. He was not perhaps always popular among his brother officers; he was too taciturn, quiet and reserved. He was not a brilliant talker, he was not a brilliant writer. But he was a strong *doer*, and that fact saved India to us in the fifty-years-ago time when we so nearly lost her.[1]

The problem with such a controversial figure as Nicholson is that often the fundamental point about the person is lost. He was probably the finest front-line battlefield commander in the Victorian British empire. Time and time again, Nicholson cleared the field of the enemy. Even one of his sternest modern critics has observed that Nicholson, 'would later go on to change the course of Indian history'.[2]

Nicholson was a lonely and a shy man, a limited man in some respects. But he was aware of those limitations, especially relating to his temper. That he was possibly homosexual or, more likely, a repressed homosexual, served only to torment his Victorian Christian soul. However, the one thing Nicholson was not, in the modern sense, was a racist. The ebullient Reginald Wilberforce, writing in the early 1890s, asserted that Nicholson 'hated Sepoys' but then goes on to say how after the engagements at Trimmu Ghat, the brigadier general had erected a memorial to the insurgent gunners who had died at their post as well as adding a footnote with the equally sweeping statement, 'Nicholson loved his Mooltanees, Pathans, and Afreedis'.[3]

Nicholson's negative perceived attitude towards Indians does not stand up to scrutiny. He certainly considered himself to be of a superior culture, yet that inner prejudice is contradicted by the relationship he had with his Indian troops and officials. One gets the distinct impression that, apart from a handful of close friends, Nicholson preferred the company of Indians to Europeans. It is not difficult to conclude that the 'wild hillmen' of the North-West Frontier, with their set views and staunch loyalties, struck a chord with someone who had spent some years of his youth in the heartland of Protestant Ulster.

Nicholson, like many of his contemporaries, learnt several Indian languages and spoke to the locals in their own tongue. There is overwhelming evidence that Nicholson cared for his Indian troops and went to extremes to see to their welfare. Indeed, by July 1857 he was permanently accompanied by a large cohort of irregular soldiers from the hill tribes. Of course, famously, there was also a religious sect, albeit small, who worshipped him, much to his irritation. In a short but telling postscript to a letter scribbled in the field while on campaign, Nicholson urges one of his field officers to make sure that the men get a good biryani at government expense.

Nicholson's occasional comments about getting out of India for good have a hollow ring to them and, in any case, were not followed by action. This was the timeless chatter of the exile. Equally, there is also no evidence that Nicholson was a jingoistic imperialist. He certainly believed Britain to be top dog, but who in Britain then did not? Nicholson had no difficulty in considering joining the Turkish Ottoman army, and equally, in the right circumstances, he would have willingly led a division for the Persian army.

If Nicholson was often unpopular with his fellow officers, the rank and file felt otherwise and at the time considered him to be great. When he marched his military column into the British camp outside Delhi in August 1857, his reputation was second to none, inspiring hope and confidence among the army on the ridge as they faced a seemingly impossible situation.

It is often forgotten that Nicholson was an effective, if stern, colonial administrator. Ironically, the latter gave him the freedom he needed to be a good soldier, independent and unfettered by regimental ties and obstructions. For Nicholson was a frontier's man, with all that implies about being betwixt cultures; beyond the mores and laws of established society; and a figure of depth and mystery, echoing the terrain and uncertainties of those regions where British India stopped.

As early as 1980, a scholarly book of documents relating to the Graham family and the Indian Mutiny criticised Nicholson.[4] But it was not until the 2000s that Nicholson has become the target of severe attack by several authors. In his book on the fall of Delhi, William Dalrymple talks of 'this great imperial psychopath', and uses a range of words describing Nicholson, from brutality, cruelty and merciless, to taciturn and piety.[5] So it is that heroes become villains. And it cannot be denied that Nicholson's approach and methods of dealing with rebellion shocked even some contemporaries. The case against Brigadier General John Nicholson is that he showed no or little mercy on his enemy. That perception is correct. But it is not the whole story.

Nicholson's reputation for being brutal is interwoven with his undoubted bad temper, which was in part the product of temperament but probably as much the results of the poisonous cocktail of medicines he was prescribed. It might seem incongruous to compare General John Nicholson with President Abraham Lincoln of the United States, and yet they had two things in common – their behavioural patterns and the medicine they took. Both Lincoln and Nicholson were prescribed the nineteenth-century cure-all 'blue pill'. This was a bizarre concoction of liquorice, marshmallow, honey and mercury, the mercury constituting a third of the dose. The result for both men was erratic behavioural patterns and a tendency to violent outbursts. Things were not helped by the fact that for constant liver pains in the 1850s Nicholson also took doses of what is today the modern domestic and industrial solvent hydrochloric acid.

To this literally poisonous cocktail needs to be added the fact that Nicholson was psychologically damaged by a difficult childhood in a gloomy puritan household, having lost his father at the age of 9. He was then brought up in genteel poverty by a religiously fixated and probably guilt-ridden mother, whom he loved dearly. Having been posted to India, it would be eleven years until Nicholson saw his home in Lisburn again. By then, assisted by the trauma of his experience in Afghanistan, the damage was complete.

This muscular giant was a loner, socially inadequate, prone to bottle things up and then to have indignant outbursts. He bore grudges, but quite easily could cast them aside if he found he was wrong and then become devotedly loyal to the subject of his attention. He was shy, hard-working and very loyal to those whom he trusted. It is hardly surprising that he was peculiar, difficult to manage, his own worst enemy, and haunted by various demons, although the interesting thing about Nicholson is that he was not malign. He also had a dry sense of humour and his nicknames for people usually had a degree of discernment in them: the 'Rosey One', 'Little Abbott' and 'the Bovine'.

In early April 1849 an oft-quoted exchange of letters occurred between Henry Lawrence, Nicholson's superior based in Lahore. Sir Henry wrote:

> let me advise you as a friend, to curb your temper, and bear and for-bear with natives and Europeans, and you will be as distinguished a civilian as you are as soldier. Do not think it is necessary to say all you think to everyone. The world would be one mass of tumult if we all gave *candid* opinions of each other.

In reply, Nicholson conceded:

> I am not ignorant of the faults of my temper, and you are right in supposing that I do endeavour to overcome them – I hope with increasing success … I readily admit that my temper is a very excitable one, and wants a good deal of curbing.

It needs to be pointed out that Nicholson having men flogged was not always, or even usually, the product of anger. He believed that a sharp punishment was preferable to either a fine or imprisonment as both of these caused great long-term hardship both for the individual but also for his extended family, who too frequently depended on the pittance paid to a government servant, clerk or sepoy.

Nicholson has been accused by several modern writers of brutality. The nature of that brutality needs to be commented upon. But first it needs to be pointed out that on several occasions during his career Nicholson did show clemency and a pragmatism that might seem counter to such comments. While Nicholson had prisoners killed after the battle of Trimmu Ghat (1857), after the battle of Gujrat (1849) he released captured Sikh soldiers and sent them quietly back to their homes. But those Sikhs, of course, were not mutineers. Also worth noting is that there is not a single example of Nicholson involving himself in a camp brawl with a fellow officer. Nicholson's violence was institutional violence, primarily the violence of campaign and battle.

It is said that he knew no fear. The psychologist might well add that Nicholson's social dysfunctionality resulted in a tendency to drive him to extremes. He was certainly an officer who led from the front and it might be argued with justification that a lack of fear meant a lack of restraint. And yet this is the officer who pressed on one occasion for the sparing of the lives of young insurgency troops whom he considered had been misled. The oft-quoted matter of his private advocacy for flaying those who killed women and children is discussed later. Suffice it to say here, Nicholson flayed no one and had no one flayed.

And yet, all this conceded, Nicholson was not 'normal'. He had a furious and frightening temper. He frequently did treat his military enemy without mercy, behaving in a way that would be completely unacceptable in 2018.

A great deal of the Nicholson stories can be dismissed out of hand as either fiction or exaggeration. Wilberforce created the myth of the archetypal masculine Victorian soldier, since when his name has been irrevocably associated with imperialism, first positively and more recently negatively. But apart from Wilberforce, these stories usually have no contemporary source material to collaborate them: the hanging of cooks who were allegedly about to poison the officers' soup; or his confronting an angry adult tiger and riding in circles around the beast to disorientate it, finally administering the coup de grâce. The same tiger story is told also of Sir James Outram.[6] Then there was the sabre work; in one battle Nicholson allegedly sliced a rebel sepoy completely in two with a strike of his *tulwar*. More to the point, Nicholson was not in command and not even at Peshawar in August 1857 when 700 sepoys were killed, the worst of the British atrocities in the Punjab; and Nicholson was dead by the time the concerted work of retribution commenced after the fall of Delhi in late September 1857.

Once in 1852, when writing to his superior about dealing with a case of murder, Nicholson noted, 'I hope all this does not read very blood thirsty – I do not believe that I ám cruel.'[7] The accusations of brutality all relate to his official duty, none to his private life, where he is invariably described as quiet and gentle. One must also disaggregate stories of being stern and uncompromising as an administrator in Bannu with his activities when on active service during time of war.

Nicholson was not slow to assist those who fell foul of the establishment. Of fellow officer Arthur Cocks, Nicholson wrote in 1855, 'He wrote me that "the world was turning a cold shoulder" to him since his downfall, and I always feel inclined to be civil to a man in misfortune when his misfortune is not owing to the commission of any moral wrong'.[8] Nor did he join in popular denunciation of colleagues who were perceived as having done wrong. Indeed, he defended the memory and good name of his old bête noir Frederick

Mackeson after he had been murdered at Peshawar in 1853 and the officers' mess resounded to the whispers of Mackeson's womanising. When a young child it is said that Nicholson's mother found the boy with a towel, striking the air in a great rage. When asked what was wrong he replied that the devil had come and tempted him and he was fighting him. This saga of upstanding child morality was seen as an early example of his rectitude, but it equally might just have been his trying to impress his mother and gain her attention. Sometimes with Nicholson one just does not know for sure what was going on.

## A NOTE ON NAMES

There was a variety of spellings for the group whose members worshipped John Nicholson. I have used the version that Nicholson himself referred to himself and the group: Nikolsein and Nikolseinee.

As any historian of nineteenth-century India well knows, there was a bewildering variety of spelling of place names. Sir Henry Yule (1820–89), the Scottish orientalist, bravely asserted that it was difficult 'in a book for popular use to adhere to one system in this matter [of uniformity of orthography] without the assumption of an ill-fitting and repulsive pedantry'. Following this dictum, I have left all spellings as they are in quotations and usually used the modern form of the name elsewhere, except where either the name has changed or where the old name still retains international currency.

Some modern historians have veered away from the term Mutiny and used such alternatives as War of Independence, Great Rebellion or Great Uprising. This is laudable, but the term Indian Mutiny is still instantly recognised internationally, whereas those alternatives are, for the moment, not. While the war was at once a civil war, an anti-imperialist war and a popular manifestation of cultural resistance, at its core it was a military mutiny, and the subject of this book is a soldier whose primary role was to try and deal with that military uprising. Because of this I have used both Indian Mutiny as well Great Rebellion.

# 1

# From Ireland to India

## IRISHNESS

Sitting in Benares 5,000 miles away from his mother, John Nicholson wrote wistfully to her in 1839, 'Has Alex been at dear Castle Blaney this summer? … I often when I am sitting alone here in the evenings think of you all at home, and say to myself, there is no place like home.'[1] Home and his Irish background would be important factors for Nicholson throughout his life, yet John Nicholson's Irishness has often been overlooked despite his being born in central Dublin in 1822. Before he left Ireland at the age of 16 to become a boy soldier in the Bengal Army of the British East India Company, he had grown up in Dawson Street, the suburb of Donnybrook, the village of Delgany in County Wicklow and the town of Lisburn in County Antrim.

Nicholson's biographers have been part of the tendency to play down his Irishness. Sir John Kaye devotes two and a half pages to his Irish background; Captain Trotter stretches to ten pages; R.E. Cholmeley, fewer than two pages; and Hesketh Pearson, about two pages. None of these biographers were born in Ireland, so it is perhaps less surprising their lives of Nicholson tend to portray him in the mould of a gallant English officer. Not one biographer recognises that Nicholson's 'sonorous' voice was an Anglo-Irish accent. Further, none fully brought out in their accounts of Nicholson just how Irish an enclave the Punjab was in the 1850s and how 'being among his own people' helped consolidate a character that had been fermenting on the advancing Indian North-West Frontier for at least a decade before the Great Rebellion or Indian Mutiny.

It is true that Nicholson's alleged piety is touched upon, with the occasional disparaging reference to his being an Ulsterman, but never in the fuller context of that significant evangelical revival that in the late eighteenth century and early nineteenth century engulfed the Anglican Church of Ireland. Even though Nicholson was not especially religious by contemporary standards, his Irish religious background was fundamental to his approach to life, leading to such comments as that from Robert Montgomery, that other Anglo-Irish Punjabi, who observed Nicholson was 'the soul of truth'. This spiritual influence, coupled with the traumatic events of Nicholson's youth, left a deep scar in the soul of this Victorian hero.

John Nicholson was the second child and eldest son of Dr Alexander Jaffray Nicholson (1795–1830) and Clara Nicholson (1786?–1874). Both were of seventeenth-century Ulster settler stock, Alexander's people having been said to have come over from Cumberland. Several members of the family appear to have been killed in the Irish 1641 insurrection and there was a family tradition that the baby son of the family and his mother were saved by a faithful servant who hid them behind some brushwood while the rest of the family was slaughtered, a story very reminiscent of the sagas from the Indian Mutiny more than 200 years later.[2]

The Nicholsons were Quakers, and like many Quakers became involved in the Ulster linen cottage industry in the eighteenth century. During that century the Nicholsons, the Hoggs and the Richardsons were all inter-related and involved in linen.[3] One newspaper report stated that John, the grandfather of the famous soldier, was the eldest of sixty-six grandchildren of Joseph Wakefield of Moyallon and Waterford, who was also in the linen business. Alexander's aunt was a Wakefield.

John Nicholson senior owned the oldest and at one time the biggest bleach mill at Hill's Mill near Gilford on the banks of the River Bann. He mortgaged other properties to raise £15,000 to construct 'a drying house, and for purchasing two large coppers, eight kieves, a wringing engine and cold press to develop the bleachgreen'.[4] The family home was nearby at Stramore House, an imposing four-storey Georgian mansion with a seventeenth-century oak tree avenue. The house and some of the oak trees, along with a watchtower folly built by John Nicholson senior about 1811, still remain intact.[5]

The Nicholson family also lived in Dublin and it was there on 15 October 1795 that Isabella Nicholson (née Wakefield) gave birth to Alexander, her third born of sixteen children.[6] The lad was bright, and after Trinity College, Dublin (1813–16) he studied medicine at Edinburgh before, in 1818, being elected to the College of Physicians of Ireland. It was in 1814 while Alexander was at Trinity that his father's business 'faltered' and he had to sell his bleach mill to Benjamin Haughton. There was an uncanny repetition in the fortunes of father and son, John and Alexander. Both died young, in their 30s, leaving a widow in financial straits.

Alexander Nicholson had a sister called Christina, who in December 1813 married the affable Anglo-Irish gentleman, Alan O'Bryen Bellingham (1770–1859). This was the second of what would be his four marriages. He was one of the Bellinghams of Castle Bellingham in County Louth, whose forebears' castle had been burnt by the forces of James II and who subsequently fought for William of Orange. Alan O'Bryen Bellingham's own home was Dunany House at Togher in County Louth. During Nicholson's childhood, the Bellinghams farmed in the rather idyllic countryside near the small hamlet of Castleblaney in County Monaghan. It was here that as a special treat the Nicholsons came for holidays.

On John Nicholson junior's mother's side were Hoggs. Clara Hogg's people had settled in the north of Ireland in the seventeenth century. She was probably born at Stoneyford near Lisburn. The family home was at 46 Castle Street in Lisburn. Her brother James Weir Hogg (1790–1876) was an Indian nabob, having made a fortune between 1822 and 1833 when registrar of the supreme court in Calcutta. Hogg established himself back in London in Lower Grosvenor Street and later Grosvenor Square. It is no exaggeration to say that in the decades that followed, Sir James, as he became in 1846, was the voice of the East India Company in the British parliament, where for twenty-two years he sat as a Conservative MP. He was a director of the East India Company from 1839 until the company's demise nineteen years later and was twice chairman of its court of directors. He refused the governorship of Bombay in 1853, but was a member of the original 1858 Council of India and became a British privy councillor in 1872. James Hogg was not a man to trifle with, but he was a good man to have as one's uncle. More than anyone, Hogg determined the fate of his sister's family following the tragedy that befell the Nicholson household.[7]

Alexander Nicholson was a Trinity College Dublin graduate and clearly enjoyed his time as a student in what Lady Morgan would refer to about that time as 'dear, old and dirty Dublin'. While at Trinity, Alexander fell in with George Bellett, a charming and intelligent young man who had fallen under the influence of the radical evangelical set within the established Anglican Church of Ireland.

As Alexander's family was a Quaker home and Clara's Anglican, theirs was in theory a mixed marriage. In practice, Alexander and the Quakers parted company and he became a member of the Church of Ireland. Whether or not this caused acrimony in the wider Nicholson family is uncertain. The couple married on 24 April 1820. Afterwards, they lived in Lisburn for a while before heading for the Irish capital. As is often the case with young newlyweds making their way, they lived a peripatetic existence in Dublin. We know that at various times they lived in 14 Moore Street; 23 Gardiner Street (March 1823), near to Mountjoy Square; 48 Lower Gardiner Street (April 1823/May 1824), close to the celebrated Customs House on the River Liffey; and in an attractive artisan's two-storey cottage with basement at 6 Vergemont Terrace in Donnybrook.[8] By 1828 the Nicholsons were back in Lisburn, where Alexander was in private practice, but after about a year they had returned to Dublin and were living in pleasant quarters at 35 Dawson Street, opposite St Ann's Anglican church.

Alexander was as restless in employment as he was in residence. The pull between the hometown of Lisburn, where Clara's mother lived in Castle Street, and Dublin, where Alexander's mother lived in Lower Pembroke Square, was clearly great. It is interesting to note that while Alexander was working at the Rotunda Hospital in Dublin, Clara gave birth in Lisburn to two of their children, Lily and James (1827–40).

For a period Alexander worked in the Mater Hospital in Merrion Square in Dublin. Between 1825 and 1828, he was assistant master at the Rotunda Lying-in Hospital at the end of Sackville Street, the present O'Connell Street. Back in Lisburn for a sojourn in 1828, he was in private practice, as he was again back in Dublin by 1830, this time possibly in partnership with a Dr Thomas Bell, who may have been a relative.

In all, seven children were born to Alexander and Clara in the years 1821 to 1831:

Mary Hogg, born in Lisburn in October 1821. Married Rev. Edward Maxwell on 11 February 1845. Their son Dr Theodore Maxwell inherited some remaining papers relating to his uncle, John Nicholson. Mary died in 1889, aged 67.

John, born in Dublin on 11 December 1822. Baptised St Thomas Church, Dublin, 18 December 1822.[9] Died in India, 23 September 1857, aged 34.

Alexander, born in 1824. Died in Afghanistan on 3 November 1842, aged 18.

Lily Anna Maria Floyer, born in Lisburn on 23 February 1826 and baptised on 12 March. Married the local Lisburn curate, Rev. John Hobart Seymour (1820–97), on 16 May 1856.[10] Children were Dr John Nicholson Seymour (Royal Navy) and Clara Seymour. Lily died on 14 January 1862 aged 36, possibly in childbirth.

James Weir Hogg, born in Lisburn on 29 January 1827 and baptised six weeks later on 14 March. Died 15 March 1840, aged 13.

William Maxwell, born about 1828. Died at Sukkur in India on 1 June 1849, aged 21.

Charles Johnson, born about 1829. Died in India on 17 December 1862, aged 32.[11]

Confusion has arisen regarding the birth year of John Nicholson, with Sir John Kaye in 1867 and the original *Dictionary of National Biography* erroneously stating it to be 1821.[12] Similarly, Nicholson's gravestone gives his age at death at 35. He was in fact still 34 when he died. Such confusion is compounded by the once-common belief recorded on the statue of John Nicholson in Lisburn that he had been born in that town. Field Marshal Lord Roberts also believed this.

Nicholson was probably born in Gardiner Street, Dublin, though possibly at Vergemont Terrace, as claimed by the *Belfast Daily Mercury*.[13] Certainly, there is a document dating from the time he entered the service of the East India Company stating that he was born in the parish of St Thomas, which would confirm the Gardiner Street location. A week to the day after the birth, on Wednesday, 18 December 1822, Alexander rode out to North Lodge, the home of John Bellett. Staying there was Alexander's close friend, Rev. George Bellett (1797–1886).[14] Bellet was then at North Lodge awaiting the arrival of documentation that would result in his leaving the large parish of Dromore in County Down and moving to become vicar of the village of Sampford Arundel in Somerset, where he was to remain until 1827.[15]

In his *Memoir*, George Bellett wrote of Alexander Nicholson:

And later in the season came one of whom I formed a very strong and intimate friendship – dear Dr Nicholson, whose name I have mentioned before.

He was a physican at Lisburn, and brought his wife to the Spa [near Magherahamlet where Bellett was curate], he coming there on Saturday and remaining till Monday. He afterwards settled in Dublin, and my dear brother John – though the colour of their theology was very different – formed as strong an attachment to him as I did; the sweet, unblemished simplicity of his mind, and his warm-hearted benevolence, strongly attracted him.

In the same *Memoir*, the 25-year-old George Bellett also recorded:

When I was left alone at Magherahamlet it was the greatest possible treat for me to go to spend the day with him [Alexander Nicholson] and Mrs Nicholson at Lisburn. After settling in Dublin he became intimate with my family, and once when I happened to be at North Lodge, he rode out from Dublin, to bring me in to baptize a little child of his just born; so I had the honour of baptizing the great General and hero of India.[16]

The Nicholson–Bellett association extended beyond Alexander and George. Alexander's sister and George's hot-tempered sister Bessy had gone to the same school run by a Unitarian called Dr Taylor across the Grand Canal in Harold's Cross in Dublin.

In people such as Rev. George Bellett, Dr Thomas Bell and the Waterford-based Dr Fleury, Alexander Nicholson had friends with one thing in common: they were, even by the standards of the time, religious devotees, if not the Calvinist zealots in John Bellett junior's immediate circle. John Bellett senior is perhaps more comprehensible to twenty-first-century eyes than are his sons, George leaning towards Armenianism and John junior to Calvinism. John senior had been a prosperous businessman who had fallen on hard times. When reading his story, one is reminded of his contemporary, Sir Frederick Shaw of Kimmage in Dublin, who dryly noted, 'it is the privilege of a gentleman to get the worse of any bargain throughout life.'[17] Because of a bad investment, Bellett senior had to retire to his modest home, North Lodge near Kilgobbin, just north-east of the Three Rocks Mountain and 7 miles outside the capital on the Dublin–Enniskerry road. North Lodge, beside Lilliput House, was on a new road that veered off the main road just before Kilgobbin and led to Carrickmines. It was not far from Leopardstown House. Today the area is part of Dublin's suburban sprawl. North Lodge no longer stands, the site now being transversed by the Dublin tram or light railway system, the Luas.

We know that the Nicholsons stayed at North Lodge in 1823 for in one letter to Alexander, George Bellett says how pleased he was that Clara had 'tried the benefit of the Kilgobbin air'. One report talks of 'the village of Kilgobbin, remarkable for beauty of situation, for salubriousness of atmosphere, and for the mouldering ruins of a castle'.[18] The castle at least is still to be found, mouldering as of old. Here in Kilgobbin John Bellett senior led a quiet country life. His attitude to religion was relaxed and tolerant, unlike that of the local rector. This was the 'pure and saintly' Rev. Henry Kearney (1782–1855), another significant actor in the formation of the Nicholson religious personae.

Kearney had been born in Birr and was another Trinity College Dublin graduate. His father, John Kearney, had been both provost of Trinity College

Dublin and then bishop of Ossory. Through his wife, Grace O'Hara, he had links with County Antrim. Said to be 'thoroughly unworldly', Kearney served as a curate in Delgany between 1810 and 1817, after which the accomplished evangelical was assigned the parish of Kilgobbin. Kearney was a good preacher and greatly influenced the Bellett boys in their religious quest. In 1824 this parish was joined with Kilternan, the old Kilgobbin church was abandoned and in 1826 its roof was removed. Today the ruin is the haunt of the graffiti artist.

Up north, Lisburn was 'a tight Protestant town' and would continue to be so. Given this environment, added to their mixing with the Church of Ireland's radical intellectual evangelicals of the time, it is little wonder that the Nicholsons were pious.[19] Not only were there daily family prayers and Bible readings in the Nicholson household, with questions on these readings for the children, there was also Sunday school and the 'keeping of the Sabbath'. Learned religious tracts were studied and discussed. From a surviving letter to Alexander dated 9 October 1823, George Bellett, commenting upon Thomas Erskine's recently published *Essay on Faith*, observes that it was:

> well calculated to obviate the evil effects, which result from a system of religion which I fear is very prevalent, particularly in Dublin. I mean that system that is tainted at least with the laven of Antinomianism. Erskine shews that Faith is not what many people would make it, a mere assent of the mind to certain propositions, but that it is an operative principle.[20]

Nicholson's circle had scant regard for the laxity of approach to religion among their counterparts in Dublin, though it is important to state that neither the Nicholsons nor their circle of acquaintances and friends were connected with political Orangeism.

The evangelical movement within the Church of Ireland was in no small part due to the activities of an extraordinary cleric called Thomas Tighe. Like so many in this surge, he was of the middle/gentry classes, well-educated and inclined to shun worldly goods and advancement for spiritual well-being.[21] That a man with such ability and talent as Tighe should, having been to St John's Cambridge, devote thirty-four years of his life to the parish of Drumgooland is testimony of his faith and dedication. Drumgooland, on the Annesley estate near Castlewellan, was an impoverished hill region not far from Slieve Croom. Here peasant farmers eked out a living on potato plots of some 10 acres each. Tighe lived among these people ministering to them and supporting them. He lived in a small cottage, 'not as good as the residence of a gentleman's steward'.[22]

By the time Tighe had died in 1821 the evangelical movement within the Church of Ireland was well rooted and converts both from Presbyterianism and Catholicism were not uncommon in those regions of south Antrim, Down, Dublin and Wicklow where it was strongest. It is no exaggeration to say that one of the repercussions of this movement was the founding in England of the Plymouth Brethren. George Bellett's brother, John Gifford Bellett (1795–1864), was a leading light.[23] He was at Trinity College Dublin when Alexander Nicholson was there, as was John Nelson Darby (1800–82), a Trinity Gold Medallist in 1819 and the other great founder of the Brethren. Darby was to be curate in Delgany in County Wicklow in 1817, undertaking extraordinary work converting some Catholic inhabitants of the Calary Bog up in the Wicklow Mountains until the archbishop of Dublin scuppered this dubious exercise by demanding converts swear an oath of allegiance to the British Crown. If Dr Nicholson was not in the inner circle of this group within the established church, he was certainly on the periphery. And, it has to be said that in later years, while staying within the security of the Church of Ireland, Clara Nicholson's demeanour and attitude was very much in keeping with the Brethren.

We know very little of the children's schooling at this time. One report has John Nicholson being able to read at the age of 4, but in reality there is little to indicate that John was anything more than average while at any of his many schools. One gets the impression that John would concentrate only on that which interested him. Throughout his life this focus on only what caught his attention was to be a significant characteristic.

Around 1828, when the family were back in Lisburn for a while, John may have attended Benjamin Neely's academy in Castle Street.[24] When in Dublin, those children old enough seem to have gone to Dr Wall's school in Hume Street, just off St Stephen's Green.

Moral rectitude and responsibility were the order of the day. One story has survived of how Alexander Nicholson, having collected the rents from some properties he owned in trust, obtained a bill of exchange for £100 and, pinning it to the inside of the young John's pinafore, sent him out into the Dublin streets alone with the responsibility of taking the large sum to his grandmother's house. Needless to say, the task was completed successfully.

# DEATH OF ALEXANDER NICHOLSON

All this puritanism, of course, does not mean that there was not love and affection in the home and there is no evidence that there was any acrimony

while the family were together. What the future might have held, no one can
surmise, but the pious devotion and security of the young doctor, his devoted
wife and their young brood was dramatically shattered when on 15 December
1830, four days after John's eighth birthday, Dr Alexander Nicholson died at
their home in Dawson Street in Dublin from a contagious fever contracted
from one of his own patients. He was only 35 years old, just a year older than
his famous son would be when he died.

Sir John Kaye, in his sketch of the life of John Nicholson, described Dr
Alexander Nicholson as a true Christian and of 'spotless integrity of life'.
A simple and elegant plaque in the upper porch north wall of St Ann's
Church opposite the former site of the Nicholson home commemorates the
young doctor:

SACRED to the Memory of
ALEXANDER JAFFRAY NICHOLSON
M.D. Died 15th. December 1830
Aged 35 Years.
Awake thou that sleepest and arise
from the dead and CHRIST shall give thee
light.
Ephesians Ch.5 v.14.


# DELGANY

Clara Nicholson was not the person to cope with such a body blow. Her
simple faith and devotion, and the bitter realisation of the hopelessness of her
situation, made her turn in on herself. For the next decade she was like a cat
with her kittens, taking her growing family hither and yon, trying to cope
with her own loss and at the same time having to bring up a large family on
a shoestring. Clara was proud and strict, and religion became the focus of her
existence, her protective ship to cope with the stormy seas of life.

She lived off the rent of several properties. These brought in a modest annual
income, which proved a lifeline for Clara and were the residue of a sizable
property portfolio built up in the 1770s by John Nicholson Seymour. They
included: 10 Anglesea Street; Churchtown; 12 College Green; 63, 64, 65, 66
Dawson Street; 15, 16, 17 Dame Court; 2 Dame Lane; 40 Dame Street; 80, 83,
84, 91, 92, 93, 94 Grafton Street; 18, 19 Lower Erne Street; 6 Merrion Square;
15 Trinity Street and 20, 21 Westmoreland Street.[25]

In addition, there were properties at Derrinraw and Derrykeeran, as well as the big house at Stramore in County Down, and part of a bog in County Armagh. A proportion of this property portfolio permeated down, first to Alexander Jaffray, then to John Nicholson and finally in 1819 to Alexander Nicholson. They were held in trust for the lifetime of the holder and then passed on.

Though only about 44 years old when her husband died, Clara Nicholson never remarried. The spectre of death haunted her from there on. By the time she died in 1874 at the remarkable age of 88, only one of her children, Mary, was left alive.

Clara's support group was small. There were Alexander's aunt Christina and her husband Alan O'Bryen at Castle Blaney, a friendly couple, without children, and lacking the religious intensity of the Nicholsons. Holidays here in this remote wild region were clearly a treat for all. But living there permanently was not realistic, even if invited. Clare had to consider schools for the children as well as her ties to the evangelical community.

The initial and obvious place of refuge was Clara's mother's home in Lisburn. There Clara went, employing a private tutor for the older boys. Mrs Hogg had been a Dickey and was originally from Randalstown. She was now old and also a widow who was not terribly well off. A child's comment at the time by young James Nicholson about there being 'no papas' in the house clearly hit home with Clara. She appears to have moved her family for a while to another house in Lisburn, possibly 37 Bow Street, for a more independent existence. Her survival depended on 'two small estates' that appear to have been the rents from the Dublin properties, maybe given to her by Alexander's family. We find her living back at Vergemont in Donnybrook after her husband's death, but it was in the quiet, quaint village of Delgany in County Wicklow that Clara made her home from about 1831 to about 1835.

Delgany was not like many Irish villages. It was more like Goldsmith's 'Sweet Auburn'. It was built by Elizabeth La Touche, whose family owned the nearby estate, Belleville, and was one of Dublin's leading bankers. In the nineteenth and early twentieth centuries Delgany particularly had a reputation for being dominated by the old ruling class, the ascendancy or Anglo-Irish. This is confirmed to an extent by what population statistics exist for the period. For example, in 1831 Delgany parish had a population of 2,268. Of that, 1,032, or 45 per cent were Protestants, this being the highest proportion of Protestants in any parish in north-east County Wicklow at that time.[26]

Delgany is 20 miles south of Dublin and 3 miles inland from the coast and the fishing village of Greystones, where the railway reached in 1855. Just over a hill from Delgany are the famous beauty spots of the Glen of the Downs and the Sugarloaf Mountain. This was hunting and fishing country. In 1822 Rev. Wright described Delgany as:

> laid out with judgement, and the cottages are built with excellent taste in rustic architecture. There is a day-school for poor children in the village … next after the delightful situation and view from the village, the church is the object most worthy of attention; it is a light Gothic building, 102 feet in length by 34 in breadth: over the western entrance a steeple rises 90 feet in height, containing a clock and bell … There is always in the summer season a very full, and what is usually termed a very fashionable congregation at Delgany Church.[27]

Twenty years later the village had 201 inhabitants with thirty-four houses 'built in a very pleasing style'.[28]

Clara Nicholson selected this sleepy village because she knew people of like mind were there. Indeed, difficult as it is to imagine now, Delgany was then a hotbed of establishment evangelicalism. Kearney and Darby had been curates there and George Bellett had close ties with the village. Clara could also obtain cheap accommodation from Tom Bellett, the brother of George, who had been Alexander's great friend. She appears to have lived in several different houses during her stay in the village.

The rector of Delgany was at that time William Cleaver (1789–1860). He was the son of a former bishop of Dublin and was a highly educated man. The historian and polemicist James Froude described the bookish, aquiline-nosed Cleaver as 'a dignified, stately clergyman of the evangelical school … the perfect type of a Christian gentleman, cultivated, pious and well read … a man of moderate fortune who could be hospitable without pinching'. His curate was Thomas Gregg, whom Clara already knew, no doubt another incentive to come to the village. But Gregg was only at Delgany from 1834 to 1835. He ended up in the unenviable position, though perhaps spiritually uplifting for such a zealous evangelical, as chaplain at Dublin's Bridewell prison in 1846, the year he died at the relatively young age of 51.[29]

Clare Nicholson may have lived in the Delgany area for upwards of five years. We know very little of her during this period. She seems to have been what was described as a 'district visitor', which presumably meant that she visited homes on behalf of the parish to ensure that both spiritual and physical well-being was cared for. Clara herself recalled that on one occasion when John, who must then have been 10 or 11, accompanied her she passed by a house and on the boy enquiring why she had not called in, she replied,

'Because they are bad people there.' To this the precocious child stated, 'Oh, mother, God makes His sun to shine upon the evil and the good, and sends His rain upon the just and the unjust.' She was doing her job well.

There is some confusion about what schooling the children had while in County Wicklow. On the one hand, Captain Trotter talks about the private tutors. But we do know that John attended the local parish school as well, later on the Holywell school run by the celebrated Dr Lewis Rowland Delamere.[30] As the name suggested, this was near a famous well that was regarded as being 'efficacious' for various ailments. Delamere's school was not in Delgany, though, but about a mile away on the right-hand side as one drove south, of the main Dublin–Wicklow road, beyond the Glen of the Downs but before the deceptively insignificant hamlet or clachan of Kilpedder. Today the house is an ivy-clad ruin, though it survived into the second decade of the twentieth century, local folklore having it that its last occupants were the notorious Black and Tan British auxiliary troops of the Anglo-Irish War. It was a long, double-storey building with a central bow entrance that extended up to the second storey. It was rather barracks-shaped, which befitted its later use.[31]

While John appears to have enjoyed the nonconformity of Delamere's establishment, Clara clearly became increasingly worried. Dr Delamere's boys were certainly nonconformist, but in a secular sense. When Achilles Daunt of Tracton Abbey at Kinsale, County Cork, visited the school, a local boy told him, 'The young gentlemen would sooner have the crows than any mate you cud give them.' Every respectable Irish boys' school had its 'sergeant' – not surprisingly as he was often an old soldier who worked as handyman, groundsman and assistant to the headmaster. He was also inclined to act as protector of the boys against the school establishment. And with a military air about him, the school sergeant was a figure respected by the boys, treated with some awe and, in later years, long remembered after the names of masters had faded away. In the case of the Kilpedder school, the sergeant was a sergeant major, or so it was said.

Though details are few, this sergeant appears to have been looked upon with disfavour by Clara Nicholson. Certainly, there would have been dramatic, over-dramatic, tales of wars and fighting. Though that in itself cannot have overly disturbed Clara, after all, as in a few years she would send the 16-year-old boy off across the world to be a soldier. More likely it is that given the intense evangelical nature of the Nicholson household, the earthy and worldly opinions of the sergeant major, as brought home by John, alarmed the strait-laced Clara. Reports of John writing humorous verses on the backs of school window shutters also cannot have pleased Clara. But there may have been another reason for Clara to take John out of the Delgany school and send him to a stricter regime far away, to the Moravian settlement at Gracehill, outside Ballymena in County Antrim, while she remained in County Wicklow.

## A BULLY

Biographers of Nicholson have tended to portray Nicholson's childhood antics as signs of a young budding hero, of early masterful leadership qualities and of an innate recognition that evil had to be confronted. But there is another explanation: the young John Nicholson was a bully.

The surviving snippets of John's childhood, carefully preserved for posterity by Clara Nicholson, present us with two characteristics. First there was the quiet, serious and reserved child. This is the clingy child who says to his mother, 'Don't fret, mama dear. When I'm a big man I'll make plenty of money, and I'll give it all to you.' Interestingly, despite Nicholson's biographers saying otherwise, there is no evidence that he in fact ever did send his mother regular payments from India, which is not to his discredit for it was many years before a young officer could build up any kind of savings from his tight pay.

But then there is another and apparently contradictory Nicholson, a precocious child who fought.[32] Every biography recounts the incident when John was 3 years old and his mother came into a room and found him lashing out at thin air with a knotted handkerchief. When his mother asked him what he was up to he replied; 'Oh! mamma dear, I am trying to get a blow at the devil! He is wanting me to be bad. If I could get him down, I'd kill him!'[33] Then there is John's attitude to his elder sister, Mary. There was the pulling of her long hair plaits and forcing her to carry him upstairs. Many years later Mary would write that John was 'just a great, big bully'. What is surprising about this is that the other children seem to have been relatively normal, playful and at times naughty youngsters, whose punishment was not being allowed to go to church.

Claire Gillman has written that children who bully are often tense or anxious about important aspects of their lives, fighting to find a means of control over their environment as well as an outlet for their anger. Some become aggressive due to harsh home backgrounds or, it has been suggested, because they feel inadequate or unloved.[34] It is difficult not to link such comments to the young Nicholson.

Whatever the reason or reasons, John was taken out of his Delgany school and in May 1832 packed off as a boarder to the Moravian preparatory school at Gracehill. His mother, however, remained in Delgany for about three more years, after which she was again living at 6 Vergemont in Donnybrook.

Charles and William in turn were packed off to a school in Carrickfergus. Mary remained in Delgany until April 1839. Until then, she was living a few hundred metres across the valley of the insignificant, if rustic, Three Trout Stream at a private school in a house called Mount Pleasant. This was on the Delgany road to Kilcoole via Pretty Bush.

Law and order was strictly maintained for humans and animals alike at number 6 Vergemont.[35] The animals in the Nicholson Donnybrook home then were Pompey, who was a dog; Muff, who was likely a cat; and Pretty, who was probably also a cat. Pompey would be beaten for going into the rabbits in the coach house and barking at them. But an equally austere regime had awaited John Nicholson at Gracehill. In the middle of the eighteenth century, the Moravians had settled in Gracehill in the heart of Presbyterian Ulster. Never a large community, they carried on their religious, personal and working lives as much as possible in the tradition of the east European region out of which they had been driven. By the early nineteenth century the community had established for itself a reputation for being devout and upstanding, and the school had a good reputation, both for the quality of education it offered as well as for impregnating a sense of moral rectitude into its pupils. It was, therefore, sought after by nonconformists as a suitable place to educate their sons.

John Nicholson was at this German-run school at Gracehill from 8 May 1832 to 29 April 1833, a few weeks under a year. This short stay might explain why neither Kaye nor Trotter mention in their biographies of Nicholson his being at Gracehill. And even Hesketh Pearson only learnt about it because Rev. Berry, a Moravian minister in Jamaica, wrote to him in 1955 telling him of the omission in Hero of Delhi.[36]

Nicholson was nominated for a place in the school by Samuel Archer of Belfast. The headmaster was Rev. Christian Frederic Harke and in that period the teachers included William Henry Oates, William John Robinson, Theodore Roepper, Henry von Werger and Joseph Waugh. The school register has survived, John's number being 548. The name Nickolson has been corrected to Nicholson and under this name has been written at a later date, 'After General Nicholson who fell in the heroic attack on Delhi'.

It was while John was at Gracehill that, through George Bellett, Clara obtained blank enlistment forms for a Protestant orphans' society. That she was thinking of getting rid of John or one of his siblings by this means is possible. Certainly putting out to orphanage was not uncommon at the time and indeed her husband's younger brother, Meadows Taylor Nicholson, born about 1807, had been dealt with in this manner a generation before, being sent as an orphan to North America in 1821 when about 14 years old. Bellett noted in his lengthy and wordy letter to Clara, 'I trust John will proceed under the care of the Moravians as you could wish. The thought of launching them all on the troubled waters of this world is I am sure at times a very solemn one to you.'[37]

Why Nicholson left Gracehill when he did in April 1833 is another mystery. He returned to his mother's home in Delgany, where he appears to have stayed until being sent to his new school in 1834. From an inscription in a book to the little Lily Nicholson from her older sister Mary, dated 8 August 1834, the family appears to have been living in Kendlestown Castle, Delgany. Mary seems to have been the most normal member of the household. The inscription in the story book has a sense of humanity about it lacking in much of the Nicholson papers: 'Lilly Anne Floyer Nicholson from her affectionate sister Mary as a reward for behaving well when her two teeth were pulled.' The name Kendlestown Castle is confusing, not least because the townland was called Kendlestown. But that aside, by the 1830s Kendlestown Castle was an extensive ruin. The Nicholsons must have lived in Kendlestown House, also near Delgany on what is now the back road to Greystones. Quite how Clara Nicholson afforded to rent such a large house, complete with a strange, square-shaped Italianesque tower, is unknown.

That several of John's classmates also went on to the Royal School at Dungannon suggests that Gracehill was possibly a feeder for the old grammar school. Another Victorian hero who followed in Nicholson's path at Gracehill was William Olpherts (1822–1902), who, like Nicholson, was born in 1822. Olpherts's military career extended beyond the boundaries of the British raj to Burma and the Crimea. He was as great a daredevil during the Mutiny as Nicholson, won a Victoria Cross and was known throughout the army as Hell-fire Jack. He was knighted in 1900, retired as a general and died on 30 April 1902. In August 1882 Olpherts, who lived at Dantry Lodge, Armagh, revisited his old preparatory school to place his niece there in the separate girls' section. On that occasion he wrote in the school register, 'The moral and religious tone of Gracehill is beyond my praise, and it is to that chiefly that I feel I owe any success which has attended my career in life.'[38] One suspects that the wayward Nicholson might not have had the same views.

That said, this small country village school had remarkable success. By the 1880s, it could boast as alumni a whole host of eminent Victorian military figures such as General Charles Barr, General Ross Moore, Lieutenant Colonel Forde, Major John Lyle and Sir Francis Reilly.

As well as Nicholson and Olpherts, the Indian army officer Major General John Lowry was also a former pupil. Years later Lowry made a comment about Nicholson that echoed what many others had to say about the contradictory nature of the future Bengal Army infantry officer: 'Olpherts, Nicholson and I were about nine years of age when we went to Gracehill, a Preparatory School. In two years we three went to Dungannon. Nicholson was tall for his age, not of a spare habit, and of a quiet and gentle disposition …'[39]

Apart from the Gracehill–Dungannon link there was the other draw card for Clara Nicholson in that the headmaster, Rev. John Richard Darley (1799–1884), had gone to Trinity with her husband Alexander. And, like the Nicholsons, Darley had been swept into the religious fervour of early nineteenth-century Trinity. He gained his BA in 1820 and was ordained in 1828. Later, in April 1841, there would also be a family link with the marriage of Richard Hogg, the headmaster of the endowed school in Carrickmacross, to one of the Monaghan/Cavan Darleys, Catherine. The ceremony was performed in Dungannon by Rev. Dr Darley.

In April 1837, replying to a begging letter from John at Dungannon, Clara Nicholson made it very plain that she was not going to ask her brother, James Hogg in London, for money for him. She had had a pain in her side that had prevented her replying sooner and perhaps made her sharp, and events may have made her anxious and gloomy. She told him that he must live within his allowance and not be ashamed of saying that he could not afford something. 'What other boys have or do, cannot be a rule for you, who are the son of a Widow with five boys to educate. Do not dear John feel any false shame at not having money, such a feeling might lead to serious ill consequences.' That is fair enough, but she continues, 'My Aunt Dickey was found dead in her bed other morning, eyes and mouth both closed so it is thought she went off in sleep. Such a fate might be ours, are you prepared to meet it.'[40]

And what can be said of Nicholson at the college in Dungannon? Sir John Kaye states, no doubt fed to him by Clara Nicholson, that:

In after years he [John Nicholson] sometimes expressed regret that he had not availed himself more fully of the opportunities then presented to him of increasing his store of learning; but he made very good progress all the same, and at fifteen was probably as good a scholar as the majority of boys at that age.

From what little evidence has survived, the contradictory character traits emerge once again. Captain Trotter, in his life of Nicholson published in 1897, quotes Darley commenting after Nicholson's death that he 'was a retiring boy, but brave and generous, the very soul of honour, and always ready to take the side of the oppressed'.[41] On the other hand, there was that fiery temper. The problem is that the reports from later life come with the mantle of hero. So what might well have been bullying is portrayed as early evidence of heroic behaviour. Fighting for right and fighting to defend weaker boys against attack was one thing, but the worldly Hesketh Pearson was perhaps more accurate when he surmised that Nicholson's reputation for fighting bullies and protecting the weak was not so much because he had any particular sympathy for the weak, but rather because he simply enjoyed fighting. Fighting was the one response Nicholson knew and the one strategy that usually worked for him because he was big, strong and fearless. Pearson also hits the nail on the head when he surmises that Nicholson cannot have been very popular at school because 'though reasonably idle in class, he was of a retiring disposition and awkwardly honest'.[42]

An interesting glimpse of Nicholson's character comes out in a story that Kaye and Trotter both relate. As a small boy back home in Ireland, Nicholson had been playing around with gunpowder. There had been an explosion that had blackened the boy's face. He could not see. The doctor bandaged his face and for ten days the family had to sit and wait to discover whether the child had lost his eyesight. During this time, the lad never complained once, just sat and waited. When the ten days had passed, the bandages were removed and it was discovered that the child's sight had been saved. It is an insightful story. The inward-looking boy, so alone as to be without fear.

## TO INDIA

Why did Clara Nicholson send her devoted eldest boy across the globe to be a child soldier in India, knowing at the very least, if he survived, she would not see him for a further ten years? One is tempted, given her character, to suggest that it was a sacrifice she made to martyr herself. But more practically, Clara recognised that the army might calm down her strange, brooding and at times violent son. What is not supposition is the stark reality that Clara had access to relatives with influence who could get John a cadetship.

Two of Clara's relatives were closely connected with India House in London. As already mentioned, there was her brother James Weir Hogg, four years back from a successful legal career in Calcutta, now Conservative Member of Parliament for Beverley in the West Riding of Yorkshire. Within the year, Hogg would be a director of the East India Company. And in India House in London's Leadenhall Street was Henry Alexander, father-in-law of John's cousin, Captain Melville Hogg.[43] Alexander initiated the process of a cadetship for John just before Christmas 1838. It would have been appropriate for the boys to follow their father into the medical profession, but that involved considerable additional expense. Ultimately, James Hogg's nepotism on behalf of his impecunious sister did not excessively inconvenience such a wealthy man. There was the cost of a cadetship, of an outfit for the lad and his keep in London for a short period, maybe some cash to set him up, but that was about it. In the end four of Clara's five boys – John, Alexander, William and Charles – were shunted off to India in the same manner, all with dire results.

On 20 December 1838, nine days after his sixteenth birthday, John Nicholson was granted permission to fill up a petition for a cadetship in the infantry of the Bengal Army of the British East Indies Company. The prospect of becoming a soldier at that young age was daunting enough, but to be sent halfway across the world to a strange country where John knew no one was little less than terrifying. And yet the boy seems to have taken his fate well enough. In early 1839 he travelled to Dublin to see his mother, now living back in her terrace cottage in Donnybrook. The house still stands. Here most of the paperwork was undertaken for his enrolment. He also had to get a medical certificate, which was signed by two doctors, Thekleton and Colles, possibly friends of his father. George Bellett had to provide a statement relating to his being baptised and the parent's declaration form was signed by Clara on 8 February 1839. Mary gave John a Bible and his mother's parting words to her child soldier son were, 'Never forget to read your Bible'. A week later, on Friday, 15 February, Nicholson was signing his declaration form in Great Marlborough Street in London.[44]

There remained the final hurdle; the swearing and oath-taking on the Bible in the India House before the chairman and twenty-four directors of the East India Company. This was completed on Tuesday, 19 February 1839 in the imposing Court Room. What the cadets were urged to achieve was in fact laudable enough for the age: 'care for the natives of India, keep out of debt and live upon their pay: learn the languages, and behave themselves bravely and honourably'.[45] So by nepotism, albeit openly public, but not bribery, John Nicholson became a cadet ensign in the Bengal Army of the British East India Company.

## CADET IN THE EIC

It is possible that the tall and lanky Nicholson had a crush on the 34-year-old Mary Claudine Hogg (née Swinton), who had married Hogg in 1822 when she was aged 17 and he 32. They were to have fourteen children, including Isabella, who became Lady Tweedmouth and who said that her cousin John was, 'always the leader in games'. The Hoggs lived in some style at 40 Upper Grosvenor Street in London, and it is there that John must have stayed in the few weeks he was in London prior to departure to India.

There is little to say of Nicholson's voyage to India, for the simple reason Nicholson wrote next to nothing about it. Several things are clear, though. Nicholson kept himself to himself, aloof from the other Company cadets, who had attended the Company's training college at Addiscombe. Nicholson indulged in no high jinks and was, as Pearson probably correctly surmised, regarded as a prig by his fellow boy soldiers. While this is true, it is at the same time unfair. Children will clique and as Nicholson had not attended the East India Company's infantry training college, he was at a disadvantage both professionally and socially. The captain of the *Camden*, however, noticed this strange, gauche boy and took to him. It was to be a familiar pattern for Nicholson: regarded as an outsider and as being peculiar and aloof by his fellow soldiers, but greatly respected and admired by his superiors.

Captain Trotter asserts, probably accurately, that the ship 'for certain' touched at the island of St Helena, which was then a possession of the British East India Company. There is no evidence that Nicholson ever landed at the Cape of Good Hope, where many East India Company soldiers and civil servants spent their furlough. This was both because living costs and travel were cheaper than returning to Britain, and also because it meant if they did not venture west of the Cape they retained their full salary and did not have to resign any staff or civil position they held at the time of leaving India.[46]

Nicholson arrived at Calcutta as a third ensign and reported to Fort William on 20 July 1839. As Captain Trotter recorded, it was the height of the monsoon rains.[47] Nicholson stayed with a barrister called Theodore Dickens, a friend of James Hogg. On 8 August he was ordered to do duty with the 41st Native Infantry Regiment at Benares.[48] Not surprisingly, Nicholson was lonely in his little bungalow and badly missed the security of his old home, though in typical Nicholson fashion he set to and found something constructive to do, in this case beginning to learn Hindi.[49] On 12 August 1839, he left Calcutta and three weeks later, in early September, he arrived in the bustling town of Benares. Dickens had put him in touch with Dr Lindsay, the civil surgeon, where he stayed for the rest of September before he moved into a bungalow within the military cantonment near Lecroll. Here, surrounded by servants who could not speak a word of English, or chose not to, and with only '50 Hindustani ones' of his own, unhappy and homesick, he was soon down with 'a severe bilious attack'.

This was not Nicholson's first illness in India. He had gone down with fever during his short stay in Calcutta. Indeed, there is a series of references to Nicholson being unwell during the following eighteen years. There is little doubt that ill heath and Nicholson's notorious temper are linked. No doubt initially acclimatising both to the food and to the extremes of temperature was a factor.

Later it is nearly certain that Nicholson contracted malaria. His life became one of living in the open, of patrolling, of riding across arid plains, wading through swamps and drinking from wells. Malaria was one of the inevitable consequences. That one can add to the mix psychosomatic illness is highly likely. And then, later, there were the dangerous drugs he was prescribed. Writing to his mother in July 1840, Nicholson comments, 'You can have no idea how the hot weather enervates the body, and if you do not take special care, the mind also.'[50]

In Benares, Nicholson again landed on his feet. By an extraordinary coincidence, his father's younger brother, Richardson Nicholson, lived near the city. Uncle Richardson appears to have landed up in India off a ship in Calcutta, where he had been a 'shippy'. He appears to have been involved in the then quite respectable opium trade, running an agency at Benares.[51] From snippets that have survived here and there, it is clear that the Nicholsons were kindly folk who gave comfort to both John and William, and though they do not seem to have met Charles, at least in the early days, nonetheless sent him presents.[52] They even gave John his own horse, the first of many Nicholson was to go through.

One of the characteristics of Nicholson throughout life was that he was rarely content. He was a great grumbler. Now he grumbled to his mother in a letter that there was also clothing and postage and the like to be bought, and, if he were ordered upcountry he would have to buy a tent at 400 rupees and to hire camels. Yet Nicholson, having done with his rant, as was his way, calmed down quickly and added, 'I am very well off and have no reason to complain.' He said his main expenditure was:

| | |
|---|---|
| 45 rupees for nine servants | 17 rupees to military funds |
| 40 rupees for his bungalow | 12 for ale |
| 30 rupees for food | 7 to maintain and feed his horse |

An assurance followed that he went to church every Sunday and read his chapter from the Bible Mary had given him, 'as you advised'. Indeed, in one letter he recommended to his mother a work by one of the great evangelical Anglican theologians of the age, Rev. George Stanley Faber, *A dissertation on the Prophecies that have been fulfilled, are now being fulfilled, or will hereafter be fulfilled relative to the great period of 1260 years, the Papal and Mahommedan apostasies* … This thick book for the faithful first appeared in 1807 and had gone into many editions by the time Nicholson came on a copy. It was not perhaps the ideal reading for a young man needing to learn about the cultures and religions of the region where he was to spend the rest of his life. In fairness, however, to Nicholson, the references to religion and evangelical fervour dry up very quickly in his letters home. He also clearly took an interest in learning various Indian languages.

Nicholson arrived at Benares in October 1839 and was out of the place in early January 1840. It must have been during these months that the sergeant major drilled some discipline into the youth. Not having attended one of the company's colleges meant that he was at a disadvantage to some of his contemporaries. On 5 December 1839 he was posted to what would be his permanent regiment, the 27th Native Infantry Regiment, then stationed far away on the frontier. This meant an epic journey up the Ganga (Ganges) River and onward to the frontier post of British India – bleak and hot Ferozepur on the Sutlej River, where he arrived on 23 March 1840 after nearly three months on the road.

At Meerut one of his own servants stole his spoons and forks. Then at Karnal his tent was cut open and a small trunk taken. This contained about £10, his pair of pistols and, most precious, his 'poor father's' dressing case.[53] The rookie was learning the hard way.

What Nicholson did not learn, and never was to learn, was how to control his temper. Captain Trotter unearthed a story from the then surgeon at Karnal, a Dr J. Campbell Brown. He told him that Nicholson had arrived in the town in the company of another ensign called James Rattray of the 2nd Native Infantry, both with a sepoy detachment. Rattray was senior over Nicholson by some months and fairly inevitably the young men fell out. Nicholson, however, was always one to chew over an old bone and would not let the matter drop, trying unsuccessfully to get a second to organise a duel.[54] Needless to say, this episode was not recounted to his mother in Lisburn.

The 27th was neither an old regiment nor a particularly distinguished one. Its origins dated from the 1790s and in its present incarnation it dated from only 1824, when it had been commanded by Major C.H. Baines. In its thirty-three years of existence, between then and its abolition in 1857, the regiment was to do good service. But be that as it may, Nicholson did not like Ferozepur. Few would have. It was miles from anywhere, hot and the encampment hastily erected. This gave ample opportunity for Nicholson to indulge himself in further grumbling. To his mother he complained, 'This station is a perfect wilderness; there is not a tree or blade of grass within miles of us, and as to the tigers, there are two or three killed in the neighbouring jungle every day.'

Soon a parcel from Ireland arrived containing letters from members of Nicholson's family, including slippers embroidered by his little sister Lily, which he said he would get soled. News that his brother Alexander had been offered a cadetship by his wealthy uncle, if the family paid for the uniform, elicited a response, 'I do not besides think Alexander at all fitted for it.' Instead he had suggested that the Bellinghams might be able to find him something else. He hesitantly offered to pay for the outfit if able when the time came, a clear indication that financially things were tight for him. Before sending love to a host of people at home, Nicholson cautioned his mother in a worldly manner about extracting rent from a family member who had not been able to pay her as yet. The letter was addressed to Vergemont, Dundrum, near Dublin.

And to his Uncle James back in London he did concede that he liked his regiment very much, saying, 'it is a corps highly spoken of'. He explained to the nabob and his benefactor that:

The Station is a very unpleasant one for a new comer, as there are no houses to be let. Ten years ago there was not a habitation of any description to be seen here, and it was only when the Army of the Indus marched past last year that orders were given for three regiments to hut themselves for the approaching winter.

At present each officer on his arrival builds a bungalow for himself. I must follow this plan, as the hot weather is coming on, and build a couple of rooms, which will last me as long as the Corps remains here.

I am now sharing with a brother officer the stable of an officer who has gone to Cabul. We are all on the qui vive for intelligence from China just now. Cabul, by all accounts, is quite quiet, and has almost ceased to afford us any interest.

On my way up here I passed through Ludhiana. Whilst there I was introduced to Colonel Wade, the great political agent in this part of the country. He was very kind to me and gave me a Perwannah [order] to the Jemadar [the Indian officer] of all the villages I should pass through on my way, ordering them to supply me with everything necessary on my paying for it. However, at several of these villages (which are in the Punjaub), the Jemadars desired the people to give me nothing, adding 'What do we care for Colonel Wade? We are Seiks [Sikhs], you may _____ unless you bring an order from Nas Nihal Singh.' Fortunately I had a Naicks guard with me, and by threatening these refractory Seiks with a good flogging I managed to procure enough to eat.

It is reported here that we cannot keep on good terms with the Lahore Court much longer, and what I have just mentioned, shows, I think, they do not like us.[55]

Taking a short cut through Sikh territory and demanding supplies along the way was exactly the attitude that resulted in bad blood. So Nicholson was right, and, as time was to prove, they had every reason for disliking the Company's army on its doorstep.

By mid-summer Nicholson was down with fever. Then in October 1840 word was received that the 27th was to see service in Afghanistan. In November the regiment crossed the Sutlej River complete with 'a second army of followers' and began a slow march across Sikh territory on its way towards the even then legendary Khyber Pass. By January 1841 the 27th was ensconced deep in Afghanistan in the ancient and dilapidated fortress city of Jalalabad, where the regiment kept its headquarters until May 1841. The first great drama of John Nicholson's life was about to begin.

# Afghanistan

The first Anglo-Afghan War would be especially difficult for Nicholson, so it was particularly unfortunate that this was his first experience of warfare. Afghanistan was also an especially difficult problem for the British generally. It was sparked by Russian intrigues in Persia and a perceived threat to western Afghanistan, and so to British India: 'Persians dancing to the Russian fiddle'. The domino theory kicked in with disastrous consequences for the British army of the Indus. So it was that in 1839, even though the Russians had by then clearly lost interest in encroaching on any perceived sphere of British influence, the armies of Bombay and Bengal invaded Afghanistan,

After initial encounters, the British expeditionary force, with its long lines of communication, appeared to have matters under its control. Shah Shuja was now on the throne in Kabul in place of the more masterful, intelligent and at times chivalrous Dost Mohammad. The establishment in November 1839 of the outstation at Ferozepur, near the British India–Punjab border, was part of British scheming in this endeavour. The death in June 1839 of Punjab ruler Ranjit Singh had created an unstable base, facilitating British operations into Afghanistan.

## ALEXANDER NICHOLSON COMES TO INDIA

Once the British were into Afghanistan 'the Government was a government of sentry-boxes, and that Afghanistan was not governed so much as garrisoned', Archibald Forbes pointed out.[1] The 27th Regiment was not a unified force when in Afghanistan, but broken up into detachments with groups of companies scattered here and there. Indeed, an advance group was already in Afghanistan when Nicholson joined the regiment in Ferozepur. He was, however, with the main body of the regiment at Jalalabad. Here letters from home were awaiting him. One of these brought with it the unwelcome news confirming that his brother Alexander was coming out to India as a cadet soldier.[2] Clara was, as usual, not to be moved and plans for young Alexander's enrolment had been set rolling despite John's advice.

More than twenty years later, in 1862, Charles Nicholson had a spat with his Uncle Richardson, who had loyally served as a lifeline to successive Nicholson boys who had arrived in India without friend or support mechanism. To his mother, Charles admitted:

> Richardson wrote me rather a cross letter reminding me of all he had done for Alexr and of what a backward lad he was as a grilf [griff[3]]. This was probably caused by my having in a private letter commented on his sons backwardness, and also by my having omitted to see any of his children.[4]

As for James Nicholson and his going to India, the question did not arise as he died on 15 March 1840 at home only aged 13, much to the grief of his sister Mary. A sad little 'Memoir of the life and death of James Weir Hogg Nicholson' was written by Mary and her brothers at home in Lisburn and is preserved in the British Library.

That winter of 1840–41 we find Clara living at 6 Waldon Terence, Torquay. This was due to ill health in the household, particularly affecting Lily and Charles, although the evangelical ethos on the Devon coast must have aided Clara's decision on where to go.[5] The death of young James also probably spurred Clara to make a change of scenery. But the family did not remain permanently in Devon and by early spring 1842 they were again back in dreary Castle Street in Lisburn.

Back in February 1841, John Nicholson at last got up the energy to write his letter of condescending advice to his younger brother. The document says more about Nicholson's past than anything else. It must have annoyed young Alexander greatly, who in any case, and unknown to John, was already in India:

> As Mamma writes to me that you will probably come as a Cadet in Spring next, I sit down to write you a few words of advice, which I am sure you will take, as I mean them, in good part. I must first say, however, that I was really sorry for your own sake to hear that you were rather idle. Depend upon it, you will deeply regret it, if you do not to the best of your ability improve the time you have left before you arrive in India. On board ship, you will have little to do; if you borrow a Straith's Fortification from one of the Addiscombe Cadets on board, and study it well, you may find a

knowledge of fortification of great advantage to you hereafter.[6] You should also endeavour to improve your manners, on your passage, as without good manners you can never advance yourself.

Be reserved and prudent in your communications with your fellow-passengers, and with those with whom you may be associated on your arrival in this country.

I suppose you know that I have been in Cabul for some time; it is a dreary tract of country, and I hope you will not be ordered up there.

We go out the day after to-morrow, to reduce some small but strong hill forts at a place called Peish Bolak; and there is no saying how long we shall be out. How do you like England? not so well as Ireland, I suppose. I was very sorry that circumstances rendered a move necessary. … I hope to pass my examination in the native languages. I should have done so months ago, were it not for this marching continually. Let me hear from you before you leave home.[7]

In March 1841 a letter to Nicholson from Mary dated 26 September 1840 eventually caught up with him at Jalalabad, on the Kabul River. It contained details of the death of James, which John had already heard about from his mother. In an unusually newsy reply, he told Mary that it looked as if they would march on to Kabul in the middle of April. He says he is 'reading hard with a Moonshee and hope to pass my examination by the end of the year … Tell my Mother as she wished to know the way in which I pass my time, when not marching, (which happens very seldom) … How do you like Torquay, not so well as Delgany I dare say.'[8]

Unfortunately, few details survive of Nicholson's first military encounter. This was a skirmish out of Jalalabad against 'a refractory tribe, called the Sungho Kheil' who were situated across the Sarobi Pass in the Nazian Valley, some 25 miles distant. The party was led by Brigadier Shelton. As well as Indian levies and some of Shelton's own Queen's 44th Regiment, there were two companies of the 27th Native Infantry led by Lieutenant Colonel Palmer with the young subaltern John Nicholson. Both regiments were out on skirmishing parties and, as General Shelton reported, on 'many occasions displayed a conspicuous bravery that ensured success'. But casualties were high, at about twenty-six British troops killed and fifty-nine wounded.[9] It was a taste of things to come. This was the kind of seek-and-destroy mission at which Nicholson was to excel in the years to come.

There was unrest elsewhere, too, for soon fractures in the British–Sikh partnership opened up and unrest began to spread. In May 1841, when

Nicholson's regiment was still based at Jalalabad, it was sent back down the 28-mile-long Khyber Pass again to Peshawar. It was ordered to help a convoy under Captain George Broadfoot on its way upcountry and threatened by a cohort of 'mutinous Sikhs'. The convoy allegedly contained Shah Shuja's harem. If true, this cannot have delighted Nicholson. On the approach of the reinforcements, the Sikhs fled. The 27th, under Colonel Palmer, turned, and in sweltering hot conditions marched to Kabul without halting again at Jalalabad.

# GHAZNI

From Kabul, a section of the 27th was ordered to march 60 miles south-west to the ancient walled city of Ghazni, where they relieved the 16th Bengal Native Infantry. Nicholson's future close friend, the blue-eyed Neville Chamberlain, was then a subaltern in the 16th.[10] In June 1841 Nicholson, writing to his sister, commented that Ghazni 'is a quiet spot and I like it very much'. He had given his opinion of the locals in an earlier letter: 'The inhabitants [of Afghanistan] are a fine looking race, and superior to Hindoostanees in everything but their relish for murder, which is carried on to great extent.'[11]

Many years later, the then Field Marshal Chamberlain recalled of his new young Irish friend:

> He was then a tall, strong, slender youth, with regular features and a quiet and reserved manner. We became friends at first sight, as is common with youth, and we were constantly together during the time that intervened between his regiment taking over the fort and my regiment leaving for Candahar. After my arrival at that place occasional correspondence passed between us, but neither of us was given to letter-writing.[12]

As will be seen, Chamberlain and Nicholson did not always get on, yet of the three men who were to love Nicholson – Henry Lawrence and Herbert Edwardes being the other two – Chamberlain was to have the mental strength equal to Nicholson. The story is told of when Chamberlain needed a leg operation, with a diseased bone being removed. The operation took ten minutes, and the surgeons say they never knew a man to bear torment like poor Neville did; not a muscle of his face altered. He refused to take chloroform.'[13]

By June 1841, a spasmodic peace had descended on Afghanistan. Unfortunately, though perhaps inevitably, the British commander, General Elphinstone, had divided his army of occupation into three: Kabul, where the British cantonment was on an exposed plain outside the city and not in the imposing Balla Hissar stronghold; Kandahar, where the fearless and no-nonsense General Nott held sway; and between them, the small garrison in the ancient and walled town of Ghazni, where Nicholson and his regiment stood sentinel.

Nicholson cannot have been too hostile to the country. He was clearly bored, however, as in August 1841 he writes about the possibility of joining the service of the British puppet ruler, Shah Shuja. He said the pay would be better. But then, he also thought that once he passed his language exams, his uncle might be able to swing something 'in Hindoostan better worth having'.[14] Nicholson took his language study seriously. In March 1841, writing to his sister Mary, Nicholson had commented, 'I exercise for an hour or so before breakfast, after which I read with my Moonshe, for a couple of hours; then read or amuse myself, till dinner time after which I study again, and I generally have regimental duty of some kind to fill up the intervals.'[15]

Afghanistan now had an unpopular army of occupation bolstering an unpopular puppet ruler, who retained a modicum of peace with large bribes of gold to various key chiefs and leaders. And it was the last of these that sparked the uprising. The subsidies to the chiefs were reduced. Matters were by no means helped by the fact that the British envoy, Sir William Macnaghten, though an admirable Arabic scholar, was less competent in other respects, and the military commander, General Elphinstone, was worn out and just wanted a quiet life.

However, a quiet life was not what was awaiting any British commander in Afghanistan. In September 1841, the governor-general, Lord Auckland, cut the subsidy the British had been paying the Afghan tribes, who soon erupted in violence as the hill fighters set out to eject the foreigners from their territory. In Ghazni the 27th Regiment found itself isolated in a town cut off by snow, living among a hostile population and besieged, albeit in a desultory manner, from without. That situation lasted from September until 6 December 1841, when thousands of Barukze fighters infiltrated the city, causing the defenders to retreat to the citadel. Conditions were grim. Colonel Palmer decided that there was nothing for it but to try to negotiate a safe passage out.

## THE KABUL RETREAT

Meanwhile in Kabul, unrest was contagious. On 23 December, the severed head of Macnaghten was being paraded around the streets of the capital. The decision to evacuate the city was not long in coming. Negotiations gained promises of a safe passage out of Afghanistan via the passes into the Punjab. So on 6 January 1842 the ill-fated British army of 4,500, 85 per cent of whom were Indian troops, moved out of its encampment, complete with 12,000 soldiers' families and camp followers. Only a handful would survive.

This disastrous and panic-induced decision to cut and run led to the greatest retreat in British imperial history prior to the May 1940 retreat from Dunkirk. Unlike a century later, it also led to one of Britain's greatest defeats. Nearly the entire column of 4,500 military and 12,000 civilians were either killed by the Afghan jezail musket shot, or sabre, or by the bitter cold. Most of these were Indians, only 15 per cent of the troops being European. The civilian cohort was overwhelmingly Indian. Though the opposition to the British column came from the mountain peoples, a degree of Afghan organisation came from Dosh Mohammad's very capable son Mohammad Akbar Khan.

On the retreat, the lucky ones, who were all Europeans, were taken prisoner or 'hostage' by Akbar Khan. One of these, the strong-willed Lady Sales, commented that she was grateful for a tumbler of sherry, which at any other time would have made her 'very unladylike', but which now merely warmed her.[16] Only a handful of survivors made it to the besieged city of Jalalabad, including most famously Dr William Brydon, immortalised in Lady Elizabeth Butler's painting 'Remnants of an Army'.

## GHAZNI FALLS

Back in isolated Ghazni, things were also turning grimmer. At 7,200ft, the town was extremely cold in midwinter. Water was a great problem as the citadel had no permanent supply and melting snow was time-consuming. Those who simply ate snow raw experienced severe stomach cramps. According to Haig and Turner, the British made no effort to use the artillery guns within the citadel. They also did not organise an intelligence network. However, one wonders realistically how the British could have extricated themselves with such a tiny force. Discussion about cannon and artillery was rendered academic by the infantry having no training in artillery. Archibald Forbes was to say that the 'bitter winter and scant rations' took the heart out of the sepoys of the 'warm and fertile Indian plains, who seriously spoke of escaping the besieged fortress and making their way to Peshawar'.

In mid-February, a month after the retreating Kabul army had been destroyed, Colonel Palmer received a despatch under a flag of truce from Major General Elphinstone via an Afghan chief. This instructed him to evacuate the town under the same worthless agreement that Elphinstone had evacuated Kabul. Surrender or even a negotiated retreat was hard to stomach. Indeed, Nott in Kandahar and Sales in Jalalabad ignored the order of their broken commander. But Palmer had no brigade behind him, very little water, and he did not know what was happening in the outside world.

Given this situation, and despite Nicholson's hostility to the idea, Palmer decided he had no alternative but to try to negotiate with the Afghan leader Shumshooden Khan for safe passage to the British line, with colours, arms and baggage. He achieved this on 6 March 1842 and the British garrison moved down from the citadel 'with colours flying' to quarters that were awaiting them, the force being divided between various buildings.

The truce did not last long, though. The next day Afghans attacked the British. Nicholson and several others were occupying a row of houses detached from the rest of the regiment. Lieutenant Andrew Crawford, of the 3rd Bombay Native Infantry, recorded what happened to him, his fellow officer, John Nicholson, and their two companies of Indian troops:

I was in the next house with Burnett of the 54th and Nicholson of the 27th, there being no decent room for me in my own proper quarters. On hearing the uproar I ran to the roof to see what was the matter; and finding what had taken place amongst my men, and that balls were flying thick, I called up Burnett. He had scarcely joined me when he was struck down by a rifle-ball which knocked his eye out; and as he was then rendered *hors de combat*, I assumed command of the two companies of the 27th that had been under him; and Nicholson and myself proceeded to defend ourselves as well as circumstances would permit. We were on the left of the heap of houses occupied by our troops, and the first and sharpest attacks, were directed at us; the enemy fired our house, and gradually, as room after room caught fire, we were forced to retreat to the others, till at last, by midnight of the 9th, our house was nearly burnt in halves. We were exhausted with hunger and thirst, having had nothing to eat or drink since the morning of the 7th. Our ammunition was expended; the place was filled with dead and dying men, and our position was no longer tenable; but the only entrance, in front of the house, was surrounded by the enemy, and we scarcely knew how to get out and endeavour to join Colonel Palmer. At last we dug a hole through the wall of the back of the house: we had only bayonets to work with, and it cost us much labour to make a hole sufficiently large to admit one man dropping into the street below; but we were fortunate enough to get clear out of our ruined quarters in this way, and to join the Colonel unperceived by the savages around us.[17]

This was Nicholson's first experience of serious fighting. It was also his first and only experience of urban warfare until the assault on Delhi sixteen years later.

The situation was hopeless and the regimental colours were burnt. The unfortunate sepoys, without water and far from home and miserable in the freezing weather, were pressurising the officers to allow them depart for Peshawar, 'which to their wild imaginings was only fifty or sixty miles off'.[18] Palmer saw no alternative but to surrender. Quite what the circumstances were is uncertain but it is said that Nicholson refused to give up his sword and on three occasions with his men drove back Afghans at bayonet point. Finally, when forced to give up his sword it is said that he burst into tears 'in the agony of shame and grief'. He did not forget and was never again to surrender.

The surrender was also, in effect, a death sentence for most of the sepoys and their followers. Some made it out of the city into the snow, where they were hunted down and killed. Forbes pulled no punches when writing of this:

> The unfortunates would have done better to have died a soldierly death, with arms in their hands and the glow of fighting in their hearts. As the event was, faith with them was broken and save for a few officers who were made prisoners, most were slaughtered or perished in a vain attempt to escape.[19]

In fact, a number of sepoys did survive. On his march from Kandahar to Kabul, General Nott rescued nearly 300 Indian troops from the 27th Regiment, who had been made slaves in the neighbourhood of Ghazni.[20]

The news that Ghazni had fallen reached George Lawrence, elder and more normal brother of Henry and John, on 12 March. George Lawrence was then, as will be seen, well to the north-east, beyond Kabul, as a hostage with a number of European women and children to Akbar Khan.[21]

John Nicholson was one of the ten European officers whose life was spared in Ghazni, without doubt as a possible bargaining counter down the track. The nine others to survive were Colonel Palmer, Captain Alston, Captain Barrett, Lieutenant Davies, Lieutenant Harris, Lieutenant Poett, Lieutenant Williams (nephew of Captain Henry Havelock), Lieutenant Crawford and Dr Thompson. Alive they might have been, but the form of their imprisonment at Ghazni was basic in the extreme.

They were confined to a single room in the citadel, which measured 18 x 13ft (5.4 x 3.9m). When they lay down at night, their bodies occupied the whole floor. With such confinement and the most basic sanitary arrangements, it was not surprising that they soon shared the room with the local rat and lice population. According to Nicholson's skimpy official military record, the garrison surrendered in March 1842. Week after week was spent in this airless unsanitary room. Food was poor and exercise seldom allowed. It is astonishing that only one person died of disease.

Undoubtedly, Colonel Palmer and his men received harsh treatment. News of the killing of Shah Shuja on 5 April gave their gaolers confidence.[22] On 21 April, Palmer was tortured by the Afghans, who believed he had buried treasure, some four lakhs of rupees. A rope was tied around one of Palmer's feet and a tent peg used as a lever to tighten the rope. Later Captain Trotter would drily comment that 'some of the victims would have liked to apply a similar experience to certain critics in the Anglo-Indian press, who denounced the surrender of Ghazni as a military crime'.[23]

They also turned their attention to the other officers, stripping them of any valuables. This led to an interesting altercation between Nicholson and his captors:

> I do not know whether I mentioned to you that I had managed to preserve the little locket with your [Clara's] hair in it. It was the only thing worth a shilling that was kept by any of us; and I was allowed to keep it, because, when desired to give it up, I lost my temper and threw it at the Sirdar's head, which was certainly a thoughtless, and head-endangering act. However, he seemed to like it, for he gave strict orders that the locket was not to be taken from me.[24]

When Major General Elphinstone ordered the evacuation of the cantonment at Kabul he ordered the British force at Jalalabad to evacuate also and return to the Punjab. Sensibly, General Sales, whose wife Lady Florentia was soon to be the hostage–guest of Akbar Khan, and the redoubtable George Broadfoot (1807–45) would have none of this, distrusting the Afghan assurance of safe conduct. They stayed put, although Sales was to waver later. Nonetheless, Nicholson's hero, Broadfoot, held the line and Jalalabad remained in British hands. Indeed, Sales with three infantry columns and some infantry were soon to march out of the besieged town's Kabul Gate and give Akbar Khan a sharp rout.[25] They were pestered no more by Afghans and when General Pollock's relieving force arrived at Jalalabad two weeks later, General Sales' 'Illustrious Garrison' welcomed it with the band of the 13th playing, 'Oh, but ye've been lang o'coming'. Pollock's comment on entering the city was that the defenders were better off than he was 'except for beer and wine'.[26]

To the south-west was the stout and stout-hearted General Nott, who with two brigades had stubbornly held out in Kandahar, had bloodied the nose of an Afghan army that had appeared near the city, and had, like the British

Jalalabad garrison, ignored General Elphinstone's order two months previously to evacuate the city. But the new circumstances were such that Nott now heeded the call by the governor-general in Calcutta that he withdraw. There is, though, withdrawal and withdrawal. The old general sent part of his army back via Sind, but elected to return to India the long way round, via Kabul. As soon as Pollock heard this, he advanced also on Kabul to meet up with General Nott.

So the British moved out from the Jalalabad fortress, Captain Broadfoot's Gurkha troops scattering what was left of Akbar Khan's resistance. This route through the passes was the one attempted by Elphinstone's doomed army the preceding winter. What the British encountered was not unlike like that of the later massacre at Cawnpore. Backhouse wrote:

> The bodies lay in heaps of fifties and hundreds, our gun wheels crushing the bones of our late comrades at every yard for four or five miles; indeed, the whole march from Gundamuk to Cabul may be said to have been over the bodies of the massacred army.

And as Generals Pollock and Sales's 'army of retribution' moved steadily in one direction on Kabul, so General Nott moved from another.

News of the British massing an army at the bottom of the Khyber Pass must have reached the Afghans in Ghazni, for on 12 May 1842 the treatment of the prisoners improved slightly, with better food and their being allowed out of their room on Fridays for exercise and fresh air on the terrace of the citadel. But this relaxation of conditions was too late for Lieutenant Davies. After a four-day nightmare struggle with typhus, unaided by medicine or even simple comforts, he died on 19 June.[27]

The prospect of their prisoners all dying and so losing their prize value clearly registered with the Afghans. Next day matters improved further, this time considerably. Their quarters were moved and now included an open courtyard to which they had free access. These officers' psychological state can only be imagined. So relieved were they to be out of the dungeon and into fresh air that they chose to sleep out in the courtyard covered in sheepskin cloaks rather than in a confined room. It later emerged that Akbar Khan had wished the Ghazni prisoners to be united with his own in Kabul, but Shumshooden Khan in Ghazni had refused to give up his prize. With the advance of General Nott and his army from the south-west, Khan moved out of Ghazni to meet them. This gave his brother, Gool Mahomed Khan, an opportunity to transfer the prisoners to Akbar Khan.

Suddenly, on the night of Friday, 19 August 1842, five months after their surrender, the prisoners were hurried out into an outer courtyard where a chaotic scene faced them. Camels were being assembled for a journey. They were ordered into paniers, slung onto the sides of camels. The caravan eventually set off, and the remnant of the 27th Bengal Native Infantry Regiment lurched towards the Afghan capital, where it arrived three days later.

Here they were greeted in the great Bala Hissar fortress by the urbane Akbar Khan and several British officers who were already captives there, including the Irishman Major Eldred Pottinger. Akbar welcomed the new arrivals in a friendly fashion and gave them a good dinner, an account of which Nicholson subsequently wrote to his mother:

> The day we arrived in Cabul, we dined with Mahomed Akbar. Many of the principal men of the city were present; and I never was in the company of more gentlemanlike, well-bred men. They were strikingly handsome, as the Afghan Sirdars always are, and made most polite enquiries regarding our health, how we had borne the fatigue of the journey, etc. Immediately opposite me sat Sultan Jan, the handsomest man I ever saw in my life; and with a great deal of dignity in his manner. He had with his own hand murdered poor Captain Trevor in the preceding winter; but that was nothing. As I looked round the circle I saw both parricides and regicides, whilst the murderer of our Envoy was perhaps the least blood-stained of the party. I look upon our escape as little less than a miracle. I certainly never expected it; and to God alone thanks are due.[28]

After this interesting meeting, the remnants of the officer corps of the 27th were moved to Shewaki, where Akbar Khan's other prisoner–hostages had been taken during the disastrous retreat of General Elphinstone's now annihilated army. At Shewaki, life was good. George Lawrence recorded of the newcomers:

> Their joy at getting among us was great, for they had suffered severe hardships and been treated with much indignity, being deprived of all their servants. Although lean and hungry-looking, they were all in good health. Their treatment had been very different from ours, which was soon exemplified by their amazement on seeing me suddenly rush downstairs and summarily eject from the square sundry of their guards who had followed them inside the building.[29]

Now there was food, money, a garden to walk in, and when George Lawrence received a consignment of clothes from his brother Henry, he handed up Nicholson a new shirt from the box. Quite what the redoubtable Lady Sales and Lieutenant Nicholson thought of each other, we do not know. Nicholson probably kept his distance from the sophisticates in the party.

But this strange life was not to last for long. As Nott's army rapidly approached Ghazni, scattering Shumshooden's army with ease, General Pollock's army of retribution drew nearer to Kabul. So it was that after only two days of pleasant captivity, after dinner on the afternoon of 25 August 1842, Nicholson and the other hostages found themselves being moved once more, this time deep into the mountains to the west. The British army was getting close.

On 6 September, General Nott marched unopposed into Ghazni. He gave his engineers two days in which to blow up the city. Lieutenant James Rattray, in his book on Afghanistan, notes that the last he saw of the ancient city that had been known to Ptolemy was a pile of smoking ruins. In fact, Rattray exaggerated somewhat, although the fortifications were badly damaged. Nott then set his army to march north-east to Kabul. A race was on, as General Pollock approached the Afghan capital from the east. And on 15 September, just after nine months since their ignoble evacuation, the British under General Pollock marched back into Kabul. Here too, as in Ghazni, the British were unopposed. Two days later, Nott arrived in sight of Kabul to see the British ensign flying over the great Balla Hissar fortress – Pollock had beaten him to the prize.[30]

Apart from some destruction, with the bazaar the selected target, all that remained for the British was to find their captured troops and the women and children. This task rested on Pollock's shoulders as Nott would have nothing to do with sending forays out into the west of the country. So Captain Richard Shakespear and old General Sales, whose wife and daughter were captives, without waiting for further orders, set out across the mountains to the west in search the British prisoners.[31]

## THE HOSTAGES FREE THEMSELVES

When the small column of British hostages moved west on 25 August, they were escorted by eighty Afghan horsemen and 300 infantry under Saleh Mahomed, in a blue frock coat and riding a large white horse. He was accompanied by a man named Ahmed, whom Lawrence thought was probably there on Akbar Khan's instructions to spy on Saleh Mahomed. And there was good reason to spy on him; George Lawrence recognised him as a former *subedar* in the forces of the pro-British Afghan camp of Shah Shuja. This was useful information. A man who had betrayed once might do so again.

The Afghan infantry soldiers carried British muskets and made much of copying British drill and military procedure. But they were 'a good-humoured set of fellows, and laughed and chatted with us as we marched along'.

The column moved off at 11 p.m. Lawrence recorded:

> We marched all night, and avoided the city of Cabul, passing though gardens and orchards, the escort plundering them as we went on. About 7 A.M. of August 27 we halted near the fort of Killah Kazee … towards evening we were joined by Dr Berwick and fifty-seven sick soldiers, who had been left at Cabul when our army retreated, and who were now able to march. At 1 P.M. of the 27th we resumed our march, Lady Macnaghten leading the way in a kajahwah, and the other ladies and children following, two on each camel, the officers and soldiers riding or walking … We met to-day many camels and asses laden with [the root spice] assafœtida from Turkestan, their drivers regarding us with much amazement.[32]

On that second day out, George Lawrence approached Saleh Mahomed and suggested that he make short marches, giving General Nott's troops time to catch up with them. In return, each hostage would contribute towards a 'considerable sum' for him. Saleh Mahomed feigned anger, but the seed was sown.

Their journey took them via or near Urgundhab, Tockhana, Sir-i-Chusmah, across the Hadjee Yuk Pass of the Koh-i-Babu and then the Kaloo Pass until, on 2 September, the procession pitched its tents at Bamyan. This was not far from the caves and famous giant Buddhist figures carved into the rock – destroyed 159 years later by the Taliban in March 2001. Even in 1842 these giant statutes were looked upon by some with contempt and Lawrence wrote of 'the caves and colossal figures for which the place is famous, at which our guards fired as they passed, cursing them as idols'.[33]

Nearby were the ancient ruins of a city destroyed by Genghis Khan, once a key settlement on the ancient Silk Road between China and the West. And beyond lay the great peaks of the Hindu Kush Mountains.

Here, where the days were warm and the nights cold, the prisoners remained for a short while in 'wretched' conditions at an old fort infested with bugs and fleas. Preferring to live outside the fort, relations between prisoners and Saleh Mahomed were tense. Here they remained for over a week.

On 11 September, the hostages learnt that should the Afghans be defeated and the British take Kabul they were to be taken across the Hindu Kush range of mountains to Khooloom. Here, the prisoners believed, they would be sold into slavery. But other rumours also were circulating: that offers of monetary reward were being made in Kabul for the release of hostages, a sort of 'futures market' in the hostages. But Saleh Mahomed would not benefit from such commodity trading, so he asked several officers what they would do for their liberty. Five of the officers, Captain Johnson, Captain Lawrence, Captain Mackenzie, Major Pottinger, and Lieutenant Webb – not including Nicholson – immediately agreed to and signed a deal. This offered Saleh Mahomed a straight gift of 20,000 rupees, plus 1,000 rupees a month pension, plus the command of an army regiment. Having agreed to be true – 'or if otherwise that we shall acknowledge ourselves to be false men, even in the presence of kings' – the five then went off to see their superior officers. Not surprisingly, Brigadier Shelton and Colonel Palmer were uneasy at the terms to which these brother officers had tied the Indian government as well as the likelihood of angering Akbar Khan, who as far as they knew had yet to be defeated. A compromise was quickly reached, by which each hostage signed a document agreeing that if the British government refused to pay the sums required, every hostage would pay his share of the ransom.[34] Fortunately for Nicholson, the government kept to the bargain.[35]

The 'flag of independence' was immediately hoisted and Akbar Khan's spy and his men sent packing, which they seemed pleased to do, having heard ominous reports of British successes. Rather brazenly, Major Eldred Pottinger (1811–43) now took command of the ancient town.[36] Pottinger was an odd fish. He had all the eccentricities of the Anglo-Irish; had relatives in high places, including an uncle who was then governor of Hong Kong; and, not unlike Nicholson, had to have adventure or he became bored and troublesome. Gaining for himself a lowly position with a relative in Calcutta, Pottinger managed to persuade the authorities to send him into Afghanistan as a spy disguised as a horse dealer. Having wandered about the place, in 1838 he came to Herat in the west. This was a key strategic stronghold that the Persians, backed by the imperial Russians, dearly wanted. There was a half-hearted siege under way, with the Persians trying to capture the Afghan-controlled city. Pottinger went to the Afghan commander, revealed his true identity as a British officer and promptly took over command of the city's defences. Now in Bamyan, Pottinger cheerfully took command of a group of his previous captors, led them out on patrol and waylaid an unfortunate trading caravan, from whom he robbed sufficient for his colleagues' current requirements.

On the morning of 16 September the party turned and set off back towards Kabul. Salah Mahomed offered the British his spare muskets. It is a reflection of the psychological state of some of the troops that while the Horse Artillery gladly took the muskets, many of the men of the 44th Regiment refused to take one. Lady Sales, however, had no such mental block and willingly carried a musket.

When they camped that night, a horseman was heard to approach. He carried a note from Captain Shakespear saying that he had left Kabul and, with a force of 600 Kuzzulbash Horse, was on his way to rescue them. Needless to say, this led to much rejoicing and little sleep was had that night. Whether the money promised to Salah Mahomed had been a wise investment is questionable, though, of course, the hostages might have been murdered before Shakespear's horsemen descended on the Afghan ranks.

On 17 September the former hostages had made it to the fort at Kaloo and were resting under the shade of the fort's wall when, in the distance, they saw a cloud of dust. It was Captain Shakespear and his column of irregular horsemen. George Lawrence wrote, 'Oh, what a joyful moment was that when I saw my old friend Shakespeare, and felt that we were really delivered! We made the hills around us ring again with our cheers of delight and thankfulness.' The ordeal of Lady Sales, Lady Macnaghten and their party was over, an ordeal that had, among other things, witnessed the birth of four babies. In a dramatic gesture, Shakespear took off his turban and placed it on the head of Salah Mahomed.

The united column moved out, turning south along the Hajigak Pass. Three days later there was even more rejoicing when General 'Fighting Bob' Sales's scouting column was sighted and the general, riding ahead with an escort, was reunited with his wife and daughter. On Sales's personal staff was George Lawrence's brother Henry, with his detachment of Sikh irregular horse. Also in the column were the 3rd Dragoons and the Queen's 13th Light Cavalry. Any fear of Akbar Khan intercepting the rescue was now gone. Further on, on the top of Sufed-Koh, Captain Backhouse and his sappers were met. He had rounded up many of Salah Mahomed's men who, armed with British muskets, had been in danger of summary execution.

On 21 September 1842 the military column entered the ghost city of Kabul, passing through the grand bazaar. That evening they were warmly welcomed by General Pollock into the British camp east of the city.

We know that Nicholson was part of this drama, although he is absent from the standard accounts. Reading between the lines, as one has to do so often with Nicholson, it seems that he was either physically unwell or psychologically stressed, or both, by his six-month ordeal. This is hardly surprising. A fellow Irish officer from the 48th Native Infantry and distant relative, Lieutenant

Richard Olpherts, took the 20-year-old under his wing. Nicholson admitted to his mother, 'Indeed, but for his kindness, I don't know what I should have done. He supplied me with clothes and other necessities, and I lived with him till I reached Peshawur.' Nicholson was not the only soldier to be shaken by the Afghanistan ordeal. George Lawrence, who was to later become a close friend, was forced by ill health to take leave and was back in Britain for nearly three years before he could face returning to India.

And yet the old Nicholson was not too deep below the surface. He looked extraordinary after his ordeal and his wearing Afghan clothing heightened the 'wild man' effect. The story was told that, while in Kabul at this time, Major Chamberlain was walking along when he was struck by a stone. Spinning around, he saw a tall Afghan whom he made for as he reached for his sword. Seconds later, he stood before a laughing Nicholson. There was a warm reunion. It was also then that Nicholson met the young Harry Lumsden. They remained friends until Nicholson died fifteen years later.[37]

On 12 October 1842, the orderly British retreat out of Afghanistan began as Generals Pollock and Nott marched out of Kabul. It would be nearly four decades before a British army returned, and once again it would be an avenging army. On 22 October, the army passed Jalalabad, the British sappers blowing up the walls of the fortress. There was a pleasant surprise awaiting Nicholson on that slow retreat out of Afghanistan. On 1 November, at Dhaka, at the Afghan entrance to the Khyber Pass, Nicholson ran into his brother Alexander. Alexander, now 18, was serving as an ensign in the 30th Native Infantry in the Bengal Army, having joined that regiment in April 1841.

But yet again disaster loomed for Nicholson. While General Pollock managed to extricate his army from Afghanistan largely unscathed, old General Nott had a much more difficult journey, his rear being harassed by Afghan raiders. These attacks, often on the civilian component attached to the army, were driven off by regular troops. Needless to say, John Nicholson was in the thick of this rearguard action. But also, and unbeknown to him, so was Alexander. In one of these actions, during the night of Thursday, 3 November 1842, near the hill fort of Ali Musjid within the pass, young Alexander Nicholson was killed. Far below the fort was a narrow defile, an ideal place for an ambush. As fate would have it, it was John Nicholson riding down the 28-mile-long Khyber Pass with Lieutenant Julius Dennys of the 38th Bengal Native Infantry who found the body. Dennys's account of this ran as follows:

He was riding along with me one day on our ever harassing rearguard duty. Pollock's force was always marching one or two days ahead of ours,

and Nicholson had a brother in that force. Our attention was attracted to
something lying some two or three hundred yards off the road on our right,
which gave us the idea that it might be the nude body of an European. To
leave the column of route was against orders and unsafe, as you could never
tell but that an Afghan from behind a rock would be at you; but we cantered
up to see what the object was. I got there first and found the body of an
European, naked with the exception of some remnants of a shirt about his
neck, and the whole of the stomach mutilated, being crimped like a codfish,
with the bowels protruding. Jumping off my horse, I observed the texture
of the shirt to be quite superior to that worn by private soldiers and, as
Nicholson came up, I remarked upon this. I saw him gaze at the body and
for a moment he could not speak. He had recognised it as that of his brother.
I rode back to the column and procured a dhoolee and then pushed on with
it, accompanied by Nicholson, till we reached our halting ground. I had a
small Shouldaree tent of my own to go to, and we dug a hole in the ground
inside it and put the poor fellow in, covering it with earth so as to leave a
mound. We then collected all the wood we could and burned a large bonfire
over it, leaving only the ashes, that the Afghans might suspect nothing, as
they were very fond of disinterring our dead and heaping indignities on
the bodies. It was a strange and sad circumstance. Poor Nicholson felt it
keenly and the tears coursed down his cheeks, which I fancy in him was a
rare and unusual thing; but it drew him and myself a good deal [closer] to
each other and, on our arrival at Meerut, we lived in the same bungalow
together. I never met him after that but came to know much of him at that
time … He made me feel that he had probably in him what must make him
a man of mark. Fear of any kind seemed unknown to him and one could see
that there was a great depth behind his reserve, and at times almost boorish,
manner. I never met him again after those days.[38]

Nicholson had been in a bad enough frame of mind without this disaster.
Alexander was buried on the Sunday. The first evidence we have are two
letters written to Clara Nicholson on the Monday and the Tuesday. This was
the first contact Nicholson had made with his mother for more than a year. So
the excitement of a letter from her favourite son was shattered with the news:

Poor Alexander is no more. He was killed in action, when on rear-guard on
3rd instant, but I know that you will not sorrow as one without hope, but
rather rejoice that it has pleased the Lord to take him from this world of
sorrow and temptation. Poor boy, I met him only two days before his death

at Dacca and a happy meeting it was for neither of us anticipated such a melancholy termination of it. He was buried by a Clergyman of the church of England which few have been who have perished in this country. He was much liked in his regiment who all speak highly of his gallantry.

Now my dearest Mother let me entreat you not to grieve more than you can help, Alexr. met a soldier's death, in the execution of his duty, and a more glorious death he could not have died.[39]

However, two days later Nicholson was compelled to write again to his mother, who was now back living in Lisburn:

I wrote to you yesterday, but as letter bags are sometimes lost in this country, I sit down to inform you again, of what I entreat you to bear with Christian resignation and fortitude, and sorrow not for him that is gone as one without hope, but rejoice, rather, that it has pleased God to remove him from this world of sorrow and temptation. How true it is that 'In the midst of life we are in death.' Just this day week I met poor Alexander at Dacca, and you may imagine we were both happy at meeting after our long separation. Three days after I placed him in his grave; but it is a consolation to me that he met a glorious death. He was killed in action, near Ali Musjid, on the night of the 3rd inst. He was a great favourite with the officers of his corps, who all speak in high terms of his courage and amiable qualities. Indeed I never saw a boy more improved than he was, and deeply do I feel his loss. It will be a consolation to you to know that he was buried by a clergyman of the church of England. Few have been, who have perished in this country. I am keeping some little things of his which I will send you by Lieutenant Olpherts of H.M. 48th, who is going home soon. The rest of his property when auctioned will, with his back pay, amount to about 100£. This I will make arrangements for having sent to you, immediately on our arrival in Hindustan. He was entitled to a silver medal as one of the army at Jellalabad. When it arrives I will also send it you. There were many subjects on which I had intended [writing] to you, but I must keep them for my next. I hope both you and grandmamma enjoy good health now and are not troubled with rheumatism. Pray write soon and frequently; my greatest pleasure is hearing from you. Have Lily and Charles quite recovered from their several complaints of last year. With love to all I remain my dearest mother … Excuse the shortness of my letter, but I am not in spirits to write anything at present.[40]

Two postscripts can be provided to this Afghanistan saga as a letter Nicholson wrote to his mother in April 1843, five months after Alexander's death, shows he was never one to forgive and forget:

I duly received your and Mary's letters of January, and I was glad to learn from them that you had been enabled to bear up so well against the shock occasioned by the news of poor Alexander's death. The President of the Committee of Adjustment will, ere this, have communicated with you about his property. But some delay must necessarily take place before the accounts of the Cabul army are adjusted, and till then, the exact amount can scarcely be told...You ask me to write you the details of the last year fully. I sent you from Ferozepoor a newspaper, containing a brief but well-written account of the siege of Ghuznee, and our imprisonment, after which nothing of any interest occurred. I cannot help being amused (though disgusted) at the ideas of the people at home, regarding the war in Affghanistan. One would suppose that the Affghans, instead of being the most vicious and bloodthirsty race in existence, who fight merely for love of bloodshed and plunder, were noble-minded patriots. The stories told, too, of the excesses committed by our troops are false, or greatly exaggerated. The villages or forts of only such people were destroyed, as had signalised themselves by their treachery and hostility towards the force of 1841. Cabul itself, for instance, Chareekor, where a whole Regiment was destroyed without pity. Lydabad, where an officer and 100 men were murdered in cold blood, as the Affghans always do commit murder. I do not think myself the retribution was heavy enough, and I was sorry to leave Cabul while one stone of it remained on another.[41]

In similar combative mode, Nicholson wrote to his aunt in London, venturing to criticise, probably correctly, the great Duke of Wellington for saying that Ghazni 'surrendered without any pressure … the want of water, or I should rather say of snow, for we never had any water, would by most military men, I imagine, be considered rather a severe pressure'.[42] According to army regulations, Colonel Palmer had to face the ordeal of a court martial over his surrender at Ghazni. Given the circumstances, it is not surprising that he was acquitted.

That will have pleased Nicholson, but what he thought of Lord Ellenborough, the governor-general, and the 'garish pageant' as the army finally entered British territory at Ferozepur we do not know. The Afghanistan venture had been an utter disaster: a disaster for the British army and a personal disaster for Nicholson. As if he had not had enough to cope with in his repressed upbringing and then being sent away as a soldier to a completely alien land at 16, now added to that had been his grim imprisonment, what he can only have seen as being encaged, and his subsequent discovery of the mutilated body of his younger brother. That the insular Nicholson did not snap is surprising. This was probably due in the short term to the kindness of the Olpherts and in the medium term to the fact that in Afghanistan he also met Henry Lawrence, sixteen years his elder but carved from the same evangelical Ulster stock as Nicholson. In the years to come, Henry Lawrence was to watch over young Nicholson and give him the anchor he so badly needed in life.

The second postscript is to note that, despite the shocking recent death of his younger brother, Lieutenant Nicholson was among thirty of the former prisoners, including Lady Macnaghten and Lady Sales, who subscribed toward an article of plate and a testimonial to be presented to Elden Pottinger for the 'cheerfullness [sic] and determination' with which he had extracted the party from the clutches of the Afghans.[43]

# War Against the Sikhs

Nicholson grumbled a great deal about how he had been treated by the British authorities after his release from captivity in Afghanistan, but in that he was by no means alone. He had lost some personal belongings for which he was not fully compensated. But there was some good news. On 14 December 1842, three days after his twentieth birthday, Nicholson was promoted to lieutenant, backdated to 13 January 1842. He had begun to climb the career ladder.[1]

Soon John Nicholson found himself back with his regiment at the large military cantonment at Meerut, only 45 miles from Delhi. To Mary Hogg, Nicholson spoke of a mutual friend, John Swinton of the 53rd Native Infantry, whom Nicholson liked and with whom he offered to share a house should Swinton return to the plains. In the end, he shared accommodation with Dennys, who recalled some years later, 'in general he was reserved almost to moroseness in those days, and I was one of the very few who were anyway intimate with him'.[2] Captain Trotter, in his biography, was later to comment that Nicholson 'had come out of this fiery ordeal in Afghanistan hardened in body, and perhaps a little in mind'.

For a while, Nicholson had the pleasant company of Richard Olpherts and his sister Mrs Dunkin, but Olpherts went off on furlough leave. Nicholson was soon bored, very bored, and grumbling: 'I dislike India and its inhabitants more every day and I would rather go home on £200 a year than live like a prince here.' He expressed satisfaction to his mother on the news that both his brothers, William and Charles, were thinking of not joining the army in India, although conceded that Charles might distinguish himself as a soldier. But grumbles such as Nicholson's were common enough in the Company's officer corps as a means of occasionally letting off steam. In September 1857 Lieutenant Roberts, who had many decades ahead of him still in India, wrote to his mother in Waterford of 'this horrid country'.[3]

Despite such grumbling, as Nicholson recovered from the shock of imprisonment, he admitted to his mother, 'At the same time I have so much reason to be thankful, that I do not grumble at my lot being cast in this country.' To his youthful and pretty aunt back in London, he said that he was studying hard. This was for his indigenous language exam. But he found the great heat made language revision very difficult.

Soon Nicholson was turning over in his mind an offer to become adjutant of the 27th. In the end, on 31 May 1843, he took the job as nothing much else was on the horizon. Very shortly after this, the regiment moved slightly east to the much more pleasant outpost station at Moradabad in the Rohilcund district, to the east of Delhi and within sight of the Himalayas. Here, on 7 August 1843, Nicholson wrote an uncharacteristically long letter to his mother. It is clear that Clara Nicholson's comment about his financial situation needled him. He was, truth to tell, not earning enough to retain his station in the regiment and remit regular sums of money home to Lisburn. And one can well believe that Nicholson was not extravagant in anything except his weaponry and his horses:

In your letter you say I must have plenty of money, as I drew arrears as a lieutenant. I was, it is true, a Lieutenant during my imprisonment, but I did not get even [an] ensign's allowances, nor was I allowed the 1450 Rupees generally granted for compensation on account of loss of baggage in war. For the six months I was a prisoner I drew only 120 rupees a month, and this did not even half cover my losses or pay for a new outfit, so that I am really thrown into debt through no fault of my own.

Before I knew that Compensation allowance would be retrenched, I wrote to Uncle James [Hogg] promising him 1000 Rs of it, but that is out of the question now. I must first pay off my debts here, and then save the money. An Adjutant's allowances are about 200 Rs a month more than his pay as a subaltern, and he has to keep up a charger and a writer or clerk. I have just paid 600 Rs for the former.

In six months I have every reason to believe that I shall be out of debt, after which it is my intention to remit home 100£ yearly. This, when Uncle James is paid, you, of course, will receive. I have written this much to prove that it is through no carelessness or extravagance of mine that I have not money at present, and I know many people at home labour under the delusion that poor Subalterns in this Country live luxuriously. Half the time I was in Affghanistan I paid 150 Rs a month and upwards, for camel hire, and that when my pay was 195 Rs great luxury!

Once over his financial woes, Nicholson moved on in the letter to more interesting matters. He was clearly shocked that Clara did not know that the Afghans were Muslim ('Mahomedans'), '… as I thought was well known at home, and they themselves claim descent from Saul, which I think not unlikely to be the case'. He then touches on political events in Ireland, something he rarely did in correspondence. Daniel O'Connell's mass movement for the repeal of the union between Ireland and Great Britain was by then at its height. Indeed, on 15 August 1843, a week after Nicholson was writing, O'Connell held his famous monster meeting at the Hill of Tara, where it is said he addressed 750,000 people. Nicholson comments, 'You say nothing in your letter about the probability of a rebellion in Ireland, though the papers are full of it. The knowledge that you are in one of the most loyal parts of Protestant Ulster makes me feel less uneasy about you than I otherwise should.' He followed up on this theme in a letter to his sister Mary four months later, commenting on the effects of such agitation in County Down, 'If the people are as loyal as they used to be, it will not make much way there.' Clearly, Nicholson was not over-anxious about 'Swaggering Dan', as O'Connell's opponents called him. He was more curious about the great swarm of locusts he had recently seen: 'at a distance they looked exactly like clouds. They have done great mischief in this part of India since summer.'[4]

A month later, Nicholson, in September 1843, having scraped together £100, wrote to his mother with a proposal. It is obvious that Nicholson felt that he had gone out to India without either military training or knowledge of the region. He was not going to allow this situation to repeat itself with his brother Charles, who now seemed destined for the Bengal Army. Charles must be sent to the Company's training college at Addiscombe, believed Nicholson:

> Young men who come out to India with direct appointment have no knowledge of their profession whatever, either practical or theoretical; and are sometimes, very shortly after their arrival, placed in responsible situations (as many subalterns were in Afghanistan, the other day), when a military education would be of invaluable advantage to them.

Charles must have arrived in India sometime in the second half of 1846, joining his regiment, the 31st Bengal Native Infantry, in September. Three years later, in September 1849, he moved to become adjutant of the 2nd Punjab Cavalry, in which position he remained until the fall of Delhi.[5]

The two and a half years between Nicholson's arrival in Moradabad and the outbreak of the first Anglo-Sikh War are somewhat shrouded in mystery, although it is most likely that it was a dull enough time for the lieutenant. They were important years, however, as he was learning the ropes of the British administration. Nicholson is remembered as a famous – or infamous – soldier, but there is no denying his contributions as a political officer and deputy commissioner on the frontier were significant. During this period Nicholson at last managed to get his Indian languages up to scratch and in November 1845 he travelled more than 200 miles to Ambala and passed the interpreter's exam without any problems.[6] This now allowed him to be considered for positions on the general staff. No doubt it was on his return that he found a small pocket Bible in black leather binding with a pressure clip fastener that his mother had sent out and which she had inscribed:

> John Nicholson from his
> fondly attached mother
> Sept. 15. 1845.
> Psa 34-37-103-119-121-46
> Jho. 14 – Rom 12 – Gal 6. Cl3
> 1st Thes.5 – Heb 12. 1st Peter
> Psa 119-11
> In February 1845 Heb 13.20.21[7]

One further note needs to be added concerning the Nicholson family at this time, and that is the marriage of John's sister Mary to Rev. Edward Maxwell. He had been a curate at Leeds, but now with his wife transferred to the industrial town of Barnsley in Yorkshire.

## FIRST ANGLO-SIKH WAR 1845–46

On 12 December 1845 the Sikh army, or Khalsa army as it was called, crossed the River Sutlej, with a force of some 100,000 men. This army was not to be underestimated. It was organised into thirty-five regiments and included 15,000 'splendidly mounted cavalrymen'. In addition there was an enormous body of irregular troops numbering perhaps 150,000. The bulk of the army were on the Sutlej, with cohorts at Peshawar and at Lahore. On 13 December, Britain declared war.[8]

At this time Nicholson made another change and joined the army's Commissariat Department, supplying the lumbering army of the commander-in-chief, General Sir Hugh Gough. Charles Allen says that Nicholson obtained this position through the influence of his uncle, James Hogg.[9] As things turned out, Nicholson, while still being a member of the 27th, was never to serve with that regiment again. Not surprisingly, Nicholson was not particularly 'partial' to working in this section. Nonetheless, it was in the commissariat that Nicholson saw service in the first Anglo-Sikh war. He was not a prominent figure in the campaign. This might in part have been because throughout the whole of 1846 Nicholson was in constant ill health.

But he was present 'as a commissariat officer, and not, to his regret, as a combatant', at the hard-won British victory at the battle of Mudki on 18 December 1845 and again at 'that bloody bull-dog fight', the battle of Ferozeshah on 21–22 December 1845.[10] In the latter, Nicholson's hero General George Broadfoot ('brave as he was able') was mortally wounded, so depriving the government of its political agent in the Punjab and consequently opening up a career promotion for Henry Lawrence. And it was in this campaign on the Sutlej that Nicholson re-met Henry Lawrence, who had been with General Sales when the Afghan prisoners had finally been found in 1842. Lawrence was to become one of the key influences in the young Nicholson's life, and would himself soon be appointed British Resident in Lahore.

The might of the Sikh army was not smashed until Sir Harry Smith's victory at Aliwal on 28 January, the arrival of a substantial British artillery force and Sir Hugh Gough's victory at Sobraon on 10 February, culminating in the East India Army, including Nicholson, advancing across the Sutlej and entering the Punjab capital, Lahore, on 20 February. From there, Nicholson wrote to his mother, admitting that the British losses had been heavy but less so than those of the Sikh army.

Instead of the British government doing the obvious and annexing the Punjab, an ad hoc political solution that satisfied few was patched together by the governor-general, Sir Henry Hardinge (1785–1856), an associate of Henry Lawrence. The British chipped off sections of the Punjab, including the Doab between the rivers Ganga and Jumna, but most notably Kashmir, which it promptly transferred to the raja of Jammu, Gulab Singh (1792–1857), 'the best Politician in India',[11] along with a war indemnity price tag of 75 lakh (7.5 million rupees).

## KASHMIR (APRIL 1846–FEBRUARY 1847)

Having handed over Kashmir to Gulab Singh, the British then assigned two army officers as military advisers and, more to the point, as tokens of Britain's support for the new usurper. These two tokens of empire were Captain Arthur Broome of the Bengal Artillery and Lieutenant John Nicholson of the 27th. Their instructions were sensible enough:

> Your business will be to instruct the Maharajah's troops, but you will not accompany them on military expeditions. Should however an outbreak occur on the spot where you may be located you will use your best exertions to quell it. You have no political duties, and no authority but such as the Maharajah may invest you with. As instructors of his Troops, Lieut. Nicholson and yourself will treat the Maharajah with respect and attention. Whenever he wishes, you will attend his public Darbars, but as far as possible you will avoid private interviews. When asked your opinion, you will give it plainly and, with reference to each particular case, as publicly as possible; but unless so consulted you will altogether abstain from interference in the Maharajah's affairs.[12]

Attached to the two officers were to be six infantry and four artillery non-commissioned officers, a sub-assistant surgeon and a *munshi*, making a total in the British contingent of fourteen.

The decision to send Nicholson to this most beautiful part of India was that of Henry Lawrence, although the position was offered personally by Sir Henry Hardinge, who remained governor-general through to 1848. Of course, Nicholson as usual did not know when to keep quiet and said he would accept the assignment on condition that if he did not like it he was to be allowed to return to his seconded post in the commissariat department. The governor-general hinted that at the end of the assignment there might be something better for Nicholson. This would not be the first time that Nicholson was made vague promises that were not quickly kept and which tended to fester in his mind and to lead to much grumbling in his correspondence. He was also now constantly ill, which did not help matters. How much of this illness was psychosomatic can only be guessed, but there is no doubt that inactivity and inaction had a serious detrimental effect on his physical and mental health.

On Thursday, 2 April 1846, Nicholson arrived at Jammu. He was soon very bored; his accommodation was poor and he was eager to proceed to his new posting over the mountains. But Nicholson was probably correct in his assessment that the maharaja had little interest in having his troops disciplined along Bengal Army lines. What he wanted was to be seen with uniformed British army officers by his side to show 'the terms of intimacy he was on with the British Government'.[13] Four long months later, the maharaja decided to travel to his new province and set off over the passes to Kashmir with Nicholson and Broome in tow.

## A WILL FOR FAMILY AND FRIENDS

Before departing on this adventure Nicholson made a will. With the Afghanistan experience and a Sikh war behind him, the 24-year-old had seen his fair share of death. One had to be prepared. In fact, like many a young Company officer, Nicholson had very little in the way of worldly possessions. Not surprisingly, his mother was to inherit nearly everything: his money in the Lahore Residency treasury; any pay owing to him; his furs and pashminas; and his Bible. Nicholson's Company papers, worth about 5,500 rupees along with interest, and in the hands of his uncle James Hogg, completed this bequest. Nicholson's writing desk, which was at Lahore, went to his Uncle Richardson; and the balance, including his horses, gun, pistols and books, went to his brothers Charles and William.[14] Charles Nicholson was his executor and the will was witnessed in Peshawar on 8 August 1848 by Major Lawrence (11th Light Cavalry), Lieutenant C.V. Bowie (Artillery) and Lieutenant Herbert Edwardes (18th BNI).

The last name was to become a key figure in Nicholson's life. Herbert Benjamin Edwardes (1819–68) was born in Shropshire in 1819, just a few years before Nicholson.[15] In some respects, they were very similar in that both lost their father while boys, Edwardes when he was only 4. Both were brought up in a strictly evangelical household; neither went to military college; both first made their name in the Anglo-Sikh wars (Edwardes more than Nicholson); both fell under the spell of Sir Henry Lawrence; both were seconded to the civil administration where they excelled; both were fluent in various Asian languages such as Hindi, Urdu and Persian; and both were extraordinarily able military commanders, gaining in particular the trust of Indian troops. It also has to be said that both were very eccentric, to the point of being peculiar.

However, there were also fundamental differences between these two characters. Edwardes was bookish, looked dishevelled but was good company and had a ready wit, whereas Nicholson was no great writer, had a laconic wit rather than good humour, dressed smartly and stood upright with his head held back as he walked, a trait copied from his mother. This mannerism in particular, combined with his natural reserve and shyness, gained for Nicholson a reputation for arrogance. Edwardes was diplomatic and could hold his temper; Nicholson achieved neither. Edwardes could 'work the system'; Nicholson had little appreciation of finesse in handling his superiors. It also has to be said that there is no factual evidence to support the claim made in one online blog that Nicholson and Edwardes were lovers.

Frederick Steele wrote of Edwardes:

> He is the nicest man I have seen in India. He has made me a present of several Hindustanii books, and when I had the fever he used to send me over great blocks of ice, which is no small luxury out here, and he now frequently sends me baskets of mangoes, peaches and grapes. By the bye I was greatly disappointed in the mangoes, which in my opinion are not so good as a good apple or pear at home. However the Lahore mangoes are I believe considered a very bad specimen of their kind.[16]

## TROUBLE IN SRINAGAR

Nicholson arrived in Srinagar on Wednesday, 12 August 1846. Things had started going wrong for the maharaja in this predominantly Muslim state and a full revolt was soon under way, with the new ruler having to escape the region as quickly as he could. Nicholson and Broome made their own escapes separately via the southern passes, arriving back in Jammu about 20 September.[17]

By November 1846, though, the insurrection had been brought to submission, through the diplomacy of Herbert Edwardes and 'the intimidation by an army of 10,000 under Henry Lawrence', which until recently had been the enemy of the British. The insurrection petered out and Nicholson was reinstalled back in Kashmir along with Henry Lawrence and several other British officers, including Harry Lumsden. In a letter to his father, Lumsden recalled:

> Nicholson and I had just got to the end of a long march, on our way up to Cashmere, when he dismounted, and I, following his example, gave my horse to a villager to hold. The man had scarcely taken hold of the bridle when the horse shook himself, and bang went the brace of pistols, blowing out the end of the holsters, and the ball from one taking the point of the poor man's nose off, for which I had to recompense him to the best of my power.[18]

On 16 November, though, the British party moved out of Srinagar to return to Lahore, leaving only Nicholson and Patrick van Agnew.[19] Soon the latter was recalled and Nicholson found himself alone, bored and again fell ill: 'I shall not be sorry to get away from Cashmere,' he wrote, 'which at this season is anything but a terrestrial Paradise. My fingers are so cold that I can scarcely hold the pen, and glazed windows are unknown here.' Admittedly it was very cold, but this is strange coming from someone who had as a child experienced the gloom and cold of the dank Lagan Valley winter. One suspects Nicholson was just finding things to express his frustration. A week later, on 23 November 1846, he told his brother Charles in a letter:

> I would have written to you on my arrival here a fortnight ago, but I was then, and have been since, laid up with a severe attack of fever and ague. I am now getting better, but living in an open house. I dread a relapse, as the weather is very raw and cold. Lawrence, Broome and the others started on their return on the 16th, and I am quite alone here.
>
> Between ourselves, Lawrence has appointed me to officiate in the Agency pending a reply to his application to Govt, to have me permanently appointed to it. In the event of its being favourable, I shall leave Cashmere when my work is finished, and go down either to Lahore or the Jullender, wherever it may be decided, to station me, in either case, I hope we shall have the pleasure of meeting one another.
>
> Gowan likewise enclosed me a letter from our mother asks me if I intend availing myself of my furlough when entitled to it?
>
> I have suffered so much from ill-health within the last eight months that, unless some improvement takes place, I fear I shall be obliged to go out of India somewhere on the S.C. before long – I have had more sickness within this twelvemonth than in the previous 6½ years, and I sometimes fear that my constitution is going.
>
> Nothing brings home to a man's mind more readily in India than illness; he then thinks of the nursing and grateful acts of attention he would receive were he among his own friends. Here, I have not even the sight of a white face to cheer me. May you never be in a like predicament.[20]

It would, however, be more than three years until Nicholson saw the green fields of home again. In the meantime, he had recurring bouts of illness. On record, we know that for nine days he was confined to bed with fever in September 1847. He was again laid low for a week in April 1849, and from his letters these were by no means the only times. When Nicholson's *munshi* also took ill in September 1847, 'business [was] at a standstill'.

In the immediate term in Kashmir, Nicholson had to deal with the maharaja, who was hoarding rice to push up the price and profiteering from the venture. Nicholson remonstrated with him and obtained a promise that some rice would be brought into the city. By 20 December, though, none had yet arrived.

## BACK TO THE PUNJAB

The imperial world, though, had not forgotten Nicholson, and to his great delight Henry Lawrence secured him a new appointment, first in an acting capacity in the North-West Frontier Agency, but soon a confirmed appointment by Calcutta as assistant to the Resident in the Punjab capital, Lahore. This was a 'political' not a military posting. It is interesting that Nicholson was not a failure at this and that for one who complained bitterly about his inability to write letters home regularly, he was to prove to be a first-class political officer.

It was with no regrets that Nicholson set off from Srinagar on Sunday, 7 February 1847 on his journey to the plains, 'crossing eight and a half feet of snow in the Poonah [Poonch] Pass'. On arrival at Ramnagar, not too far from Lahore, he was ordered to make the long journey south-west to Multan. [21] Nicholson wrote to Henry Lawrence:

> I shall be much obliged if you can lend me or borrow or buy for me a map, with the part of the country I am about to visit, in it: will you also kindly send me ½ dozen doses of salt and jalop, and a little calomel and quinine, as many of my servants are suffering from fever; a little ink, a comb, toothbrush, and cake or two of soap. [22]

This diversion suited Nicholson just fine as he had heard that his younger brother Charles was with his regiment, the 31st Native Infantry, at Multan. Having reached his destination on about 24 March, Lieutenant Nicholson breakfasted and then strode off through the army camp in search of Subaltern Nicholson. When they met, neither recognised the other. Eight years had passed and the schoolboy had grown into a tall lanky young man, even taller than John's 6ft 2in. John Nicholson wrote of the encounter:

> Fancy neither of us recognising the other. I actually talked to him half an hour before I could persuade myself of his identity ... You may remember my saying to you, some time ago, that the want of society had [rend]ered me low spirited. Well, I have within the last few months become so reconciled to living alone, that really were not Charles here, I should wish myself away again in the Cashmere hills or Jummoo forests. [23]

Many of Nicholson's psychological problems stemmed from the fact that he was a deeply lonely man. But from now until his death, Charles was never too far away and the presence of a friendly younger brother at least helped keep the demons at bay for Nicholson. And for his part, for such a young and inexperienced young man, Charles behaved in a most mature manner in relation to his ever more famous elder brother, in whose shadow he was destined to remain for the rest of his life. Charles kept his quiet Ulster good humour and common sense, qualities not always uppermost in his elder brother's character.

Initially, Nicholson was sent around the Punjab on various reporting missions by Colonel Henry Lawrence. But he spent May and part of June 1847 in Lahore surrounded by the pleasant and rather like-thinking young men of Lawrence's kindergarten. At one time or another, these included such as James Abbott, Johnny Becher, Arthur Broome, Arthur Cocks, Henry Coxe, Herbert Edwardes, Harry Lumsden, and Reynell Taylor. Some of these were regular army officers and others were seconded politicals. Later, these young men were to look back upon this time as halcyon days. Henry Lawrence's wife, the gentle and devout Honoria Lawrence, who had spent her childhood in the idyllic setting of Fahan beside Lough Swilly in County Donegal, acted as surrogate mother to the young, muscular Christian officers.[24]

They all lived in the old tomb of the legendary Anarkali at Lahore. The word tomb gives a false impression. It was more like a palace, with high ceilings, wide passageways and open verandas. Writing to Nicholson from Nepal some years later, Honoria described it as, 'a wilderness of a house, so hot and so cold, and so noisy'. In her boudoir, the young officers lounged about chatting and sorting out the wrongs of the world. How many of these young men were either homosexual or latently so is a matter for speculation but the salon ethos of the place was not one to attract the heartiest of heterosexuals.

## INTELLIGENCE WORK IN AMRITSAR

Nicholson was not entombed in Lahore for long. In June 1847 he was sent on a special mission to Amritsar to check up on the local Sikh officials and the state of the district. He paid special attention to the great fort of Govindgarh, assessing its guns, stores and ammunition. He listed details of the guns. To a list of seven brass, eighteen iron and fourteen hill guns without carriages, he added: 'There are also 20 zemboors 70 wall pieces and 500 muskets and matchlocks.' In the arsenal, there were 73,029 balls; 3,614 shells; 36,214 grape and canisters; 34,910 zumboor balls. There were also 3,645 maunds (160 tons) of gunpowder, 2,500 of it still good, as well as 14,984 maunds (650 tons) of lead and 2,412 (105 tons) of iron. As part of his spying operation, Nicholson also listed food stocks, which included 103,721 maunds (4,550) of wheat, 10,649 (167 tons) of salt and 4,617 (200 tons) of rice.

He found Amritsar to his surprise to be 'as clean as Lahore; there is at present little or no sickness in it'. He discussed in his letter to Henry Lawrence various characters in the city establishment. 'With regard to Bhaie Maharaj, I believe him to be a harmless man himself, whose object is to acquire a name for great sanctity and benevolence, but I think it would be advisable to put a stop to the daily assemblage at his house of all the idle vagabonds in the country, who go to partake of the food, he is in the habit of distributing.'[25]

Nicholson was sent at the end of June 1847 from Amritsar to what was meant to be his permanent posting in the south to Multan. But he was soon back north as 'political officer in command' in the Sindh Sagar Doab between the Indus and the Jhelum rivers, in which was situated the town of Rawalpindi. This was a region full of differing peoples. Captain Trotter rather sweepingly listed them as ranging from 'the warlike Ghakkars, Pathâns, and Rajputs, to the cattle-lifting Gujars and the peaceful Jats'. It was also very rugged country with a plethora of 'fort-crowned hills'. This stretched from Attock to Rawalpindi and on to Jhelum, south-west to Jhang and north to where his area adjoined both that of the maharaja of Kashmir and his new friend Captain Abbott's domain in Hazara. Nicholson tended to make his headquarters at Hasan Abdal, about 25 miles north-west of Rawalpindi. As when in Bannu, Nicholson travelled endlessly, visiting the small towns and the villages, some of which were walled. This was indeed a difficult and enormous territory to control, for he had to ensure that justice was fairly administered and revenue collected. This was complicated because he had to work through the previous Sikh order. Alongside, there were local leaders to placate, also the ever-present threat of trans-Indus raids. Writing to Nicholson, Henry Lawrence laid out his instructions:

You are requested to cultivate the acquaintance of the two Nazims [regional governors], Sirdars Chutter Singh and Lal Singh, as also of their deputies, as indeed of all the respectable Kardars that you meet. Much may be done by cordiality, by supporting their just authority, attending to their moderate wishes, and even whims, and by those small courtesies that all natives look to, even more than they do to more important matters. I need only hint at these points to ensure your zealous attention to them. The protection of the people from the oppression of the Kardars will be your first duty … your next most important care will be the army … without allowing the troops to be unduly harassed, see that parades and drills are attended to. I insist upon insubordination and plunder being promptly punished; and bring to my notice any particular instance of good conduct. Avoid as far as possible any military movement during the next three months; but should serious disturbance arise, act energetically.[26]

Nicholson got off to a bad start with John Lawrence, who was commissioner of the Jullundur district. Lawrence obviously considered that Nicholson had not done a particularly good job in assessing the returns of cultivated lands in his sector. This elicited a defensive response explaining the difficulties of assessing such matters. That Nicholson's hero, Henry Lawrence, was John's older brother cannot have endeared Nicholson to his new boss. John and Henry were frequently at loggerheads. After Henry found his written instructions that Nicholson had left behind on a table when riding off on an allotted mission, all he said to the miscreant was, 'you are a neat youth'.[27] John's reaction would have been very different. Matters were not helped by the fact that Nicholson was frequently ill and as such even less diplomatic than his usual taciturn self. But in fairness to Nicholson, his reports show a balanced approach as well as assiduous attention to detail, albeit succinctly stated. One can well believe that it would be difficult for a new official to grasp immediately the details of something as complicated as land occupation and ownership, especially after such an unsettled period, and when the new, alien official can hardly have been welcomed. Perhaps rather naively, Nicholson stated – and no doubt believed – that fair government as he perceived it would, as he stated to Henry Lawrence in December 1847, 'make the people content'.

No sooner had Nicholson established himself in his new fiefdom in the doab than he was called upon to assist in the neighbouring mountainous terrain of Hazara. Nicholson had to move north with two military columns to assist the Punjab boundary commissioner, the redoubtable Captain James Abbott (1807–96), in his quest to bring to heel the leaders of Simulkund, who were raiding Bakkar. It is probable that this was Nicholson's first fully independent military command. Needless to say, he exceeded his mandate and instead of staying in reserve on the border of Hazara, he crossed it and occupied Simulkund without opposition. This was to be the way of things to come. Nicholson was also ill again, commenting from Hazarra in September 1847 to Edwardes that he must follow Sir Henry home to Britain and Ireland, as, 'I don't think I can stand another hot season in the plains.'[28]

# NICHOLSON'S WORK DIARY (1847 TO 1849)

It is illuminating to look at Nicholson's official daily diaries while he was administering the Rawalpindi doab region to see what interested him as well as his style of governing.[29] Though he carried the unprepossessing title of Assistant to the Resident and until March 1849 was a mere lieutenant, Nicholson's de facto role was that of military governor of the doab.

Nicholson's energy and determination emerge clearly in his official diaries. Unlike so many administrators, Nicholson had a good retentive memory and was constantly following up on whether his orders had been carried out. In the Rawalpindi district, this was crucial because of the recent war. Without an effective central government authority, administration of this doab district had largely degenerated, with a great variety of petty rulers, warlords and officials quick enough to pocket those revenues they continued to collect and which had previously been forwarded to Lahore.

Six main groups of administrative matters concerned Nicholson in the twenty-six-month period between March 1847 and April 1849:

**Taxes**
In the Sindh Sagar Doab, Nicholson spent much time assessing the agricultural revenue of each district and assigning a 'settlement' of how much Lahore would be paid in a two or a three-year period, depending on circumstances. Nicholson achieved this by personally marching with his troops around the vast area forming his territory. He invariably tried to trace revenue books from the previous dispensation so he could form some idea as to how much a specific region might be expected to produce. Surprisingly, many of these had survived. But where they had been destroyed Nicholson went to great lengths interviewing people and looking at the land before determining a reasonable rate of tax. By studying the revenue books at Khatur, he was able to prove that 'Mukun Sing, the rebel Kardar' had embezzled 8,000 rupees. Singh admitted this and agreed to pay back the amount within a few days.

**Roads**
Whether to fill up space in his sometimes rather scanty reports or to comment on conditions for military operations, Nicholson frequently commented upon the conditions of the roads. These were generally good, although sometimes they were bisected by ravines that had to be negotiated. Only once did the road condition seriously affect his progress. On journeying to Leree, all went well until it rained. Nicholson commented, 'Rain having fallen during the night,

nine [camels] were 24 hours in getting up the last four miles, – indeed, so much assistance was necessary that they may be almost said to have been carried up.'

Nicholson also sometimes noted the type of terrain through which the road passed. For example, the road in the Bhawana area passed 'almost entirely through grass jungle' and that further on, the soil is 'wholly unproductive owing to its being impregnated with saltpetre'.

## Crime

Throughout his career in the civil sector, Nicholson was always zealous in his pursuit of criminals, particularly murderers. He went to endless trouble badgering and even threatening local rulers to hand over miscreants who had fled across borders in search of safety. Nicholson found himself caught up in a time-consuming murder investigation of a woman called Shah Khanum, concerning which case a leading local official appeared to have been bribed. Nicholson commented, 'The inhabitants of the province have so much Affghan and Eusofzye blood in them, that they think little or nothing of taking life, and the example would have much greater effect, if made on the spot [at Chuch], than at a distance.' Later he commented, 'The fact is, that Chuch Patans think the murder of a woman, no murder, and to this creed of theirs it is owing, that I experienced so little difficulty in arriving at the truth in this case.'

Thanks to a contact, Nicholson managed to extract the runaway villain from the frontier hill country. He persisted with the case and finally recommended that the guilty man be executed. But the matter did not rest there. John Lawrence questioned Nicholson's authority to pass sentence, especially one of death. The matter dragged on and had not been resolved by the time Nicholson moved on to a new appointment.[30]

The widespread use of 'green salt', smuggled across the Indus from the Lachi salt mines near Kohat, in preference to the government-owned locally mined 'red salt' from the Surdhi mines, gave Nicholson much concern. As the smuggled salt was a fraction of the price of the local product, it is not surprising the former was widely used. In April 1849, Nicholson recovered 12,000 maunds (525 tons) of government salt that had been stolen by locals in the Rhotas region in the closing phase of the first Anglo-Sikh War.

Though Nicholson generally had a good sense of reality, occasionally he could not resist making a sweeping statement in his reports. He declared, for example, that the 'Awns', while not as noted for quarrels and blood feuds as those in the Gheb region, were less honest and petty thieving and highway robbery were common in their area. Highway robbers were one category of criminal that Nicholson sought out to punish severely.

One unique cache plundered by local *zamindars* (landowners) in the Arrah district that fell into Nicholson's hands was said to be the wedding garments of the daughter of the Sikh general and leader Chutter Singh. She had been meant to marry the maharaja of Kashmir. As will be seen, these Nicholson had to send to Lahore, but with the request he be allowed to keep one 'for a lady'. On other occasions, he was content to try a case and leave the verdict up to a local official or a military sirdar. In the case of a cow killing, for example, Nicholson's only stipulation was that the culprit was not to suffer death or maiming.

On another occasion, Nicholson bluntly refused to allow a murderer who had already been tried and only fined to be retried, stating that the murder 'could not be again punished for the same offence'. Then in the case of 'a courtezan desiring to abandon her trade and marry', Nicholson decided that she was at liberty to do so. News of Nicholson's field justice seeped back to the attorney general's office at Lahore and he received an officious letter demanding to know by what authority he was acting as a magistrate. In typical Nicholson style, he did not answer but just sent it on to his boss, Sir Henry Lawrence. No more was heard of the matter.

### The Army and the Military Situation

Nicholson was not averse to sending 200 to 300 troops to burn a few houses in a recalcitrant village and, of course, had assisted his friend Abbott with additional troops. At one time Abbott had several Sikh regiments on loan from Nicholson. But during this period there was no military emergency for Nicholson as would later be the case so often with raids into Bannu from the Afghan mountains. Accordingly, Nicholson could concentrate on reforming the regiments under his control, for example introducing British forms of drilling the troops and at least on one occasion undertaking the training himself. Many of these units had been part of the Sikh army that had recently been defeated and had in consequence low morale.

This was not helped, Nicholson found, by the fact that many of the local regiments had not been paid for at least five months, one for nine months. He made more than one representation to Lahore on the matter. He also addressed the issue of Indian non-commissioned officers who complained that they were given fifteen days less leave than the ranks. But the large number of troops who did not return from leave prompted Nicholson to advise that they should be tracked down and punished *pour encourager les autres*. And, like Herbert Edwardes a few years later, Nicholson was nervous about the number of old, small, mud-built forts in the region. Where he considered them unnecessary, he had them pulled down.

Another aspect of Nicholson's role as a military commander was to attempt to disarm the local population. By April 1849, he had managed by cajoling, threatening and seizure to bring in 13,000 firearms. On one occasion, he found good-quality swords hidden in mule saddles and matchlocks carefully wrapped in tent canvas and buried. This arms dump Nicholson believed to have been stashed by the defeated Khalsa army as it marched to surrender at Lahore.

Nicholson was also proactive in using the army to prevent possible civil unrest. News that rioting was likely at the Katas fair between rival sects of fakirs prompted him to despatch 200 soldiers to the town to maintain law and order. The other aspect of Nicholson's military endeavour was to give orders for the laying out of cantonments or military settlements at both Rawalpindi and Jhelum. He ensured that compensation was paid to those whose land had been expropriated for this purpose.

## Dealing with the Locals

On the whole Nicholson did not meet with hostility from the locals, who were frequently pleasantly surprised by the fairness of his tax settlements. They also cannot but have appreciated the fact that he largely eradicated plundering of crops by strong neighbours. And Nicholson was also responsive to what had happened to villagers in the immediate past, such as how along the main thoroughfare between Lahore and Attock, troops had lived off the land causing farmers to suffer. The impact of this was assessed by Nicholson and taken into consideration when fixing various tax settlements. Nicholson was severe, too, with soldiers who would 'openly plunder' the country people. But he added in one diary entry that as regards good order and discipline, 'the contact of the Sikh troops has in this respect been *most exemplary*'.

Nicholson spent days listening to complaints and either taking decisions or referring the matter to Lahore. One problem was that of the 'gold-washers' who sifted the river sand for gold fragments. On each *droon*, or wooden trough, they paid a hefty tax of seven rupees. This was considered excessive by the workers, and indeed revenue had declined by 50 per cent. Nicholson reduced the tax down to five rupees per trough. At Jhelum, the boatmen were disgruntled because the Sikh army had destroyed their boats and the new regime was now demanding a third of their takings. Nicholson increased the number of ferry boats from eight to twenty. He also released to its commander the steamer *Conqueror*, which had been commandeered as a ferry. Nicholson tried to sort out the issue of the famous bridge of boats at Attock as well; army engineers had instructed the boat bridge to be reassembled in what the boatmen considered the wrong place and when the river rose the construction began to break up.

Nicholson was on the side of the weavers, too. An entry in his official diary reads: 'The weavers (ibafindahs), complained of being used as *legarees*: forbade the practice in future. It is strange that this class of tradesmen seem throughout the Punjab to be selected for oppression.' And at one place Nicholson comments drily, 'The people are certainly much less litigious than those of Chuch, Khatur or Rawulpindee, and are on that account perhaps, worse off.'

As well as caste and ethnic divisions in the region Nicholson controlled, there were also religious divides that sometimes surfaced. At the town of Cukowala a number of Muslims complained to Nicholson that 'certain Khutrees forbid their calling to prayers; also that they were prohibited from yoking female oxen or buffaloos in their ploughs. I told the Kardar that interference with the *azan* was not authorised. On the latter point he said he had received positive instructions to prevent the employment in labor of female oxen.'

Gifts were occasionally offered and Nicholson was careful about how he handled such seemingly friendly gestures. On one occasion, he accepted some fruit and a Tibetan dog from the maharaja of Kashmir. He declined, though, even to open two shawls proffered by Gulab Singh's messenger. On another occasion, Nicholson accepted two pashmina chogah shawls from a local *nazim* (which no doubt ended up in Lisburn), but the following day Nicholson presented the *nazim* in return with a brace of pistols and a canister of gun cotton.

Of course, all was not innocent good neighbourliness. Nicholson did his homework well and had no hesitation in using spies to gather information or informers (known as approvers) to gain convictions in criminal cases.

In September 1847 he sent 'two Guides sepoys who understand Pushtoo [Pashto], desiring them to conceal their knowledge of that language while among the Khan's [Khan-i-Zeman] people'. Nicholson also had no qualms about sending his men across the frontier to scout around, on one occasion sending a Guide across the Indus into Afghan territory and into the lands of the Eusufzye people, who had a reputation for raiding and plundering and against whom the British were to send a force of 1,000 men in late 1849. Nicholson was also always on the lookout for those spying on him or stirring up dissent by means of the postal service, as several letters to his friend Arthur Cocks illustrate:

**5 July 1848.** We seized a Gooroo and Bhaee yesterday under somewhat suspicious circumstances, though I don't think we shall be able to prove anything against them: The latter is an uncommonly holy man, and has just come from Huzara where according to Abbott he was engaged in other work than praying.

**8 July 1848.** We have also intercepted some treasonable correspondence here amongst the followers of the prophet but the plot is not one to alarm.

**17 July 1848.** The seal and handwriting were both recognised as those of the Sirdar and his confidential Moonshee. Since then two or three chits from men in the neighbourhood to the Sirdar have been intercepted. There has evidently been no settled plan, but I think there is equally little doubt that E's [Edwardes'] operations in Multan were anxiously watched by many both here and to the westward who would gladly have availed themselves of any opportunity to create disturbances.

Nicholson was never a snob when mixing with ordinary people and frequently he struck up the most unusual friendship. One November in 1847 he came upon some traders from Kabul and chatted away to them about what they traded – tobacco and snuff to Kashmir and finely woven *puttoo* and *toosh* back to Afghanistan – and the problems they faced, the principal danger ironically for them being the road from Peshawar to Kabul.

Nicholson, both in the doab and later in Bannu, was not easily deceived by the superficial, something that assisted in his being regarded locally either with resentment or respect. An example of his looking beyond the obvious can be gained from the following diary entry for 24 October 1847:

Rode through the village [Pindee Gheb] in the evening. It is large and the houses are well built and comfortable. The bazaar contains nearly 100 shops. The land in the immediate vicinity, being very low (probably the lowest in the district), is irrigated from wells, and the crops look green and promising. Indeed, judging only from the appearance of the village and the land attached to it, one would suppose the country was in a highly flourishing state and the people in comfortable circumstances. The fact is, however, that the houses are those of the Mullick's friends or retainers, or of wealthy Khuttrees [Khatri], by whom the land in the vicinity, which is the best in the country, is rented on terms much more favourable than would be granted to any Mussulman [Muslim].

Nicholson, like many reserved people who watch more than talk, was a good judge of character. Several pithy pen sketches can be found in his official diary. Of one kadar at Kot in Gheb he recorded: 'I believe him to be a well-intentioned man, but he has neither ability, tact, nor energy, all of which are necessary to bring this long unsettled country into good order.' A week later,

Nicholson commented of this man's deputy, 'He has in my opinion quite a sufficient force to preserve tranquillity and collect revenue; but, like most of his class, I imagine he is afraid to do his duty with a moderate force, and is a tyrant when he has an overwhelming one at his disposal.'

News of the formal annexation of the Punjab arrived on 31 March 1849 when Nicholson was at Rawalpindi. He commented that this caused 'no excitement whatever'.

### Friends and Visitors

As Nicholson's diary entries are very short and certainly not chatty, they contain few personal observations. On 14 March 1847, he noted that in the Chenab River he 'Saw an alligator swimming about, said sometimes to do mischief'. He also commented on the fact that the 'very old town' of Chiniot was famous throughout the Punjab for the bows sold in its bazaar.

Both in his correspondence and in his reports, Nicholson was careful not to mention the friendships that he made with Indians. Charles Allen has highlighted that with his protégé Muhammad Hayat Khan but there were others. A cryptic note in Nicholson's diary entry for 12 April 1849 reads, 'Dismissed Sirdar Ibrahim Khan (Sirdar Sooltan Mahomed's son) to Afghanistan with a gratuity of Rs 1,000. He was anxious to go to India, but for various reasons I thought he would be better beyond the Khyber.' Another protégé about whom we know next to nothing about was Sodhoo Nehal Sing.

Occasionally, and much to his delight, Nicholson had a visitor of whom he approved, usually en route between Peshawar and Lahore. He was greatly annoyed to miss George Lawrence because a letter had taken ten days to reach him. But another time the two did meet and he had 'the pleasure of seeing that officer'. Harry Lumsden, then a lieutenant, stopped off at Hasan Abdal on his way to Lahore with his Guides to see Nicholson, taking on with him also those Guides who had been seconded to Nicholson's care. Nicholson was sorry to see these men go as they had been useful spies and were 'of course more to be depended on in case of emergency than Sikh soldiers'. Unfortunately, while with Nicholson, Lumsden sprained his ankle while out walking one morning. The equally eccentric James Abbott sometimes came over to see Nicholson. On Christmas Day 1847, Nicholson recorded, 'Rode over to Kahoota [Kahuta], 28 miles, in the evening, to see and dine with Captain Abbott. Road good, except last four miles, which are much intersected by ravines.'

## WAR CLOUDS LOOMING

For the moment all was quiet. Then in January 1848 Henry Lawrence took long leave and sailed for Britain, his place being taken by the more mundane Sir Frederick Currie (1799–1875). At this time, there are indications that Nicholson was again not terribly well. In February he stated, 'Pray believe that I am not sparing myself, I can conscientiously say, that I could not work harder.' The coming years of pressure and illness were to take their toll. A letter dated 28 April 1848 stated, 'Nicholson is very far from well, but we hope the change will be of service to him.' That very day Nicholson himself wrote another grumpy letter, this time complaining, probably justifiably, about the slovenly manner in which a 70-year-old was running the great fort at Attock. And at Peshawar itself, Nicholson was soon sniffing around and finding examples of corruption and skulduggery among officialdom. Nicholson then, or indeed at the time of the Great Rebellion a decade later, was never overtly concerned about townsfolk themselves, from whom 'we have nothing to fear'. He was, however, never completely sure of the regular troops.[31]

Early in 1848, the murder of two political advisors at Multan in the south had the Punjab once again heading for war. The remarkable activities of Edwardes, assistant commissioner in the turbulent Bannu region, with his mounted police and locally raised Pakhtun levies contained the rebellion, in particular winning a victory at Kineyri near the Chenab River. Edwardes was forced to withdraw strategically, regroup the Bannuchi levies and then advance, again defeating the enemy at Sadosin beside Multan. But once more without reinforcements, he could not storm Multan itself. Nicholson became extremely annoyed about how Edwardes was being left without military support. Writing to Cocks, he stated:

> If anything happens to him [Edwardes], his blood will be on the Resident's head and in such a case, should all else be so – but weak as my voice is, I would use it to the best of my ability. I trust however with you, that E's talent and courage, and what he places most reliance on himself, God's providence, will bring him safely and creditably through all the dangers to which he may be exposed. He is a truly noble fellow and neither the Residency nor the service can afford to lose him.[32]

Needless to say, soon Nicholson was asking Cocks to put a word in for him at Lahore for a transfer to be with Edwardes and the action down south. When Edwardes gained his famous victory outside Multan, Nicholson had a gun salute fired in his honour in Peshawar.[33]

## THE CHAIN OF LETTERS

All the action in the south of the Punjab was not matched by Currie, who, while quick enough to gain any kudos from Edwardes's exploits, was stubborn in his refusal to commit additional troops to assist his district officers in the field. Nicholson, never a lickspittle, referred to Currie as 'the Rosy One'.[34] The common practice of exchanging both their own and other's letters, while dangerous occasionally, helped to keep the British Punjab politicals an informed and sometimes united cohort. That unity was now cemented against Currie's lack of action in sending them reinforcements. In early May 1848, Nicholson drily commented to Arthur Cocks (1819–81), the assistant commissioner, 'is there no one at Lahore to remind Sir F.C. that *two days* inactivity lost us Cabul'. Cocks remonstrated with Nicholson about this comparison and Nicholson had to explain laboriously to Cocks that he was making the point only that delay could lead to problems.

Nicholson liked Cocks, whose mother came from Killarney, and when Cock's wife gave birth in early June 1848, Nicholson wrote, 'I am glad to hear that the son and heir is all right, and I shall propose his health at dinner this evening.'[35] He also sent Mrs Cocks a pair of slippers, which seems to have pleased her. Nicholson was relaxed enough with Cocks to philosophise, 'How little any of us know what is really best for us, or what is in store for us.' Though, in Nicholson fashion, several lines later he was instructing Cocks about mining the defences of a town.[36]

Nicholson also did something that set a pattern for his dealings with colleagues to whom he was closest and who happened to be stationed at Lahore – he sent lists of requirements to be forwarded to him. In the late 1840s, this role fell on Cocks, who received requests from Nicholson to be sent such items as two or three nightcaps; six merino or flannel banyans (undershirts); a penknife; and patent leather shoes and pumps ('being shoeless at present'). Cocks was also used to fight various battles Nicholson had with the Post Office ('I have received none [overland letters] in 2½ months'), with an insurance broker who held onto a parcel of his for a year, and with the Bengal Bank, where his relative Charles Hogg looked after his financial affairs.[37]

When Currie criticised Abbott for some outburst, Nicholson asserted that, 'there are very few men who possess Abbott's courage and firmness. Moral and physical.' Of course, two weeks later he was himself criticising Abbot for being over-anxious.[38] But some years later, Nicholson recounted to Henry Lawrence that Abbott, having once written to Currie in 'an unbecoming style', felt bad about it and next day sat down to write 'an apology much worse than the letter he was trying to excuse!'[39] In the late 1840s, Nicholson and Abbott were in 'almost daily communication' with each other and, according to Nicholson, were generally in agreement over subjects. Surprisingly for Nicholson, he commented to Cocks that Abbott, a 'chivalrous and kind hearted little man', sometimes 'carried his suspicions a little too far and [I] advised him to send no more rumours to Lahore, save such as he had good reason for believing well founded'.[40] By the end of May 1848 and again in early August 1848, Abbott was giving Nicholson grim warnings that 'the whole or part of the [Sikh] Army is in a plot to rise'.[41]

Unity, however, was created among British officialdom for a while by an attack on John Lawrence in a Delhi newspaper editorial for his defending his brother Henry. This was most likely the *Delhi Urdū Akhtār*.[42] The strange accusation, given Henry Lawrence's character, was that 'Col Lawrence was daily in the habit of insulting the Durbar by going with bare arms and throat in pajamahs and slippers; and using language which foul mouthed men employ to their menial servants.'[43] The 'rascally' editor was fortunate that Nicholson was many miles away. Nonetheless, Nicholson sent off a letter, which he described to Cocks as 'couched in much stronger language than yours'.

But greater indignation in Nicholson's mind was caused in July 1848 by the Rosy One in Lahore. Writing to James Abbott, Nicholson fumed:

> We are without further news from Multan or Lahore, save that the Resident [Currie] talked of the success of *his* 'Mohammodan combinations' and of the way in which *he* 'humbugged the Khalsa [Sikh army]'. This is remarkable verging upon the extreme confine of coolness! I imagine he will make a favourable report of E. [Edwardes] for so well carrying out *his* plans and instructions. I will get [George] Lawrence to send you a letter he had from him yesterday, an amusing but disgusting production. I return Inglis's letter with thanks. With kind regards to you and your circle.[44]

Nicholson's request to join Edwardes had been rejected by Currie, who no doubt was well aware that Nicholson had been bad-mouthing him. On being reassured by Cocks that he was not out of favour in Lahore, Nicholson was, somewhat naively, extremely grateful to Cocks. But Patrick van Agnew, one of the two British emissaries who was murdered at Multan on 20 April, had told Nicholson before leaving Lahore that the resident was not well disposed towards him, although Agnew tried to backtrack on this later.[45] One suspects that Cocks was trying to pour oil on troubled waters rather than disclose the truth about the Rosy One's feelings towards Nicholson.

## HOLDING THE LINE

Back in the northern Punjab, the formidable combination of George Lawrence, James Abbott and John Nicholson held the line. Nicholson was now officially under Major George Lawrence, which must have pleased him, given his dislike of Currie and John Lawrence. George Lawrence and Nicholson already knew each other as they had been captives together in Afghanistan. Though born in Ceylon, George Lawrence had attended school in Derry and was as much of an Ulsterman as the rest of the clan. He had less of the evangelical fervour and imperial zeal about him than his two more famous brothers, and, being eighteen years Nicholson's senior, was generally a good, if unconventional, influence on the highly strung young man, on occasions even in *méchant* fashion encouraging him in his bucking against authority.

In May 1848, following a multiple murder of men and women by villagers at Adeyzye, Nicholson and some Sikh troops were despatched. By a rapid march, they were able to surprise the village before it could resist. The murderers were apprehended and some arms seized.[46] Elsewhere, rebellion was in the air. On 17 May, writing again from Peshawar to his friend Cocks in Lahore, Nicholson declared, 'I believe our long inaction threatens us. Rumours are already rife of risings in Bannoo, and the Derajat, also in the Dhooab country. John Sing who in his cups used only to lament his governor's long sleep, now swears that he shows symptoms of waking, and commits his Pundits for an auspicious day.'[47]

Nicholson was not far wrong. The failure of Currie and General Gough to act during the warm season, however, gradually tilted the balance in favour of open insurrection, which was now only a matter of time.

# Unleashed: The War Renewed

On 8 August 1848 George Lawrence had a holy man, a fakir, hanged in Peshawar. A local chief had brought in a fakir after he had been allegedly preaching sedition. Interrogation extracted the information that the fakir had been as far as Kabul urging Afghan intervention. The next day George Lawrence received news that the rebel general, the ageing Chutter Singh, was mustering his forces in the Bannu and in the Hazara regions, with the intent of marching on Lahore. This was the self-same man whom Henry Lawrence had advised Nicholson to cultivate when he was appointed to his Sindh Sagar Doab posting. When news of the uprising reached Nicholson, he was yet again ill and lying in bed with fever. It is said that on being told what was afoot, he immediately threw off his sheet and announced that the fever would not hinder him. A fellow officer present at the time later recalled:

> Never shall I forget him as he prepared for his start, full of that noble reliance in the presence and protection of God, which, added to an unusual share of physical courage, rendered him almost invincible. It was during the few hours of his preparation for departure that his conduct and manner led to my first knowledge of his true character, and I stood and watched him, so full of spirit and self-reliance, though only just risen from a sick-bed, with the greatest admiration.[1]

The immediate object of the British was to secure the strategic fort at Attock on the Indus River. George Lawrence allowed Nicholson to lead the expedition and he immediately rode out at the head of a column of Muslim militia. As was his way, Nicholson travelled like a whirlwind through the midsummer night of 9/10 August. When he entered Attock, 50 miles distant, only thirty of his horsemen had kept up. With this small force, he entered the fort just in time to prevent the gates being closed on them. The governor had remained loyal to the British, keeping the fort so far out of the hands of Chutter Singh, but the garrison was doubtful. George Lawrence sent a follow-up contingent of men received from Eusufzye (Yusafzai) chiefs. The infantry did not arrive until late on the night of 10 August. Nicholson then, in gung-ho fashion, turfed out the Sikh garrison and closed the gates of the mighty Attock fortress.

Next, leaving the garrison at Attock accompanied only by 100 men, forty of whom were on foot, Nicholson moved further east to his old headquarters, the village of Hasan Abdal on the main Peshawar–Rawalpindi road. Here Nicholson arrested the ringleaders of the Sikh agitation and lined up the rank and file of the miscreants, threatening them with stern retribution if they did not come to heel. This extraordinary piece of bravado worked and, with the ringleaders despatched back to Peshawar, Nicholson added the rebel Sikh troops to his own force.

But he was not out of danger yet. Further east was Rawalpindi, where there was big trouble for the British. Captain Abbott's Sikh force at Kurara had deserted and arrived in the town to join other insurgents. The other local area of insurgency was in Hazara. To cut the Rawalpindi force from joining up with this other section, Nicholson determined to hold the narrow pass in the line of the Margalla ('cut-throat'[2]) Hills that separated Rawalpindi from the frontier towns of the north-west Punjab. Here Nicholson and a hastily raised local levy to support his tiny force waited to meet Abbott's mutinous regiment.

## ATTOCK'S AVENGING ANGEL

This strategy proved to be another of Nicholson's daredevil moves. On 15 August, Nicholson positioned his small force in the bush lands near where the Kurara force was encamped at Janika Sang. He then rode forward alone to where the Sikh army was encamped behind a Muslim cemetery wall. He demanded to see the colonel in command and, within earshot of the Sikh troops, he called on the commander and his force to return to their former allegiance or he would attack them and be merciless. Then, sitting bolt upright on his horse, Nicholson produced his pocket watch and told the colonel that he had just half an hour to declare that the army would return to its duties. He asserted that if they refused, within the hour he would destroy them. Considering that his opposition was a well-armed, disciplined force with cannon and Nicholson had 800 local ill-disciplined 'raw levies' with a handful of regular troops, this was brave talk. But the sheer stature of the man and his deep, sonorous and powerful voice succeeded. The insurgent Sikh body turned themselves over to Nicholson's command and marched off in orderly fashion towards Rawalpindi.[3]

The incident, while certainly confirming Nicholson's persuasive ability and indeed effrontery, also well illustrates the ambiguous and uncertain state in which the Sikh forces found themselves. The victory was not simply due to Nicholson pushing his luck. Nor, it has to be said, did Nicholson's actions sort out the mess in which the British found themselves in the Punjab. Indeed, five days after Nicholson's successful bluff, Chutter Singh formally rose in revolt against the British occupier. The cat-and-mouse game began in earnest. The armies of Chutter Singh in the north in Hazara and that of his son Utar Singh further south at Rawalpindi attempted to unite but they were being harassed by Abbott, Edwardes, Robertson and Nicholson, who vainly tried to persuade their superiors to send reinforcements immediately. The British commanders could do little more than attempt to cut Sikh communications, hinder their flow of supplies, carry out raiding expeditions against the enemy's rear and prevent rising in other parts of the territory.

In the middle of all this excitement, we find Nicholson writing from Hasan Abdul trying to raise the morale of his friend Arthur Cocks: 'Don't go away old fellow … [since] my first acquaintance with you, I regard as a sort of era in my existence, and you won't suspect me of insincerity in saying so.' As with Chamberlain and Edwardes later on, Nicholson's male friendships had an intensity of loyalty and respect about them, and indeed love. Cocks did not run away, and indeed served in the second Anglo-Sikh War on the commander-in-chief's staff with such bravery that on one occasion General Gough took off the sword he was wearing and gave it to him. But after the war, Cocks faded from Nicholson's orbit, becoming an efficient district administrator and eventually a country gentleman in Worcestershire.

Now in August 1848, though, was the hour of action. Nicholson had a fixation with the fort and river crossing at Attock. Time and time again he rushed back from a military sortie to check that all was well there. Gradually he brought in more and more Muslim troops from the hill country or from Afghanistan. George Lawrence in Peshawar had placed an ally, Nizam-ud-Dowla, in charge of the fort. But Nicholson did not trust him and this made him even more edgy. Things came to a head when Nicholson gained intelligence that Chutter Singh was making forced marches to capture Attock by surprise. Such a challenge had to be met. Nicholson's force outmarched that of Singh's army in the race to occupy Attock. Nicholson now appealed to George Lawrence to send down a Company officer to hold Attock, so releasing him to undertake what he was best at, guerrilla warfare harassing the rear of enemy lines. The next morning, 31 August, Lieutenant Herbert was there with 200 men. Now Attock was garrisoned with eight guns and three months' supplies, Nicholson, his mind settled, set out as an avenging angel to act along with James Abbott in harassing the enemy – though without official permission.[4]

There is an interesting comparison to be made between Nicholson and 'Little Abbott', as Nicholson increasingly referred to him.[5] Both were distinctly peculiar; both fierce fighters; both ended up more at home in Indian than European society; both liked the trappings of 'oriental power'; and both were quintessentially frontiersmen. And yet, while Nicholson had the ear of Sir Henry Lawrence, Abbott had not. Nicholson, despite his constantly pushing the limits of his authority, moved gradually from strength to strength on the frontier, whereas James Abbott was regarded as having, in the parlance, 'gone native' in Hazara. As will be seen, he became so powerful there that the British authorities removed him in 1853. It was at the town of Abbottabad, which retains its name in Pakistan to this day, that Osama Bin Ladin was killed in May 2011.

## CLEARING THE MARGALLA PASS

Meanwhile, in mid-September 1848, Nicholson and what was in effect his personal army arrived once again back before the defile of the Margalla Pass. The saga of what followed is one of the great Nicholson stories. The pass and the stone tower or *burj* that commanded it was held by Chutter Singh's forces, and in particular Baba Pendee Ramdial's regiment. In usual fashion, Nicholson led the assault. But only a few of the raw troops in his levy dared approach the base of the tower, from which the enemy poured out fire. The timidity of his troops infuriated Nicholson and, in a rage, he tore at the stonework of the tower with his bare hands. Like an Irish round tower, the *burj* was constructed without a ground-level door. Instead, the door 10ft up could be approached only with a ladder.[6] Not surprisingly, those holding the tower opposed Nicholson's assault. A rock thrown from the tower struck him in the face, forcing him and his small force to withdraw to the nearby British camp for the evening. Nicholson would play down the incident later, saying that it was a 'slight hurt from a stone in a skirmish in the hills a week or two ago – I have often had a worse one however when a boy at school', a statement that would seem to confirm his reputation as a fighter at Dungannon Royal.[7] It is not known how badly Nicholson was injured but by the following morning he was all for renewing the assault. On approaching the tower once more he found, however, that both it and the pass had been vacated. The enemy had fled in the night. The British force fell back and re-joined Abbott at Hasan Abdal.

The skirmish at Margalla Pass is noteworthy for another incident with long-term repercussions. During the fighting Nicholson had got into difficulties and was rescued by a local leader named Sardar Karam Khan, who had sided with the British. Some months later Karam was murdered by his half-brother and his widow and children fled to James Abbott in neighbouring Hazara. Abbott in turn sent the family down to Nicholson, who ensured that they were looked after and the wrong done to the family was rectified. From then on the 15-year-old Muhammad Hayat Khan's fortunes were inextricably linked with Nicholson's. He became Nicholson's assistant, orderly and protector, and was rarely parted from his side.[8]

Today, here at Tarnol where the battle was fought stands a 40ft obelisk in granite dedicated to Nicholson, sandwiched between the old and the new Grand Trunk Roads. This monument was erected in 1868 on the initiative of Edwardes. Below the hill on which the edifice stands, two derelict 'gate houses' still poignantly recall this vanished age.

Nicholson's efforts aroused British morale but, apart from the key occupation of Attock, were an inconvenience rather than an obstruction to the rising Sikh insurrection. Nicholson's force was too small and certainly could not have met a Sikh regiment in the field. Indeed, shortly after the Margalla pass skirmish, Utar Singh's Sikh army advanced in force on the British camp at Hasan Abdal, forcing them to withdraw and so opening the path for the two Singh generals, father and son, to unite at last. They now determined to march north to Pakli and Nawashahr to relieve the Sikh army that Lieutenant D.G. Robinson was successfully harassing.

Nicholson, of course, was soon in pursuit of the Sikh general. Cutting north-west through the mountains and then swinging east, he hit the Damtur Pass before the Sikh army. Abbott, exposing his western Hazara flank, was soon alongside Nicholson as they dug in awaiting the enemy. Early the next day, the enemy appeared, spread out with skirmishing parties and moved quickly forward, pushing back the British levies with ease. Nicholson climbed the side of one of the surrounding hills only to find that his men were not holding their positions. It is said that he ran down the hill to rouse reinforcements and that when the levies saw this they thought he was running away, so they too took to their heels. Soon there was a stampede of men. Even Abbott's steadier musket men could do little to stop the more professional (and committee-run) Sikh army, which swept easily through the pass and on to relieve the Pakli brigade. Although ignored or played down by most of Nicholson's biographers, Damtur was a frustrating defeat.

## NICHOLSON'S FLYING COLUMN

The two British sections withdrew westward, uniting some hours later among the hills. Nicholson and Abbott then parted, the former moving to Jhang near Hasan Abdal and the latter deep into Hazara to Narra. Later Abbott would hole up at remote Srikot, causing annoyance to the Sikh army whenever possible. Hasan Abdal, the T-junction where the road from Hazara met the main Peshawar–Rawalpindi road, and the attractive Hasan Abdal valley were to become the birthplace of the Nikolseini sect who advocated the divinity of Nicholson, a unique phenomenon in the annals of the Irish diaspora. But this Nicholson worship was also an indication of the reputation that he acquired in those months when he and his mounted irregulars acted against what was in effect an insurgent force: hitting and running, inflicting damage on small Sikh columns and intimidating villages and areas at very least into remaining neutral.

Meanwhile, in the deep south of the Punjab Sher Singh's army, which had been assisting the British, declared for the insurgents and marched north. Still the governor-general Lord Dalhousie refused to commit further troops. And in the field, Abbott, Edwardes, Nicholson and Robinson were alone having to deal with Sir Frederick Currie, the dithering acting resident at Lahore.

The cat-and-mouse war continued in the region into September 1848. Nicholson wrote to his mother complaining vociferously that the state of affairs in the Punjab had been 'brought on by the incapacity of our rulers, civil and military. It is a month and seven days since I wrote for troops, and I believe a single man has not yet started from Lahore.' But this lack of regular British troops meant that Nicholson increasingly came to know and respect his irregular horse levies. Indeed, the time would soon come when his preference was to fight with these hillmen. And, of course, always one for strong opinions, as Nicholson's respect grew for the 'wild men of the mountains', so conversely did his suspicion of the sepoy army of the East India Company.

Far and wide Nicholson ranged across the northern Punjab, making the 'trustworthy garrison in the fort of Attock' his retreat in time of crisis. He admitted, 'I am leading a very guerrilla sort of life with 700 horse and foot hastily raised among the people of the country. Sirdar Chutter Sing and his son, who are in rebellion, have 8 Regular Regts and 16 guns, so that I am unable to meet them openly in the field.' But all this military action on Nicholson's part was against orders. Perhaps to pre-empt any later political retribution, in a letter to his mother, Nicholson asked her to tell his uncle James Hogg in London that 'it is 10 days since the Resident [Currie] wrote me to retire on either Attock or Lahore but I consider it my duty to maintain my position in the field as long as possible.'[9]

At one point during the war, Nicholson complains about looting by British troops, remarking that flogging culprits made no difference. He suggested a solution to this problem would be granting him the powers of provost-marshal – in other words, give him the power to hang looters. 'Rely on my bringing the army to its senses within two days,' he added. As for the levies under Nicholson, they saw in the Irishman a powerful and resolute figure who did not waste words, led from the front and respected them as soldiers. The legend of Nikkel Seyn dates from this period, a clear nine years before the Great Rebellion itself.

The next we hear of Nicholson, he is again back with the main body of the Company's army commissariat, serving in General Colin Campbell's division. This in turn was under the general command of fellow Irishman General Hugh Gough, of whom Nicholson clearly did not think much. Nor indeed did he like Campbell, writing to Cocks on one occasion, 'Campbell is becoming downright rude. I should have quarrelled with him yesterday could I have afforded it.'[10] There is no evidence that Nicholson was the source of Campbell's nickname, the Crawling Camel, but he certainly would have approved of it. Despite such personal dislikes, though, Nicholson had a close working relationship with Gough's staff. And while officially in the rather dull commissariat, Nicholson had the elevated task as 'a political' to influence 'the nobles and the people of the country'.[11]

According to Captain Trotter, Nicholson was not so popular in the general's camp. The manner in which Nicholson threw back his head when walking was viewed by many as the mark of a 'stuck-up political'. In his new role, Nicholson reconnoitred a lot, one suspects in part because he could not abide inaction. He was forever grumbling at the inactivity of the field command. On 19 November 1848, for example, he wrote: 'I cannot understand why HQ Qrs camp has not been making longer marches.' Almost three weeks later, on 8 December 1848, he wrote:

> I shall be sorry to think the Chief [Gough] a humbug, but he told me two days ago, that the GG [Dalhousie] was sending him Mackeson, to explain his views and intentions more freely than could be done in writing; and he said not a word of his having applied for M. I quite agree with you however that we must stifle our present feelings and not allow them to get the better of our sense of public duty.[12]

Nicholson was good at ferreting around. As Chamberlain was to note many years later, the British neglected to make a military survey of terrain both during the Anglo-Sikh wars and, across the Indian Ocean in southern Africa, during the Anglo-Boer war, a generation later.[13] While not denying the axiom that there was nothing so dangerous on a battlefield as an officer with a map, nonetheless, basic knowledge about river fords and the extent of jungle would have been an immense benefit to Gough and his army of the Punjab.

## CHARLOTTE LAWRENCE'S CRY FOR HELP

A fresh crisis focused Nicholson's energies on a rescue mission. After the garrison had mutinied at Peshawar on 24 October 1848, George Lawrence and two other Europeans, Lieutenant Bowie and Dr Thompson, with a detachment of fifty men escaped to Kohat 'not a moment too soon'. Charlotte Lawrence, George's wife, and her daughters had initially been sent, in anticipation of such an eventuality, into the caring hands of Sultan Mohammed Khan. In turn, he sent them east across the Indus towards British lines, but at such a slow pace to make Charlotte Lawrence suspicious. She found herself at Chakwal to the north-west of Lahore, effectively a prisoner. She managed to get a rider to send a message for help – and it is significant that she addressed the plea to John Nicholson. She well knew who was the man of action. And she was not wrong.

On receipt of her message Nicholson, enraged by the treachery of Mohammed Khan and always one to assist a lady, gathered a cohort of reliable horsemen together and set off at breakneck speed to intercept the convoy taking Charlotte Lawrence and her children back westwards. But he was too late. The prisoners had been moved back deep into enemy territory before the Nicholson rescue party had arrived at Chakwal. It is reported that he hanged several people who were suspected of delaying Charlotte Lawrence on her abortive flight to freedom, though whether that is another apocryphal Nicholson story is unknown.[14] Meanwhile, Bowie, Lawrence and Thompson were being held west of the Indus as prisoners of Chutter Singh, who now put to siege the great fortress of Attock, occupied by Lieutenant Charles Herbert and, as it proved, a treacherous garrison.

The rest of Nicholson's force followed him and in early October 1848 he marched with about 900 men 30 miles south from Chakwal to Pind Dadan Khan, near the Jhelum River. This march involved traversing the Salt Mountains, which were in enemy hands. Nicholson achieved this by the simple but effective device of approaching the selected pass with stealth, then, as dawn broke, sending forward his entire force screaming, shouting and firing. The sleepy pickets fled and Nicholson's column could move on towards and then into the occupied town. The rebel Sikh garrison soon fled to the sanctuary of the town's fortress, which also housed the much-prized treasury. This was unfortunate and in contrast to Gujranwala, where William Hodson and his notorious levies managed to secure the principal Sikh treasury in Govindgarh, some 60 miles south of the British camp at Ferozepur.

Nicholson now found himself in a stalemate, with the road along which he had advanced closed behind him by massing enemy forces. Sher Singh had vacated Multan to the south and was moving with his sowars along the banks of the Chenab River with the intention of eventually swinging east and marching on Lahore. When Nicholson heard this, he determined to intercept Sher Singh at Ramnager, 40 miles due west of Lahore. So yet another forced march was ordered. Nicholson's force crossed the Jhelum and then the Chenab rivers, before pushing south, experiencing some opposition as they progressed. But Singh's army was four times the size of Nicholson's band of irregulars and a slowly advancing Company relief army was still at least 60 miles away.

## NICHOLSON REBUKED

Matters were beginning to turn nasty. Nicholson was forced to fight a rearguard action as local communities turned out and sent the invaders packing: 'Cutting up some stragglers, plundering some baggage, and releasing my prisoners, amongst whom were the Chaikwal Choedrees, whom I had seized for refusing a passage through their country to Mrs G. Lawrence.' This would seem to give the lie to the story that Nicholson hanged those he believed had been involved in the Charlotte Lawrence kidnapping.

The expeditionary force seems to have been saved from destruction only by Nicholson's appearance in front of his troops to rally his men.[15] He was leading the expedition alone now, dashing here and there, striking the enemy and then retreating. The following year a despatch in *The Times* recorded the advance of the British army:

On the 4th [November 1848] they had a march to Goojranwallah, upwards of 20 miles, over a dry, barren, sandy country. On the way, at a distance, they saw the appearance of a body of men which they supposed to be enemy, and immediately gave chase, For five miles some 2,000 mounted troops were seen at a gallop or hard trot across the country, when it turned out that it was a portion of the friendly troops under Lieutenant Nicholson on their way towards Ramnugger that had been mistaken for insurgents.[16]

We know that in late November 1848 Nicholson, 'with his Pathan Horse', was on the left or southern bank of the Chenab River, at Wazirabad in a fairly direct line north of Lahore. Here, Nicholson's men had collected seventeen boats, which meant that the Bengal army pontoons were not needed. This allowed Sir Joseph Thackwell to cross the river with an army of 8,000 men, though his subsequent failure to pursue the enemy somewhat negated the advantage Nicholson had given him.

The insurgents were aware of Nicholson's presence as Sher Singh sent him 'an impertinent letter'. Singh had noted to Nicholson that he was near Akalgarh, a mere 20 miles to Nicholson's south-west and also on the left bank of the Chenab River. Singh stated that he had a large force but that he had no wish for war with the British. Nicholson, instead of ignoring this or forwarding the document to Campbell, wrote 'the rebels an ambiguous reply' advising the Sikh general to 'devise therefore some measure to avert [war] and acquaint me with the results of your deliberations. You say that Major [George] Lawrence is with your father Chutter Singh in Peshawar. You will also be aware that Sirdar Gulab Singh is in Lahore.'

In fairness to Nicholson, and surprisingly given his previous tart remarks about the acting resident at Lahore, Sir Frederick Currie tried his best to defend Nicholson. Yet he had to concede, 'I cannot account for the error he has committed.' Of course, Nicholson never knew when to keep quiet and wrote a lengthy defence of his action, making the point that he had acted in the government's best interests by not frightening Sher Singh into retreat, which would have stymied the British plan of attack. This was a fair enough point, but Nicholson was rather naive to suppose that the generals would countenance any captain exchanging letters with the enemy command.[17] He received an official rebuke, part of which ran, 'I received the latter document with astonishment, with indignation and with shame ... I cannot conceive how you could consider yourself having every authority to hold written communication with the rebels regarding the desire and intentions of the Government. You must have known that in doing this you were assuming to yourself power possessed by no party in the Punjab but myself.'[18]

Meanwhile, John Lawrence, with some levies, a sprinkling of regular European Company troops and a couple of field artillery pieces, descended upon a Sikh regiment that was suspected of being about to mutiny. Without warning and showing no mercy, his force crushed the regiment and followed up by driving all rebel Sikh forces out of the district. And far to the west, Reynell Taylor would facilitate a reversal of allegiances with the British, recently allies of the Sikhs against the 'wild men' of Bannu, by joining with the Bannuchi and effectively sweeping the Sikhs south into the fortress of Lakki, which they besieged. This made any Afghan intervention in support of the Sikhs more difficult.[19]

## THE SIKH RISING SPREADS

But there was trouble elsewhere. At Attock, Herbert had been holding on in the fortress on the Indus River for as long as he could. But he was running short of cash and firewood, and his credit was not good. Worse, he had unrest in the ranks. In a tiny note, partly written in ancient Greek and folded twenty-eight times and smuggled out of Attock, Herbert urged Nicholson to press the governor-general for relief:

> I wrote to you yesterday to represent _____ was becoming more difficult and beg you to represent to the C in C that unless speedily relieved I fear much for the safety of this Fort. Not from the physical force of the enemy but from the increasing efforts to create treachery among my people ... discouraged at the non arrival of succour and doubt that any is coming. Serious symptoms of insubordination have shewn themselves ___ It is only by continually giving small presents and disbursing money – in addition to giving liberal rations that I can keep them together.[20]

And in one postscript to Reynell Taylor dated 11 December 1848, Herbert commented, 'I am unable to answer for my men from day to day and any hour might oblige me to relinquish my high hopes of holding out till you can arrive.'[21] And so it was to prove. Within days, Lieutenant Herbert's irregular force went over to the Sikh army and he had to flee. But the British commander-in-chief, faced with thirty guns and eight regiments and pressed by Frederick Mackeson to wait until Multan fell, was in no hurry to do anything.[22] Nicholson found himself wishing he was 'up again with Little Abbott in Hizarra than with this Army'.

A few days later Nicholson was congratulating Edwardes on his knighthood, 'I tell you, you are about the only man of my own standing in India, of whom I think I would not have felt some degree of jealousy.' In the same letter, he comments on the current situation in the Punjab:

> I am not free from anxiety on poor little Abbott's account ... The general feeling as you may perhaps have experienced yourself is very strong against any man with politics to his name. He is looked upon as fair game by the mob ...

the man in the whole army who is if possible the most rabid against us, is no other than our formerly courteous friend, Brigr Campbell. He has done his utmost to injure me with the chief, but failed most signally I am happy to say.

That year did not close without Edwardes seriously injuring himself. In the heat of preparing for battle, he had crammed his pistols into his belt and the hammer of one of the guns became entangled. Pulling it down, there was 'A loud report, a short pang, and I had lost the use of my right hand for life! The ball had passed through the palm, and lodged in the floor at my foot.'[23]

## MENTIONED IN DESPATCHES

On 13 January 1849, both Nicholson brothers were involved in the battle of Chillimwala near the Jhelum River. The British were victorious but suffered high losses. John Nicholson was under Sir Hugh Gough's command. He and Colonel Henry Lawrence were mentioned in Gough's despatch dated 16 January 1849. Nicholson, nevertheless, was growing increasingly irritated by his commander-in-chief's sloth. This had become a regular theme of Nicholson's nearly daily notes to Henry Lawrence, who had been back in Lahore and who was wont to receive a reprimand if he did not reply to Nicholson within a day or two. The arrival in camp of 1,600 captured camels did not improve Nicholson's humour as he did not know what to do with them. After a few days, he dumped the problem on the commissariat.[24]

When Chutter Singh's army suddenly came out of the mountain and encamped on the plains near Karee, Nicholson was beside himself: '… what are we to do, God only knows. I don't think the C in C has any plan … It is a disheartening indeed a maddening reflection, that an army like this, on which so much depends, should be without a head.'[25]

As was to become a feature of much that he did later, Nicholson kept a close ear to the ground and frequently made use of spies and informers. It was in this way that he heard the Sikhs had been making overtures to the Company's troops to come over to their side. His comment on this was simply, 'I think that the native army knows which side its bread is buttered.' Eight years later, during a halt on the long and hot march to crush mutinous troops at Sialkot, Nicholson told his men an amusing anecdote about the Anglo-Sikh War to improve morale, which unlike most of the Nicholson fables, has a ring of truth about it. He recalled how the British were on one side of a river and the Sikh army on the other. A great bonfire was burning on the Sikh side. Nicholson, disguised as a Sikh water carrier with a sewn-up pigskin full of water on his back, swam across the river:

> On my arrival amongst the Sikhs, I straightway advanced to the immense pile of burning faggots, and observed on the top of it a large cauldron charged with boiling water. Forthwith I disburdened myself of my pigskin and joined the men squatting around the fire and smoking at the hubble-bubble. Taking me for a native water-carrier, they freely discoursed with me. They said, in answer to my questions, that in the cauldron they intended to boil Nicholson. I had a whiff or two at the hubble-bubble, and adding more fuel to the fire, said, 'There, I've made it hotter for that rascal Nicholson over yonder.'[26]

Nicholson's keenness for battle was enhanced by the fact that he heard of Shumshooden Khan, 'my old jailor at Ghazni is said to have left Peshawar with 1000 horse a week ago'. Nicholson was not one to let bygones be bygones. Indeed, Nicholson suggested to Henry Lawrence that the British foment what in effect would be a civil war in Afghanistan. Ironically, the core of this idea was underpinned by the fact that Nicholson got on so well with his mountain levies, who occasionally took leave to return to the Peshawar district. Nicholson probably gained his spies from this source and for the next decade, they ensured he was usually one step ahead of the game. 'What do you think of putting the Eastern Ghilzies to rise at Cabul?' he suggested to Henry Lawrence, 'I think it might be managed without difficulty.' But the idea of opening a second front in the war did not go down well. Indeed, Nicholson running off to assist Abbott without authority gained for Henry Lawrence a grudging admission from Nicholson, 'I erred in not informing you.'

But Abbott was more optimistic about the way the wind was blowing. The day Nicholson wrote to John Lawrence about the appearance of Chutter Singh's army, Abbott commented to Reynell Taylor:

> As soon as our army crosses the Jelum all our partisans in Peshaur and Cabul will be ready to aid us in expelling Doost Mulk. The Mooltan Force is marching up, I trust rapidly … The Maharaja continues his liberality. May his shadow never be less.[27]

Another reason Nicholson was champing at the bit to get at the Sikhs was because George Lawrence and his family remained prisoners behind enemy lines. From his spies and informers, Nicholson knew where they were and even knew when George was brought down to Chutter Singh's camp.

## CAT AND MOUSE

Now there developed a leisurely race between the Company and the Sikh armies for Dunjee, with neither side in much of a rush. A cat-and-mouse game developed, much to Nicholson's annoyance. This restlessness was exacerbated when on 1 February Nicholson had word that Chutter Singh was on the move again.[28] Writing from Chillianwala on 5 February, Nicholson complained bitterly to Arthur Cocks, 'Chutter Sing has actually come out of the pass into the plain near Karee. The Chief after a long consultation with the generals has decided on nothing. I am very miserable at such a display of indecision and want of common sense.' And the same day to Henry Lawrence he complained, 'What are we to do, God only knows. I don't think the C in C has any plan … It is disheartening indeed a maddening reflection, that an army like this, on which *so* much depends, should be without a head.'[29]

Ten days later Nicholson was encamped a mile from Sadulapur. It is surprising that Gough had been able to keep Nicholson and his horsemen in check. But the general's aim had been to bring up as much support as possible before pressing on with any attack. When upbraided by Henry Lawrence for his negativity, Nicholson responded bluntly: 'You have misunderstood what I wrote yesterday. I am not down in the mouth because I doubt the result of our action, with our new over-whelming force, but because we have an imbecile Chief with imbecile advisers at the head of the finest army ever assembled in India.'[30]

The arrival of three new regiments and a battery of artillery changed matters, and with the prospect of 'thrashing' the enemy, Nicholson calmed down somewhat. The arrival of colleagues such as Coke, Lake, Lumsden and Hodson helped also. Mackeson was already with the commander-in-chief, but Nicholson did not warm to that equally strange character, no more than Henry Lawrence had.[31]

The battle of Gujrat was fought on 21 February 1849. The day before it was said, 'Nicholson seems to be valued on all hands as the man to do whatever is done.'[32] It is estimated that the Company's army faced an enemy double its size. However, the Company had something of an advantage with a third more field pieces.

It proved a very hard-fought battle and one the British had great difficulty winning. Nonetheless, ultimately the enemy were, in Nicholson's phrase 'well licked', although Nicholson's friend John Coke had been severely, but not mortally, wounded. 'The Sind Horse are heroes,' Nicholson asserted. And again Nicholson was mentioned in despatches (28 February 1849), as 'that most energetic political officer'.[33]

It was said that twenty years later visitors to the Chillianwala and Gujrat battlefields would have local guides keenly pointing out where Nikkel Seyn had stood. Such are the timeless ways of battlefield guides. In the two Anglo-Sikh wars, Nicholson fought in the battles of: Moodkee (18 December 1845); Ferozeshah (21/22 December 1845); Sadullapur (1 December 1848); Chillianwala (13 January 1849); and Gujrat (21 February 1849).

## UNLEASHED AT LAST

It goes without saying that Sir Walter Gilberts' 'column of retribution' had Lieutenant Nicholson and his hillmen as well as John Coke well to the front, although Nicholson had needed to lean on John Lawrence to get himself included. But even before that Nicholson was out in the field, in what capacity is uncertain, using his contacts with the hill tribes to ensure that the retreating Afghans who had supported Chutter Singh, 'run the gauntlet as they go by'. And after several days of scouting, Nicholson had captured nine enemy artillery pieces.[34]

One issue greatly annoyed Nicholson's puritan soul and his raising it made him unpopular with many of his fellow officers. Writing to Henry Lawrence, he exclaimed:

> Plundering is carried on to a disgraceful extent by both Sepoys and camp followers. I quite <u>dread</u> taking an army of ours among my people whom I used to protect from my Sikh troops. The C in C has offered to make over camp followers to me. I feel convinced that till one or two are summarily <u>hung</u> the evil cannot be checked. Will you sanction my doing this? The evil is an extreme one, and requires an extreme remedy. We have tried flogging for 3 months to no purpose and I would rather not be with the Army than be compelled to witness the treatment the wretched people of the country receive at our hands.

Soon, in a bid to settle this matter, Nicholson was asking General Gough for the powers of a provost marshal. That he bothered to ask anyone's permission to hang looters shows that Nicholson still had some reserve. For, even by 1849, in matters not relating to the death penalty, Nicholson increasingly did as he pleased, asking sanction after the event. A case in point was after the battle of Gujrat. Nicholson collected all the prisoners whom the British had captured and told them they should go quietly to their homes.[35] There was all the difference in the world in Nicholson's mind between these soldiers, who had fought in the Sikh army, and the insurgent sepoy prisoners who were captured by the British eight years later.

There was no betrayal in the former, no killing of their officers, no murdering of women and children. To him, the situations were clean different.

Meanwhile, Mackeson was annoying Nicholson. Writing to Henry Lawrence on 26 February, Nicholson stated:

> If I am to have my old district [Sindh Sagar Doab] back pray place it at once under my charge – I know whom to trust and whom to distrust, who deserve reward and who punishment, for their conduct in the late rebellion, and I fear Mackeson's interference unless I have an order in writing from you, to assume charge.

Nicholson's underlying attitude at this time was that 'we should hold all guiltless, whom the force of circumstance has compelled to join the rebels'.[36] It was Nicholson who persuaded Mackeson to issue a proclamation allowing disarmed Sikh troops to go quietly back to their homes. Haigh and Turner wrote in 1980 that such an attitude 'comes as something of a surprise to anyone still clinging to the traditional picture of Nicholson as the hard, inarticulate, ruthless soldier'.[37]

But such leniency, of course, did not apply to some of the insurgent leaders, especially those who had betrayed George Lawrence when he gave his family into their care. They required a 'severe example' – a phrase that on Nicholson's tongue could mean only death.

He was soon writing of Mackeson's 'extreme jealousy' of him, since Mackeson was clearly sidelining Nicholson as a fellow field political officer. Mackeson was certainly an odd fellow, described by Charles Allen as 'shadowy'.[38] Four years later, in September 1853, when Colonel Mackeson was commissioner of Peshawar, he was stabbed to death while sitting on his veranda. A story circulated that there was more to the murder than met the eye and that Mackeson had been interfering with Afghan women. Interestingly, and as will be seen, Nicholson rejected this story out of hand.[39]

## BACK IN CHARGE

Henry Lawrence granted Nicholson's wish and from 1 March he was assigned to resume his civil charge of his old district, Sindh Sagar Doab. This was clearly an attempt by General Gough to prevent Nicholson from roaming about 'like a partizan'. But in his reply to Lawrence's granting his wish of his old district, Nicholson pushes his other request to raise 1,000 men for him to lead against the retreating enemy. Lawrence gave a firm 'No' to the suggestion and told him that there was a government order forbidding enlisting of fresh troops. To this,

Nicholson rather boldly enquired 'does this extend to police?' Having been on the civil side of affairs, Nicholson was au fait with recruiting and employing police.

Nicholson was technically on the civil side, answering to the Lahore Board rather than to his regimental colonel. While in Bannu, he reorganised the police into five rassalahs. As the years went by, Nicholson increasingly used 'police' as his military force to circumvent military obduracy and to establish, at least in part, an independence of the military command.

On one occasion in 1855 Nicholson actually persuaded the chief commissioner in Lahore, John Lawrence, to permit the minimum height of police recruits to drop from 5ft 7in to 5ft 6in and, if 'unusual strength and activity', even 5ft 5in. This gave Nicholson a bigger pool from which to recruit but also opened up the police to stockier men from the hill country, where Nicholson's powerbase increasingly lay.[40]

It is unclear whether Nicholson went recruiting or whether he simply disobeyed orders. Within days, though, Nicholson had rounded up many of the irregular forces he had used before the second Anglo-Sikh war. These amounted to 300 infantry and 150 cavalry. He soon also picked up 100 extra troops who had stayed loyal to George Lawrence when at Peshawar during the insurrection. Loyalty meant a great deal to Nicholson and he had no qualms whatsoever in flouting regulations to ensure that what he regarded as justice was done to those who had remained faithful in extraordinarily difficult circumstances. On 7 March he complained bitterly to Henry Lawrence about the treatment British loyalists in the Punjab were receiving during the emergency: 'A most extraordinary policy certainly that of treating friends and foe alike.'

The shortage of supplies and ammunition was another grumble, Nicholson penning a note on the subject to Lawrence and then telling him to pass the letter on to General Gough. Meanwhile, Mackeson tried to make Nicholson responsible for guaranteeing the supply line, something that infuriated him:

> I cannot be responsible for feeding the army on a days notice … I cannot understand M. Independent of his jealousy and mistrust, he talks to me as a school master, giving an idle boy a lark, and not as to an officer who has the interests of Govt just as much at heart and who at all events, works just as hard, as himself … Poor Sadi Sham Sing has died of his wound, which by the bye Mackeson would have was a make believe one.[41]

There was nothing personally against Henry Lawrence in these rants, and in the middle of them Nicholson would ask for things to be sent to him – more stationery (in three consecutive letters), or 'a bottle of my old blue ink', or a pair of hunting spurs. He also asked for a dozen brace of pistols to reward his Indian officers who had given good service. That in particular, and to Nicholson's rage, caused a bureaucratic storm. More than a month later, he was still asking for the pistols, something officialdom was very reluctant to give him to hand out to his Sikh friends. We also rather strangely find Nicholson looking for employment for the son of Sultan Mahommed Khan, who had, albeit from circumstantial necessity, betrayed George Lawrence.[42] In the end, Nicholson gave the young man 1,000 rupees and despatched him to Kabul.

Nicholson was in his element with all this action, dashing from place to place. For part of this time in March, Nicholson also teamed up with Harry Lumsden, who had been George Lawrence's number two at Peshawar. Together Nicholson and Lumsden occupied the dramatically situated hill fort at Rohtas. Overlooking the Son River, it was north of where the battle was fought at Chillianwala and some 10 miles from Jhelum. The ancient fort had recently been evacuated by the Sikh army, which was now at Dhumiak. And it was towards the escarpment they rode, reaching the pass unopposed on 7 March 1849, just in time to be in on the capture of the Sikh leader Sher Singh.

Lumsden had been collecting intelligence information when Nicholson joined him. Nicholson continued his complaint about a lack of troops to support him and the necessity of raising what had now become 1,600 irregulars, 'otherwise I will not be responsible for the peace of the district'. In that same letter to Henry Lawrence, Nicholson again attacks Mackeson for his attitude to those Sikh leaders of whom Nicholson clearly approved:

Boodh Sing man has just come in [to camp]. He was wounded by my side at the commencement of the rebellion, did good service with your brother afterwards, and has since been allowed no command in the rebel army, yet I have had the greatest difficulty in prevailing on Mackeson to receive him, and I doubt very much whether he will receive Khan Sing Majestic, who is coming in today. It is a most extraordinary policy certainly that of treating friends and foe alike … M sits on my head for supplies, and yet can't let me leave his tail to collect them. Altogether, I never was so 'hairan' [confused/at wits end] in my life, and shall bless the day, we part company.[43]

## PEACE AND BACK TO CIVIC DUTIES

The surrender of the Khalsa army came on 8 March. By 13 March, thousands of Sikh soldiers surrendered unconditionally to the British. Nicholson was at

Humak near Rawalpindi when most of the Sikh army laid down their arms. That day Nicholson wrote to Henry Lawrence:

> I believe we have got all the Sikh guns and upwards of 3000 of their infantry laid down their arms yesterday. I suspect the greater part of the rebel force has gone off quietly to its homes and that we shall not find many left to disarm today. I have put Kardars into Jelum and Rotal ...[44]

A poignant story is told of an exchange between Nicholson and a surrendering Sikh soldier:

> How is this, friend, did you not say you would drive us all into the sea, your guru should have advised you better.

To this the sanguine veteran replied:

> Ah, Sahib, there's no striving against fate. There's no fighting on a diet of cabbage. Just try it yourself, Sahib.[45]

Nicholson was now inexorably drawn south-west towards Attock and the Indus, and the fort he had done so much to keep from enemy hands. On St Patrick's Day, Nicholson was on the left bank of the Indus and could see the enemy across the river withdrawing from the old fort, cutting loose the boat bridge and burning four boats. But his 'Attock mullahs' associates were quick to materialise. In twelve hours the boat bridge across the great river had been repaired, 'A shorter space [of time] than ever the Indus was bridged in before.' Nicholson handed out 1,000 rupees and gave the leader of his group a shawl.

Nicholson was always a stickler about such matters, at least when it came to paying for favours or supplies obtained in friendly or at least neutral territory. The day he crossed the river and took possession of the fort at Attock, he wrote to Colonel Henry Lawrence criticising the commander of the pursuit column, 'Genl. Gilbert's force in its passage of this Doab has not paid for its forage, but I have begged the general to order all detachments left in the Doab or which may hereafter have occasion to pass through it, to take no crops, or supplies of any kind without paying for them.' Here again is an aspect of Nicholson's character that needs to be included in the balance of any assessment.

Later in the same letter, Nicholson asks once again for pistols to present to those 'superior officers' who had come to his assistance, and finishes off the communication, 'I have not heard from you for 3 days and I am *still* without the oft asked for stationery'.[46] Not surprisingly, the paper and envelopes arrived by return of post. And, ever suspicious, Nicholson sends Lawrence the wax seal of a letter he had sent on 21 March: 'I am doubtful', he comments, 'whether the impression of a thumb which it bears is that with which you despatched it.' The saga of the pistols dragged on, with Nicholson now lowering his demands to two brace. Nicholson's suggestion about an ad hoc arrangement for a tax on the spring harvest was, however, sensible and fair. But then on such broad-ranging matters Nicholson was usually level headed. It was smaller matters such as his need for a bottle of ink or a few guns as presents for hill tribesmen that tended to make him irascible.

Meanwhile, many of the Sikh soldiery quietly slipped away to their homes. On 16 March, George Lawrence accompanied the Sikh army commanders Chutter Singh and Sher Singh as they inspected their army for the last time, before moving over to the British camp, where the Sikh leaders surrendered unconditionally. The Punjab was annexed as a province of British India on 30 March 1849 with Henry Lawrence appointed lieutenant governor, based at Lahore. Nicholson on hearing of the British decision to add to its empire, merely commented, 'I am not surprised to hear that the country is to be annexed. No fear of anyone in this quarter however, getting up a row about it. All regard it, as annexed already.'[47]

## PROMOTION IN RAWALPINDI

The districts were then portioned out with deputy commissioners. Although Nicholson had wanted the Singh Sagar Doab, on 4 April he was writing to Henry Lawrence, 'I am greatly obliged for your permission to change a district. I will take Rawalpindee, if Jelum goes with it, but if not, Pind Daduce Khan.' This was the reverse of what he had written to Sir John Lawrence a month before. Then he had said he would not take Rawalpindi, but after John Lawrence wrote to him, Nicholson changed his mind once more, saying it 'was a pity my experience of this part of the country should be lost to the state'. In the end, Nicholson was officially appointed deputy commissioner to Rawalpindi from 14 April 1849.[48]

On 10 April 1849 Nicholson was breathing fire and brimstone again because General Gough had again not listed him among the officers whom the commander-in-chief had thanked in a general order communiqué. He pointed out that since November 1848 he had been mentioned no fewer than three times in official despatches. At the end of this complaint, he adds, 'I was a little doubtful as to the propriety of writing you on this subject, but George [Henry and John Lawrence's elder brother] says he thinks I am right to do so and not unreasonable.' George Lawrence was not quite of the same mould of either of his two more famous brothers and seemingly was not beyond gently stirring the pot on occasions. Nicholson himself, for all his principles, could be pragmatic when it suited him. On sending his weekly diary to Henry Lawrence in mid-April he commented, 'I know you will approve of my treatment of the levee people, but if you think the GG won't, do not send him the Diary.'[49]

In fairness to Nicholson, he did question the proclamation that the property of rebel soldiers should be confiscated. While he had no qualms to 'ease the wealthy of their superfluous riches', he did object to seeing 'every poor man's cattle, bed and cooking utensils taken from him'.[50]

Nicholson's position was such that, like Abbott, his authority far exceeded that even of a captain, so on 7 June 1849, Nicholson was officially elevated to brevet major, 'for his services in the Punjab'.[51] He had in fact been using the title since the end of March 1849 when first told about the acting promotion. He complained bitterly that he had not received the pay increase this carried with it. James Abbott, who had been a captain in the artillery since 1841, had been made a major a year earlier, in April 1848. In his old regiment and, sadly for pension purposes, Nicholson remained a captain. The key posting of Peshawar went to his friend George Lawrence. One of the first things Lawrence initiated there was to construct a proper military road between Peshawar and Kohat, something that would prove invaluable at the time of the Mutiny. It was also a great convenience later when Nicholson had to travel from Bannu to Peshawar.

With the second Anglo-Sikh war over, Nicholson did two things. First he disengaged his levies, and, second, he asked for compensation. No doubt, he had not forgotten the shabby treatment he had received regarding the loss of his property after the Afghan affair:

> I suppose compensation will be allowed me for my property lost at Peshawar, Attock, and Hussun Abdal. I estimate it at 1000 rupees, which George [Lawrence] says is even under the mark. – I also rode a horse worth 400 rupees to death on Government service – not running away.[52]

He was still looking for his compensation that November, five months later. He had written to James Abbott, 'my fine chestnut died during the night of the effects of a gallop to Margalla and back again'.[53] This would not be by any means the last horse Nicholson would literally ride to death.

## CORRESPONDENT AND ADMINISTRATOR

Nicholson kept up a regular line of advice to Henry Lawrence, whose tolerance for the young man was quite exceptional. Nicholson continued with his long-running theme that irregular levies were sorely needed in the Punjab. He also proposed the demolition of various forts, an enterprise subsequently and famously undertaken by his friend Herbert Edwardes in Bannu.[54] Nicholson was not so enthusiastic about preparing the requested cash accounts for Henry Lawrence. After some prodding, Nicholson agreed to keep a day book of expenditure, although there is no record of him subsequently having done this. But what has survived of Nicholson's account is telling enough. During the campaign in August 1848, for example, he was responsible for receiving 30,101 rupees. His expenditure for the district he controlled was 19,302 rupees, or 64 per cent of income, but that included a requisition of 11,000 rupees for James Abbott to run his show next door in Hazara. The overall favourable balance was 10,799 rupees. More to the point, the accounts give an idea of the Indian force Nicholson controlled. This numbered 2,297 sepoys and sowars or mounted irregulars. In addition, Nicholson's right-hand man, Boodha Sing, was paid 1,704 rupees for the sepoys he controlled. That would bring the total force up to about 3,000 men. The other payments were small. Interestingly, Nicholson spent exactly the same amount on spies as he himself received as his own pay that month, 147 rupees.[55]

In late March 1849 Nicholson proposed the establishment of a 'Flying Force' of 1,500 or 1,600 men, which would spend a year moving around the north-eastern part of the frontier maintaining law and order. It was an idea he would propose again, with success that time, eight years later. What is interesting in this 1849 instance is the distrust which Nicholson felt towards Britain's sepoy army: '… I would very much rather have old soldiers of the Empire, or men whom I could raise myself than our own regular troops.'[56] Time proved Nicholson correct.

So it was that Nicholson spent several months doing what he enjoyed, riding around maintaining the peace. At one place he disarmed former Sikh soldiers. At another he organised the revenue systems. In a third he handed out firm judgements in resolving disputes. As far as tax gathering was concerned, his technique was simple enough. When he found that his proclamation had been ignored and due warning given, he burnt half a dozen houses belonging to those who paid no attention to his demands. But it was not so much the burning of poor Indian homes that got Nicholson into trouble but rather his short temper when dealing with his fellow officers, especially if they were obstructionist or resentful of what they saw as interference by an overzealous and over-moral brother officer. In April 1849, matters came to a head over what we do not know, with Henry Lawrence in Lahore writing to Major Nicholson:

> Let me advise you, as a friend, to curb your temper, and bear and forbear with natives and Europeans and you will be as distinguished as a Civilian as you are a Soldier. Don't think it is necessary to say all you think to every one. The world would be one mass of tumult if we all gave <u>candid</u> opinions of each other. I admire your sincerity as much as any man can do, but say thus much as a general warning. Don't think I allude to any specific act; on the contrary, from what I saw in camp, I think you have done much towards conquering yourself; and I hope to see the conquest completed.

And as usual, instead of keeping quiet and taking the advice to heart, Nicholson could not resist replying:

> <u>Very many</u> thanks for yours of the 7th, and the friendly advice which it contains. I am not ignorant of the faults of my temper, and you are right in supposing that I do endeavour to overcome them – I hope with increasing success. On one point, however, I still think I am excusable for the plain speaking which, I am aware, made me very unpopular with a large portion of the officers of the Army of the Punjab. I mean with reference to the plundering of the unfortunate people of the country, which generally prevailed throughout the campaign, and which was, for the most part, winked at, if not absolutely sanctioned, by the great majority of officers. I knew from the first that I was giving great offence by speaking my mind strongly on this subject; but I felt that I should be greatly wanting in my duty, both to the people and the army, if I did not, to the best of my ability, raise my voice against so crying an evil. For the rest, I readily admit that my temper is a very excitable one, and wants a good deal of curbing. A knowledge of the disease is said to be half the cure, and I trust the remaining half will not be long before it is effected.[57]

## A FEVERED TEMPER

Henry Lawrence was undoubtedly correct but Nicholson was a complex character. Much of what he was attacked for was true enough, and yet there was another side. He had great tenacity. He was not extravagant. He could harbour deep friendship and loyalty to those whom he liked. He was reliable. He refused to panic or be panicked in time of crisis. And, he was, as the letter above illustrates, self-conscious about his own failings and was neither slow to admit fault nor to accept the dictates of his superiors when they denied him one of his many requests. What changed over the years was Nicholson's standing, and of course his health deteriorated. All this tended to exaggerate or at least emphasise his strongest character traits. The one consistent negative was his temper. Back in 1847 Lieutenant, later Major General, Young met Nicholson when the two officers had just returned from Kashmir. Giberne Sieveking, in her invaluable, if rather ramshackle, Mutiny book, described what happened as follows:

> They had come out by different routes, and Young on his arrival found another tent pitched. On hearing that Nicholson was in this tent, Young, as junior officer, called upon Nicholson. Nicholson received him with no particular cordiality, and, for something to say, remarked, 'I'm the senior officer, and ought to ask you to dinner, but I have no plates and not much food.' Young replied that that did not greatly matter, as his own plates and dinner could be brought to Nicholson's tent, and they could thus dine together. Nicholson agreed, and it was arranged. During dinner, Nicholson's table servant offended him in some way, and in a sudden anger he took up his tumbler and threw it at the man. It missed aim, but hit the tent pole and was broken to pieces. 'There goes my last tumbler!' was all Nicholson's comment on what had occurred.[58]

Such stories of displacement anger are no doubt true, though their impact on others was enhanced by Nicholson's great physical stature.

By 1849, Nicholson had grown into a great bear of a man, well over 6ft in height, with broad shoulders, powerful arm muscles (the product of training with and using a sabre), a large head with a proportionately large dark beard, dark eyes and a very deep rich Anglo-Irish voice. One commentator said that facially Nicholson resembled the Victorian statesman Benjamin Disraeli, but that might have been wishful thinking. Nicholson's hair was thinning (something ignored by later portrait painters), though as he tended to wear a forage cap that was not so noticeable. But in his high leather riding boots and military tunic, John Nicholson made an imposing and somewhat frightening figure.

In part, Nicholson's temper also depended on whom he was with. There are no reports of his ever losing his temper with Sir Henry Lawrence, and Nicholson himself admitted a ploy he had for dealing with matters of dispute on the rare occasion that he and his friend Edwardes disagreed. Referring to his soldier hero,

Major George Broadfoot, who, as mentioned, died of wounds sustained in action in December 1845, Nicholson was wont to say, 'Let us think how Broadfoot would have acted in the present case.'[59] But the reality was that Nicholson's temper, never the calmest, was exacerbated by the fact that he was often unwell. That on occasions he drank too much when he was alone is also highly likely and probably contributed to a liver problem. In March 1848 he had asked his doctor at Lahore to send him 'another packet of physic-jalap (in a phial) salts, calomel, emetics quinine, and box of blue and colycith, and another of opium pills'. He also asked for him to be sent copies of *Harnam Das's Diary*, grumbling that others received this publication and he did not, so that, 'I frequently find my ignorance of all that goes on out of my own charge, prove very embarrassing.'[60]

A year later, in April 1849, Nicholson wrote to Henry Lawrence apologising for a letter he had written on 23rd: 'I don't know at all what ails me. I am writing now with a warm chagah on at 1 PM. Half the night, I lay naked, and half with two rezais over me. Still it is not my old enemy fever and ague, at least it does not resemble it in other respects.'

## GIVEN CREDIT

Nicholson also apologised for complaining about the work he had done in the war, and says he now felt that perhaps he should not have written it, 'but 'George urged it on me'. One suspects that his health and humour would have improved considerably had he known that the next day in the House of Lords, in a notice of thanks to the army in India, Viscount Hardinge, fresh back in London from his stint as governor-general of India, singled out four officers (Edwardes, Lake, Pollard and Nicholson) who 'had distinguished themselves' in the recent Anglo-Sikh War.[61]

The other factor that needs to be taken into consideration when judging Nicholson's quick temper was that he was essentially a loner in life. Like many such, he was quintessentially shy, bottling up emotions, which sometimes then had a tendency to burst out in a fit of rage or over-dramatic and exaggerated expressions.

Early May 1849 found Nicholson pressing the administration at Lahore concerning a list of names of Indians who had given good service to the British during the war and who should be rewarded. In every case, these men had stuck with Nicholson when the tide of events appeared to be turning against the British. This list had been sent in March and he had heard nothing. No names of European troops were on the list. The names as given by Nicholson included:

Major Boodh Singh: With Nicholson at battle of Margulla, where wounded; then with beleaguered garrisons at Attock and Peshawar. Sing came with his own troops, probably about 700 or 800 men, whom Nicholson paid a lump sum of 1,700 rupees a month.

Colonel Baboo Pandy: With Nicholson from time he was at Hazara until October 1848.

Colonel Nooroodeen: With Nicholson from time he was at Hazara until October 1848.

Sodi Nehal Singh: With Nicholson from October 1848.

Sirdar Abbas Khan: Joint commander of Nicholson's Afghan Horse.

Syud Isamudeen: Joint commander of Nicholson's Afghan Horse.

Kurrum Illahee: Joined Nicholson with his sowars at Pind Dadun Khan and fought alongside him for campaign.

Malik Feroze Kan of Shumsabad in Chuch: Commanded Nicholson's irregular infantry in the forts of Gujranwala and Gujrat. Nicholson observed of Khan, 'I know no one of the many who served under me, to whom I consider myself under greater obligations. His house was burned, his property plundered and his family compelled to fly the country by the rebels.'

Saadullah Khan of Sama in Chuch: Nicholson left him with Lieutenant Herbert at the fort of Attock.

Another accusation against Nicholson has been his reluctance to correspond. This was sometimes true enough, but depended in part upon circumstance. His mother reprimanded him for his tardiness in lifting a pen. But overall, this is somewhat unjust. Nicholson was essentially a front-line field commander. Such individuals, like tightly wound springs, are generally not good correspondents. What is astonishing about Nicholson though, as the late 1840s and early 1850s were to prove, is that he was also an excellent administrator. And that meant endless reports, correspondence, logistical paperwork and, to a degree, revenue book-keeping. Biographers have forgotten that Nicholson undertook this written work, so making him even less inclined to shift his frame of mind to rush in answering relatives' letters about the goings-on in overcast Lisburn. But furthermore, his lengthy list of correspondents included his mother, his brother, his sister Mary, his Uncle James, his Aunt Mary, his Uncle Richardson, Charles Lawrence, Henry Lawrence, John Lawrence, James Abbott, Herbert Edwardes, Neville Chamberlain, John Becker, Arthur Cocks, John Coke and no doubt others who came and went. Then it must also be remembered that there was a system of exchanging letters, or demi-official letters as they were called, between Company army and civil officers. Where the official ended and the private began was clearly a grey area.

# DEATH OF WILLIAM NICHOLSON

At the end of one of his numerous notes to Henry Lawrence, Nicholson states, 'My brother is <u>not</u> fit for the Guides, but I think would make a tolerable Adjutant of a common Irregular corp.'[62] Despite his brother's initial misgivings, William Maxwell Nicholson had joined not the Bengal Army but the sister Bombay Army of the East India Company. This was on 12 June 1847. He had actually joined his regiment as an ensign only on 11 November of that year. A few of this young 19- or 20-year-old's letters from India to his mother and sister Mary in Barnsley have survived. To the latter, he wrote, 'Are there any Chartists in Barnsley. Judging by the newspaper accounts the north of England seems to be full of them.' And to his mother, William wrote about the Famine in Ireland and about Daniel O'Connell's death. From these letters, we learn that Clara Nicholson usually went to Bangor, County Down, for an annual holiday, but in 1848 stayed instead with her daughter Lily at Ardglass. William writes about the abundance of European table vegetables available in India and about the problems of getting and paying for a *munshi* to teach Indian languages, who then expected a substantial cut of the allowance a subaltern was paid having passed the examinations. All very chatty and unlike his brother John's letters.

William was in the military fort at Belgaum, near the Portuguese enclave of Goa, then at Bombay, and so on to Karachi. Then in December 1848 William wrote to his mother:

> You will see by the 'Delhi Gazette' that Lord Gough has highly complimented John for energy and decision which he displayed in procuring boats for the passage of the River. I cannot give you any particulars, as John and I never correspond and Charley has not written to me lately.[63]

From Karachi, William's regiment preceded into Sindh, where he arrived in November 1848, being stationed at Sukkur, one of the hottest stations in India. Seven months later, on 1 June 1849, William Nicholson suddenly died.[64] Charles Nicholson read the news of this in a Delhi newspaper three weeks later and immediately wrote to John:

> We are now alone in the world. You and I, the eldest and youngest are the only 2 left out of five brothers.
>
> Poor William is dead – the companion of my childhood is no more – I saw his death mentioned in the Delhi [Gazette] yesterday as having occurred at Sukkur on the 1st June a whole month ago. Poor fellow a whole month unwept and unmourned for.[65]

Years later Clara Nicholson stated that William had died of fever, but the truth appears to have been more sinister. In 1896 Captain Lionel Trotter, then writing his life of Nicholson, in one of his many fishing notes to the Maxwell family, the repository of Nicholson family memory, posed the following question:

> From one of the documents you kindly forwarded me, I gather that the mystery about Will Nicholson's death was never cleared up. It was only conjectured that he walked in his sleep and fell over a cliff from his verandah. On the other hand his brother Charles, who visited the house long afterwards, found that it had remained shut up since W.N.'s death, was known as murder house, and that no native would live in it. And the writer of the Memo. (your wife? [Mary Nicholson]) says that this 'speaks for itself'.
>
> Did she or her mother believe that he had been murdered? and by whom?

If death resulted from an accident, how was it that none of the servants threw any light upon the matter?[66]

No reply has been found to this probing letter, not that it probably would have said very much. If there was skulduggery over William's death, the family would not have wished that to go down in posterity and, besides, most likely would in any case not have known the truth.

In writing to his sister Mary in September 1849 in relation to the tragedy of the death of the 20-year-old William, Charles quoted her several stanzas from Thomas Moore's most haunting song, 'Oft in the stilly night':

> Oft in the stilly night,
> Ere slumber's chain has bound me,
> Fond Mem'ry brings the light
> Of other days around me.
> The smiles, the tears,
> Of boyhood's years,
> The words of love then spoken,
> The eyes that shone,
> Now dimm'd and gone,
> The cheerful hearts now broken!
> When I remember all
> The friends so linked together,
> I've seen around me fall,
> Like leaves in wintry weather;
> I feel like one

Who treads alone
Some banquet-hall, deserted,
Whose lights are fled,
Whose garlands dead,
And all, but he, departed!

Charles, rather than John, was able to express the tragedy that had been and was to be the Nicholson family.[67]

## CHARLES NICHOLSON AND THE IRISH CONNECTION

As fortune would have it, that June 1849 John and Charles found themselves together for the month at Rawalpindi. India had by now taken two of their brothers. Maybe it was that as much as being thousands of miles from Ireland that drew the two very different men together, for until the death of John eight years later, it is clear that John and Charles sought and liked each other's company. In April 1849 Nicholson had expressed thanks to Henry Lawrence for putting, 'my brother's name down for an adjt. in one of the new inf. corps'.[68] Touchingly, Charles secretly implored his sister Mary not to take any money from John to pay 'Willy's debts', as John had paid for too much and he, Charles, had yet to pay for anything.

The growing closeness of the two brothers is interesting. They were of very different temperament and character, but they had two things in common: family and their Irish background. The Irish link between Henry Lawrence in particular and his difficult protégé, whom he guided and protected, was clearly important, not least because of the north of Ireland connections. But the matter went further. The Irish in the Punjab establishment were a community and thought of themselves as such. This was nothing so vulgar as having a hooley on St Patrick's Day, but rather a consciousness of the fact that the Irish were a significant element in the colonial dispensation of the newly acquired Punjab.

Leaving aside the traditional Ulster battle cry, the old defiance not to surrender that Henry Lawrence gave his troops as he lay mortally wounded on 2 July 1857 in the ruins of the Residency at Lahore during the Great Rebellion, there is other evidence to substantiate this Irish consciousness. Perhaps a more subtly poignant example is an incident that occurred at Christmas 1849. Sir Henry Lawrence was now president of the Punjab Board of Administration, a deceptively prosaic name for the very powerful Irish troika that ruled the Punjab from 1849 to 1852 and which comprised Henry Lawrence, his brother John and Robert Montgomery. Not only were these Irishmen, but they had gone to the same school together, Foyle College in Derry, an institution that the late Will Ferguson, the historian of that school, estimated had between 1814 and 1834 provided the British establishment in India with no fewer than twenty-six former pupils. Lord Radcliffe, in an excellent public lecture delivered at Magee University College, Derry, in 1957, recounted the following anecdote:

> It was from Lahore that the three of them, sitting at Christmas dinner under the sparkling alien sky, remembered the 'two poor old Simpsons' who had been ushers at Foyle College in their schooldays, under-paid and unregarded, and Henry made his proposal to the others: 'Let each of us put down £50 and send it off to-morrow as a Christmas box from the Punjab Board of Administration.' So the kindly gift reached two old brothers in Londonderry; and a letter of thanks, written in a shaking hand and blotted with tears, reached Sir Henry Lawrence, K.C.B., in Lahore.[69]

Now home called Nicholson. Initially he was granted leave for three months, from 3 October to 26 December 1849, and subsequently he was granted full furlough leave in Europe for one year, commencing on 17 January 1850. As will be seen, this was in turn extended. Nicholson did not hurry away from India, leaving only after the New Year. In the interim, his claim for 1,000 rupees compensation for losses incurred during the war was turned down, along with one for 15,000 rupees from George Lawrence. An official note recorded, 'With every disposition to take a favourable view of the claims of officers whose conduct has been so eminently meritorious, we must decline.'[70]

Not surprisingly, in November 1849, Nicholson was grumbling that 'India is like a rat trap, easier to get into than out of'.

# Home on Furlough

Permission for Nicholson to depart from Bombay, the nearest major port to Peshawar, was granted on 17 January 1850, signalling the official start of his furlough leave. The excitement in Lisburn must have been great. It was more then ten years since the family had seen John and in that time he had made a name for himself in the Company's army. Both Alexander and William, though, had died in India.

Despite the anticipation, there was a professional disadvantage of going on furlough. Company policy demanded Nicholson resign his assistant commissionership, with the chance, albeit unlikely, of his not getting an equivalent position on his return to India and so having to return to the 27th Regiment at his lower but substantive rank of captain.

## THE JOURNEY HOME

Nicholson took a boat starting from Ferozepur down the Sutlej River and then all the way down the Indus to Karachi, and from there a steamer to Bombay. The plan was for him to travel with his old friend Herbert Edwardes. A complication was that Edwardes had been entrusted with the care of the young Lawrence girls, the daughters of John Lawrence. This daunting task says something about whom the gruff bureaucrat trusted with his children.

The plan was to sail to the Red Sea and then land at Cosire [Quseir] on the African coast, 'march' over to Thebes and thence travel by boat down the Nile to Cairo. Nicholson seems to have treated children as he did women, as sacred objects to be protected. Unlikely as it might seem, the Edwardes–Nicholson–Misses Lawrence group had the potential to be a rather fun travelling party.

The *Bombay Overland Times* of 17 January 1850 reported:

Major Edwardes and Captain Nicholson – two of the officers who so eminently distinguished themselves throughout the Punjab war, and received brevet rank, and the former a C.B.-ship – have been residing for some days amongst us and receiving the honours and attention that are their due. They return on a twelve-month's leave to England to take breath after their adventures.[1]

At Bombay, they boarded a packet for the Red Sea. As luck, or ill luck, would have it, a fellow passenger was General Gough, whom Nicholson had so often criticised during the recent Anglo-Sikh war. But all went well and Hugh Gough was pleasant enough company. The journey went as planned and Nicholson, Edwardes and the two Lawrence girls crossed the desert from the Red Sea to the Nile and from there steamed slowly up the great river, seeing the sights on the way before exploring Cairo.

Because of the girls, Edwardes had to head straight for Britain from Egypt, but Nicholson was intent on steeping himself in as much culture and history as he could. He was in no great rush to run home to his mother. We know Edwardes came quickly back to England because a photograph of a painting of Edwardes resplendent in Afghan dress survives. It was taken by H. Herring of 137 Regent Street, London and is dated 20 March 1850.

From Alexandria, Nicholson took ship and was in the Ottoman capital of Constantinople from 26 February to 15 March 1850. In a letter to his mother dated 20 March he noted, 'Why I remained three weeks instead of only one as I intended, I will tell you when we meet, and you will not disapprove of my motives.'

## THE KOSSUTH CONSPIRACY

The story goes that Nicholson became involved in a bizarre entanglement with an émigré from Austria, who happened to be an Englishman referred to only as 'General G'. Given other circumstantial evidence, this can only have been General Richard Debaufre Guyon (1813–56). Though the family was of French origin, Guyon was born in the sedate and very English village of Wilcot, near Bath, in Somerset. He joined the imperial Hapsburg army in 1834 and in 1838 married Mária Slény, the daughter of a Hungarian general. When his father-in-law died, Guyon retired from the Austrian army and settled in Hungary. But his was not to be a peaceful retirement. With the Hungarian revolution of 1848, Guyan joined the insurgent army with the rank of major, rising to colonel and finally major general. When the Hungarians were defeated in August 1849, Guyon crossed the border into the Ottoman empire and made his way to Constantinople.

Guyon is an interesting man in many respects, both because of the cosmopolitan credentials of this Somerset gentleman and also because he converted to Islam, not, it has to be stated, out of any necessity. The Turks welcomed him into their army, where he did much good in reorganisation. He was to die at Scutari outside Constantinople in 1856 during the Crimean war.

How Nicholson met this extraordinary man is not known. Guyon certainly retained contact with the famous British diplomat at Constantinople, Sir Stratford Canning (1786–1880), who had close Irish connections including an Irish father. Possibly it was through this link that Nicholson and Guyon met.[2] Whatever the circumstances, Nicholson and Guyon obviously got on very well together and soon Nicholson found himself embroiled in a hare-brained plot to rescue the Hungarian leader Kossuth from an 'honourable' castle arrest 'in a fort in Asia Minor' where the Turks were holding him.

After Kossuth crossed the frontier into the Ottoman empire, in what is today Bulgaria, on 17 August 1849, he had been moved several times by the Turks. From 30 August to 3 November, he was in the picturesque fortress of Babavida in Vidin on the Danube river, only 60 miles from the Hapsburg border, but some 435 miles from Constantinople. Between 3 and 21 November, Kossuth had a difficult journey to Shumen, much nearer to the Black Sea, but still in Turkish-held Bulgaria. In Shumen, Kossuth was accommodated in a comfortable house. He was now only 160 miles from Constantinople. Finally, on 15 February 1850, Kossuth was moved to Bursa in Asia Minor, much nearer the imperial capital. The exiled Hungarian leader was there when Nicholson landed in Constantinope on 26 February, so the dates match.[3]

Kossuth may have been at Bursa for a while, but his final places of house arrest were a barracks and then a house in Kütahya. Bursa and Kütahya are both in Asia Minor and within riding distance of the sea, Bursa particularly being only 12 miles from the Aegean. Sir John Kaye's account of this episode in Nicholson's life specifically says the place from which the rescue of Kossuth was to be staged was in Asia Minor.

The story goes that when in Asia Minor the Turks permitted Kossuth to ride out once a day accompanied by an escort, the route altering every day. The conspirators' plan was to intercept this riding party, as they had knowledge of when the group would be riding in the direction of the sea. Once liberated, Kossuth would be hurried to the coast and transferred to a boat, from there to an American frigate and so to America. So there were Americans also clearly involved in the scheme.

Nicholson agreed to help but, fortunately for his head, the plot was discovered by the Austrians because of the gossiping of 'an American lady whose husband was in on the secret'. From a letter written by Honoria Lawrence some months later, she quotes Nicholson as saying, 'The American Counsel told his wife, and she of course let out the secret.'[4]

The guard on Kossuth was strengthened and the route of his ride altered. The plan was abandoned and the conspirators avoided arrest only no doubt due to the fact that General Guyon was popular with the authorities. Sir John Kaye's comment on this ridiculous episode was, 'The Kossuth enterprise he [Nicholson] had felt to be in truth little business of his, and he had only joined in it from natural curiosity and a kind of professional shame at declining danger in any honourable shape.'[5]

## PRISON POSTMAN

But the Guyon story does not end there. General Guyon allegedly persuaded Nicholson to leave Turkish territory and travel to Austria. His purpose was to deliver a letter to Mária Guyon, who was imprisoned in an Austrian fortress. This Nicholson achieved by walking up to the castle gate, requesting to speak to the officer on duty and identifying himself, quite openly, as a major in the Indian army, who wished to see Madame Guyon. After some hesitation, the officer granted Nicholson a brief interview. Once in the cell, Nicholson removed a boot and produced a letter from Richard Guyon and said, 'You have just five minutes to read it, and give me any message for your husband.' This was duly done, 'gratitude was looked rather than told, the door opened, the sentry reappeared, and John Nicholson departed with a few words of courtesy and thanks to the officer at the gate'.[6]

In a strange way, the second saga rings more true than the first, though in fairness to Nicholson nothing ever actually happened to release Kossuth – the scheme was a busted flush. Nicholson presumably was all the while in Constantinople. But the cheek and devilry of Nicholson as the prison postman was not out of character. A question mark, however, must be raised over the logistics of the Madame Guyon mission. Travel in the Balkans was extremely difficult. For Nicholson to travel to Austria, undertake his mission and return even within the whole eighteen days he was ashore at Constantinople would have been very difficult.[7]

Six months later, Honoria Lawrence wrote to Nicholson that 'you can hardly believe the interest and anxiety with which we watched the result of your projected deed of chivalry. Kossuth has taken his place in my mind as one of the true heroes.' Whatever the truth, Nicholson stayed longer in Constantinople than he had planned and departed by ship on 15 March 1850.

A day out of Constantinople there was, of all things, a snow storm and the ship, the *Lycurge*, ran aground in the Dardanelles and stuck fast. The passengers were transferred to a British gunboat, the wooden paddle-steamer HMS *Porcupine*, and taken to Piraeus.[8] Nicholson must have enjoyed being on board the Royal Navy vessel. After a short time in Athens, Nicholson moved on to Trieste.[9] He appears then to have travelled to Hamburg via Vienna and Berlin. Haigh and Turner speculate that he used this opportunity of freedom from authority to perhaps 'cut loose', though they concede that there 'is very little evidence to go on'. Certainly, it was not until near the end of April 1850 that John Nicholson landed in England.[10]

## HOME

Having reached London, Nicholson made his way to his uncle's elegant residence at 16 Grosvenor Square, Sir James and Lady Mary Hogg having migrated up the social ladder somewhat from 40 Upper Grosvenor Street. Later Hogg would move again, south of Hyde Park, to 11 Grosvenor Crescent. It appears that Clara Nicholson was staying there, which is hardly surprising.[11] No record has survived of their reunion after ten years' separation, but both must have been nervous. Trotter, in a letter to Rev. Maxwell, says he had learned from Quintin Hogg, Sir James's son, that Nicholson stayed 'some weeks' in the Hogg house on his arrival in Britain.[12]

That John and Clara Nicholson did not immediately return home to Ireland is confirmed by the fact that we know on 24 April 1850 the Goldsmiths' Company held a banquet in honour of General Sir Hugh Gough, now Viscount Gough of Goojerat and Limerick, to admit him as a member of the guild. Guests included the Duke of Wellington, Lord Stanley, the bishop of London and former governor-general Lord Hardinge. Also present were Edwardes and Nicholson. A year before to the day, Wellington had proclaimed in the House of Lords, 'It is impossible to speak too highly of Major Edwardes and the other gentlemen who have been engaged in these services [in the Punjab].' In that same debate, Lord Hardinge had mentioned Nicholson by name. Edwardes and Nicholson were therefore known to the distinguished guests.[13] Maybe it was at this banquet that Nicholson raised a notion of:

applying for my whole three year furlough, and employing it in learning Turkish, and making myself acquainted with the principal localities (in a military point of view) in Turkey and Egypt, from a conviction that we must one day have to oppose Russia in the former, and France in the latter country, and that an English officer with some active experience and knowledge of the country and language would have a fine field open to him. Sir J. Hogg and Lord Hardinge, to whom I mentioned my plan, thought the contingency too remote. I begin to suspect that it is not so, and that I should have done wisely had I adhered to my original intention.[14]

At the City of London banquet, Edwardes proposed a toast to the East India Company army. During his short speech, Edwardes gestured towards Nicholson and in magnanimous fashion said, 'Here, gentlemen, here is the real author of half the exploits which you have been kind enough to attribute to me.'[15] Gough tried to persuade Nicholson to come home to Ireland with him 'and enjoy a share in the ovation which awaited the old hero'.

From London, Nicholson made his way across the Irish Sea and back to his mother's home in Lisburn. There, on Thursday, 23 May, a grand banquet was held in his honour in the old Market House. The Lisburn and Lambeg Volunteers had paraded in front of it sixty-eight years before in honour of the Dungannon Convention. A dramatic statue of John Nicholson, carrying sabre and pistol, would be unveiled there seventy-two years later in 1922.

The dinner was chaired by the Very Rev. James Stannus, dean of Ross and rector of Lisburn. Thomas and Walter Stannus of Manor House, Lisburn, were also present, as were between forty and fifty local dignitaries. Women, with the exception of Clara and Mary Nicholson, were restricted as observers in the gallery of the hall. The room's central decoration was a banner proclaiming 'Cead Mille Failte' surrounded by laurels. And on the walls were other banners with the names in yellow lettering on a blue background of 'Ghuzhee', 'Ramnaggar', 'Chillianwallah', 'Goojerat', 'Gough' and 'Sutlej'. Music was provided by the Lisburn Amateur Band.

Rev. Stannus talked about his time at Lahore, when he had been able to 'paralyse all their efforts at insurrectionary movements'. Nicholson himself spoke of the opportunities he had had to shine, mentioning Major Edwardes and General Pollock.[16]

## A WIFE

Two things strike one about Nicholson's furlough home. The first is that he did not spend all his time back in Lisburn with his mother, but instead spent a lot of time in Britain and on the European continent.

Second, Nicholson did not 'find' a wife, nor is there any evidence that he made the slightest effort to do so. The pressure relating to this was great and predated his departure from India. There is a much-quoted letter to Nicholson from Sir Henry Lawrence, dated 23 October 1849, part of which reads, 'Get married and come out [to India] soon; and if I am alive and in office, I shall not be at fault if you do not find employment here.'

The rather unseemly practice of seeking out a wife having spent ten years on service in India was well established and no doubt much family plotting and conniving went on behind the scenes to facilitate this open season marriage mart. And, as in the queen's army, this often meant that the new wife was considerably younger than her husband. This had interesting social repercussions, as either battle or old age left many British and Irish women widows at a relatively young age. Nicholson's close friend Neville Chamberlain would marry only in 1873, when he was 53 years old.[17]

Another example of an 'Indian' quickly finding a wife while on home leave was no less a figure than the future Field Marshal Lord Frederick Roberts. Roberts was Nicholson's junior by a decade, and, as will be seen, was on his fellow Irishman's staff for a short period. On his furlough in 1859, Roberts was at the family's home in County Waterford. Two years before he had asked his mother in a letter to look out for him, 'some nice girl with "blue eyes and yellow hair"'.[18] After a little judicial family management, the dashing young lieutenant proposed to his cousin, Nora Henrietta Bews. And, as with Edwardes, Roberts took his new bride back with him to the very different cantonment life of the British, or in the case of the Punjab, 'Irish raj'.

## 'NOBLE SELF-DENIED'

Nicholson cut a striking figure: 6ft 2in (1.88m) tall, broad shouldered, very dark brown hair and piercing eyes. There was a quiet and at once 'dangerous yet vulnerable aura' about him – and he already had established reputation as a swashbuckling fighter. Added to this were Nicholson's sonorous Anglo-Irish accent and his Grosvenor Square contacts.

Clara Nicholson was aware of the pressure on her son, and indeed added to that pressure. She wrote about the subject to Rev. William Pakenham Walsh (1820–1902), then deputy secretary of the Church of Ireland Church Mission Society and later doctor of divinity:[19]

> I often wanted him to marry when he was at home, but his answer was so characteristic that I remember it well: 'After what I have seen the Lawrences suffer, I would not take a wife across the Indus, and I do not think a good wife ought to be left behind. If I married, I must ask Government to change my appointment, and I know the Punjab so thoroughly that I do not think I could serve my country as well in any other part of India.'

Forty years later the then Rt Rev. Dr Walsh, bishop of Ossory, Ferns and Leighlin, pompously asserted that Nicholson's declaration to his mother were 'Noble, generous, tender, self-denying words!'

Flora Steel suggested in her Mutiny novel *On the Face of the Waters* that perhaps Nicholson had been 'disappointed in love', but there is no evidence for that. The *Edinburgh Review* of 1898, however, informed its readers that Charles Nicholson had pointed out that, next to his mother, John Nicholson 'respected his aunt, Lady Hogg, better than any women' and Nicholson and Mary Hogg, with whom he had established a good rapport, certainly corresponded. The same journal also, more drily, quoted Captain Trotter, that 'perhaps his [John Nicholson's] heart, for all its tenderness, was less inflammable than his temper'.[20]

So what 'went wrong'? Of course, it might just have been that Nicholson met no one whom he cared enough about to spend the rest of his days with. But there are also two fairly stark suppositions that are difficult to avoid. First, that John Nicholson was psychologically damaged beyond repair and either potential brides picked up on this or he alternatively avoided attachments because of this. The second point is that John Nicholson was homosexual.

Up to relatively recently, and indeed, often still by inference, homosexuality was treated by officialdom as sinister. One could not have a Victorian military hero who was homosexual. This is quite extraordinary when one considers that the Victorian army was, by definition, a gathering of males only. The existence of male brothels around military barracks remains a largely closed book to military historians. That homosexuality existed in the army and establishment circles is beyond doubt, as the 'Dublin Scandals' of the 1880s well illustrated. If outwardly homosexuality as 'a bad thing' was the stereotype in the minds of the Victorian public, this negative attitude continued far into the next century and in some quarters beyond.

Not marrying did not, however, mean Nicholson was homosexual and he certainly did not fall into the 'Cairo corps' of officers, of whom fellow Irishman Kitchener is probably the most infamous. When Nicholson's brother Alexander was killed by Afghani tribesmen, Nicholson wrote to his mother saying that Alexander was now beyond the realm of temptation. Temptation was a real issue for such a haunted person as John Nicholson. It is impossible to say for certain, but Nicholson's temperament, his experience in life, and his affection for certain men as Henry Lawrence and Herbert Edwardes would tend to point to his possibly being a homosexual, repressed or otherwise. One cannot take it further without more evidence. The religious strictures embedded in his mind make it highly doubtful if matters ever surfaced and nearly certain that he was not a practising homosexual. In a throwaway comment to Nicholson in a letter, Honoria Lawrence wrote of her baby girl, 'on whose beauty I could descant but I'm afraid the subject is beyond you'.[21]

But that in itself is important, for it contributed the contradictions of his character. His fiery temper, the sternness of his punishments; the ferocity of his killing on the battlefield – contrasted with the fairness of his judgements; a decency towards ordinary Indian people who fell on hard times, the devotion to those, men and women, whom he loved; and his restraint in social recourse.

Be all this at it may, John Nicholson did not find a wife while back in Britain and Ireland. Probably, we can safely assume, because he did not look for one.

## WEDDING BELLS

On his immediate return from Ireland, ironically, he was attending a wedding. Herbert Edwardes, having none of the qualms or inhibitions of his friend Nicholson and being the 'hero of Multan', very soon became engaged to and then married Emma Sidney, the youngest daughter of a deceased Richmond Hill gentleman called James Sidney. On Tuesday, 9 July 1850, they were married at St Peter's parish church at Petersham in Surrey. Nicholson was best man. According to *The Times*, about fifty relatives and friends attended. After the ceremony, the wedding breakfast was held in the residence of Dr and Mrs Grant, where a gold medal that was soon to be ceremonially presented to Edwardes by the East India Company was displayed for guests to admire. The newspaper recorded that the honeymoon was to be in Wales.[22]

Writing to Nicholson in September 1850, Honoria Lawrence expressed her delight of hearing about his exploits in Turkey and once again raised the issue of his finding a wife:

Do you remember that eve of your quitting Lahore, when you and Major Edwardes and I sat over the embers in the office, waiting for Sir Henry's return from the GG's camp, and talking of home? – We rejoice that (*Inserted:* Major Ed) his wooing has since sped so well, and most earnestly hope that his married happiness has only begun.

Piling yet more pressure on poor Nicholson, she ended her eight-page missive by urging, 'Now do try and see our boy [in England], and you will be doubly welcome back.' She also reminded Nicholson that her son Harry, in India, liked liquorice.

In addition to finding a suitable wife when on furlough, Edwardes went all the way down to Devon to visit Honoria's sister-in-law, Mrs Hayes. The daughters of John and of George Lawrence had been farmed out to the Hayes. Writing to a man servant or agent, a Mr Libby, on 11 September 1850, Edwardes expressed shock at having received a tradesman's bill for £68 for china and glass and noted:

> I have returned here for the rest of September; and think we shall leave on 1st October to spend a week with Sir Henry Lawrence's sister Mrs Hayes, at their summer residence, Lynton in Devon, nr Ilfracombe; and if so we shall touch at Seymour Street, in passing, to take in 'coal and fresh vegetables'.
>
> Will you enquire for me at Bentleys [publishers], if the portrait of Sir Henry Lawrence has been altered as I suggested; and if so, get me another proof to look at.[23]

A visit to the opera was organised when Nicholson returned to London – no doubt at Hogg's invitation as Nicholson certainly would never have gone on his own initiative. It is difficult to picture Nicholson in evening dress, even in a box, sitting relaxed and watching opera. Nicholson's discomfort can only have been matched by the irritation of others having to put up with his fidgeting. Writing to Honoria Lawrence, Nicholson made his views very clear, 'We have nothing so bad in India.' Honoria was '*delighted*' with this assessment.

No doubt Nicholson was more comfortable attending the half-yearly cadet prize-giving and dinner at Addiscombe Military Seminary near Croydon, the Company's training college, on Friday, 14 June 1850. Sir James Hogg was there and it was probably at his suggestion that Nicholson and Edwardes came along, too. Next day *The Times* reported that one of the distinguished speakers said to the young cadets that present with them was Major Edwardes, 'of whom they had all heard; also Major Nicholson, Colonel Alexander, and Major Rawlinson. (Cheers).'[24] The following year General Frederick Abbott, the brother of Nicholson's friend James Abbott, was to take over as Addiscombe's lieutenant governor, the last incumbent of the post.

## FAMILY VISITS

According to Chamberlain, Nicholson then made his way back across the Irish Sea to his mother's home in Lisburn. Here he met his siblings and old friends and acquaintances. But Lisburn cannot have held Nicholson's interest for long. From the fragmented evidence that has survived, we know that he travelled in Ireland and, much more in character, went sailing along the Irish coast with his sister Mary.

After the Edwardes' wedding in July, Nicholson took himself off on a tour of the Continent, where he appears to have visited France, Prussia, possibly Austria again and Russia. Nicholson was particularly impressed with the Russian imperial guard. Even the sight of the Czar coming out onto the parade ground and saying good morning, then receiving the response of the assembled troops, impressed him. And the guards' physical stature was also impressive. Nicholson was no blind patriot. In a typical sweeping statement, he wrote to James Abbott: '[the Russian] guard were as superior to the British Household Brigade as were the British Household troops to the ordinary infantry of the line.'[25]

Needless to say, this greatly annoyed 'Little Abbott', but Nicholson raised an interesting point. After all, Russia was perceived as a real threat to British India. It would also not be too many years before Britain and Russia clashed in the Crimean War.

Nicholson was in Brussels in late October 1850, writing to his brother-in-law Edward Maxwell and trying to extricate himself for some indiscreet comment about him not staying with them when in Barnsley. Nicholson's sister Mary, as noted previously, had escaped the gloom of the family home in Ireland and married Edward Maxwell, who was appointed to a parish in Barnsley in the West Riding of Yorkshire. This was one of the new industrial towns of the north, with coal mining, linen weaving and glass making. Nicholson pleaded their 'limited' income, the Seymours' small house and the fact that his mother, who was to join the family reunion, liked to have her own room. In truth, he added, 'I have of late years been oftener without than with shelter, so that my own accommodation is [a] matter of indifference to me.' Having dug this large hole for himself, Nicholson concluded, 'I shall therefore feel obliged if you will take a room for me somewhere in your neighbourhood; provided it be <u>clean</u>. I care not how small or how plain.'[26]

Nicholson seems to have made this trip to Barnsley in late November 1850. The Maxwells had a 4-year-old boy called Theodore, who quickly made friends of the giant who was his uncle. In later life, Theodore was to do much to preserve what remained of Nicholson's papers and to assist Captain Trotter in writing his life of Nicholson. He was probably that little bit too young to remember the stories of India that the strange visitor told him. But he was not too young to recall the boisterous nature of Nicholson's games, such as when the army major lifted him onto the top of an open door frame and left him there, or hung him upside down by the feet over the stair banisters in his home.

Nicholson told the child that if he came to Bannu, he should have butter on one side of his bread and sugar on the other. The youth replied, though, that he did not wish to go to somewhere where there were lions and tigers. Nicholson assured him that he would write to his Uncle Charles and have them all killed.[27]

On 7 December 1850, we find Nicholson in Chester, not so far from Liverpool. From the letter, it is clear that he and the Edwardeses parted in a rush from Euston Station that morning, or rather that Nicholson got into a fluster about catching his train 'abruptly', taking with him in his haste and in error Emma Edwardes' snewspaper and *Bradshaw*'s guidebook. In Chester, he visited the cathedral and the Roman wall, 'both well worth seeing'. From there, Nicholson went on to Castle Street in Lisburn but, not surprisingly, he was back in London a couple of weeks later.

Christmas 1850 was spent in the congenial and festive surroundings of the Hogg household in Grosvenor Square. Here Nicholson was much interrogated by the young and somewhat precocious 5-year-old Quintin Hogg, who had ensured that his famous soldier cousin was by his side during the annual Christmas children's party.[28]

## EUROPE

With Christmas over, Nicholson set off to the Continent again. This trip seems to have taken him to Paris, Berlin, Vienna and finally St Petersburg. It is, however, possible that the St Petersburg trip happened before Christmas, maybe on the journey when he visited Brussels in October.

The highlights of this grand tour seem to have been military rather than romantic. In Berlin, Nicholson was greatly taken by the new rifle that had recently been added to the inventory of the ever-expanding Prussian army. This was Johan Dreye's needle-gun. These guns were breach rather than muzzle loaders. Equally important, they had carriages that contained both a gunpowder charge and a lead bullet, so greatly simplifying and hastening the gun's discharge. A needle-shaped firing pin was used, hence the name. Soon the smooth bore in these guns would be replaced by a rifling within the barrel, something that greatly increased accuracy, as was dramatically illustrated at the battle of Sadowa in 1861 when the Prussians defeated the Hapsburg army.

Nicholson brought an example of this rifle with him back to London and made his way to the War Office in an attempt to persuade it to discard the old muzzle-loader, the Brown Bess, and switch over to the modern breach-loaders. But the mandarins of the War Office were not interested in being lectured to by a captain in the Company's service. Subsequently, Nicholson took the rifle back to India.

We know that on 5 February 1851, Nicholson was granted an extension of his leave by ten months, meaning that he would not need to be back on duty in India in November 1851.[29] He was for the moment clearly enjoying being away from the Punjab, probably not surprising given this was his first time in the British Isles since he had left as 16-year-old boy.

## EDWARDES'S BOOK

Herbert Edwardes had had the bright idea of adapting the official reports he had written when based in the Bannu District and those of his subsequent military adventures around Multan, with some additions, into a two-volume book that would be entitled *A Year on the Punjab Frontier, in 1848–49*. Volume one was 608 pages and volume two 734. The book was brought out by the reputable London publishing house of Richard Bentley. It was advertised for sale in *The Times* on 19 November 1850, though the title page carries the date 1851. On 13 February 1851 a second and cheaper edition appeared. That day Edwardes wrote from Portland Square:

> I hope my dear Nicholson you can conscientiously rejoice also over the work; for after all, the book to be worth anything must be approved by those who know what it is about. Indiscriminate praise is as beneficial as the holy water sprinkled by a Romish Priest over all his congregation; ignorant alike

of good or evil. Above all I desire that the book do good to our political service, and show that we are not nusiuk-huzaions.[30]

There were various plans and illustrations, including a frontispiece of Sir Henry Lawrence, to whom the following was inscribed by Edwardes: 'If I have been able to serve Government to any purpose, I owe it to your teaching and example; and as the only way I may ever have of proving myself grateful for your friendship, I inscribe your name upon these records of the days I least regret.'

Particularly useful to the reader (and the historian) was a map of the frontier region stretching from Peshawar in the north to just beyond the confluence of the Indus and the Chena River in the south. The map was compiled from a series of district maps drawn for the frontier assistant commissioners by a man named Arrowsmith. But to this draft map, Edwardes added the names of the passes that would lead through to Afghanistan, as well the area controlled by Dewan Moolraj around Multan; tribal areas in the Bannu district; and the route followed by Edwardes in his narrative. The map measures about 1ft x 1ft 3in (30 x 43cm). [31]

Ironically, Henry Lawrence had wanted to send Nicholson on this expedition into the southern Punjab but considered he could not at that time be spared from his duties up in the Rawalpindi region. Because of this, Nicholson does not feature in the book apart from several honourable mentions in passing, such as Nicholson's 'distinguished' record in the recent second Anglo-Sikh war. In an oration in the conclusion of the book, Edwardes also intones in relation to the work of the army's political officers: 'See how the Huzaruh tribes took James Abbott for their Khan. See how the Eusofzyes loved Lumsden. See how the men of Rawul Pindee followed Nicholson.' [32]

On 12 February 1851, Edwardes called at India House to collect his specially struck gold medal. This was a grand item with the queen's image on the obverse and the Edwardes's details of the award on the reverse. It was a closed court, so Emma Edwardes was not able to witness the ceremony. The next day, writing from 37 Upper Seymour Street off the Edgware Road, Edwardes told Nicholson of this event, of his book's appearance and of his own departure back to India.

It appears that he and Nicholson kept missing each other. Nicholson was in London on 20 February, but the Edwardes were out of town, first in Sansaw in Shopshire and later Bath, then back to Shropshire. Nicholson was on his way again to the Continent, first to Paris where he stayed in the Hotel Folkestone. He had been grinding himself to learn French for some months, and now in Paris he focused on this project.

## HONOURS

On his way to the Continent, in London, he picked up some gossip from Sir James Hogg that annoyed him. For their efforts in the second Anglo-Sikh campaign, George Lawrence had petitioned for a knighthood and Mackeson for a colonelcy. George Lawrence he liked, but Mackeson he did not. Writing to Edwardes from Paris, Nicholson entered into one of his rants against such a proposal, his line being that he had done Mackeson's work for him, 'I should be very unhappy to see M receive additional honours, and I should be sorry to receive any myself which were not alike bestowed on Abbott, Taylor, Lake and others who are equally perhaps more deserving than myself.' He also added in petulant manner that he had been told, 'the staff all thought I should have had the Bath'.[33]

Be that as it may, that British spring of 1851 brought news that Nicholson was entitled to a medal with bar for his action in the battles of Chillianwala and Gujrat.[34] Some time after came the equally welcome news that Nicholson's request that gratuities or pensions be awarded to five of the Indian troops who had served under him in the second Anglo-Sikh War had been granted.[35]

On 8 March, Nicholson was writing from 26 rue Mont Thabor, a narrow street near the Tuileries Gardens in Paris.[36] After talking about visiting people in England and asking in which county in Ireland Raphoe was located (Donegal), he continues, 'I am living here very quietly in the old quarters of last summer [1850]. Early next month [April 1851], I go on to Italy.' In all he stayed about six weeks in Paris before going on to Italy.

The Edwardeses and a female servant went back to India ahead of Nicholson and sailed on the *Indus* from Southampton direct to Calcutta on 20 March 1851.[37] On the 20th, the newly married Edwardes wrote to his friend in Europe from Hadley's Hotel in Southampton, not letting up on the pressure:

> if your heart meets one worthy of it [matrimony] *return not alone*. I cannot tell you how good it is for our best purposes to be *helped* by a noble wife, who loves you better than all men and women, but God better than you.[38]


## CAPTURING THE IMAGE

On his return from France and Italy, Nicholson spent most of his time about London, though he may well have visited Ulster again to see his mother. Indeed, it appears as if his mother came back over to London, probably to be there when he finally left to return to India. It was also probably about this time that both he and she had their photographs taken, one for Clara to take back to Lisburn and the other to travel thousands of miles back to the Punjab. We know that there was family pressure for such a portrait as Nicholson's grandmother wrote to him from Lisburn in mid-November 1850 saying she may never see a photo as her eyes were failing, though adding defiantly, 'I do not require your picture to remind me of you or to endear you to my fond heart as a very much loved grandson.'

Today both the original daguerreotype photographs of John and a twin daguerreotype of Clara are kept safe in the British Library. The photograph of John Nicholson is particularly significant because it is the only authenticated true likeness of the man.

Daguerreotypes were widely available in Britain on a commercial basis only from the mid-1840s. This image of Nicholson was taken by William Edward Kilburn (1818–91), whose studio was then at 234 Regents Street. He was popular with the royals and celebrities of the day, most notably Prince Albert, Miss Jenny Lind and later Florence Nightingale. This greatly helped Kilburn's reputation, so by going to Kilburn, Clara Nicholson was sending her son to the reputed best.

Kilburn's photographs present great character in the sitter. With the Nicholson portrait, we are hampered by the fact that what was and is frequently reproduced is not the original daguerreotype, but a stipple engraving of it by J.W. Knight. This was subsequently reproduced by the publishing house of James Sprent Virtue (1829–92).

In the original photograph 2½ x 3½in (6.35 x 8.89cm), placed in an elaborate closing display case, Nicholson is in civilian dress, an interesting matter in itself. He wears a seemingly dark jacket, waistcoat and trousers, with a starched stiff-faced dress shirt and a broadly tied cravat. He wears a single ring and a gold watch chain. His receding hair is waxed down, but curls emerge at the sides. The eyebrows are quite thick but otherwise he is almost entirely clean shaven. He has a small, shaving cut and a shaving rash, possibly indicating that he had recently shaved off his beard, for there is not even a hint of the great dark beard he was to grow later in the decade. The sideburns reach only to mid-ear length. His ears and nose are quite large. His expression is one of restraint, with his famous piercing stare. He does not smile, no one did in pictures then, and he looks away to the left of the photographer. Evelyn Thomas thought that there were signs of 'laughing lines' at the outer corners of the mouth, though many would regard that as wishful thinking. She goes on, 'The outstanding characteristics of the portrait are the domed head, with its beautiful high and broad brow; The intensity of the penetrating gaze; and the beauty of the mouth.'[39] The hands are large, which is hardly surprising given his prowess with a heavy sabre or tubular sword.

Several recently discovered studio photographs can be identified with strong probability as portraying Nicholson in civilian dress, with a felt hat and a silver-topped cane. Characteristically, the photographs show him with his full dark beard. His eyes are less sunken than in the 1851 daguerreotype photograph, and the hair line appears less receded. This would suggest the photographs predate his only return trip home, meaning they would have been taken in India in the late 1840s.

Although Dickie's large painting of Nicholson resting on the hilt of his sword became famous, it was painted after his death. The other image believed to be Nicholson, shown as a man in a goatee-type beard, is possibly his brother Charles. Two versions of this exist – a drawing by W. Carpenter (reproduced in Cave-Browne's Mutiny book) and an 'amateur' painting copying this sketch. This image was borrowed from Dr Maxwell, Nicholson's nephew, by Sieveking for his book *A Turning Point in the Indian Mutiny*, published in 1910. Confusion, if confusion there is, has arisen due to the simple fact that at some point someone has written John Nicholson's name on the sketch. In Sieveking's book the illustration is given as one of Charles Nicholson. A print of this image is in the National Portrait Gallery in London and is listed as John Nicholson.[40] There is yet another version of the illustration in a scrapbook owned by General Sam Browne (1824–1901): a framed sketch above a pasted-in Nicholson signature.[41]

## COUNTDOWN TO INDIA

Nearly sixty years later Neville Chamberlain wrote, 'John Nicholson came home to rest [in 1850], but to a nature like his rest was impossible.'[42] And in November 1850 Charles Nicholson had written to his mother, 'How lonely you will feel when John is gone! Tho' he has been but a short time at home [Lisburn] it must have been a comfort to know that he was comparatively speaking near you.'[43] Four months later, he might have felt differently after receiving a grumbling letter from his brother: 'I have not heard from you 3 months – is it yr intention to cut me.' He reprimands Charles for not subscribing to the Lawrence Asylum, a military school for the children of poor European soldiers in India that was established at Sawawar near Simla in 1847. Nicholson had been a supporter of this endeavour of his mentor and in September 1855 had congratulated Edwardes on a speech he had made in Peshawar in support of the institution, adding 'I saw it [report of Edwardes's speech] just in time to stop a rather furious letter I was about to despatch to the papers, and wh. might possibly have done more harm than good.'[44]

In this letter to his brother, Nicholson repeats his anger at the thought of 'Fanny Mackeson' possibly getting an honour. More interestingly, he instructs Charles, who had joined the 2nd Punjab Cavalry, that he is to tell Lieutenant Sam Browne that he would be glad to take anything back to India for him. The celebrated inventor of the Sam Browne belt duly wrote to Nicholson, who was able to buy the pipes he wanted as well as ensuring a new rifle he had ordered was ready for the September steamer. In a postscript to that March letter to Charles, Nicholson adds, 'I am going to take tea – with whom do you think – Louis Napoleon,' the then president of the French Ssecond Republic.[45]

Of Nicholson's Italian sojourn we know nothing, beyond that he made it as far south as Sicily. While on the island, a letter had come from Sir Henry Lawrence telling Nicholson that on his return to India Lawrence was trying to get him posted to Bannu. On Nicholson's way back to Britain from Sicily, he stopped off again in Paris, where he appears to have attended the famous Grand Banquet of the Paris Fêtes in the Hôtel de Ville. He comments on, 'our [London] lord Mayor and Aldermen, who as you may suppose, made great fools of themselves in the French Metroplis'.[46] Seventy-one years later, in 1922, a letter in the *Irish Times* from 'W.A.S' recounted a delightful episode involving his cousins, the daughters of William Armstrong of Farney Castle near Thurles in County Tipperary, when they were in France visiting their French sister-in-law:

> Their visit concluded, they got into the train for Paris, *en route* for home. They found their carriage already tenanted by 'a tall, dark, noble-looking gentleman', seated at the further end. The sisters were chatting away in English, when one of them remarked in an undertone, 'Hush; perhaps, that gentleman understands English.' To their astonishment he bent forward and said, with a very sweet smile. 'Indeed, ladies I speak English just as well as yourselves, for I am Irish.' This led to further conversation, and he told them that his name was John Nicholson, home from India on furlough, and that he intended shortly to return there. My old cousins (long since dead) frequently alluded to this incident, and used to dilate on the perfect courtesy of his manner and how charmingly he rendered the little aids incidental to travel.[47]

One can only wonder as how fortuitous it was for the Irish Land League of the early 1880s that Nicholson had not married one of the Miss Armstrongs and had residency of Farney Castle, a house as eccentric in appearance as Nicholson was in character. Boycotting Nicholson would not have been such a lark as it was the hapless Captain Boycott of Lough Mask House.

Nicholson was back in London on 9 August 1851. Another letter to Charles dated 23 August was written from Barnsley, where he was again with the Maxwells. The family party was increased by the presence of Nicholson's mother and of his other sister, Lily. No doubt to break the tedium of such a family gathering, Nicholson cajoled the party to come to London by train and spend a week as his guest and visit the Great Exhibition. Young Theodore seems to have been left back in Barnsley. James Hogg's central London home was to be the base camp for the adventure.

The Great Exhibition of the Crystal Palace was held in Hyde Park between 1 May and 15 October 1851. This spectacular glasshouse designed by William Paxton was 1,851 x 454ft (approx. 564 x 138m). Attendance reached 6 million people. For novelty and excitement, there was nothing to equal a visit. Nicholson was particularly interested in the firearms on display, which included the new revolver designed by Samuel Colt, a sample of which he took back to India for his brother Charles.

Nicholson seems to have left England on 23 September 1851. Six weeks later, he reported officially at Fort William in Calcutta on 3 November, just over two months ahead of the expiry of his leave.[48] It was by no means unusual for 'Indians', as these Company officers were called at the Cape Colony, to return early from furlough, whether because they were becoming bored back in Britain, feeling out of place in the metropolis, or simply because of penury. In 1846 Neville Chamberlain had returned after only half his leave was expended.[49] This was not the case with John Nicholson, which was just as well for he would not see his home again.

**Daguerreotype photo of Nicholson, 1851**. Until 2017 this was the only known photograph of John Nicholson, and the only authenticated illustration of him, as the oil portraits and sketches were painted after his death or are of uncertain provenance. Copies of this photograph and sketches made from it usually softened the eyes and reduced the bags under them. In this original there is a shaving cut and shaving rash, perhaps a sign that his beard had just been removed. His characteristic firm stare was remarked on by contemporaries. (© The British Library Board, All Rights Reserved: Daguerreotype photo 246/(2) 1.0.)

**Oil painting of Nicholson by John Robert Dickee**. This portrait was painted for Clara Nicholson in 1867, a decade after John Nicholson's death. A similar but larger portrait, which hangs in the East India United Service Club in London, was painted twenty years later by Comley Vivian. Neither Dickee nor Vivian ever saw Nicholson. According to Captain Charles Griffiths, the Dickee portrait was not a good representation. Nonetheless, if it was accepted by Clara Nicholson and remained in the family's possession, it must have had some resemblance to her son. (© Armagh County Museum Collection; ARMCM21.1951)

**The Nicholson home, Lisburn**. After Nicholson's father died in Dublin in 1830, the family eventually moved north to a terraced Georgian residence (46 Castle Street, covered in ivy) where Clara Nicholson made their home. The house was marked with a commemorative plaque in 1938, the year before Hesketh Pearson published his call-to-arms, *The Hero of Delhi: A Life of John Nicholson Saviour of India*. The house was demolished in the 1970s. (Sieveking, *A Turning Point in the Indian Mutiny*, 1910)

**Clara Nicholson (***c.* **1786–1874)**. Nicholson took back this photograph of his mother with him to India after his furlough in 1851. Clara lived in genteel poverty after being widowed with seven children until receiving an East India Company pension of £500 a year after John Nicholson's death. A supporter of the evangelical section of the Church of Ireland, she raised her children with a strict puritan ethos. She sent four of her sons to be soldiers in India, where they all died. Clara was strong-willed and narrow, and outlived all her children apart from her eldest daughter Mary Maxwell. (Sieveking, *A Turning Point in the Indian Mutiny*, 1894)

**Charles Nicholson (1829–62).** Like John, Charles Nicholson was sent out to India as a soldier. A much less colourful character than his famous brother, Charles and John nonetheless grew close to each other in the 1850s. Charles lost his right arm in the assault on Delhi. Later he was appointed to command of the Gurkha regiment but died suddenly on his way upcountry to assume his post. (Sieveking, *A Turning Point in the Indian Mutiny*, 1894)

**Sir James Hogg (1790–1876).** In 1839 Nicholson received his cadetship in the East India Company's Bengal Army thanks to the nepotism of his uncle James Hogg, a wealthy nabob and director of the company. Hogg was Clara Nicholson's brother, and like Clara was not someone to trifle with. Yet he was kindly disposed towards his nephew, who stayed with the Hoggs in their palatial residence at 14 Grosvenor Square when he was on furlough in the early 1850s. It is possible that Nicholson was, at least in his younger days, in love with James Hogg's young wife, Mary. James Hogg outlived the Nicholson clan, excepting Mary Maxwell, dying aged 85. (*Illustrated London News*, 9 October 1858)

**Ghazni (1840s).** In this imposing city fortress Nicholson and his fellow officers of the 27th Bengal Native Infantry were held prisoners of war from March to August 1842 during the first Anglo-Afghan War. Nicholson never recovered from his bitterness at the harsh conditions.

**'One by one dropped through into the narrow street below'.** H.L. Shindler's drawing of the escape of the remnant of the 27th Native Infantry (Nicholson with the black beard) from a burning house in the Afghan city of Ghazni in 1842. (R.E. Cholmeley, *John Nicholson, c.* 1909)

**Ali Musjid on the Khyber Pass.** This photograph shows the place in the defile below the small fort of Ali Musjid where Nicholson's 18-year-old brother Alexander was killed in an ambush on the night of 3 November 1842 during the British retreat from Afghanistan. John Nicholson found his younger brother's body next morning and buried him nearby. Though this photograph by W.D. Holmes of Peshawar was taken a generation later, little has changed save for the improved path winding its way along the Khyber Pass. (Donal McCracken)

**The citadel of Attock.** The great fort of Attock, with the adjoining bridge of boats across the Indus, was a key fortress in the Anglo-Sikh Wars as well as in the 1857 Great Rebellion. Nicholson was obsessed by this fort's strategic importance and spent much time here during the second Anglo-Sikh war. (Engraving c. 1885)

## THE FORT OF RHOTAS, IN THE PUNJAUB.

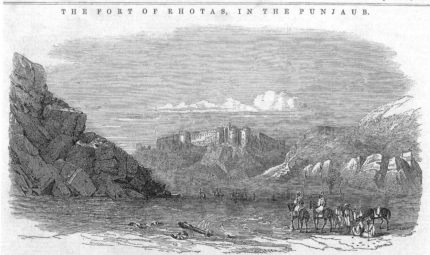

PART OF THE FORT OF RHOTAS—FROM A SKETCH BY A CORRESPONDENT.

**The great fort at Rohtas.** Just before the conclusion of the second Anglo-Sikh war, in early March 1849, Nicholson and Harry Lumsden occupied the great hill fortress of Rohtas unopposed with a small force. (*Illustrated London News*, 21 April 1849)

**The worldly and jovial Sir Harry Lumsden (1821–96).** The Lumsden brothers (William, Peter and Harry) all knew Nicholson but the most extrovert of them, Major Harry Lumsden (later Lieutenant General Sir Harry Lumsden of the Corps of Guides) was closest to him, both having campaigned together in the second Anglo-Sikh war. During the Mutiny, Peter Lumsden would be killed in battle while serving under Nicholson. (*Carte de visite*, Donal McCracken)

'**They seated themselves and fixed their eyes upon the object of their adoration**'. The cult of the Nikolseinee developed in the 1840s long before the 1857 Great Rebellion or even before Nicholson became a legend on the frontier. Occasionally 'Nikolsein' would allow members of the sect into his tent on the condition that they sat and did not speak. On one occasion, he had some members flogged for annoying him. At another point, Nicholson tried to hand over the cult to his friend Major James Abbott, who sensibly declined the honour. (R.E. Cholmeley, *John Nicholson*, c. 1909, drawing by H.L. Shindler)

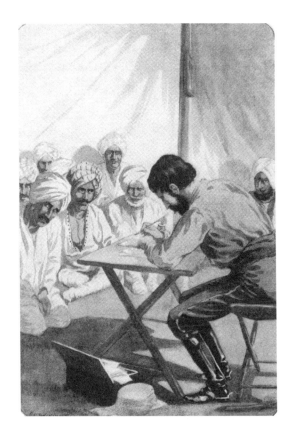

'**Fort of Duleepgurh in Bunnoo**'. This was the great fort, mostly made of dried mud, which Major Edwardes built when stationed at Camp Duleepgurh, Bannu. Between 1852 and 1856 Nicholson was in charge here. This drawing by the equally eccentric Major Reynell Taylor in 1850 well illustrated both the majesty of the Afghan mountains and the fort's importance as a strategic stronghold guarding the passes to the west. Along the mountain frontier it was one of fifteen forts servicing another fifty military outposts. Camp Duleepgurh held 1,200 troops and the European cantonment was situated inside its walls, an indication of unrest in the region. In 1874, it was renamed Fort Edwardes. (Edwardes, *A Year on the Punjab Frontier*, 1851)

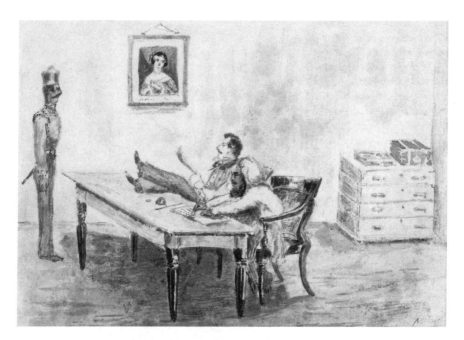

**'The subaltern and his moonshee'.** This humorous pen-and-ink of an East Indian Army subaltern was drawn by Henry Macdonald of Sandside in Caithness in Scotland. For attitude and period (1850s) it might as well be a sketch of Nicholson, who employed a munshi to teach him various Indian languages. Nicholson could converse in Hindi, Urdu and several of the hill country dialects. (Donal McCracken)

**Chiefs of the Derajat.** One of Nicholson's greatest achievements was to win the respect of the local Bannu region leaders when he was deputy commissioner of the Punjab–Afghan frontier's Dera Ismail Khan district. He achieved this through a combination of rapid military response to trouble, rough justice and a quiet determination, a combination that earned Nicholson a reputation for toughness and reliability unrivalled on the frontier. (Edwardes, *A Year on the Punjab Frontier*, 1851)

**Panoramic view of Peshawar with the Khyber Pass beyond.** Nicholson knew and was well-known in the frontier garrison town of Peshawar with its narrow streets and high buildings. Here he was deputy commissioner when the 1857 Great Rebellion broke out and here his close friend Herbert Edwardes was commissioner and the older General Sydney Cotton army commander. Not far distant was Major Neville Chamberlain and his Punjab Irregular Frontier Force. And from these surrounding hills were to be drawn the irregular troops led firstly by Chamberlain and then by Nicholson in the Moveable Column. (*Harper's Weekly*, 21 December 1878)

**The Edwardes Gate, Peshawar.** The gate was originally called Kabuli Darwaza and was one of the entrances to the old city of Peshawar. It was renamed after John Nicholson's close friend and superior officer Herbert Edwardes, for whom Bannu was named Edwardesabad for a period. (*The Graphic*, 6 October 1883)

**Herbert Edwardes (1819–68).** Major General Sir Herbert Edwardes was one of the great eccentric geniuses found on the British Indian frontier. An excellent and successful soldier and an able administrator, he became a very close friend of Nicholson's. There is no evidence of a homosexual relationship between them, but there is little doubt that a deep affection existed between the two very different men. Edwardes published a book entitled *A Year on the Punjab Frontier*, (1851). This *carte de visite* belonged to General Sir Peter Lumsden. (Donal McCracken)

**Emma Edwardes.** Emma Sidney married Herbert Edwardes when he and Nicholson were home on furlough in 1851. She came to India with her husband but her health deteriorated and fortuitously she returned to Britain before the outbreak of the Mutiny. She acted somewhat as a surrogate mother to the insecure Nicholson, but also managed to gain the approval of the matriarchal Clara Nicholson. After Herbert Edwardes' death in 1868, Emma devoted much energy to compiling a two-volume collection of letters and documents relating to her husband. This *carte de visite* belonged to General Sir Peter Lumsden. (Donal McCracken)

**Field Marshal Sir Neville Chamberlain (1820–1902).** Nicholson and Chamberlain met during the Afghan campaign in the early 1840s and their friendship was at times turbulent. Chamberlain, like Edwardes, could handle the military and civil hierarchy better than Nicholson, as his career path illustrated. Though severely wounded during the siege of Delhi, Chamberlain was an outstanding second in command, dealing with the nervous and cautious commander, General Wilson. It was Chamberlain who was left with the onerous task of managing Nicholson's affairs after his death and comforting Nicholson's family and inner circle of friends. (Forrest, *Life of Field-Marshal Sir Neville Chamberlain*, 1909)

**'Blowing from the guns'.** This dramatic representation of the distasteful yet traditional execution of insurgent troops from cannon at Peshawar shocked Victorian Britain perhaps more than any other reports of atrocities on the British side. (*Illustrated London News*, 3 October 1857)

**'Disarming the native regiments'.** One of Nicholson's major contributions to the British retention of military control of the Punjab was the unswerving assurance and authority he exhibited when disarming regiments that he suspected were on the brink of mutiny. In no instance when Nicholson undertook this difficult assertion of power was there any violence. (Trotter, *The Life of John Nicholson*, drawing by W.S. Cumming)

**'Mutiny in India: Peshawur land transport train'.** During the 1857 Great Rebellion, while commanding the Moveable Column, Nicholson balanced the danger of moving troops during the Indian summer against the necessity of rapid force deployment. To address both issues, at times he commandeered supply wagons and used them to transport some of his infantry force. (*Illustrated London News*, 3 October 1857)

**Signature of John Nicholson.** The distinctive signature of John Nicholson was cut from a letter and kept as a souvenir in a scrapbook by his friend General Sir Peter Lumsden (1829–1918). (Donal McCracken)

**'Attack on the Sealkote mutineers by General Nicholson's irregular cavalry'.** Engraving of the battle of Timmu Ghat, one of two set-piece battles that Nicholson fought and won.

**'He saw Nicholson's great form riding steadily on as if nothing was the matter'.** One of Nicholson's legendary yet confirmed acts was his epic 1857 march in pursuit of an insurgent army that left Delhi in an attempt to disrupt British lines and prevent reinforcements arriving. Cutting across country to intercept the enemy, Nicholson successfully led his force through a swamp and caught up with the enemy at Najafgarh, where he won a significant victory. (R.E. Cholmeley, *John Nicholson*, c. 1909, drawing by H.L. Shindler)

**The city of Delhi as seen from a Bengal Artillery position.** This extraordinary panoramic sketch of Delhi, looking from siege battery number 1, shows clearly the daunting task that the British faced in capturing this large and well-fortified city. The great Jama Musjid and the walled palace are clearly seen. The wooded area to the left gives cover for the British troops' assault. (*Illustrated London News*, 31 October 1857)

**'Roberts' last sight of Nicholson'.** This poignant scene depicts Lieutenant Fred Roberts, later Field Marshal Lord Roberts, finding his former superior officer and mentor, John Nicholson, just outside the walls of Delhi after the stretcher-bearers had deserted him to join in the looting of Delhi. Roberts ensured that Nicholson reached the field hospital at Ludlow Castle. (Trotter, *The Life of John Nicholson*, drawing probably by W.S. Cumming)

**The Delhi/Dungannon Nicholson statue.** This superb watercolour is reproduced in Major A.C. Lovett's *The Armies of India* (1911). It shows the representatives of thirteen regiments, including the Gurkhas, which took part in the September 1857 capture of Delhi standing under the statue of Brigadier General John Nicholson in Nicholson Park, Delhi. The statue, which now stands in the grounds of Dungannon Royal School, was the work of the celebrated sculptor Sir Thomas Brock R.A. (Lovett, *The Armies of India*, 1911)

**Lisburn statue, erected 1921.** On the centenary of Nicholson's death on 11 December 1922, this remembrance ceremony was held in Lisburn, County Antrim. The dramatic statue of Nicholson by F.W. Pomeroy had been unveiled the previous January by General Wilson. Significantly, the guard of honour was constituted by the A Specials, a paramilitary wing of the recently created Royal Ulster Constabulary. (Irish Linen Centre and Linen Museum, Lisburn)

**The Nicholson frieze in Lisburn Cathedral.** This dramatic frieze by J.H. Foley RA commemorating John Nicholson was erected in Lisburn cathedral in 1862. Clara Nicholson vetoed a proposal that Nicholson should be depicted in the frieze on the fundamentalist grounds that this would be idolatrous, though most observers will suppose the wounded figure cheering on the advancing troops to be him. The church in the background is St James', Delhi. The inscribed tablet below this bas-relief also honours Nicholson, the fourteen lines running to a lengthy 274 words. The opening sentence is, however, elegantly succinct: 'The grave of Brigadier-General John Nicholson, C.B., is beneath the fortress which he died to take'. (*Illustrated London News*, 10 May 1862)

**When Nicholson Kept the Border.**
A generation after Nicholson died,
he became a *Boys' Own*-type hero.
From then until the 1940s, Nicholson
and his legendary exploits appeared
in a number of children's books.
Possibly the best is the fictitious and
action-packed, *When Nicholson Kept
the Border: A Tale of the Mutiny Days*
(*c.* 1925), by J. Claverdon Wood,
illustrated by Stanley L. Wood.

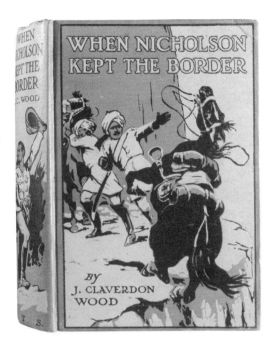

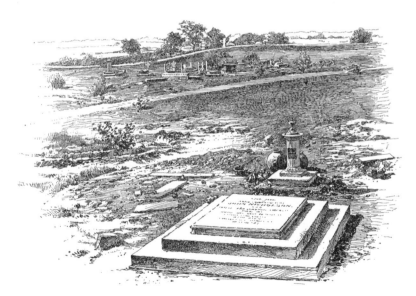

**Nicholson's grave, Delhi.** In 1880, General John Younghusband commented, 'Some of his
[Nicholson's] old soldiers have been known to visit the cemetery at Delhi, and place a *chiragh*
(oil lamp) at the head of his tomb. For some years after Nicholson's death the guards of the Sikh
Regt stationed at Delhi, when going past the cemetery near the Cashmere gate, always saluted
by carrying arms when passing his grave; and to within the last few years many of his men came
long distances to visit the spot and make their Salaams to it' (BL, Eur F 197/37). (Wilberforce, *An
Unrecorded Chapter of the Indian Mutiny*, 1894)

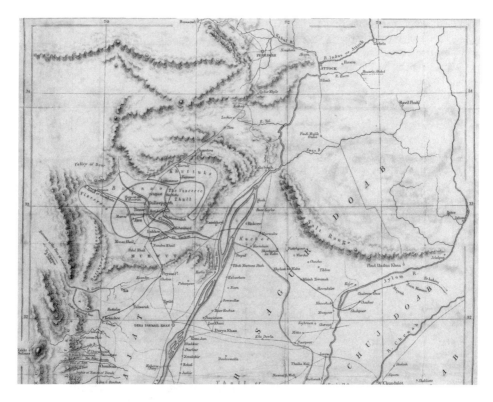

**Map of the Bannu region (1850).** Detail from an 1850 map by the famous cartographer John Arrowsmith of the Punjab and the Multan region showing Afghan passes to the west, the tribal areas in Bannu and that region's relationship to Kohat, Peshawar and Attock to the north. (Edwardes, *A Year on the Punjab Border*, 1851)

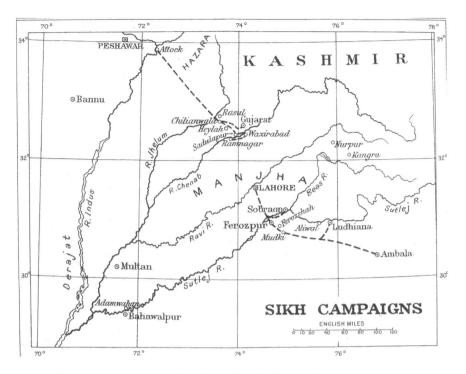

**Anglo-Sikh campaigns (1840s).** (Taylor, *General Sir Alex Taylor*, 1913)

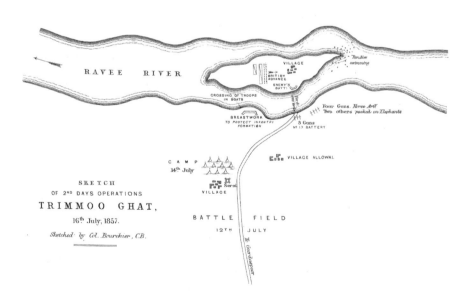

**Map of battle of Timmu Ghat, 16 July 1857.** (Bourchier, *Eight Months' Campaign*, 1858)

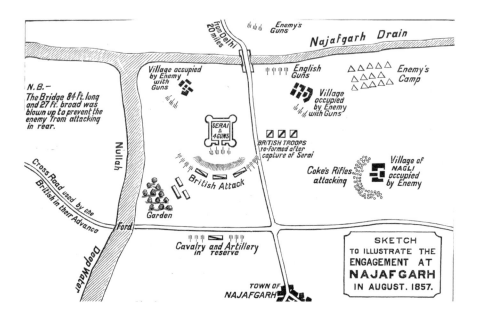

**Sketch map of the battle of Najafgarh, August 1857.** Nicholson led a force against an insurgent army which had left Delhi attempting to intercept the British relief column and cut the British communications from the rear. The ensuing battle was a complete victory for Nicholson. (Roberts, *Forty-one Years in India*, 1897)

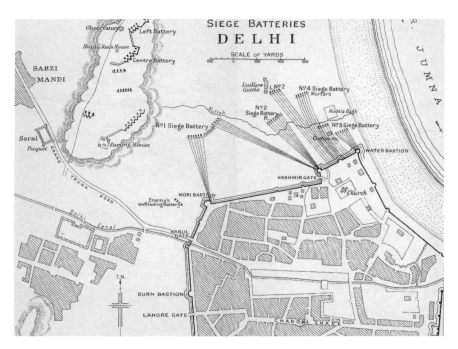

**The line of fire at Delhi, September 1857.** Sketch map by Alex Taylor showing the British siege batteries at Delhi and the area which was assaulted by the force led by his friend John Nicholson. (Taylor, *General Sir Alex Taylor*, 1913)

*Above and overleaf:* **John Nicholson in civilian dress.** These recently discovered calotype photographs are most probably of Nicholson and in the possession of a descendant. He wears the same clothing in both the standing and the seated poses, which were taken in the same studio. The head and eyes are distinctive and there is the famous thick dark beard and wings of hair above the ears. The shoulders are broad and although the body is leaner than might be expected, this would result from a very active life in the saddle and also recurring illness. The face appears to be younger, the eyes less sunken and the hairline less receded than in the 1851 daguerreotype taken in London so these photographs were probably taken in India, dating from the late 1840s. (Roger and Pam Hamilton)

# On the Frontier: The Making of a God

Nicholson seems to have proceeded slowly back upcountry from Calcutta to the Punjab frontier, taking advantage of the time before his furlough expired to catch up with old friends during this journey. At Benares, no doubt he visited Uncle Richardson. At Jalandhar, he met up briefly with Herbert and Emma Edwardes, probably reliving once again in chat and gossip their recent adventures in England. Edwardes was now a deputy commissioner just southeast of Amritsar.

At Lahore, in a bungalow near the city, Nicholson stayed with his old friend Neville Chamberlain, then military secretary to the governor-general. Nicholson proudly showed Chamberlain the needle-gun he had purchased in Berlin, and 'descanted lovingly upon its peculiar merits, and spoke strongly of the imperative need for its introduction into the British army'. He also, in Nicholson fashion, then proceeded to rant on about something of which he knew little – the Bourbon monarchy in the Kingdom of the Two Sicilies.[1]

It was generally agreed among his associates that the leave had helped Nicholson, even if he had not returned with a wife. This certainly was the view of Henry Lawrence and of Sir James Hogg, who wrote to the latter in February 1852: 'I agree with you in thinking that Nicholson has greatly improved by his trip to Europe. Having gone out to India again his views though always noble and generous were a little contrasted by his temper was somewhat insubordinate. Those imperfections were much abated if not entirely removed by his home visit.'[2]

Nicholson had arrived in India as a precocious, insecure boy. A tough decade later he had learnt many lessons, but army and colonial life had left him rough around the edges. His time in Europe, not just home in Ireland and in London, let him see the metropolitan world for the first time as an adult. The romantic ideal of his youth was dispelled and he could now see both India and home in a more balanced and realistic light.

Nicholson's home background is the key to the aspect of his life that most baffles modern detractors: the admittedly strange phenomenon of his popularity not only among those Indians with whom he was closely associated but also among Punjabis who were divided from him by every social, cultural and religious gulf imaginable. Behind the veneer of those constructs, though, there was in reality not a great deal of difference in attitude between his childhood among puritan Ulster folk and life for the hill-dwelling Indians. Admittedly, there was also a push factor that facilitated Nicholson's appeal across the colonial racial divide. Nicholson was not very popular among many fellow European officers, especially those in the Queen's army, whose posing and truculence he looked upon with unconcealed contempt. In his memoir, John Bayley of the 52nd Regiment, denounced Nicholson for his rough manners and his negative attitude to European troops and officers.[3] Bayley was not alone, which was probably one of the primary reasons why after Nicholson's death it took a generation for him to emerge as a 'national hero'. The other obvious contributing factor was rising imperial jingoism.

Leaving aside the more wobbly modern claims against Nicholson, there is sufficient evidence that he was a hard taskmaster in his civil role and ferocious in battle. In fact, these were two qualities that India knew well enough, then and historically, and did not find particularly outrageous.

## THE NIKOLSEINEE

Among the Indian population with whom Nicholson lived, respect and veneration blended *in extremis* into cult adoration. At various times, Nicholson was referred to as the Nikkul Seyn, Nikalsain, Nickalsain, Nikalsayn, or, as Nicholson himself wrote, Nikolsein. It is, however, important to distinguish the Nikolseinee from the band of Indian irregular cavalry who attached themselves to Nicholson, considering that they owed allegiance only to him. According to Herbert Edwardes, the sect arose as early as 1848. Isabel Giberne Sieveking gives the date as 1849, when 'a certain Gosain, or Hindu devotee, discovered in the popular hero a new Avatar, or incarnation of the Brahmanic godhead'.[4] This was during the second Anglo-Sikh war when Nicholson was let loose in the region between Jhelum and Attock. The numbers of Nikolseinee were never great. They were said to have a 'monastery' in the valley of Hasan Abdal.

This was an area Nicholson knew well. Indeed, according to James Abbott, it was to this valley that Nicholson sometimes retreated for solitude. Abbott was probably correct that a desire for solitude rather than spirituality was what attracted the young officer. Fishing, too, perhaps as the mountain streams and rivers contained large fish. It is said that Nicholson, with an element of romantic nostalgia, erected his tent on a wooden platform over a stream that he named the Bendemeer. This name Nicholson took from the epic poem *Lalla Rookh*, which had been written by the famous Irish poet and balladeer, Thomas Moore some thirty-two years earlier:

> There's a bower of roses by Bendemeer's stream,
>     And the nightingale sings round it all the day long;
> In the time of my childhood 'twas like a sweet dream,
>     To sit in the roses and hear the bird's song.
> That bower and its music I never forget,
>     But of when alone, in the bloom of the year,
> I think – is the nightingale singing there yet?
>     Are the roses still bright by the calm Bendemeer?
> No, the roses soon wither'd that hung o'er the wave,
>     But the blossoms were gathered, while freshly they shone
> And a dew was distill'd from their flowers, that gave
>     All the fragrance of summer, when summer was gone.
> Thus memory draws from delight, ere it dies,
>     An essence that breathes of it many a year;
> Thus bright to my soul, as 'twas then to my eyes,
>     Is that bower on the banks of the calm Bendemeer!

New lyrics were added to Moore's tune at the turn of the nineteenth century by Percy French with the result that it is now better known as 'The Mountains of Mourne'. This remains appropriate to Nicholson, given his link with the Bellinghams of County Louth, from where, looking north, the mountains of Mourne do sweep down to the sea.[5]

But renaming his pavilion Bendemeer was more than a deliberate choice for John Nicholson and romantic harking back to the songs of his youth. Moore's ballad tells of the daughter of the Emperor Aurungzebe in Delhi sending his daughter Lalla Rookh in a great cavalcade to Kashmir, where she was meant to marry the son of Abdalla, who had abdicated his throne as king of Lesser Bucharia in Persia in favour of that son. But a young Kashmiri poet called Feramorz accompanying the procession wins the heart of Lalla Rookh, much to the discomfort of her protector, Fadladeen. However, all is eventually well. At journey's end, in keeping with the theme of romantic quest, Feramorz is revealed as the prince Lalla Rookh had come to marry.

## NICHOLSON'S FAITH

Two issues are raised by the Nicholson cult, the first being Nicholson's own spiritual beliefs. Herbert Edwardes once said that Nicholson was not a Christian. Such things mattered greatly to Edwardes, who still remembered the stark question Letitia Lawrence had asked him, whether he 'thought her brother Henry was *merely* a Philanthropist or really a Christian'? That is perhaps harder to answer for Nicholson than for Sir Henry. Was Nicholson a timeless soldier or a Christian? There can be little doubt that once free from the oppressive puritanism of his mother, Nicholson became less religiously orientated. In his letters, remarks relating to Christianity are not particularly frequent and when mentioned are of a practical rather than a devotional nature. For example, when a hare-brained scheme was launched to establish a Christian mission in Islamic Peshawar, Nicholson duly did what he considered to be the correct thing and donated 500 rupees, equivocating as he did so as to whether or not his name should be published among the subscribers. But Nicholson was all too clear about the reality of the situation. On 19 February 1854 he wrote, 'I wish your mission at Peshawur every success, but you require skilful and practical men as well as good men.'

In another letter, Nicholson comes out with a straight attack on the type of missionaries he had seen in India: 'As far as my experience of missionaries goes they are generally selected with infinitely less care than [military] Recruits – The most uncouth brute I ever saw in my life I think was a missionary on his way to Jerusalem, of all places in the world.'

The ranting Christianity to be found in Edwardes' letters – 'When the Mahomadan and Hindoos have done their worse and the Christian will triumph unmistakeably' – is absent from Nicholson's letters. This does not mean the two men were not very close and remained so until Nicholson's death, there being no record of a discord between the two – a rare thing for Nicholson. One day in 1853, in Bannu, a local tribal leader, attempted to undermine Edwardes's name and flatter Nicholson. 'I turned the speaker out', Nicholson wrote, 'very unceremoniously to his great surprise and disgust.' And as early as September that year he was pressing to be posted alongside

Edwardes, should Sir Herbert gain the commissionership at Peshawar. This the largest division in India, encompassing not only Peshawar itself but also the fortress towns of Attock, Rawalpindi, and Jhelum. Also included was the hill station at Murree. The division's garrison numbered about 6,000 Indian and European troops. Next to Meerut, Peshawar had the largest artillery force in India, most of whom were Irish.[6]

Nicholson did not lose his Christian faith but he certainly became more pragmatic as the years rolled by on the North-West Frontier, far away from the puritan Lagan valley. His periodic attacks on the Afghanis – 'I hope you will never forget that their *name is faithfulness*, even among themselves; what then can strangers expect?' – were the product of circumstance. But, the fact remains that the peoples of the frontier mountain lands were not so different in their approach to life from Nicholson himself and it is not really surprising that he grew increasingly close to them as the 1850s progressed.

## EXPERIENCING THE CULT

The second issue raised by the Nikkul Seynee cult is Nicholson's own reaction to it. This was contradictory. Much has been made of the order he gave to have several members of the sect flogged 'on several occasions'. The innuendo here has been that this was partly a reflection of brutality and partly sexual deviancy. In fact, it more likely reflects simply Nicholson's notorious and flaring bad temper. Nicholson did not flog these unfortunates himself, nor did he call for flogging as a matter of course. Indeed, it may well be that this was a single incident. That he 'sometimes imprisoned' a few sect members probably also reflects on his ill temper and should be viewed as a 'period in the cooler' rather than any long-term imprisonment. And looking more broadly, Nicholson also was not slow to flog others who had nothing to do with the sect.

Yet there are snippets that suggest that Nicholson was not totally hostile to these worshippers. Indeed, in his suggestion that they shift their devotion to Nicholson's friend Johnny Becher there is what can only be described as *méchant* humour. From the little evidence we have on the matter, it appears that Nicholson came to terms with these camp followers, respecting the tradition from which they came and allowing parties of them to enter his officer's tent and sit and watch him as he sat at his small wooden camp table doing his endless administrative work. As long as they were quiet, they were let be. So there developed a kind of symbiosis between the old and the new ways.

ngineer whom Nicholson had known since they were on
in the mid-1840s, recalled how some years later he also
ange cohort:

y small bungalow at Hassan Abdal half way between
̶a̶w̶a̶l̶p̶m̶d̶i̶ and Attock, some twenty helmeted men, very quaintly dressed,
filed in, one after another, and after a courteous salute, but without speaking
a word, squatted down in a row opposite me. I was much taken aback at this
strange apparition. I looked to them, and they at me, till at last one of them
gave utterance to their thoughts and objects. 'We are Nikkul Seyn's Fakirs,'
he said; 'you are a white Sahib, and we are come to pay our respects to you
as one of Nikkul Seyn's race.' I had never even heard of the existence of this
strange sect before. After a little conversation I dismissed them, and they
passed on Southward, towards Dera Ismail Khan, where the object of their
adoration was then to be found.[7]

According to Gilberne Sieveking, after Nicholson's death several of the
members asked to be instructed in Christianity, saying that if they ever wished
to see him again, they must worship Nicholson's god. According to Sir Donald
Macnabb, later commissioner of Peshawar, writing to Sir James Hogg in 1860,
one of the cult members on hearing of the death of Nicholson slit his own
throat and died. Sir John Kaye commented that the 'brother-hood of Fakeers
in Hazarch abandoned all forms of Asiatic monarchism, and commenced the
worship of "Nikkul Seyn", which they still continue!' That was in 1868, a
decade after Nicholson's death. But Kaye contradicts himself in a footnote
where he quotes Edwardes asserting that the last of the 'original disciples dug
his own grave, and was found dead, at Hurripoor, in the district of Hazareh,
not long after John Nicholson fell at Delhi. Whether any successors have
arisen is not known.' Another version has survived in a letter Johnny Becher
('one of the gentlest, best and most charming of Lawrence's Young Men'[8]), the
deputy commissioner of Hazara between 1853 and 1859 and successor there
to the legendary Abbott,[9] wrote to Edwardes in December 1858:

Did I ever tell you that the Nicholsenee fakir who committed suicide was
buried in [Sirdar] Hurree Sing's garden [in Gujranwala] in the grave yard,
with Carne and Tapp[10] – he dug his own grave, and determined he wd be
buried there – is not this a curious end!.[11]

A passing comment by Sir John Ross in 1929 in the *National Review* that the cult still existed cannot be taken too seriously, though revivalist movements do happen.

## ATTEMPTED ASSASSINATION

Assassination attempts on frontier officials were not unusual and on 19 January 1856 one was made on Nicholson. Herbert Edwardes recounts in some detail various attempts to assassinate himself in Bannu just a few years before.[12]

What is interesting about the assault on Nicholson was not so much the attempt by a 'poor wretch' to cut down with a sword the now-famous Nicholson, but the picture of Nicholson it offers from the time. Firstly, the would-be assassin did not recognise Nicholson because of the Indian clothes he was wearing. Nicholson's group consisted of about eight men: himself, two other European officers, Sladen and Cadell, with four or five orderlies or *chupraisses* from Nicholson's much-valued police battalion:

> when a man with a sword rushed suddenly up, and called out for me. I had on a long fur pelisse of native make, which I fancy prevented his recognising me at first. This gave time for the only chuprassee who had a sword to get between us, to whom he called out contemptuously to stand aside, saying he had come to kill me, and did not want to hurt a common soldier. The relief sentry for the one in front of my house, happened to pass opportunately behind me at this time, I snatched his musket [with attached bayonet], and presenting it at the would be assassin told him I would fire if he did not put down his sword and surrender. He replied that either he or I must die, so I had no alternative, and shot him through the heart, the ball passing through a religious book, which he had tied on his chest.[13]

According to Nicholson, the man was 'religiously mad'. His named was Martwutee, and he was a Marwari speaker. Perhaps the most interesting aspect of the incident is that when the police orderly who had confronted the deranged attacker was asked which man was Nicholson he replied, 'All our names are Nikolsein here.' In other words, the name and the concept that went with it were everyday parlance by that time, especially among Nicholson's own men.

There is a famous postscript to this drama. Robert Montgomery spread the story that following this incident he had received a note from Nicholson that simply read, 'Sir, I have the honour to inform you that I have just shot a man who came to kill me.'

# RAWALPINDI

For a time in the immediate post-war period, Major Nicholson was posted to Rawalpindi, where he was deputy commissioner. By this time he was becoming so well acquainted with local people near and far that he was the source for obtaining various military curios for the new British rulers at Lahore. These included an Afghan firelock (40 rupees); a suit of chain armour (200 rupees); and an Afghan dagger (60 rupees).[14]

Scattered throughout Nicholson's letters are references to indigenous manufactured or artisan-made goods to which he had access and which he was giving to people or was obtaining on request. Three things strike one about this matter. First, that Nicholson with his extensive contacts and friendship among the hill tribes had access to difficult to obtain artefacts for others. Second, from his comments Nicholson clearly knew the difference between quality craft goods and shoddily made items. Third, that there was a great demand among the British, both male and female, for such products.

On 5 October 1849, six weeks after he had supplied Lahore with an ancient suit of Afghan chainmail, we find Nicholson writing to John Lawrence:

> I have not been able to get any good Affghan Knives nor any Swords worth sending. I am however despatching to you by coolie a jazail [long-barrelled muzzle-loading gun] and a couple of indifferent specimens of knives with a blunderbuss [short muzzle-loading flintlock] or two – also a petarrah containing four of Miss Chattar [Chuttar] Singh's dresses as the patterns and texture of all four are alike, perhaps the Board will allow me to keep one, for a lady.[15]

Nicholson's stubborn sense of justice and right was seen in the months following the war. He was determined to obtain rewards for those Indian leaders of his irregular forces who had fought alongside him during the recent Sikh campaign. And being Nicholson, he never let the matter drop. So four years later, in December 1853, we find him still pushing the claim of Sayad Hassan Uddin and the *sardar*, Abbas Khan. Six months after this, Nicholson was trying to get Lahore to agree to compensate the son of Ali Khan Gandapur, one of Britain's supporters in the previous Anglo-Sikh war. The son, Kaloo Khan, had himself fought alongside Herbert Edwardes and had been severely wounded.[16] This compensation was consequently agreed by John Lawrence.

On the other hand, on St Patrick's Day 1856, Nicholson was a veritable storm cloud of rage and indignation when Syed Mohsun Shah put in a claim for having supplied the British garrison at Ghazni during the Anglo-Afghan war fifteen years earlier: 'I consider his claim a fraudulent one, and should like to see him put on his [sic] trial in a criminal court, for making it.'[17]

Another injustice that annoyed Nicholson, and which clearly illustrates that he had next to no realpolitik in his make-up, was the case of Kardar Daulat Rai, who admittedly played a dangerous game of ingratiating himself both to the Sikhs and the British. For some time after peace had come, Nicholson was out for revenge on Daulat Rai for his role in his humiliating retreat from Pind Dadun Khan. Nicholson ensured that his former deputy, Lieutenant Henry Coxe, arrested Daulat Rai, who unsuccessfully tried to bribe Coxe with 10,000 rupees. Rai was sent as a prisoner to Lahore, then a melting pot of the Sikh elite and English baronets, where revenge on the wealthy was not the order of the day. So 'to the astonishment of the whole country', Rai returned home, unscathed and none the poorer. Nicholson saw this as 'an example to the people of the Punjab, of what a man may effect who has the means to bribe and knows how to use them'.[18] Not that Nicholson was beyond using bribery, or at least rewards. It is said that he kept a bag of rupees in his office and if an informer gave particularly valuable information to him, he would permit the informer to plunge his hand into the bag and keep as many rupees as he could extract.[19]

Many of the legendary, and sometimes probably apocryphal, stories about Nicholson date from this time on the frontier. As much as Nicholson's eccentricities, the stories often have varying versions and embellishments, testament to the hunger among the British on the frontier to manufacture their own entertainment from gossip and hyperbole. In the Rawalpindi district, one of the Nicholson stories told of the award of 100 rupees, doubled by Nicholson, which had failed to bring in a well-known local outlaw. Acquiring the name of the villain, Nicholson rode alone to his village. He confronted the man, who rushed at Nicholson only for him to cut him down. Thorburn recounts that 'When the body was brought in, Nicholson had the head cut off and placed in Cutcherry [the administration building] beside himself, and he contemptuously asked every malik who came to see him if he recognised to whom it had belonged.'[20]

# 'A PARADISE PEOPLED BY FIENDS': BANNU
## 1852–1854

Of the Afghanistan debacle a few years earlier, the erudite Scottish war correspondent Archibald Forbes had noted that the old and reliable General Nott 'had in full measure that chronic dislike which the Indian commander in the field nourishes to the political officer who is imposed on him by the authorities, and who controls his measures and trammels his actions'.[21] Such, however, could not be said of Nicholson. It is ironic that the great fighting hero of Victorian Britain should draw attention to himself when living as a good administrator as much as a daredevil soldier. But after the Anglo-Sikh wars Nicholson spent far more time as a political officer than as a regular army officer. Lieutenant Frederick Roberts, eventually the famous field marshal, remembered years later his father, General Sir Abraham Roberts, saying that 'the political department was *the* one to aspire to, and failing that the Quartermaster-Generals'.

On 3 February 1852, Nicholson arrived in the Dera Ismail Khan District, a long tract of land more than twice the size of County Antrim where his mother lived. The district stretched across about 155 miles between the Indus in the east and the great mountain chain in the west, beyond which was Afghanistan. The population was about 360,000, around the same as County Antrim, which included much of Belfast city. Fifty-three per cent of Dera Ismail Khan's inhabitants were male, with a total population density of around eighty-eight people to the square mile. This compared to the whole of the Punjab with its 10 million people and a population density of around 140 to the square mile. The religious divide in Dera Ismail Khan in the 1850s was approximately 89 per cent Sunni Muslim and 11 per cent Hindu. About 60 per cent of the population was engaged in agriculture for a living. No metalled roads existed.

Though only a section of Dera Ismail Khan, this whole area was sometimes referred to as Bannu, the site of Edwardes's great period as soldier–administrator. It had originally been proposed that Nicholson would accompany Edwardes to Bannu when he had been posted there in the 1840s, but circumstances had prevented that.[22] Then as now, this area was important both because it assisted north–south communications and also because slightly north-west of Dera Ismail Khan lay the Gomal River Pass, beyond which the great pass of Gwaleyrie connected into the heartland of Afghanistan. There were three great trading passes into Afghanistan on the British frontier, the Khyber, the Gomal and the Bolan, further south in Sindh. The Gomal was in Nicholson's domain.

Though less famous than the Khyber, it was described in the mid-1850s as 'scarcely inferior'.[23] However, the Khyber was regarded as more significant because of its proximity to the key town of Peshawar, the memory of the 1842 British army debacle and because it was via this route that the British supposed the grand Russian imperial army would one day come. In fact, an army was as likely to come via the southern pass as the northern, and certainly much trade between India and Afghanistan and beyond found its way via this southern route.

The hill tribes of this region were described in the early 1850s as 'noble savages of pure blood, pastoral habits, fierce disposition, and wild aspect'. Though some were technically British subjects, the reality was that they gave little in the way of allegiance to either the Afghan chiefs or the British.

## TAKING OVER BANNU

After Edwardes's much-heralded period as a deputy commissioner or chief district officer had come the 'gentle and noble' Major Reynell Taylor (1822–86).[24] In 1852, Taylor was going off to Britain on his own long leave, a fortuitous occurrence for Nicholson. Though the same age, the two men were very different. Taylor was the son of a celebrated cavalry officer who had fought at Waterloo. He had himself trained at Sandhurst, where the father was in charge, and had been commissioned into the 11th Bengal Cavalry. After his furlough, Taylor was to take over as commander of the guide corps. He was thin, a fervent evangelical and advocate of Christian missionary endeavour in India. He also had the reputation of being a good swordsman. Unlike Nicholson, he enjoyed putting pen to paper.

Before he left Bannu, Taylor was meant to supply Nicholson with a memo on the frontier. Nicholson complained that this was not done. The result was that Taylor sat down and wrote Nicholson a 45,000-word document about the Dera Ismail Khan district that, when published as a district memorandum, came to 104 pages of printed text. This document is an invaluable commentary on the people of this borderland region and predates by twenty-four years the 480-page book *Bannú: Or our Afghan Frontier* by Septimus Thorburn of the Indian civil service.[25]

It is very doubtful if Nicholson ever bothered reading Taylor's memorandum to him. The home truths, advice and commentary of the at times apparently baffling inconsistencies and actions of the 'Wuzeeres' (Wazirs) and 'Bunnoochees' (Bannuchi) would, as they said back in his Lagan valley

ittered few parsnips' with Nicholson. Not surprisingly, when
d over' took place, the meeting was not a success, with Taylor
1 matters and Nicholson at his haughty worst asserting what
..as going to do. Later Nicholson would complain to Henry Lawrence, 'He
promised me a Memo on the frontier too, but went off without supplying it.'[26]
That said, later Taylor and Nicholson seem to have got on together, or at least
as well as Nicholson got on with anyone outside a small circle of friends.

Taylor had been in Bannu from 1850 to 1852, having replaced the even more
eccentric Herbert Edwardes. Edwardes had been the military commander in the
field who held no civil title in the area. It has, however, to be said that Edwardes
had done a remarkable job. It is ironic that in fact it had been Edwardes and
not Nicholson who had 'reduced the <u>people</u> (the most ignorant, depraved, and
bloodthirsty in the Punjab) to such a state of good order and respect for the
laws, that in the last year of his charge not only was there no murder, burglary,
or highway robbery, but not an <u>attempt</u> at any of these crimes'.

Today the Taliban are not without influence in this region of modern
Pakistan. One hundred and sixty years ago the district had a not dissimilar
reputation among westerners, and this had filtered through as far away
as Lisburn. In May 1849, after the Anglo-Sikh War, Henry Lawrence had
transferred Charles Nicholson, first as adjutant and later as lieutenant and
second-in-command, to the 2nd Punjab Cavalry. He was subsequently moved
to Bannu and later to Dera Ghaze Khan, far south and to the west of Multan.
In a sudden fit of panic, Clara had written to Charles some time in late 1851
recommending that he relinquish his appointment as a staff officer at Bannu
and re-join his regiment, one presumes because of the area's reputation for
being unsafe. Quite bravely and indeed boldly, Charles had replied that he was
in fact as safe in Bannu as he would be in Jullundur 'or even Lisburn', which
given the sectarian thuggery in Lisburn was probably true. He then added the
all-important detail that such a move would entail his losing half his current
pay and being away from his brother John's company, which he evidently
enjoyed very much. Charles appears to have come to Bannu about October
1851. On 3 February 1852 his brother turned up, as deputy commissioner,
the civil and judicial administrator of the vast region.[27] It is possibly then that
John gave Charles the things he had bought for him in Europe – a sword and
belt, and the new improved model of a Colt revolver. He would have bought
a saddle also for Charles, but because a money draft from Charles had not
materialised Nicholson did not have sufficient funds for that purchase.

Nicholson gave himself three weeks to settle into Bannu. Before meeting
Henry Lawrence, who was due to arrive on 24 February on one of his

periodic tours, Nicholson set out to inspect his new domain. As the deputy commissioner, Nicholson's was primarily a civilian assignment. His assistant was Lieutenant Frederick Richard Pollock of the 49th Native infantry. Charles at least thought Pollock was very good. Not surprisingly, though, at first Pollock retained a lingering loyalty to Taylor, who had actually recommended Pollock to John Lawrence as his own replacement to run the district.[28]

However, Charles did not have so high an opinion of John's close friend, Herbert Edwardes. With the jaundiced eye of a brother, he wrote this to Clara. She in motherly fashion passed on the gossip to John, so causing Charles some embarrassment. Replying to the old lady, Charles was fairly restrained, 'By the bye, I was very vexed at hearing that he [John] had seen my criticism of Edwardes, I wrote and told him that they were never meant for his eye or knowledge.'[29] But John liked having Charles around – among other reasons because there was less pressure on him to write home.

## LIFE AT THE GREAT FORT

Camp Duleepgurh, the fort at Bannu, which Edwardes had constructed, was a very large affair, holding 1,200 men and eight cannon. It contained an inner citadel with a 25ft-deep ditch and 20ft-high wall, including the magazine and a well. Unlike most British bases, the cantonment was not separate but surrounded the citadel and was itself also defended by a 10ft-high wall and 30ft-deep ditch. The bricks for the drains and water courses were dug up from the nearby ruined ancient settlement of Akra. It was the biggest fort on the frontier between Peshawar and Multan. As Edwardes drily remarked, 'The military reader will judge from the annexed plan whether he would like to have the job of taking it.' By the mid-1850s, Britain had a line of fifteen forts along this frontier servicing fifty outposts. In 1874, the Bannu fort was renamed Fort Edwardes.

Military matters in Bannu, at least in theory, were run by four cavalry, two infantry and two artillery officers. It is noteworthy how quiet the region was after a year of Nicholson's dispensation possibly because construction begun on a conventional cantonment outside the fortress. This was greatly welcomed, not least because it gave many local people work.

Charles Nicholson also claimed that he had lived under canvas since 1848 and was greatly looking forward to a house. In March 1852, Charles wrote, 'I have all lots of trees and cactus for irrigation as the East is well adapted for Gardening, so if they will but leave us quiet for 2 or 3 years we shall have a beautiful Cantonment.'

Needless to say, there is no historical record of his brother, the deputy commissioner, having the slightest interest in gardening. He did, however, read and probably widely. As his brother said, 'Remote as Bannoo is we take *The Times* and other papers and periodicals in the "Book Club" so we are not badly off for literature.'[30] This point was also made by Nicholson to both his mother and sister Lily to try to stop them sending London newspapers. Rather untypically, he adjoins this reprimand with a sweetener,: 'I have got three pieces of grey squirrels fur for cloaks for my mother, you [Lily] and Mary. There will not perhaps be enough for the sleeves but it is not customary to put fur in the sleeves in this country as it does not wear well in them – cover the cloaks with cloth and you may rely on their bidding defiance to rheumatism.' Nicholson seems to have been more relaxed when dealing with his younger sister than with his elder sister Mary. Like John, Lily was tall and her face also resembled his, though she had grey eyes and his were dark (said by Reginald Wilberforce to be dark grey with black pupils that 'would dilate like a tiger's' when excited). In a later letter than the one quoted above to Lily, John adds a rare piece of humour in a postscript: 'How did mother contrive to get 26 people into her little room? I am sure they must have felt anything but obliged to her *crushing* hospitality with a vengeance!'[31]

On 14 May 1852 Charles wrote from Bannu to his mother in Lisburn, 'John is still in the district making settlements and performing generally the very disagreeable duties that pertain to his appointment.'[32] This included sitting days on end listening to judicial cases, hearing witnesses and making judgements. Charles was grateful that he did not have such duties, telling Clara Nicholson of the difficult of 'extracting truth from witnesses with whom lying is quite as much a habit as truth telling is with a respectable Englishman'.

But poor Charles had his own worries. A brother officer had recently died, his life insurance having expired ten days before the officer, leaving Charles, who had stood surety for him, landed with a demand from the bank of 3,000 rupees. But it did not prevent Charles remitting 1,000 rupees home to his mother. Money worries aside, Charles appears to have had a rather pleasant existence at this time. His lack of activity was reflected in the fact that at this time in Bannu he had no horse and only an old gun given to him by John a few years earlier.

## HOLDING THE LINE

It was Charles Nicholson's opinion that the British front line in the Bannu region was not satisfactory. At any time a hostile force could pour out of the mountains at any point. But entering the mountains was also filled with risks. He was correct on all counts. In 1856 Richard Temple, secretary to Sir John Lawrence, stated the official view of raiding from tribes living in the frontier mountains, which would remain the British line well into the twentieth century:

> It became evident that their incursions were prompted, partly by hostility, partly by lust of plunder, and partly by the hope of concessions, and could only be checked by punitive force.[33]

In 2013 a Reuters report still commented, 'Pakistan's semi-autonomous Pashtun lands along the Afghan border, known as the Federally Administered Tribal Areas (FATA), have never been brought under the full control of any government.' Similarly, 160 years earlier, there were eleven major military actions on the frontier for which medals were issued between November 1849 and March 1857 alone.

The number of armed fighters whom these hill tribes could put in the field varied. The Wazirs, for example, could assemble an estimated force of as many as 20,000. Richard Temple estimated that in total there were some 135,000 fighting men immediately across the British frontier, with a further 80,000 in tribes within British jurisdiction.[34] These tribes were, of course, far from a coherent group. Internecine conflicts were numerous and frequent. But little did Temple realise that this reservoir of nearly 250,000 men would prove very useful to the British before many summers had passed. It should be noted that the British at this time in the mid-1850s had a mere 23,000 troops in the five frontier districts of Hazara (1,884); Peshawar (13,292); Kohat (3,626); Nicholson's region of Dera Ismail Khan (3,204); and Dera Ghaze Khan (1,615). The overall ratio of regular troops to irregulars was 46 per cent to 54 per cent, but that is a misleading statistic as 10,754 (99 per cent) of the 10,821 regular troops were stationed at Peshawar. None were stationed in Hazara, Dera Ismail Khan or Dera Ghaze Khan.[35]

The frequency of Nicholson's counter-raids annoyed some in authority, not least the frontier police under Hodgson, who saw this as his domain. On one occasion the governor-general himself remarked, 'I know that Nicholson is a first-rate guerrilla leader, but we don't want a guerrilla policy.'[36] Such raiding expeditions averaged about 2,500 troops on each occasion. In the eleven raiding expeditions, seventy-seven British army troops were killed, and 395 wounded, giving a total casualty figure of 436 men or an average of forty casualties per expedition. Of those casualties, only one European officer was killed (at Kohat Pass in February 1850) and seven wounded. So while the trans-Indus was an intriguing place to be and exotic to European eyes, it was not actually as dangerous a posting for British officers as its reputation suggested.[37]

On arrival in the district in 1852, Nicholson had found himself inheriting a long-standing raiding problem with the Umarzai, assisted by the Muhsood Wazirs. Nicholson was blunt on the matter to Lieutenant Pollock, saying 'we do not defend passively we hit back, the only way to control the Wazirs is by demonstrating that they have no safe refuge in their own hill country'.[38]

The account of the matter by the Indian government's Foreign Department was to the point:

> an expedition was undertaken against them [Umarzai] with a force of 1,500 men. The affair was planned by Major Nicholson, and was successfully executed. The Ommerzyes were surprised in the fastness near the well-known Hill of Kapi Kôt; three of their principal villages and one encampment were destroyed. Thoroughly humbled they sued for peace and re-admission to their lands in the valley. An interval was allowed to elapse, in order that their penitence might be tested. Their conduct being quite satisfactory, they were re-admitted during 1853, and are now as good cultivators as any section of the Wuzeeree Tribe.[39]

## ACTION IN THE HILLS

In addition to these rather set-piece flag-waving incursions, there were also numerous follow-ups by British forces and their allies stationed on the frontier. Nicholson had hardly settled into his new posting and inspected his district than he was champing at the bit to lead counter-raiding parties into the hills. One major problem was that there were so many gaps in the hills from which raiders might emerge. In the Kasrani Hills alone, Nicholson said, there were twenty-one passes or *durrah*. Then there were also the narrow openings in the ranges, the *choor*.

One problem Nicholson seemed to have sorted out, at least for a while in one location, was the Waziri Pathan bandits using the deep irrigation channels to access a settlement undetected at night. He placed some of his men into these with muskets loaded with buckshot. The resulting catch included a well-known Wazir headman or malik, whose body Nicholson, in medieval fashion, had 'exposed in the market place, as a stoat might be on a barn door'.[40]

A story that was probably true and repeated by the intrepid and then very junior Younghusband of the frontier police related to Nicholson's 'taming' of

Bannu. It concerned a malik who, at a council of chiefs, had spat onto the ground in front of the new deputy commissioner as a deliberate act of defiance and disrespect. Rising from his desk in rage, Nicholson had instructed an orderly to 'make that man lick up his spittle and kick him out of camp'. It has to be said that this questionable and arbitrary action enhanced Nicholson's reputation as a strongman among hills people, as did ordering that a mullah have his beard shaved off because he had not offered the salaam to the deputy commissioner as he rode past.

Another oft-told Nicholson story comes from Younghusband.[41] This related to Nicholson marching up to John Lawrence with 'his head well in the air as it always was when he was angry', complaining that one of Lawrence's escort, 'a scarlet-coated Jamadar of Chuprassies', had been levying a bribe (*dasturi*) on supply goods coming into camp. Nicholson did not wait for Lawrence to say anything but marched the culprit off and had him publicly flogged.

Younghusband was of the opinion that Nicholson was less outraged by what was an everyday occurrence than by the fact that the offender was a member of Lawrence's escort. Younghusband added a comment that perhaps says more about him than it does about the strange major he had encountered:

> Nicholson had been in India far too long to be surprised by such a minor peculation and usually winked at it, saying with unusual resignation: 'never remove a native official unless you know you can replace him by a better one, otherwise you will get an equally stupid or corrupt man, minus the experience of his predecessor'.[42]

Younghusband was not slow to praise Nicholson and in December 1852, recalling the success of military activities in the hills, remarked to Henry Lawrence, 'The chief credit is due to Nicholson alone, for no part of his plan failed.'[43]

Though Nicholson might have ranted away in letters about whatever or whoever was annoying him, this did not mean that he did not strive to be fair when the need called. For example, on 10 August 1853 Nicholson's old bête noir Frederick Mackeson was murdered on his veranda at Peshawar. A fortnight after this incident Nicholson wrote to his brother Charles:

> Bye the by I hear that some of the Mily at Peshawur have got up a story that M's murder was owing to his intrigues with married women – I have no hesitation in declaring it to be an infamous lie – poor M was fond of women, but he was not the worse public servant on that account, and he was

much too right minded and had too much regard for his private and public character to bring discredit on himself and his Govt by intriguing with married women – I am trying to trace the slander to its source and I hope you will do what you can too – it is a duty to Govt no less than to the dead.

This calmer and more rational side of Nicholson came out again in July 1852. Writing to Henry Lawrence, he threw in the comment:

Has it ever struck you that there are no field guns between Bunnoo and Asunee? ... There is no target practice here either among the police or regulars, and when I enquired why, I am told there is a scarcity of powder and lead – If these troops are ever required to use their arms it will probably be in the hills, and inexperienced marksmen are not much use there. Pray don't let the Brigr know that I have dared to write on subjects so much out of my province.[44]

Lawrence saw to it that target practice was soon introduced.


## STOCK THEFT AND FUGITIVES

In September Nicholson wrote to his friend Neville Chamberlain, still military secretary to the Board of Administration in Lahore, which ran the Punjab:

The near approach of the cold season induces me to submit for the consideration of the Board of Administration the advisability of adopting early measures for the chastisement of the most troublesome of the hostile hill tribes on the border, with a view to securing immunity from their depredations in future, and making their punishment a wholesome and salutary example to their neighbours.

Nicholson then proceeded at length to give his views of the worst miscreants, the Kasrani, the Omerzye, the Ushterani and the Wazirs. Nicholson was no doubt correct when he wrote that the hill tribes 'all look forward to getting rid of us sooner than later and would show their true colours if opportunity offered'.[45]

The Wazirs, he claimed, were being incited into a religious war against the British by 'an Affghan calling himself Syud', whom the Afghan government had sent as an agent to create disturbances. Nicholson's general approach was simple, 'I think our policy is to do all we can, without sacrificing our dignity, to maintain friendly relations with our border tribes.'[46] Soon Nicholson was on his horse and out on scouting ventures. One brief report ran as follows:

Riding out a few mornings ago to look at the Wuhoa pass, I perceived a few huts near the mouth of it, the inhabitants of which, as I approached fled to the hills, I sent some men who understood their language to reassure and bring them back, but they positively refused and threatened to fire on us if we approached. Having only a few horsemen with me, I accordingly withdrew, carrying off their cattle about 40 head. On enquiry, I learned that these men were old allies of Yusuff, and had been most active in the attack on Futteh Khan. They had since (if nothing else can be proved against them) been living at the mouth of a pass, through which a great deal of plunder is carried.[47]

The degree to which these raids were serious and to which they were an element of psychological warfare and assertion of rights emerges with some details that have survived relating to livestock theft allegedly by the Bozdar in the period 1 April 1854 to 1 September 1855. This was to the south in the Multan region where the mountain barrier of the Sulaiman range runs roughly south–north. It is near the Sungurh valley. To the north-east was Dera Futteh Khan and to the south-east Dera Ghaze Khan. Across the Indus in the arid region was Leiah.

There were some seventy-four separate instances of theft, with total losses estimated at 2,454 rupees. Not all details of each raid have been recorded, but minimum figures stolen can be noted as 510 head of livestock, made up of 181 goats, 177 camels, 130 cattle, thirteen sheep, and nine asses. Of these, 55 per cent were actually recovered.

When the figures are scrutinised more fully it emerges that several of these losses occurred in one raid. For example, 100 goats were stolen in one raid and fifty in another, while eighty-five camels disappeared in a single raid, though fifty-three of these were recovered. Indeed, the significant overall recovery rate says something for the British negotiating and/or military skills, as well as their intelligence network. The problem, of course, was that often then so-called tribes were loose conglomerations with little real unity unless in the face of an adversary. Agreement to stop raiding might be genuine enough, but applied only to one section and did not intimidate another faction from carrying on a traditional practice.[48]

The hill country of the Bozdars was, as was the way in many frontier territories across the empire, the haunt of those attempting to evade the colonial law. In 1855, Nicholson's right-hand man, Lieutenant Pollock, knew of no fewer than thirty-five fugitives in Bozdar territory, an indication in itself of the intelligence network Nicholson had established. These fugitives included: eighteen tax defaulters; five murderers; four cattle thieves; two 'bad characters'; two individuals who had absconded with someone else's wife; two non-cattle thieves; one deserter from the 4th Punjab Cavalry; and one highway man.

## CHAIN OF COMMAND

Nicholson set out a plan of campaign and pressed for semi-official rather than official instructions, thus giving him more control and helping prevent information from leaking. Being a master spy himself, he was disconcerted that he himself might be spied upon, which most certainly was the case. He was fortunate that his deputy, Pollock, was a competent military leader, complemented by Lieutenant Younghusband in charge of his police battalion. But Nicholson had no illusions about his situation, 'so few friends have we among our subjects here'.[49] Three months later Nicholson received permission to advance against the Omerzyes. But Nicholson, rather typically, had in fact already started operations against one section of that tribe and was negotiating with another. So Lahore's approval, therefore, met with a rather disinterested reaction, followed by details of how he was already manoeuvring police and infantry units around his territory like chess pieces. Nicholson's thinking seems to have been that action by troublesome hill tribes gave him the automatic authority to react without Lahore's prior approval. He also suspected connivance in some instances between the hill and some of the plains people.

Nicholson struck a stumbling block with General van Courtlandt, who controlled the Dera Ghaze Khan district to Nicholson's south. There the terrain was much dryer ('not a drop of water or a green thing visible') and the Beloch tribes were actively raiding. Nicholson wanted permission to carry on his campaign both within this territory and his own, as well as having a section of van Courtlandt's district made over to him. Unsurprisingly, General van Courtlandt had different ideas about this turf encroachment. He preferred to use intermediaries to help solve the raiding problem, rather on the principle of setting a thief. He also seems to have felt that a partial solution was that, 'some arrangement might be entered into by which their movement could be controlled'. This appears to translate into paying danegeld, either directly or more likely through employment and influence. In the end, of course, it was a mixture of British military force and local collaborators who for the moment settled the problem of infiltration through the passes to the west of the Derajat plain.

It seems interesting that Nicholson, the great soldier of legend, was in fact for much of his career more or less at loggerheads with the military but for years he was seconded to the civil service. Indeed, annoying General van Courtlandt was by no means an isolated event. Four years later we find Nicholson, now an acting commissioner, grudgingly asserting to John Lawrence that the military in the area were 'making their own arrangements for intelligence, as they have always done both here and at Derah Ismail Khan', but adding, no doubt correctly, 'My intelligence is better than theirs.'

The relationship between the British in Bannu and Lahore was not to improve and as the years passed, Nicholson became more resentful of interference from head office. This ranged from big matters to the insignificant. An example of the latter was when John Lawrence tried to persuade Nicholson to take on a well-trusted soldier, Shere Khan of Isa Khel:

> I beg respectfully to submit for the Chief Commissioner's consideration, that a man of 54 years of age, of broken health can scarcely be deemed very fit for service, and that a service requiring drill and discipline and the wearing of uniform, can hardly be called well-suited to the habits of an old border soldier of nearly 40 years service, without any of those restraints which our discipline imposes.

This was all very true, but rather incongruous coming from Nicholson, who was increasing drawn to the 'wild hillmen' as the core of his fighting force. But by dismissing Lawrence's proposal so harshly, Nicholson was forcibly making the point that these were his men, not Lawrence's superannuated imports.

## DEATH OF LADY LAWRENCE

In early 1852, Nicholson had issued a proclamation calling on the property of former rebels to be given up. This had an interesting consequence, for Nicholson found himself in possession of some plundered jewels after paying a reward of 1,700 rupees. The Indian owner or owners were identified and it was determined that the value of the jewels, minus the 1,700 rupees, would be paid unless the owner also had been assessed as having been a rebel.[50] What happened to the actual jewels is not known; they probably went to the treasury in Lahore. Had Nicholson had the authority to give them away, there can be little doubt that the recipient would have been Honoria Lawrence. In the years before her premature death, Nicholson occasionally wrote to her, often on personal matters. For example, on 16 November 1852, writing from Bannu, he was quite frank both about his wishful dreams of making his fortune to enable him to live 'at home' in Ireland and about his positive hopes for enabling local people to escape poverty, unrest and crime:

> I confess I have even thought of settling in New Zealand. I have sometimes dreamt of trying my luck as a gold digger with a view to realising enough to enable me to live at home. I am sorry I am not to see you here this winter it is a very pretty country with a very bad people, but I see such good traits in them every now and then, particularly in the children, that I am in hopes the faults are more the result of education and circumstance than of anything unusually bad in their nature, I am in the hopes of being able to improve them.[51]

The saga of Henry Lawrence's exile as British resident to Rajputana is well documented. The troika system of governing the Punjab did not work because the Lawrence brothers could not work together and Robert Montgomery was not the man to act as 'buffer between two high-pressure engines'. That they had all attended the same school together in Londonderry did not alter matters. And the rubicund Montgomery's 'benevolent nature' could not calm the regular disagreements.

In early 1853, as Kaye put i, 'Cruelly was he [Sir Henry Lawrence] removed from the Punjab, which was his public life's stage, and he was equal to the trial.'[52] This exile continued until 1856. when he was given the prestigious position of chief commissioner of Oude (Awadh), a promotion that was to prove fatal. Back in the Punjab in early 1853, the board of administration was swept away by Lord Dalhousie, the governor-general, described by Hesketh Pearson as making up for 'his physical insignificance by his dictatorial manners'. Dalhousie made Sir John Lawrence chief commissioner of the Punjab. Nicholson was beside himself with grief and anger. On 4 January 1853, he foolishly requested that Sir Henry take him to Rajputana, adding, 'I certainly won't stay on the border in your absence.' Nicholson could see the way things would go and accurately predicted to Sir Henry, 'I am afraid poor little Abbott will soon be driven out of it [Punjab].'[53] He was correct in this, for within three months Abbott was unceremoniously removed from his beloved Hazara where he was much respected – too much for the authorities' liking – and relegated to taking charge of a government gunpowder factory in Calcutta, an act of bureaucratic cruelty.[54] Edwardes moved from Jalandhar to replace Abbott in Hazara, where he stayed only a matter of months before gaining the plum posting of Peshawar commissioner.

But as it turned out, it was probably John Lawrence who had more of a headache with Nicholson under him than Nicholson did with Lawrence as his superior. Eventually, a cautious *modus operandi* emerged between them. From the start, John Lawrence had made a conscious effort to work with Nicholson, not always an easy task. Haigh and Turner quoted a despatch John Lawrence wrote to Dalhousie that year, that he:

> regarded Major Nicholson as the best District Officer on the frontier. He possesses great courage, much force of character, and is at the same time shrewd and intelligent. He is well worth the wing of a regiment on the border, as his prestige with the people, both on the hills and plains, is very great. He is also a very fair civil officer and has done a good deal to put things straight in his district.[55]

The year 1853 was a bad one for Henry Lawrence. First came his loss of authority in the Punjab to his younger brother. Then in the summer of 1853 Honoria Lawrence became terminally ill. Writing to Nicholson that September, Sir Henry quoted what Honoria had said to him: 'I often think of those fine young fellows in the Punjab and what our example ought to have been to them and how much we have neglected them es [especially] our Nicholson.'[56]

Sir Henry took Honoria to the coolness of Mount Abu in Rajputana. And from there, early one September morning, he wrote a sad letter to Nicholson relating that his dying wife had said:

> Tell him [Nicholson] I love him dearly as if he were my son. I know that he is noble and pure to his fellow-men; that he thinks not of himself; but tell him he is a sinner; that he will one day be as weak and as near death as I am. Ask him to read but a few verses of the Bible daily, and to say that collect, 'Blessed Lord who has caused all holy Scriptures to be written for our learning, grant that we may in such wise hear them, read, mark, learn.'[57]

In fact, the gentle Honora held on for a further four months, dying in mid-January 1854. The grieving widower sent Nicholson a New Testament that she had owned, a keepsake from one of the women who loved the strange young army officer. Inside the holy book, Henry Lawrence wrote: 'John Nicholson, in memory of his friend and warm well-wisher, Honoria Lawrence, who was this day laid in her grave, H.N. Lawrence. Mount Aboo, January 17th, 1854.'

Nicholson was always on the move. If not riding his district, he was taking trips to Lahore or to visit Herbert Edwardes and his wife Emma as his new posting as commissioner at Peshawar. In the endless game of British administrators' musical chairs, Johnny Becher now got the mountain province where Edwardes had been briefly. Four years later, when the Great Rebellion broke out, Becher was still there.

Nicholson said that seeing Herbert Edwardes always made him feel a 'better man'. When not on the move, Nicholson was usually grumbling about his lot and his desire to move somewhere else. Yet Nicholson had an unexpected side. When John and Harriette Lawrence turned up on a grand tour of the frontier in early 1854, complete with young baby, Nicholson went out of his way to assist, even escorting them as far as Kohat, an act of kindness the commissioner did not forget.

## THE HILL TRIBES

On 13 April 1854 Nicholson wrote to his mother from the small but strategic outpost of Kohat:

> I came in here this morning from Peshawur, where I have been spending a few days with the Edwardes … I was glad to learn from your last letter that you and Lily were enjoying yourselves so much at Cheltenham – If you have not yet received any rent from the Caldbecks, I would ask you not to take any. It would seem to me inconsistent with the friendly relations which I believe exist between you, to take rent for accommodation which one friend should be happy to have an opportunity of affording another … Where do you think of spending the coming summer? I hope you will go to the seaside; sea-bathing seems to agree so well with you and Lily.
>
> … I do not remember if I acknowledged the receipt of the gloves; they arrived safe and fit very well – I was sorry to see however, that having sent them as a letter instead of as a parcel, you had had to pay an enormous amount of postage for them.[58]

As for Charles Nicholson, he was quietly making his own name. About this time, he served for two years as captain of the Punjab Police Force while its commander was on sick leave in Europe. On his return, Charles re-joined his own Punjab cavalry regiment.[59] But Charles was not to catch up in the rankings with his more famous brother, for on 28 November 1854 John Nicholson was made an acting or brevet lieutenant colonel.[60]

# TORTURE

It was during Nicholson's time at Bannu that his fellow deputy commissioner in the not too distant district of Ludhiana, a Mr H. Brereton, was first suspended and then demoted and removed from the district. The charge was that Brereton had employed a man named Futteh Jung who, with a servant named as Alla Buksh, had extracted confessions from suspected criminals using torture. It was said that the inhabitants in the street where Jung lived 'could not sleep at night for the cries of his victims'. It appears that Brereton was 'the virtual though not the intentional cause of many deplorable cruelties and tortures, and much injustice, and has brought disgrace on our administration'. The tortures inflicted were described as: 'The hair of the head (they are Sikhs) was tied to their leg irons. Wooden pegs were driven into the joints of their elbows and other sensitive parts. Others were merely bound tightly and beaten with fists, so that no marks might remain.'

The chief commissioner, John Lawrence, recommended to the governor-general demotion and removal from the Punjab. Dalhousie, however, quite correctly noted that if Brereton was unfit for employment in the Punjab, he was unfit for employment in the North-West Provinces. In the end, Brereton was demoted to an assistant commissioner and Futteh Jung given eight years' labour in irons.

The case is significant in that it took place on Nicholson's doorstep. It was said of Brereton that: 'He seems possessed with a species of infatuation in regard to the use of espionage, the employment of personal attachés, and the application of indiscriminate severity; from this vicious system experience does not seem to deter him, nor advice dissuade.'

It was difficult not to run such a wild, newly acquired territory without the use of spies and a firm hand. What the Brereton case shows, however, is that there was a line over which a deputy commissioner could not step. But Nicholson, unlike Brereton, knew this. With all the talk of his firmness and no-nonsense approach to the inhabitants of this frontier land, Nicholson was meticulous in asking permission when it came to imposing serious sentences, such as execution. Indeed, contrary to frequent comments about Nicholson being a bad correspondent, an image he himself propagated, he kept in very regular contact with his colleagues and superiors. More importantly, Nicholson had that respect for the law, be it good or bad, which was the hallmark of many a Calvinist soldier from the sixteenth well into the twentieth century. If it was not legal, Nicholson did not do it. While he would flog, and for a capital offence 'blow a man from a gun', these sentences were in fact within regulations and widely practised at the time. He did not cross the line beyond that.

## FALLING OUT WITH NEVILLE CHAMBERLAIN

At the end of 1854, the post of commander of the 11,000-strong Punjab Frontier Force became vacant. Both Nicholson and Chamberlain applied. Nicholson, hearing that his friend had also gone for the posting, withdrew his application. He then wrote to Chamberlain stating what he had done and saying that he believed Chamberlain's claim was greater than his, and wishing him success.

Nicholson's letter apparently never reached Chamberlain. But as the weeks passed and no reply was received, the matter began to fester with Nicholson, who soon was holding a large grudge against his friend for his apparently unacknowledged gesture. This resentment grew to gigantic proportions in Nicholson's mind. When one of Nicholson's senior Indian lieutenants, Zaman Khan, was killed in a border raid, Nicholson latched onto this to attack Chamberlain's force for not having done its job properly.

John Lawrence noted of the matter:

> You know 'old Nick', what a stern uncompromising chap he is, he was frightfully aggravated at the death [of] Zaman Khan and spoke out plainly, too plainly, about the cavalry at the posts who were to blame, in this particular case, but the fact is that the detachment in the posts have done little or no good in the Derajat … I did not tell Chamberlain one tenth of what Nicholson said and much of which seemed to me to be true … the detachments at the outposts do not effectually guard the border. This is the gravamen of Nicholson's charge.[61]

Indignantly, Chamberlain refuted the allegation and letters were exchanged that, as Isabel Sieveking drily commented, 'alas, only too surely reached their destination'. John Lawrence, the chief commissioner at Lahore, was quickly dragged in and was soon in Nicholson's firing line, too. Unlike his brother Henry, John Lawrence was not a 'people's person' and the great mandarin of northern India struggled hard to end the administrative civil war in his backyard, though, it has to be said, he was not without wiles in the matter. On one occasion, Lawrence noted with some humour:

I have got an official letter from Chamberlain putting twenty queries on each of the four raids to Nicholson! Now if anything will bring Nick to his senses it will be these queries. He will polish off a tribe in the most difficult fortress, or ride the border like 'belted Will'[62] of former days; but one query in writing is often a stumper for a month. The pen-and-ink work, as he calls it, does not suit him.[63]

In December 1855 Nicholson wrote to Edwardes claiming that John Lawrence had snubbed him twice.[64] So the dispute dragged on and on. Nicholson does not come out of the fracas well. He sulked, held grudges, was intransigent and was bitter. Of course, several things were at play. He was hurt and felt betrayed; he was jealous of Chamberlain getting a position he had greatly coveted; and he was bored beyond distraction in Bannu. Nicholson may also by this time have started to drink heavily, which cannot have helped his temper.

Eventually, Lawrence cleverly quoted to Nicholson what Chamberlain had said to him in a recent letter:

I never considered the question [of the raid] personal; and even the official discussion was buried when I last addressed you on the subject. If I am correct he feels cool towards me. But I shall be happy to receive him with the same feeling of respect and admiration which I have all along borne towards him. He has only to come within reach for me to extend both hands towards him, and in doing so I shall be doubly glad, for I shall know that the Government, of which we are the common servants, will be the gainer.

Nicholson was touched by these words and agreed the two should meet at Kohat. Once together, the truth of the missing letter was soon out. Nicholson was so agitated by what he heard that he bit an ivory paper knife in two. Of course, now with the truth out Nicholson was racked with guilt and remorse. It was very much to Chamberlain's credit that once he had brought an end to the lengthy period of backstabbing, he did all he could to let the matter be and to move on. The wounds did heal, though it took a little time. In April 1856 Nicholson wrote to Edwardes, 'Chamberlain is staying with me and is very amiable, but I think he considers me in his way and wd be glad to see me out of it.'[65]

It would not be the last time Nicholson wrongly accused someone only to find out his mistake. As will be seen, the young Lieutenant Roberts had a similar, though less volcanic, experience in 1857. And to Nicholson's credit, once having behaved badly, he was not only remorseful but sealed in his own mind a complete trust in the person he had wronged. Nicholson was, however, never to change his mind about John Lawrence, whom by February 1856 he was accusing of acting with '*spite*'.

## 'RUNNING RUSTY'

One of the Nicholson stories that is probably true comes from these Bannu years. A visitor found Nicholson sitting with a bundle of official regulations in front of him. Seeing the friend, Nicholson kicked them across the floor, saying, 'This is the way I treat these things.'[66] But Nicholson was not the only restless and grumpy deputy commissioner on the frontier. Just to his north at Kohat was his old associate Captain John Coke, who had charge both of civil and military matters. They had become close during the Anglo-Sikh wars and both had been active with Sir Walter Gilbert's pursuing force after the Sikh army had been broken at the battle of Gujerat. He had, with the support of Henry Lawrence, established in 1849 the 1st Regiment of the Punjab Infantry, later called the Punjab Irregular Force (the famous Piffers), and fifty years later as Coke's Rifles. In the mid-1850s, the two became close associates again and, to quote *Blackwood's Edinburgh Review*: 'During '54, '55, and '56 there was a considerable correspondence between him [Coke] and Nicholson, from which it is evident that both men were, in John Lawrence's phrase, "running rusty". Nicholson exhorting his friend to patience in a tone which implies that he found it no very pleasing task to exercise that virtue himself.'[67]

In December 1855 Nicholson was complaining bitterly to Edwardes that he was 'not a whit better than a machine now' and he wanted out of the Punjab. Much of 1855 had been spent by Nicholson trying to persuade the authorities to allow him to go and fight in the Crimean War (October 1853 to February 1856). Officialdom just ignored him. Nicholson grumbled continuously about the failure of Calcutta to reply to his request. Only in January 1856 did he get a polite rejection along the not unreasonable lines that the governor-general could not interfere with staff appointments in the Crimea.[68] In fairness to Nicholson, he was by no means alone in his wish, nor was he alone in never getting a reply from Fort William. So persistent did Nicholson become that Sir Henry Lawrence tried to mollify him by reminding the young adventurer that Bengal Army officers were not usually treated in friendly terms by Queen's army officers and he might be better to stay put. But once Nicholson had a bee in his bonnet, it was difficult to remove it. He even contemplated joining the Turkish army, lamenting that he had not learnt Turkish, 'I feel I missed the tide of my fortune when I gave up the idea of learning Turkish at home.'[69]

The Crimean War passed. Meanwhile, Nicholson contemplated taking on the Persians, 'who are but the scouts of the Russians', and rolling them back from Herat 'like a carpet'. Nothing, of course, came of this. His restlessness grew and he wrote of quitting the Punjab, perhaps to Oude. His long-suffering friend Herbert Edwardes actually spoke to the governor-general, Lord Canning, about Nicholson and a possible Persian posting, even though the Indian army involved in that fracas was the Bombay army and not the Bengal one. It was during this exchange that Edwardes made the famous comment, 'Well, my lord, you may rely upon this, that if ever there is a desperate deed to be done in India, John Nicholson is the man to do it.' One account adds that Canning with a smile replied, 'I will remember what you say, and I will take you for Major Nicholson's godfather.'[70]

To Nicholson himself, Edwardes was less patient, writing to him, 'Why are you going away [wanting to leave the Punjab]? because an injustice has been done you. Can you not forgive it, or bear it … It is a trial of temper and pride, in which you should not let the Devil get the victory.' These points Nicolson conceded, but added that he had no prospects, he was in dispute with Chamberlain, his commissioner (Ross) gave no support and the chief commissioner (John Lawrence) was 'silent'. Basically Nicholson wanted it both ways: to be independent and to have support from above. In lugubrious but revealing fashion, Nicholson added, 'I shall retire in four years [after 20 years' service], if I live so long.' But more to the point, later in this valedictory missive Nicholson observes:

> I also believe that there is a general opinion among the natives of the Punjab, who (not owing to any fault of mine) considerably exaggerate the value of my services both here and in the war [Anglo-Sikh], that I have earned promotion and am unjustly used in not getting it, and it is not pleasant to hear this constantly hinted at.[71]

In other words, long before the Mutiny, and leaving aside the Nikolseinee cult, Nicholson was very well aware that he was a legend among the people of the North-West Frontier.

There is no doubt that by 1855, when Nicholson handed Dera Ismail Khan over to his successor Captain Busk, he had his district 'licked into shape'. Nicholson had needed to learn how to record that timeless political hot potato, crime statistics. At first he entered all crimes that had been reported to any police official. This resulted in his crime-to-population rate being a high 1 to 106. However, he discovered that the practice was not to include reported crimes that did not come to court, so producing the more palatable proportion of 1 to 217. His claim that serious violent crime had disappeared, however, seems justifiable – 'we had [in 1855] not had a single murder or highway robbery, or attempt at either, in Bannoo throughout the year. The crime has all gone down to the southern end of the district, where I am not allowed to interfere.'[72] Ironically, the exception in the new year was the already mentioned attempt on Nicholson's life by a religious fanatic.

In 1854, Nicholson wrote to Edwardes several times asking him to buy and send him some children's toys from Peshawar – spinning humming-tops, Jew's harps and the like for the 'Wuzeeree children'. He also ensured that a child who had murdered a man was not punished but sent to live with a man whom he liked and trusted and who would help bring him up in a moral and righteous way. The boy was keen on going to live with the man, according to Nicholson, because, 'He never gives any one bread without ghee on it.' It is easy from the vantage point of the twenty-first century to sneer and cast sinister motives on such things but the fact remains that among the ordinary people of these plains and hill country, Nicholson was regarded, as indeed James Abbott was up in Hazara, as someone different from other British officials. Nicholson was respected.

The stories relating to Nicholson's no-nonsense and sometimes rough justice are numerous. One often told was of a young man who, when a boy, had lost his father and inherited his lands. But this land had been seized by the orphan boy's uncle, Alladâd Khan. When the young man brought the matter to the court in Bannu, the uncle had intimidated and bullied all the witnesses. Taking the practical route, Nicholson rode out to the disputed lands, left his grey mare loose, and tied or had himself tied to a tree. When villagers found him, their hakim demanded to know on whose land the outrage of his being apprehended had occurred. They all pointed at Alladâd Khan but he, in terror of some punishment had said, no, the land belonged to his nephew. And so justice was served.[73]

This highly improbable story has the air of a fairy tale about it, nearly an Old Testament morality tale. There is a drawing of this fable in Cholmeley's charming and rare booklet *The Lion of the Punjaub*, which was published about 1908.[74]

A rather poignant end to one of Nicholson's stern justice sagas related to a man he had hanged for murder. The body was buried in the corner of a plot of a bungalow. A tomb had been erected by the dead man's friends after Nicholson had left the district and every Thursday evening diwahs were lit over the tomb, which became a place of pilgrimage, an interesting fact in itself. Some years later, the owner of the bungalow dismantled the tomb and built a hut where it had been. Eventually, one of Nicholson's more literary successors, Septimus Thorburn, occupied the bungalow. One day on entering the hut he found the tomb partially restored and a number of diwahs around it. Thorburn recorded, 'The servant occupant said he had seen two snakes in the hut, and supposing them to be the guardians of the grave, had renewed its superstructure, and that people were in the habit of coming and salaaming at it.'[75]

Nicholson's contribution to the Bannu region went beyond maintaining peace, building the town's first jail and trying to impose some form of judicial equity among its inhabitants, albeit of the rough justice variety. Another of Nicholson's achievements was to build on the work commenced by Major Taylor in attempting to reclaim the Nák jungle lands and extend the Kachkot canal from the Kúrm into a 'large waste tract' called Landídák.

The activities of his medical corps are worthy of note. Bannu had a dispensary that serviced Dera Ismail Khan, treating about twenty patients a day. In 1853 it dealt with 1,123 cases. In 1854 there were 1,295 patients, who came from a wide surrounding area.

A European medical officer was in charge and there was also an Indian doctor, described by Dr B.E. Ross as 'a good man', and a hospital establishment. In addition, Nicholson, as civil administrator, was also responsible for a smallpox vaccination programme among children. In 1854 no fewer than ninety-three villages and towns were visited by the vaccination team, some of them up to five times during the year. This resulted in 1,858, mainly children, being vaccinated, with a known success rate of 90 per cent. Including Bannu itself there were 2,579 vaccinations, of which 87 per cent were known to be successful. Many of the balance also may have been successful, the team having to move on before the matter could be verified. Dr Ross noted that while Hindus 'have never allowed their children to be vaccinated', among the tribes to the west who came into the region in the cold season with their flocks, 'the benefits of vaccination are well known and appreciated'.

In 1854 Nicholson made a Summary Settlement of the Land Revenue. This new tax system replaced that imposed by the Sikhs under which a quarter of a village's crop had been claimed irrespective of the quality of the land. Now the taxation system, although retaining the one-quarter base, took into account the rough valuation of land cultivated as reflected by estimates of the previous four years' revenue. This was an acceptable mechanism as long as the annual crop was satisfactory, but was disastrous should the crop fail or partially fail. The settlement covered 88,351 acres as well as about 11,000 acres from ten villages that had not yet been measured.[76]

It is important to note that the saga of the Bannu region was not just one of raids and counter-raids, or of bringing villains to justice. The society that Nicholson consolidated also concerned day-to-day living and the survival of the people of the district.

## THE FRONTIERSMAN

Nicholson had been in Bannu, or to be more accurate the Dara Ismail Khan district, for four and a half years. He had brought a semblance of stability to the region, at times stirred up by the rulers across the border in Kabul. He had dispensed justice in his rough and ready fashion, which had generally satisfied the locals. But then there was the press.

Nicholson was not slow to urge strong action against the vernacular press when he considered it had crossed the line of sedition. He lectured John Lawrence on what 'Freedom of the press' meant – 'not licence to publish falsehoods of mischievous tendency or to defame all individuals who will not be called into subscription'. Nicholson added:

> In a new country like the Punjab and among a people scarcely far enough advanced in civilization to be fit for liberty of the press, even as it is understood in Europe I do not think a paper like the 'Reag Noor' can safely or wisely [be] tolerate[d].

Fortunately for the troublesome editor, he was in Multan and not within Nicholson's domain.

Nicholson's fearless (or foolhardy) nature at this time also played itself out over the government of India's decision to allow Afghanistan to invade and occupy the valley of Dour, which was independent both of Kabul and Lahore. One of the contradictions in Nicholson was his preference to have Afghans fighting alongside him, while apparently holding a deep dislike of Afghanistan. Added to this was the unpleasant reality that Dour was directly over the mountain range from where Nicholson sat in Bannu. So angry was he at the British concession to the government in Kabul and its betrayal of those whose 'friendly neutrality' was known that he sat down and wrote:

> It is with extreme diffidence that I venture unasked, to offer an opinion on a subject on which Government has already come to a decision. Believing however as I do most strongly, that there are very serious political objections

to the annexation of Dour by the Booranees, which have not occurred to the Chief Commissioner because they have not been put before him I think it right to submit my views on this subject, for his consideration and that of Government, trusting that whatever may be thought of their correctness, I shall not be deemed to have exceeded my duty, in making a deferential representation of them.

The long-suffering John Lawrence noted to the governor-general, 'The C.C. has much respect for Major Nicholson's views in general; but in this particular case cannot assent to their correctness.' Needless to say, the Afghans gained possession of what Lawrence called the 'little valley'. A treaty between the British and Afghans, brokered by Edwardes and reluctantly supported by John Lawrence, was signed on 20 March 1855. Nicholson also had no great enthusiasm for his friend's diplomatic manoeuvrings. Whether or not this was the restraining influence that kept the Afghans relatively neutral during the Indian Mutiny is a matter of conjecture.[77]

These years on the frontier changed John Nicholson. Coming from an Irish frontier family, he reverted to the form of his forebears. He had the usual characteristics of the frontiersman, a loner, outside the portals of polite society, at once rough and tough, but at the same time dutiful to obligation and loyal to his side. And yet, there was an added difference less well known among frontier folk. Four days after John Nicholson died, William Graham wrote to a friend:

You ought to see the conglomeration of fellows we have fighting our battles for us now: Affreedes, Affkhans and all different race of border tribes, who have for so many years past been giving us so much trouble. All our horses were taken away from armed regts, and these fellows put on them with arms etc. complete, and sent down under their own chiefs, and the latter looked upon poor Nicholson as their head. He was the only one that had the slightest control over them; his name and they quaked.[78]

# The Irish Waziri

By May 1856, Nicholson's mental and physical heath was collapsing. He had frequently been ill in the 1840s, sometimes from 'fever' and sometimes, as now, from a troublesome and enlarged liver. To what extent this was brought on by drinking is not known. There are references to his asking Henry Lawrence to send him some beers, but half a dozen beers once a month could hardly be considered over-indulgence. Still, turning to drink was not beyond the realms of possibility given Nicholson's at times hermit-like existence, his social isolation and what appears to have been increasingly manic depressed state. He certainly would not be the first Irish officer to drink too much. But his overall decline in health was more likely precipitated if not caused by malaria, a fever that laid him low for periods but from which his 'iron constitution' eventually raised him. In August 1854 he was prostrate for a fortnight owing, he claimed, to a 'blunder of our Dr here'. This recurring illness did not improve, and certainly was not helped by Nicholson's insatiable drive to be chasing recalcitrant tribesmen through the hills. Then there was the exhausting and tedious time spent hearing legal cases, a matter Nicholson took very seriously.

By September 1855, he was admitting to Edwardes that in the past when he felt feverish he would take 'physic and slops' but how on the first signs of fever he would 'immediately open a bottle of beer and drink it on the Top of from 5 to 8 grams of quinine, and I continue as long as any feverish symptoms last, to drink *double* my usual allowance of beer'.[1]

&#42; &#42; &#42;

As for his mental state, his letters became shriller in tone as 1855 closed and 1856 opened. He would leave the Punjab. His superior Commissioner Ross did nothing for him. He would leave India and join Osman Pasha's Ottoman cavalry as a volunteer. He pestered the governor-general's office in Calcutta

with letters to get out of the Punjab. He vacillated in his correspondence
with Edwardes about what he would or would not do. To Edwardes's credit,
he acted as a restraining force on the caged Nicholson. John Lawrence was
now Nicholson's bête noir. If Edwardes had not a wife and he not a mother,
Nicholson said to Edwardes, he would settle matters 'with revolvers across a
pocket handkerchief' – though quickly added as his conscience kicked in:

> Now Mrs E [Emma Edwardes] mustn't see this, or she will think me a
> monster, which I don't believe I am ... I think there must be a great deal
> of the Wuzeeree in my nature. An old W came to me the other day to ask
> leave to kill a fraudulent Hindoo bankrupt, who had fleeced him of his little
> savings. He said he was content to be hung afterwards but that the thought
> of his wrong, *burned up his inside*, and made his life miserable.[2]

As a sober afterthought, Nicholson added that in the Punjab he could not
agree to any change that 'would be regarded as a snub or disgrace by the native
community'.

And yet, in the middle of all this anxiety Nicholson could record how
beautiful Bannu looked when he returned there after a short absence: 'The
sight of it as I rode in yesterday morning almost laid the evil spirit within me.'

That March, Nicholson asked Robert Montgomery in Lahore for permission
to spend the hot season in Kashmir. He readily agreed and recommended this
to Lawrence, adding, 'I shall be very sorry if circumstances should take you
away from the frontier – all the old hands seem to be leaving the Punjab.' Of
course, when dealing with John Lawrence nothing was straightforward for
Nicholson and the matter dragged on. Nicholson then tried a new tack to
transfer to Kashmir because of his declining medical health. An unusually long
medical certificate written then at Bannu by Assistant Surgeon W. Delprate of
the 3rd Punjab Cavalry stated:

> Major Nicholson aged 33 of sanguine temperament and intemperate habits
> has been suffering for some months past from functional derangement of
> the liver. It would appear that his liver first began to trouble him about
> four months ago [c. January 1856], to relieve which he commenced upon a
> course of blue pills, and colocynth but without finding himself very much
> improved thereby about this time he began to complain of shooting pains
> in his shoulder, and right side – shortly after his duty took him into camp
> where in tents the uneasiness increased latterly from abstaining from beer,
> and all stimulants of whatever kind he finds the inconvenience arising from

such a state to be less distressing having beyond habitual costiveness of body little else to complain of – pressure on the side though not attended with immediate unpleasant sensations produces subsequently a return of the pains in the shoulder, and side. This state of things indicating in my opinion, a somewhat congested condition of the organ requires some care and attention and should be overcome not only by appropriate remedies but by a removal to a more genial climate than can be obtained at any of the stations on the border. I have therefore to recommend that if it be practicable Major Nicholson might be permitted to reside during the ensuing hot season out of the influence of the exceeding heat of the summer months without which change his efficiency, and activity as an energetic servant of Government will be liable to become very much impaired.[3]

As mentioned earlier, this certificate is a key document to understanding, at least in part, the ill-temper for which Nicholson was known at the time and no doubt his over-excited state in his last years in Bannu. What is clear is that Nicholson's tendency to evade where possible normal social discourse, to be erratic and unpredictable in his behaviour and to suffer from periodical and violent outbursts was exacerbated by the 'blue pills', which were mercury based, combined with the equally dangerous colocynth. The result of taking colocynth is frequently severe pains, actuate headaches, irritableness and anger. Not surprisingly, this can incapacitate the person, who has a tendency to remain aloof and avoid mixing with people.[4] All of this is relevant to Nicholson's character.

There then emerged a new danger, as Captain James, Edwardes's deputy at Peshawar, tried to get the Kashmir posting, also on the grounds of ill health. But two weeks after sending his request, Nicholson was granted permission to proceed to Kashmir on full pay. This was under the understanding that while there he was, 'to act as referee in cases of complaints against British officers residing or travelling in Kashmir and its vicinity in the manner as Major Macgregor did in 1852 and Major Marsden in 1853. It is to be understood however that no establishment will be allowed.'

Lieutenant Coxe was to be acting deputy commissioner in his absence. Nicholson was to be back in his position come 15 November that year, so he had more than five months off in the mountains.[5] In confirming this arrangement with the governor-general in Calcutta, John Lawrence's secretary speaks of Nicholson as a 'meritorious officer of experience and weight'.

Nicholson decided to travel to Kashmir the long way round via Peshawar so that he could visit Herbert and Emma Edwardes. He had last been there staying with them the previous Christmas a few months before, riding back to Bannu afterwards. This time when he arrived Nicholson found that Herbert Edwardes was absent in Hazara so Captain and Mrs Brabazon Urmston acted as host. The Brabazon Urmstons had very close Irish links. Henry Urmston, at 27, was slightly younger than Nicholson. He was then in the 62nd Native Infantry. To the delight of the family, and indeed the neighbourhood, Nicholson had brought with him his Bannu police band, which played every evening in the Urmstons' garden. The gift of a magic lantern box with slides further delighted the Urmston children. The only shadow on the stay was an embarrassing incident that could provide fuel for the Nicholson conspirators. At dinner one day, the Urmstons' young daughter burst into tears because Nicholson had 'fixed his gaze upon her'. The hysteria was only quietened when Nicholson came round the table, sat himself on her high chair and put the child on his lap. The ridiculous situation of Nicholson on her high chair soon produced smiles on the little girl's face and the incident passed.[6] Worthy of note is that after the Mutiny, in 1858, the Urmstons named their new babe Herbert Edwardes.[7]

Sending their best field officer to Kashmir to recuperate was understandable enough, but sending him there 'on special duty' to monitor and arbitrate on incidents relating to Company officers on leave was a mistake. The news in July 1856 that Emma Edwardes was so ill that she and Herbert Edwardes could not join Nicholson in Kashmir cannot have helped matters.[8] News of developments in eastern Persia distracted Nicholson from his surroundings as he dreamt of leading an army of 5,000 to capture Herat and re-establish British influence in the country: 'They [Calcutta government] will ignore the lessons taught by the successful advances of Pollock and Nott, in the face of the whole Affghan nation, through as difficult a country as any in the world, and with no loss to speak of.'

But reality on the ground soon called Nicholson from his day dreaming.

By the mid-1850s Kashmir had become a magnet for those British who on leave who had neither the time nor the funds available to made the trip home to Britain or Ireland. The journey to Kashmir could be made by easy stages from Rawalpindi, with rest bungalows along the way. Some went out on expeditions into the mountains, enjoying the wild rhododendrons, bluebells and towering deodar cedar forests. Some enjoyed lotus lilies on the lake; some collected specimens of natural history; some went hunting for wild goat, wild sheep, bears and leopards, or ducks. Some stayed and relaxed in the beautiful and quaint capital, Srinagar, which stood at 5,250ft above sea level. Lieutenant Roberts wrote of Srinagar at this time:

it is needless for me to dwell at length upon its delights, which, I am inclined to think, are greater in imagination than in reality. It has been called the Venice of the East, and in some respects it certainly does remind one of the 'Bride of the Sea', both in its picturequeness and (when one gets into the small and tortuous canals) its unsavouriness. Even at the time [1854] of which I write it was dilapidated, and the houses looked exactly like those made by children out of a pack of cards, which a puff of wind might be expected to destroy.[9]

In Srinagar the visitor might walk to the gardens, a temple or the magnificent wooden mosque. They might take a leisurely boat along the Mar or Kutical canal and view the part-wooden houses and the delicate bridges over the water. Or the young soldier on leave could have a rip-roaring time, burning the candle at both ends and for a few short, glorious weeks, throw off the strictures of Victorian society. The Bannu police band, which had slogged its way up the passes with Nicholson to play every second evening to entertain the populace, was not the sort of fun that the last group had in mind.[10]

Kashmir at the time acted rather like Lourenço Marques, or one of the homelands, during the era of South African apartheid. If one was looking for a wild time and perhaps a little sin, Kashmir was the place to go. Interference from some puritan Company officer was neither expected nor appreciated. In July 1856 we find Nicholson writing to John Lawrence, 'I have observed that many of the officers here doubt my having been entrusted with any authority, save to receive complaints, and have felt disposed to resent any interference.' Nicholson deeply resented the moral high ground that Gulab Singh (1792–1857), his old associate, the British-installed maharaja, could adopt on watching the 'licentious and riotous' activities of these young officers and the retinue of Indian 'camp followers' who accompanied them. In total, Nicholson estimated the total number of these attendants to be about 1,000, with some one or two hundred English visitors. Of the former, he said that they:

are totally exempt from all control or authority of any kind. They commit theft, assault, riot, drunkenness etc without check or fear of punishment. On the habitually insolent demeanor of this class, out of our own territory, I need not dwell. I heard Affghans at Cabul and Sikhs on our first occupation of Lahore, say that the greatest annoyance which resulted to them from our presence, was the overbearing and insulting behaviour of our Hindoostanees, and I am sorry to say that I have observed a good deal of this here.[11]

In contrast to such debauchery, Nicholson found the news of the marriage
of his sister Lily to Rev. John Seymour, the local curate at Lisburn, something
to welcome. That August he wrote to Lily from Kashmir congratulating her.
Somewhat indiscreetly, he also discussed her financial situation, saying she
could live comfortably in Ireland on £400:

> but should any unforeseen circumstances ever put you in want of money, I
> hope you will apply to me without hesitation or scruple. I have purchased
> a Cashmere shawl for you, which I will take down to Bannoo with me in
> October, and there dispatch via Bombay.[12]

In August Nicholson attended a 'great dinner' hosted by the raja, who
Nicholson invariably referred to as 'the bovine', and who he said had aged
twenty years since he had last seen him. The evening went well and there was
no rowdyism, although Nicholson fully realised that many of the company
regarded him as a 'wet blanket'. In the end Nicholson felt he had to upbraid
only two officers, one for coming in a shooting coat, and the other for
familiarly addressing 'the bovine' as 'old fellow'. On the raja, Nicholson was to
the point: 'The Bovine's physical state which you enquire about is wonderfully
good, considering the life he leads. As regards the political state of the valley,
the people are more ground and more depressed than ever … If the bovine
had a spark of any good or right feeling in him, I should feel inclined to try
my fortune here.'

Nicholson was still not well and his liver was playing up again. For this he
took muriatic acid, what is today known as hydrochloric acid, a domestic
cleaning agent. And as mentioned, he also used calomel and continued with
the toxic colocynth pills.[13] It is little wonder that he was easily annoyed.

Nicholson became seriously irritated in early September 1856: he was taken
to a bungalow that had been rented by a young officer, Lieutenant Osborn,
adjutant to the 7th Irregular Cavalry. 'Extremely objectionable and indecent
writing' was on the wall of one room. This was made up of the following names
of 'well known prostitutes' who used to visit Ens. Osborn 'rather publickly':

| Janee | – | Ugly |
|-------|---|------|
| (name illegible) | – | flat |
| Gollabee | – | kept |
| Kul Bux | – | stout |
| Huree | – | scrappy |
| Heeral | – | tight (at first) |

| Ashmalee | – | all so so |
| Mahtabee | – | active |
| Malee | – | springy (very) |
| Mookhtee | – | juicy |
| Soondree | – | luscious |

4 unknown oysters.

N.B. The above are not warranted

Having recorded his fifteen encounters, Osborn ended his holiday and went back to his more mundane duties in the Punjab, either forgetting to rub down the wall or deliberately leaving it as a record of his prowess and possibly as a reference for others.

Nicholson was beside himself with rage, noting that 'similar instances of misconduct have not been uncommon'. It was not clear at first that Osborn was the guilty person as the bungalow had a fairly regular turnover of occupants. He learnt that a colonel of the Irish 27th Regiment, the Inniskillings, had been in the house. Nicholson had to be delicate in his approach to Lieutenant Colonel H. Williamson: 'I firmly believe you to be incapable of any such conduct, but …' Williamson wrote a factual note in reply, stating that he had been in the bungalow from 27 April to 27 June and he had seen no obscene writing on the walls, 'nor could any thing of the sort have been there without coming (I think) under my observation'. Osborn was the next occupant, until 11 July, and then Lieutenant J.F. Cordner came in. A letter to Cordner in the town of Nowshera elicited the news that when the lieutenant had moved into the bungalow he had seen the writing on the wall as, fortunately for Cordner, had a Captain Brougham. So having spent considerable time in detective work, Nicholson had his man, the hapless and foolish Lieutenant Osborn. The matter went to the desk of John Lawrence, who behaved more sensibly over the problem than did his deputy commissioner. He wrote to Osborn and said that if he were guilty and willing to apologise and promise not to act in a similar manner in the future, the chief commissioner 'will not deem it necessary to take further notice of the matter'.[14]

Nicholson was not oblivious to the beauty of Kashmir or to its produce. He visited the market and looked at the 'very pretty' shawls, though the four he obtained at 700, 675, 670 and 650 rupees he considered to be 'undeniably dear'. These prices seem to have included the specialised washing of the garment before delivery. Nicholson commented, 'so few men make these woven shawls now, that those who do have a monopoly.' Nicholson distracted himself in these lovely garments and became something of an agent for his family and his friends. And he had his own carrier to take the garments down to the plains for inspection. This was Hafiz Ahmed Khan:

> the only native I know whom I can really rely on to work as well in my absence, as when I am present – He has three pushmeena coats of the kind Mrs Edwardes asked me to send you – Take whichever of these you like best, and give the other two to Hafiz Ahmed, to take on to Coke and my brother [Charles] – first however show the three to Becher, and ask him to let me know which color and braid he likes best and I will have one made for him accordingly – I would offer him one of these, but I fear they are all too large for him; as they were made for myself.
>
> I have got some square woollen and sewn shawls for Mrs Ed. and again only keep them till I can get a few more, which I hope will be in two or three days – I am sorry the long ones were not quiet – James and Brougham and I all concurred in thinking them the prettiest we had seen, and we have not since found any equal to them though many higher priced ones (even up to 1100 Rs) have been bought me …
>
> You ask the price of the cloaks – The one without the hood was 42, and the small one I think 28, so was the lilac one – The two first wide capes I sent were more expensive, I forget how much but I will enquire of the seller.[15]

In another letter he grumbled that shawl merchants did not give discounts even though he had spent more than 2,000 rupees and Mrs Calthorpe 5,000. He also stated that, not surprisingly, two of these merchants, Mookhtean Shah and Hadjie Abul, preferred cash to bank drafts. In all, it appears that Nicholson spent 2,320 rupees on items for Edwardes. This did not include the ponies, which were half the price of those that might be bought on the plains. A last-minute request from Emma Edwardes for a yellow long shawl elicited the response, 'Yellow is a very uncommon color here: so much so, that I cannot call to mind having seen a yellow shawl since my arrival.'[16]

## BACK IN THE PUNJAB

From March 1855 Nicholson had received a temporary promotion as officiating commissioner and superintendent of the Leiah division. But his heart was set on being in Peshawar under Edwardes. He had raised this off and on with varying degrees of assertion since September 1853. And as this last summer before the Mutiny passed slowly by, there were indications that this prospect might indeed be accomplished. Behind the scenes Henry Lawrence was pressing his brother John to keep Nicholson on the frontier not least because this departure would give 'a handle' to 'the opposition'.[17]

But, of course, no sooner had John Lawrence indicated that Nicholson could be transferred to Peshawar than Nicholson began to have second thoughts. On 12 August he wrote a long and rather silly letter to Edwardes expressing his reservations that the two of them working together in Peshawar might not work. And once again he resurrected his dream of leading an army of 5,000 carefully selected men with 'revolving rifles' to chase the Persians out of Eastern Persia. As always, Edwardes was kind and sensible in his reply, not least in his concern about Nicholson's health. All this immediately had a calming effect on his young disciple: 'I think you do yourself and me no more than justice when you say you believe our friendship would bear the weight of many huge hookums.'

Nicholson then went into a long list of things he would do and not do, including being ordered about, especially in relation to control of his beloved police. Concerning his health, he said that he was fine, 'with the exception of a very slight pain occasionally in the region of the liver; it causes me very little annoyance, but of course I don't like it there, and am anxious to get rid of it'. It is probable that the presence of Emma Edwardes was what really concerned Nicholson. Not that he did not like her, and she certainly liked him, but she was not beyond stirring him up by supporting him in his distrust of John Lawrence, something that led on more than one occasion to her being 'scolded' by her husband.

Nicholson in turn lavished Kashmiri cloth upon her. However, the prospect of working with Herbert and his wife close by could be unsettling for Nicholson. As events turned out, though, fortuitously given the deluge that was about to descent on British India, Emma would not remain in the Punjab much longer. In early October, Edwardes told his friend that Emma must, on doctor's advice, return to Britain for her health. In a very friendly note to her, Nicholson commented, 'I quite agree with you, that Herbert and I will make the prophets of evil hide their heads with shame at the powerlessness of their forebodings.' Emma's prediction was not far off the mark.

Brevet Lieutenant Colonel Nicholson was formally transferred as deputy commissioner to Peshawar on 29 October. Nicholson's feelings on leaving his Bannu appointment were reasonable enough:

> I do not believe I shall ever regret the change. The Bannoo appointment had many great advantages, but it had its drawbacks too – I think that though a little solitude is good for a man, I lived in too great seclusion at Bannoo,

Moreover I think it is good for me to be near a good friend, and though at Bannoo I have many friends in the common acceptation of the word, there is no one for whom I can say I feel much real affection or whom I would consult in any case of doubt or difficulty.

Strangely enough, an attack on Nicholson in the Lahore newspaper did not send him into a rage. He was criticised for conducting himself in Kashmir with 'a want of urbanity'.[18] But distrust of John Lawrence persisted and Edwardes worked hard to restrain Nicholson for his own good as much for the pointlessness of pressing claims on the chief commissioner. In doing so, Edwardes made several astute comments about the relationship of a chief commissioner with the military, as well as observing:

> The temper of the European officers of Iregr [Irregular] troops is quite different from that of officers of Regulars – the latter have nothg [nothing] to do and are supremely ignorant … The former have their hands full their heads too – They know their men, and the surrounding tribes and country – They are not quite Civil officers but they are next door to it, and they fraternise with the administration very tolerably … The Police are still the weakest point, but they are angels to what they were.

When Nicholson arrived in Peshawar in early November 1856 Edwardes was away on his important mission to negotiate with the Afghans, a process that would result in a peace being agreed that in no small part served to protect Britain's vulnerable Afghan frontier in the conflagration that was on the horizon. Edwardes wrote to his new deputy, wisely giving him carte blanche. Nicholson naturally took him at his word and was soon sniffing out an 'utterly corrupt and unprincipled' *thandar*, who was clearly exploiting the villagers in his district. He also caught out a *munshi* who transcribed official documents for petitioners at four annas a sheet – using half sheets and writing with large letters. Nicholson suggested one anna per half sheet was fair.[19] Nicholson was firmly of the belief that 'a man never gets the character of being corrupt, without reason'.

Unlike Taylor when he left Bannu, Nicholson received no word of thanks for all he had done there and this was now the subject of grumbling, with the spectre of John Lawrence surfacing again: 'I confess the conclusion I have come to, is that he wishes to lure me to stay in the Punjab, till he can find an opportunity of gratifying his revengeful feelings by superseding or disgracing me.' Even talk of the commissionership of Leiah did not mollify him. He carped on about the prospect of a treaty with the Afghans and perhaps military action against Persia. Edwardes accused him of sending Lawrence a threatening letter, to which he glibly replied that 'my subsequent letter … ought to have atoned for it'. To give Nicholson his due, however, he threw himself into his new responsibilities, even doing his homework and 'reading all the old political and border correspondence'.

Lawrence passed through Peshawar in late November on his way to meet Dosh Mohammad Khan, the Afghan emir. Lawrence was 'civil but nothing more' to Nicholson, but agreed to his going off to the hills to sort out problems and thus avoid having to attend the durbars that were part of the British–Afghan negotiations. It was not that Nicholson wanted to avoid the Afghans for any reason of embarrassment He had told Edwardes in June 1854, 'The Affghans have found out that I was one of the prisoners. I had a letter yesterday from a Gguznee Mulick with Sultan Jan in Khoorrum, reminding me of our acquaintanceship 13 years ago.'[20] When the negotiations concluded and the Afghan leaders were back across the border, Nicholson returned to Peshawar from his remote camp some 50 miles into the mountains.

That Christmas of 1856, the last before the Mutiny, Nicholson spent with the Edwardes. Other officers in their circle came in from outstations and with officers, wives and children a pleasant house party atmosphere prevailed. Nicholson was his usual quiet self when not alone with his small circle, but he seems to have enjoyed himself in his own way.

While Nicholson celebrated his last Christmas with his friend at Peshawar, Chamberlain was nearby on the frontier at Kohat. John Lawrence was firmly in control at Lahore. Henry Lawrence was in Lucknow, returned from his exile in Rajputana, where his brother George was now in charge. The amiable General Cotton was military commander of the district. All the actors were in place for the last great drama about to be played out in John Nicholson's life.

## THE CALM BEFORE THE STORM

The opening months of 1857 were quiet enough for Nicholson. He retained his suspicions of the malign intent of John Lawrence against him. Yet, when the prospect of a position in Oude surfaced, Nicholson backtracked about leaving the Punjab and threw the decision on the shoulders of Edwardes and Robert Montgomery, although reminding them that in the end he had not been given the commissionership of Leiah. Yet again, as in Bannu, Nicholson threw himself into his work and was forever riding around the district sorting out problems and laying down the law to any who annoyed him. While saying he had no ambition left, he spoke of being promoted so he could save some money and retire. He envied George Lawrence getting Rajputana and 5,000 ruprees. One piece of news greatly pleased him: 'Old Coke writes me that the Bunnoochees, well tamed as they have been, speak kindly and gratefully of me. I would rather have heard this than got a present of 1000 £, for there could be no stronger testimony of my having done my duty among them.'[21]

Emma Edwardes's departure meant that Herbert had to take some long leave in order to escort her personally to Calcutta to board the ship home. Nicholson became acting commissioner in Peshawar and Henry Brabazon Urmston the acting deputy commissioner. The separation from Edwardes was not good for Nicholson's morale. By 20 March 1857, he telegraphed Edwardes that he wanted out of the Punjab. Two letters followed laying out his complaints, which summarise his sense of John Lawrence's hostility and unfairness towards him and his own feelings on the general administrative system of rewards. Nicholson admitted that there was also a matter of pride 'which I *can't* conquer'. Not surprisingly, Edwardes wrote back a stern letter saying Nicholson's letter had pained him.

Nicholson asserted in reply that Lawrence 'has inflicted no real injury on me, either in worldly prospects or honour ... As for "praying for grace to forgive him" – I *cant* do it. It would be rank hypocrisy uttering the words, while so different a feeling was in my heart.'[22] Even with Edwardes' gentle guiding hand, Nicholson was not going to change.

Paradoxically, and as is often the case, before the great combustion, the months prior to the outbreak of the Great Rebellion were very quiet for Nicholson and his small circle in the Punjab. Indeed, a year later Herbert Edwardes would look back on that time before so many of his associates had died as idyllic. Nicholson appears even to have put pen to paper to his family more frequently in this period than he had, even venturing to express a passing interest in the (failed) fortunes of his cousin Lieutenant General James Macnaghten McGarel Hogg (1823–90), formerly of the Life Guards, in the general election campaign in Lisburn in April 1857. This cousin was Sir James Hogg's son and he was defeated by Jonathan Richardson of nearby Lambeg, possibly another Nicholson relative. In the true tradition of Lisburn, oft repeated before and since, there was a robust campaign verging on riotous behaviour. This resulted in the dean and his son having to take refuge in the hotel, preventing them from voting. According to Clara Nicholson, this resulted in James Hogg losing the election. When one sees that the difference between the candidates was a mere seven votes, Richardson gaining 138 against Hogg's 131, it appears as if Clara Nicholson might not have been far wrong. The Lisburn constituency electorate was a mere 296, with a 91 per cent turnout.[23]

The same month as the Lisburn election, Mary Nicholson wrote a frank letter to her brother from her home, which was now in High Roding Rectory at Dunmow in Essex, north of London. Nicholson could be quite touchy in his letters home, even occasionally putting his mother on the defensive. On one occasion she actually had to justify on what she had spent £200 John had sent home to her. Mary's response to such was simply to ignore the offending and gauche letter. Now, in April 1857, she replied to her brother in a tone that probably only she could get away with:

I know that you are not fond of letter writing, and perhaps I have been deterred from writing myself partly by the letters I used to send in days of yore never being answered, and partly by the idea that you criticized letters rather more severely than I felt that mine were able to bear. But now that you have made a begin-g, I hope you will fr time to time favour us with a letter, even if it be but a short one, and I promise you, it will be welcomed and valued. The large furs you were so kind to send me to hand safely.[24]

But this was not a new start. It was the beginning of the end.

# The Great Rebellion Breaks Out

Much attention has been paid in recent decades to the fact that what has been called the Indian Mutiny, the Great Uprising, the Great Rebellion or the First War of Independence was in fact something much more. More correctly, it was an uprising with widespread civil dissension, as detailed studies now emerging clearly indicate. This view, in fact, echoes the understanding of the most discerning European officers on the ground at the time. Yet such awareness does not exclude the fact that the core of this uprising was a serious military mutiny. An overwhelming majority of both the regular cavalry and infantry regiments in the Bengal army either mutinied or were suspected of planning insurrection and disarmed by the British authorities.

There were two sets of British forces in India, the Queen's army and the Company's armies (Bengal, Madras and Bombay), all falling under a single commander. The various senior commands were parcelled out between Queen's and Company officers. In 1854, for example, twelve of the seventeen army divisions, as well as thirty-one of the thirty-eight brigade commands, in India were under Company officers, the balance in each case being Queen's army officers. The ratio was about three to one in favour of the Company armies. In the case of the Bengal army, Company officers held six of the eight divisional commands and thirteen of the sixteen brigade commands.[1]

## PREVIOUS MUTINIES

'The English army in India came nearer his [the Duke of Wellington's] idea of what the Roman legions were than any troops which he had ever seen in his life,' the Peel Commission heard in December 1858. This was the evidence of Edward Law, earl of Ellenborough, who had been governor-general in the 1840s during the first Anglo-Afghan War when Sindh was annexed. Ellenborough added, 'I do not think that he confined his remark to the Europeans, but that as an army there was no army superior to the English army in India.'[2]

That said, there were regimental army mutinies in India in 1800, 1813 and 1843.[3] In May 1848 James Abbott had warned Nicholson that 'the whole or greater part of the army is in a plot to rise'.[4] This unrest appeared the following year with instability in five regiments. There was again some trouble during the second Anglo-Burma War of 1852.

An unpleasant row had broken out in 1849 between the governor-general, Lord Dalhousie, and the commander-in-chief in India, Sir Charles Napier. It centred on the relatively innocuous matter of Napier, fearing a mutiny was imminent in a regiment, waiving a regulation relating to compensation for rations. This was seized upon by the excitable Dalhousie as an example of Napier having usurped his position. Napier resigned. However, a series of acrimonious memoranda passed between Napier and Dalhousie. The British prime minister, the Duke of Wellington, and Nicholson's uncle, James Hogg, were dragged into the dispute. In an attempt to flatten Napier, the correspondence between the two antagonists was made public.[5]

What comes out of this is that Napier had no illusions about how the British stood on a knife edge in relation to its Indian army: 'There was the mutiny! 40,000 sepoys were more or less infected with this bad spirit: we were in the midst of a hostile population.'

That was six and a half years before the 1857 mutiny.[6]

## THE 1857 INSURRECTION

Three-quarters of the Company's Bengal Native Infantry regiments mutinied wholly or in part during the Great Uprising. All but three of the remaining regiments were disarmed or disbanded. Only three such regiments out of twenty-nine partially mutinied in the Company's Bombay army and none of the fifty-two regiments in the Company's Madras army.[7]

The cataclysm in Bengal was sparked for the British by rumours about the Enfield rifle cartridge being greased by taboo pig fat, which finally ignited the revolt in early 1857, in the very week that Dalhousie arrived back home in Britain at the end of his posting as governor-general.[8] His approach to India and the inhabitants of the presidencies had been by no means unique.

There had developed an inherent cruelty around the Company's rule. The lack of compassion in suppressing the Mutiny has been much discussed but it was not an overnight aberration. Indeed, even earlier in 1857 those who warned about the dangers of using the new cartridges were silenced as 'insufferable croakers'.[9]

Another fundamental element encouraging mutiny in the army was the simple fact that there were just too few European troops on the ground, especially in the Indian regiments. In addition, in 1855 the Bengal Army had only 75 per cent of its official European establishment of full strength (2,329 as opposed to 3,079). In the infantry regiments the percentage was about the same at 76 per cent (1,357 versus 1,776).[10] The actual as opposed to establishment staff is reflected in Graph 1.

*Graph 1*

*Actual/establishment figures for European officers in the Bengal Army, 1855*

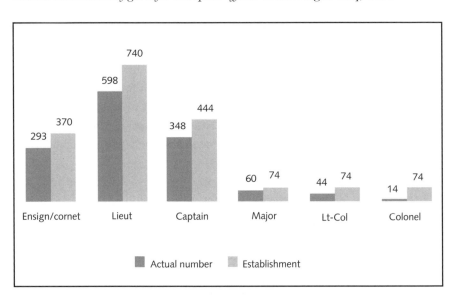

One intelligence report dated 7 August 1857 commented, 'The Sepoys thought, and (considering the rare appearance of a European Regiment) not unnaturally, that they formed the sole pillar of the Empire.'[11] Of the regiments that mutinied or were disarmed while in the Punjab between May and September 1857, approximately 23,000 troops were involved, of whom 1.5 per cent were European and 98.5 per cent Indian. It is difficult to judge whether the fact that a quarter of the army in the Punjab was on leave when the Mutiny broke out was beneficial or otherwise to the British.[12] In the whole of India, according to P.R. Singh, about 70,000 Indian troops took part in the insurrection.[13]

The British later recognised that this breakdown was a key factor in the nature and course of the insurrection. In 1844 the Bengal Army stood at about 127,000 men. Of these, 110,000 (88 per cent) were Indian and 16,000 (12 per cent) were European. By the 1870s in the Bengal presidency about 60 per cent of the troops were Indian and 40 per cent European.[14] But by then the British were recruiting heavily in the Punjab and frontier hill regions under the premise, real or imaginary, that the Sikhs in particular had largely been 'loyal' during the Great Rebellion. This assertion is questioned by many Indian historians today, probably correctly. At the very least, the alleged loyalty was neither uniform nor consistent, and very much depended on time and circumstance.[15] At the time, though, that is what the British thought and their trust in local Punjabi recruits meant that by the 1870s, of some 30,000 troops in the Punjab, there was approximately one European to every four Indian soldiers (27 per cent European and 73 per cent Indian). But in the rest of the Bengal presidency the ratio was nearly on a par, with 47 per cent European and 53 per cent Indian.[16] In the Bombay and Madras presidencies, the ratio of Europeans to Indians in the army was, as in the Punjab, about one to four. So after the Great Rebellion it was the Delhi/Ganga Valley region, which had been the heart of the insurrection, where European troops were particularly numerous.

Herbert Edwardes noted nearly a decade before the Great Rebellion:

If N.C.O.[s] do their duty, it is impossible for any mutiny to come to a head, for they live among the men; and at the first insubordinate word that is spoken, they would arrest the speaker, carry him before the Colonel, and draw down on him such punishment as would effectively deter others; at least if the Colonel is worth his salt.

The problem was that in the 1857 affair the British had lost the confidence and the trust of the Indian officers, so this disciplinary chain was already broken.[17]

The British trust in the Sikhs dated from nearly immediately after their defeat in the second Anglo-Sikh War. As early as June 1850, the adjutant general of the Bengal army pressed to be permitted to recruit Sikhs into infantry regiments. The Sikhs were already regarded by the British as a martial race, but successfully harnessing them to the imperial juggernaut only months after their being mortal enemies was quite remarkable.[18]

The focal point of the Mutiny was the greater Ganga or Ganges River valley, although many other parts of the subcontinent were affected to some degree or another. The British capital at Calcutta was relatively safe, despite such crises as Panic Sunday (14 June 1857), as were tracts of southern India and the Brahmaputra valley.[19] Another shock for the British would have been the broad-based support for the uprising. Neither religious differences between Hindu and Muslim nor caste divisions were predictors between mutineer or British loyalist, though a fair number of upper-caste Indians were in the thick of the insurgency movement. The military mutiny also affected and attracted large numbers of the north Indian population.

And yet the uprising was as much an anachronism as it was a progressive force. For a great many involved, it was looking back rather than a forward outward vision into the future. The bombardment of railway engines by a cannon at Allahabad had a Luddite feel about it. Recently India had changed rapidly in some respects. Vast tracts of territory had within the previous two decades come under foreign imperial rule – Oudh, Sindh and the Punjab – paradoxically advancing the creation of a united political entity. But this was superimposed on what was little more than a semi-feudal society. Added to the potent brew in recent decades was the spectre of an overlay of secular evangelicalism, Victorian mores and practices, with the threat of religious proselytisation to follow.

Landowning patterns, social conventions and political practices were all perceived to be undermined, in many cases with some justification. Vested interests and tradition were threatened. Even what might, in normal circumstances, be considered innocuous could cause suspicion, such as the arrival in the Punjab in early 1857 of the Anglican bishop of Madras to consecrate churches and cemeteries. Language was also threatened, despite the Company's rigorous policy regarding its European officer corps learning indigenous languages. The Indian world was being turned upside down, psychologically and physically.

The telegraph was advancing, as was road construction. As Herbert Edwardes pointed out in his post-Mutiny memorandum on the Punjab, by the time the Mutiny had broken out, thanks to the efforts of Limerick-born Sir William O'Shaughnessy (1809–89), 'the electric wire had in an incredibly short space of time, been laid down from one end of India to the other'. Something has been made in recent times of the fact that the telegraph system in India in the 1850s was not terribly efficient, which is no doubt true. Equally true is the fact that, at key moments, the telegraph was in a very real sense a lifeline for the British.[20] Frequently, 100 telegraphs were received and despatched from the chief commissioner's office at Lahore in a single day. Equally important, though, the telegraph's potential was not exploited by the insurgents, save in one rather bizarre attempt to make cannon from the iron sockets into which the wooden telegraph poles were placed to try and ward off insect attack, the telegraph wires being adapted as ammunition. But in the Punjab the telegraph line was not sabotaged on any scale.

The telegraph was broken from Delhi soon after hostilities commenced, as it was in much of the middle Ganges basis. It still operated in the Punjab, however. By being connected south to faraway Bombay, the Punjab was also linked to government headquarters in Calcutta.[21] And from as early as 17 June 1857 the telegraph was re-established between the British camp outside Delhi and the Punjab.[22] Telegraph stations were few and far between, but it was not unusual for a military column to include a mobile telegraphic station that could be attached to the wires.

Despite Captain Bouchier's assertion that carrying letters was a 'dangerous trade' during the Great Rebellion, the Punjab postal service was remarkably unaffected in many areas. The only major disruption was for a period of about twenty days in September 1857 in the Goorgaira district between Lahore and Multan. Disturbances there and in the Murree Hills near Lahore that month were put down without great difficulty. It is said that the postal service between the British camp on the Ridge in Delhi and the Punjab was uninterrupted throughout the crisis.[23]

The post carts trundled hither and yon, often at breakneck speed. As for the roads, the Grand Trunk Road was now far advanced in its route to Peshawar. Some areas in the Cis–Sutlej region were tarred. But bridges were badly needed and lengthy stretches of road in the Punjab were 'in a crude, half-finished state'. The road from the Sutlej River and the Beas River was in a poor way and that between Ferozepur and Lahore was 'unmade', so that 'it might hardly have been possible to take Delhi, at least during the autumn of 1857'.[24] Also assisting the British greatly was the flotilla of river vessels that plied between Karachi and Multan, bringing up to the Punjab three regiments of European cavalry, one of cavalry, fifty lakhs of treasure (£500,000), 'and a vast quantity of baggage and ammunition'.

As has often been pointed out, the loyalty of the rulers of Patiala, Jind and Nabha went beyond lending the British government in the Punjab more than seven lakhs.[25] Their own soldiers were sent to keep the main roads open and free of rebel forces, assisted on occasions by European troops. This was very important, not least because after the initial financial crisis, when European officers disarmed Indian regiments and the civil establishment pay fell three months in arrears, the British ensured its multi-regional and multi-ethnic army outside Delhi was paid regularly. Upwards of twenty lakhs of rupees was brought down by road from Lahore to service the army. During the Great Rebellion there was also a camel train operating between Karachi and Multan. This section was briefly closed in mid-September, but by the end of the month it had been reopened, with every European traveller being given a guard.

From Multan, the wagon train continued to the great military camp at Ferozepur and on to the Punjab capital of Lahore. This system operated from July to October 1857 and was said to have cost 97,317 rupees. There was also a daily wagon train organised from Delhi to Ambala, Ludhiana and Karnal, carrying the sick and wounded out of the Ridge encampment to Umballa and carrying in vast amounts of ordnance for the gun batteries and ammunition for the troops.[26]

The British, and Nicholson in particular, soon came to realise what a rich harvest could be gleaned by intercepting mail bags and checking the contents for seditious letters being sent between mutineers and even those not directly involved in the uprising but sympathetic to its cause. That they were in Hindi, Urdu or Persian was no barrier thanks to the Company's rigorous language policy for officers. During the five months that Nicholson survived into the Mutiny there never was a period when he was not able to communicate with whomever he chose, although admittedly he would have used military riders at times. But letters invariably got through to their destination unscathed.

The very real prospect of a railway network was on the horizon in 1857. Although at the time of the outbreak of the insurgency, there was only about 300 miles of railway in existence, a further 3,628 miles had been approved and was under construction.[27]

## PEASANT REVOLT, MASS MOVEMENT OR CIVIL WAR?

Peasant farmers tended to follow their leaders, even when alien, or at least tried to remain neutral. A great many may not have had any particular love for the British, but many remained passive in the eye of the storm. Like the peasant Clubmen during the seventeenth-century English Civil War, their attitude was 'leave us alone and a plague on all your houses'. In certain regions, however, the insurgents were supported widely and in others the traditional leaders stood firmly behind the British. William Forbes-Mitchell observed, 'it needed no great powers of observation to fully understand that the whole population of Oude was against us.'[28] Hugh Gough remarked how the inhabitants of villages in the vicinity of Delhi 'turned out against us and here and there shots were fired at us'. Robert Montgomery noted how 'lawless' were many of the villages in the Punjab.[29] And Lieutenant Roberts, writing from Bulandshahr, south-west of Delhi, was quite frank with his mother:

> What nonsense *The Times* talks about the Mutiny being confined to the Army. In this district there never was Army … With scarely an exception, all the Police and Native Civil Authorities joined at the very commencement, and many independent Rajahs raised their Standards against us. Every villager tore down European houses and robbed their property.[30]

But in some settlements villagers were very often more than willing to round up and hand over rebels, or indeed put them to death themselves. In August 1857, Sir John Lawrence observed, 'though the country [the Punjab] is friendly, we have a long border to guard, and, above all, upwards of 20,000 Hindustani soldiers to guard. The majority of these men are desperate.'[31]

It was the slightly better off who had more of a grudge against the new world being imposed upon them. And as is the way of things, their alienation might come down to relatively minor changes in taxation or the operation of the judiciary. In the Punjab, for example, after 1 May 1857 the period when magistrates would hear suits for bond debts was arbitrarily cut from debts of twelve years' standing to six years.[32]

Then there is the issue of following a mass movement and the psychology surrounding that. Hugh Gough recounted how when a regiment rose in revolt, a body of Indian troops had stood by him and escorted him to within sight of the Artillery mess and safety, then stopped and turned back. When Gough tried to persuade them to stay with him, 'They told him it was impossible for them to separate themselves from their friends and relatives, and making the officer they had so carefully protected a respectful salaam, they rode off to join their mutinous comrades.' Another case of apparent hesitation or inconsistency was at Ferozepur, where on 14 May, 'the sepoy guard, true in this respect to their trust, had procured a cart, taken the treasure to the fort, there handed it over to the officer at the gate, and then started for Delhi'.[33]

By late July 1857, it was said that even in the Punjab 'placards of an inflammatory nature were posted in every village'.[34] After it was all over, Herbert Edwardes was to write, 'The valley of Peshawur, then, at the beginning of the eventful month of May, stood in a ring of repressed hostilities.' In fact, two fundamental factors dictated British success in retaining their grasp on the Punjab. First, they pacified disgruntled elements, or at least restrained sufficient

Afghans, Pakhtuns and Sikhs in the crucial opening months of the conflict. The reasons for this varied: realpolitik; a vague sympathy for the British in some quarters; a wait and see how the dice fall attitude; or a crude 'my-enemy's-enemy-is-my-friend' attitude.

Second, the calibre of British commanders in the Punjab and their neo-seventeenth-century values, whether by intimidation or respect, caused many to pause. As Roberts wrote to his mother, Nicholson was 'about the best man in India'.[35]

But there is another factor seldom mentioned in the revisionist debate. The 1857 uprising would not have failed had it received universal support. An interesting statistic has survived that tells a lot about continuity in time of crisis: in 1857 in the Punjab 99,146 people were vaccinated for smallpox.[36] Life did go on. In addition, a tangible cohort of fighting men from the Punjab either remained loyal to or grew attached to the British cause during the conflict. This latter factor was invariably linked to a personal loyalty to such commanders as Nicholson.

Finally, and often airbrushed from the history books of the post-formal imperial world, there were those not inconsequential number of Indians who actively or passively supported the British. And, like the black troops in Europe's twentieth-century colonial armies and the nineteenth-century Catholic nationalist Irish in the British army and the Irish constabulary forces, their story is awkward and is consequently passed over as quickly as possible, if mentioned at all. The harsh reality was that in India, as in much of the anti-imperial crusade, the struggle was both that and also a civil war.

## THE LEGAL POSITION

The punishment for mutiny in time of war was more often than not death, be it under martial law, operational by September 1857, or the Articles of War, which preceded that. The Indian Legislative Council in Calcutta had on occasion passed updated articles of war: in 1840 and then again in 1844 when the 64th Bengal Native infantry under Major General George Hunter mutinied in Upper Scinde. When the 1857 Mutiny broke out, the Bengal army was operating under Act 19 of 1847. On 16 May 1857, this was revised, allowing for not only generals but 'other Officers having the command of Troops' to establish district or garrison courts martial, the death sentence being permitted by a majority vote of the court. An act passed by the Legislative Council of India (Act 11 of June 1857) prescribed the death penalty, transportation or hard labour 'upon conviction' for anyone who rebelled or waged war against the queen. Act 14 of 6 July permitted European officials to execute any Indian suspected of fermenting insurrection.[37] And a proclamation issued on 10 July offered generous awards for those who turned in insurgents.[38] But in the Punjab things went further. As one report noted:

> One of the first measures of the Punjab authorities was to empower the local officers to try and punish summarily, even with death, offences affecting the public safety. Shortly afterwards there arrived from Calcutta the Legislative Acts, authorising such like measures being taken.[39]

In addition, a proclamation was issued by Edwardes in Peshawar asserting that any deserter might be killed wherever found in the district, and the property on his person be appropriated by the captor. This led to dozens of mutineers being butchered by villagers, but more significant, as Edwardes admitted, 'destroyed all confidence between the soldiery and the people'.[40] It may well have been this proclamation to which Sir John Lawrence referred in August, assuring the governor-general that he was 'not aware of any proclamation having been issued in the Punjab, offering a reward for men, dead or alive', something he regarded as 'objectionable'.[41] Another impetus to British officers to take the law into their own hands came from Robert Montgomery, the judicial commissioner at Lahore, who issued an edict that 'any two British officers could sentence to death any person who broke the law, and then carry out the order'.[42]

## THE PUNJAB

The Afghans had in the not too distant past controlled large areas of the Punjab and might well have taken this opportunity to regain what they could well consider to be theirs, extracting revenge at the same time for the first Anglo-Afghan war of sixteen years earlier. That the British held the Punjab, despite serious outbreaks of trouble, was in no small part due to the inactivity, if not quasi-support, of the Afghans. Edwardes described the Afghans at this time as:

> vultures smelling the corpse of a battlefield, and their wings are trembling for a swoop. Dost Muhommud restrains them hitherto ... I never knew so little crime, or so much good-will on the frontier, during the four years I have had charge of it.

Or, as one report commented drily, 'there was no leisure for common crime'. For whatever reason, the Anglo-Afghan treaties of March 1855 and January 1857 held. Perhaps, as one commentator observed, this was because the 'fiercer spirits' who might have caused the British trouble were 'drained off to serve abroad' in the 'popular expedition' as part of the upcoming fight at Delhi. It should also not be forgotten that from January 1857 the British were paying Dost Muhommud a subsidy of one lakh ($£10,000$) a month to help him defend his border with Persia, a development that saw Harry and Peter Lumsden and Dr Bellew forming a British mission in Kandahar.[43] The subsequent evacuation of the Afghan city of Herat by the Persians in July 1857 was also 'most fortunate for our [British] interests'. And circumstance was all, as one British official noted, 'the moment that the Punjabees heard of the fall of Delhi, their doubts regarding the stability of our rule vanished, their respect for our prestige revived, and they became as good subjects as ever'.[44]

When the rebellion first broke out, there were in the Punjab 36,000 Indian Company troops and 10,500 European troops (eleven infantry regiments, three cavalry and 2,000 artillerymen). A large number of the European troops were, like Nicholson, Irish. Sir Patrick Cadell estimated that at the time of the Great Rebellion 'considerably more than half' of the European troops were Irish.[45] In the Punjab the European–Indian ratio was about 1 to 3.4, although the statistic is misleading because other factors came into play. From the British perpective, they soon lost three infantry regiments and one cavalry regiment, ordered south to join the British force outside Delhi. That reduced their numbers to 7,500 European troops, or a ratio of 1 to 4.4 in favour of the insurgents. But there also needs to be added to the British side 13,551 local Punjabi troops, only about a quarter of whom were from Bengal, plus the 9,234 military police, giving the British a boost of about 20,000 men whose loyalty could largely be depended upon. This was before raising thousands of local levies from the Punjab and eastern Afghanistan. Excluding these levies reduced the ratio to 1 to 1.3 in favour of the rebels. Of course, this excludes both quality of troops or the crippling levels of sickness among European troops as the monsoon and summer heat arrived in northern India.

This is not to underestimate the challenge facing the British, but it did mean that, precarious as the peace in the Punjab and the frontier hills was, nonetheless, the British were still a force to be reckoned with. As illustrated in Table 1, what the British had to face in the Punjab in a sixteen-week period between May and August 1857 were nine different sets of mutinies involving eleven infantry regiments and three light cavalry regiments or wings of regiments. To this figure should be added the four cavalry regiments and eighteen infantry regiments that were disarmed. Taking into account the hapless 26th Native Infantry, which was disarmed and then mutinied, the British in the Punjab therefore lost thirty-six regiments or parts of regiments, being seven cavalry and twenty-nine infantry regiments.

Table 1:[46] Regiments in the Punjab that Mutinied or were Disarmed (May to August 1857)

| Date | Place mutinied or disarmed | Regiment(s) | Dis-armed | Mutinied | Outcome |
|---|---|---|---|---|---|
| 13 May | Lahore | 8th Light Cavalry<br>16th NI<br>26th NI*<br>49th NI | 277<br>744<br>845 | | 26th NI mutinied 11 weeks later on 30 July. |
| 13/14 May | Ferozepur | 45th NI<br>57th NI | | 886<br>913 | Most escaped. |
| 21 May | Murdan and Nowshera | 55th NI | | 1,091 | Nearly all killed. |
| 22 May | Peshawar | 5th Light Cavalry<br>24th NI<br>27th NI<br>51st NI* | 407<br>896<br>640<br>732 | | *51st: See 28 Aug |
| 26 May | Nowshera | 10th Irregular Cavalry | 585 | | Refused to act against mutineers so disbanded. |
| 3 June | Abasye | 64th NI | | A section garrisoning the fort. | The remainder of the regiment was distributed to various frontier outstations. Many sent back to their homes. |
| 7/8 June | Jullundur Doab | 6th Light Cavalry<br>3rd NI<br>61st NI<br>36th NI | | 380<br>c. 100<br>953<br>767 | Escaped to Delhi. |
| 10 June | Multan | 62nd NI<br>69th NI | ?<br>882 | | |
| 15 June | Amballa | 5th NI | | | |
| 25 June | Phillaur | 33rd NI (Hilliarka Pulteen)<br>35th NI | 816<br>(partial mutiny) | 887<br>? | |
| 7 July | Rawalpindi | 14th NI*<br>58th NI | Part<br>590 | | *14th: See 7/8 July |

| 7/8 July | In their lines at Jhelum | 14th NI | | 722 | Nearly all killed or captured. |
|---|---|---|---|---|---|
| 8 July | Amritsar | 59th NI | ? | | |
| 9 July | Sialkot | 9th Light Cavalry (right wing) 46th NI | | 241 916 | Nearly all killed. |
| 12 July | Hoshiarpur and Noorpur | 4th NI | ? | | |
| 14 July | Derajat | 39th NI | 820 | | |
| 15 July | Ambala | 4th Light Cavalry | 259 | | |
| 30 July | Lahore | 26th NI | | 907 | Nearly all killed. |
| 19 August | Ferozepur | 10th Light Cavalry | | 334 | Escaped. |
| 28 August | Peshawar | 51st NI (already disarmed) | | 732 | Nearly all killed. |
| 21 Sept | Indus River | 9th Irregular Cavalry (partial) | | 29 | 23 killed. |

Regiments that remained loyal to the British in the Punjab and which were not disarmed include the 21st Native Infantry; the Kelat-i-Ghilzie Regiment; and seven corps of Irregular Cavalry, (1st, 2nd, 6th, 7th, 16th, 17th and 18th Regiments).[47]

Peshawar was the frontier garrison headquarters for British India. Ten regiments were stationed there, according to Saul David – two of European infantry, five of Indian infantry, one of light cavalry and two of irregular cavalry – as well as four batteries of European artillery. Members of the famous Punjab Irregular force were found in outposts.[48] In May 1857, Charles Nicholson went to visit his brother John at Peshawar, staying for ten days.[49] Writing afterwards to his sister Mary from Kohat on 10 May, the day the Mutiny broke out at Meerut, Charles comments that he had not seen his brother in some time and was clearly shocked:

John is not looking so well as he did when I saw him a year ago, his general health is not bad but hard work in this climate is undoubtedly telling on him. He talks of going home for good in 2 years when he will be entitled to his Captain's pension, but I hope he won't because his prospects [?] then that with no employment and very limited income he would not be happy after the active life he has led all the same I quite agree with him that no position or income can compensate one for living in this country if you can afford to live out of it, now in two years time he may have money eno [enough] to live quietly at home as a bachelor but certainly not as a married man, and I should be very sorry indeed if he were to resign himself to the former unhappy lot for the sake of getting out of India.

It is clear that Charles Nicholson did not think his brother to be homosexual. As for his appearance, maybe John Nicholson's advancing baldness may have helped change his appearance somewhat. To that must be added also the harsh outdoor existence he led, the unhealthy, indeed poisonous, cocktail of drugs he took, along with tobacco and some liquor. Charles himself was not feeling too grand and had told his mother that he might take a break and go up to Kashmir to recuperate.[50]

## BRUTALITY

To Nicholson, the Mutiny was a straightforward enough matter. His view was:

> Neither greased cartridges, the annexation of Oude, nor the paucity of European officers were the causes. For years I have watched the army, and felt sure they only wanted their opportunity to try their strength with us.[51]

He was equally convinced that the only way to deal with the uprising was to crush it. He was not alone in thinking this. Young Lieutenant Roberts wrote to his mother on 14 May 1857, 'All confidence in the native Army is at an end, and the most decided measures and strenuous exertions will only save India now.'

There is an impression that Nicholson was in charge of mass executions and present at them. But of 525 executions carried out in the Peshawar district during the Mutiny, he was present in the region for only sixty-five, or 12 per cent. He did kill numbers of the 55th Regiment, but that was in the field of battle during the regiment's retreat. However, we do know he executed prisoners when he commanded the Moveable Column. One must not forget, however, that by then carte blanche had been given to villagers to massacre any army deserters – something that they appear to have had no difficulty in doing on at least on three or four occasions. Chamberlain had held courts martial, specifically drumhead courts. Nicholson, though, largely dispensed with these and what he regarded as their predictable consequences, adopting the dictum, 'The punishment of mutiny is death', or, as Frederic Cooper put it, Nicholson's motto was 'à la lanterne'.[52] Even so, Nicholson did at times call a drumhead court. Whether he was wont to go to his tent and weep after such executions is another of Wilberforce's comments that must be treated with scepticism. But there is no doubt that Nicholson did have prisoners executed without any form of trial or hearing.

This mindset was not confined to the British. Woe betide any 'Khaki' soldier who fell into enemy hands. It was reported that one soldier captured outside Delhi was 'tied up and so severely beaten by men of the Nimach platoon that his whole body was in bits'.[53]

Neville Chamberlain was more of a disciplinarian than Nicholson, whose determination to enforce regulation was, unlike Chamberlain, tempered by a quaint, romantic – patronising perhaps – regard for the hill people. This extended even to the Afghans, whom he roundly denounced on many occasions, but with whom he was on excellent terms when they were in any troop he commanded.[54]

Nicholson was a very different character from either the vindictive General Neill or the rather sinister Captain Hodson. It is interesting, incidentally, to note that Nicholson disapproved of Hodson and his methods, and Captain Trotter referred to Nicholson and Hodson as 'worthy rivals'. One account has Hodson smiling as he slashed down sepoy after sepoy. There are no diary entries about Nicholson smiling as he struck down men in battle. That Edwardes and Hodson did not get on might also have influenced Nicholson, at least up to a point.[55]

Nicholson's approach on retribution is shown in a letter to Sir John Lawrence:

> I think, however, that there are Corps to whom it would be neither just nor politic to refuse pardon ... some regiments were positively the victims of circumstances and could not have held out any longer. We cannot, if we would annihilate the whole force now in arms against us ... and it is not wise, all things considered, to make every man desperate.[56]

Three forms of execution were employed by the Bengal army: hanging, shooting and the old Indian practice, adopted by the Bengal army, of 'blowing away' from the mouth of a cannon. The last of these shocked contemporary Victorian Britain and continues to shock readers today. It has been associated in particular with Nicholson, though there is no evidence to show that he employed this form of execution more than any other commanding field officer. While Nicholson did not object to this method of execution, the fact that he was eventually advising against it is generally forgotten – although in typical Nicholson style, he claimed this was because such executions wasted too much valuable gunpowder.

It has to be said that the insurgents themselves were not beyond reviving this old Mughal practice, either, no less so than they were at blowing human heads out of cannons, as was the fate of Major Burton, the political agent at Kota.[57] One of George Barnes's secret despatches to Lawrence in Lahore dated 19 July 1857 records, 'Ranji Dass reports that cow killing in the city [Delhi] had begun. But the King has ordered that anyone guilty of killing a cow shall be blown away from guns.'[58]

It is important to note that Nicholson's reputation for ferocity was based primarily on his actions on the battlefield. That ferocity is unquestionable. It is also unquestionable that he took a different attitude to prisoners of war in the Anglo-Sikh conflicts from that to mutinous Bengal army troops in the Great Rebellion. The latter in his book had no rights. The Roman diktat on dealing with mutiny, 'Flog the ranks and throw the leaders off the Tarpeian Rock', did not hold sway. To Nicholson, mutiny meant death, regardless of rank.

This was not, however, the attitude of many of the Bengal army's regimental colonels. They tended not to be of the type of the evangelical new British order. Slow and too often elderly, or at least old before their time, they frequently possessed a touching blind faith and trust in their men – and with some reason. They had led their men through the war in Afghanistan and against the powerful Sikh army. They understood how the Mutiny unleashed a human tragedy. It brought with it all the hallmarks of a civil war: bitterness, feelings of betrayal, desire for revenge, and raw prejudice all coming to the fore.

From the British point of view, several factors came into play. The Mutiny was a shock; it came out of the blue and it was seen in simple terms as a betrayal. To this was linked the Victorian attitude towards the concept of sanctity of 'women and children', exemplified five years earlier with the sinking of *Birkenhead* and the accompanying legendary 'Women and children first' command. In fact, given the total number of people killed in this conflict, European women and children were a very small minority. The civilian killings at Cawnpore did run into hundreds of women and children, and those at Delhi and Jhansi each exceeded 100, while at Meerut they numbered fifteen and at Agra, ten. So the total was in the region of 1,000.

Nicholson's nose for insurrection had a certain seventeenth-century covenanter ring about it. As he trusted few in life anyway, he was not encumbered by the sentimentality of those sepoy regimental colonels. Interestingly, Lieutenant Roberts at the time wrote of the causes of the Great Rebellion, 'The fact is, no one knows what it is. A combination of affairs I believe, but the Musalmans are at the bottom of it.'[59] Harry Gough was more of a cynic, noting that at Meerut after mutiny had erupted, the rebels showed no qualms about entering the arsenal, taking and using the controversial cartridges.

Nicholson had utter contempt for those colonels who preached restraint and moderation. From the start, he saw the struggle against the mutineers as a uncompromising fight to the end – as Forbes-Mitchell correctly observed, *guerre à la mort*. And the truth is that the mutineers would have agreed with them. On 29 May, John Lawrence, writing from Rawalpindi to Chamberlain, noted optimistically, 'Vaughan gives a much more hopeful account than Nicholson.'[60] But the proclamation issued that day promised hope for those mutineers who gave up their arms and had not been 'guilty of heinous crimes against private persons' who would be allowed 'to go to their homes unmolested'.[61]

During the Mutiny, Nicholson kept up a constant, nearly daily correspondence with the chief commissioner, Sir John Lawrence. The themes of these letters varied but boiled down to Nicholson often trying to push the boundaries of his authority. They also served as a vehicle to let off steam and vent his frustration, offering juicy meat to any detractors. Lawrence also found it difficult to express gratitude and warmth. He was cautious and quick to criticise. He lacked diplomatic skills in handling difficult people such as Nicholson. Many remembered how he had outmanoeuvred his own brother Henry when the Punjab troika had broken up. Even at the height of the Mutiny, we find Edwardes writing to Nicholson:

> Never through the whole of this struggle has John [Lawrence] said an encouraging word of all my labours – of snubs I have got my share. I do him justice in it – believe it to be his way and idiosyncrasy – and I think only of his good qualities; – but it cannot but crush real zeal … I have come to a much more sober feeling as to my own fame; and could endure a world of injustice now without writing 2 vols [*A Year on the Punjab Frontier*] to prove myself a wonderful fellow.[62]

In the same letter Edwardes, clearly answering a question from Nicholson, comments:

> No. I have never heard one adverse criticism on any of yr proceedings since you got the command, but I mix little in society. Those Officers I meet at the Generals all seem very kindly disposed to you – and I suppose they draw that feeling from all they hear in private letters.[63]

## THE COUNCIL OF WAR

Edwardes returned to Peshawar in the first week of May. He found Nicholson 'looking much better than when we left him'. The following week, on 10 May the Indian Mutiny broke out. Interestingly, that day Nicholson, writing to his mother, observed, 'I dare say you will have seen in the papers that the Native Infantry of the army are in a bad way.'[64] On the evening of the 11th Edwardes and Nicholson were dining together in the bungalow they now shared when an orderly burst in with a fateful telegram. This read:

> The sepoys have come in from Meerut and are burning everything. Mr Todd is dead and we hear several Europeans. We must shut up.

When the first news of the Mutiny broke, Chamberlain was not too far off at Kohat with his frontier force and rode into Peshawar in the early hours of Wednesday, 13 May in time for a council of war at 11 a.m. The very make-up of that initial council of war illustrates the strength of the leadership that the British processed on its North-West Frontier and which the insurgents were to face in the Punjab. Present were:

Brigadier Sydney Cotton, military commander, aged 64.
Brigadier Neville Chamberlain, Punjab Irregular Frontier Force, 37.
Colonel Herbert Edwards, commissioner, 37.
Colonel John Nicholson, deputy commissioner, 34.
Major-General Thomas Reed, president of the council of war, 61.

In attendance to record the decisions of the council were Captain Wright and Lieutenant Roberts.

Nicholson and Roberts had first met the previous month when the young lieutenant found himself camped at the hill station Cherat, 34 miles south-east of Peshawar. Returning from an expedition to survey for water supplies, Roberts found Nicholson's patrol force camped beside him. The young man was invited for dinner. It is interesting to note that Roberts' autobiography published forty years later contains considerably more comment about Nicholson than do his letters home at the time of the Mutiny. In it Roberts asserted:

> Nicholson impressed me more profoundly than any man I had ever met before, or have met since. I have never seen anyone like him. He was the beau-ideal of a soldier and a gentleman. His appearance was distinguished

and commanding, with a sense of power about him which to my mind was the result of his having passed so much of his life amongst the wild and lawless tribesmen, with whom his authority was supreme.[65]

Reed was a veteran of the battle of Waterloo who had commanded in the Sutlej, Madras and Ceylon. Freddy Roberts no doubt echoed the common perception that Reed was not thought much of, but that he did 'listen to reason'.[66] Because of ill health, Reed was to yield command of the Delhi siege operation to General Henry Barnard.[67] As commander-in-chief, Reed was soon conveniently out of harm's way at Rawalpindi and well under John Lawrence's thumb.

The situation facing the senior officers in Peshawar was a simple one. They were not only outnumbered but fewer than 10 per cent of the European troops were cavalry, whereas nearly 20 per cent of the Indian troops were cavalry. In Peshawar, the total breakdown was 2,800 European troops and 8,000 sepoys. So from the outset, the British had two fundamental problems: the number of Indian troops who were likely hostile to them and a shortage of cavalry. The matter of artillery and field guns was less serious. There were about 146 guns in the region (eighteen being at Peshawar) of which European regiments, horse artillery and batteries controlled about 60 per cent. But the remaining 40 per cent (sixty-two guns) were frequently, for very practical reasons, not taken by mutinous troops who rose in revolt and left their regimental lines.

The idea of a military moveable or flying column to operate within the Punjab had been Nicholson's. He suggested it first to Edwardes and then to Chamberlain. Nicholson clearly wanted the position. It was his ideal posting: constantly on the move, lots of fighting, pretty well independent of command. But Nicholson was relatively junior and Chamberlain, Cotton, and Edwardes also all saw good prospects of gung-ho glory in the position. By the end of the council of war, it had been agreed:

General Reed as chief military commander in the Punjab transferred to Lahore, so all civil and military establishments would be in the same place.

Brigadier Chamberlain to consult with Sir John Lawrence.

The removal of the existing Indian garrison at the fort at Attock and their substitution by a more reliable one under Futteh Khan Khuttuck and 100 Pakhtuns.

Establishment of a Moveable Column at Jhelum with General Cotton in command.

Colonel Nicholson to be political officer attached to the Moveable Column.

All this was agreed upon, with the exception of the last two, which were flatly refused by Lawrence, something that cannot have endeared him any further to Nicholson.[68] Lawrence advised that General Cotton could not be spared from Peshawar and that Chamberlain must lead the column. Calcutta had to approve the column formally but this was pre-empted when news of what had transpired at the council of war leaked and became the talk of Peshawar. The proposal had been officially telegraphed to Lawrence and, as a morale booster, to the commanding British officer at every Punjab station.

For reasons that are unclear, Nicholson suspected Roberts to be the source of the leak. He stormed into the young officer's quarters and accused him. Roberts was a small man and Nicholson large, so it was a frightening ordeal for the 24-year-old artillery lieutenant. But he stood his ground and slowly Nicholson's anger abated. Soon these two strange figures were rushing together down to the town's telegraph office. Here a second interrogation took place, with the young telegraphist denying that he had told anyone the contents of the important message to Lawrence. But he soon cracked under Nicholson's stare and was given a severe dressing down.[69]

Of course, Nicholson then had a conscience about having accused young Roberts unfairly and, if Roberts' memoir is to be believed, from then on the two were close. This indeed seems to have been the case for on several occasions Nicholson took Roberts along with him on his latest exploit. Roberts was with Nicholson in the column for a while.

And ironically, as will be seen later, in the heat of battle in the dusty hot city of Delhi, it would be Freddie Roberts who found the wounded and abandoned John Nicholson.

Edwardes and Nicholson worked closely together to consolidate the British position in Peshawar. This was facilitated by the fact that the two shared the same bungalow, not far from the officers' mess.[70] The arrangement not only worked but also helped pull Nicholson out of his now all-too-regular fits of depression. However, as matters for the British grew more and more dire, Nicholson became more and more buoyant and animated. The Victorian hagiographers were not completely wrong when they spoke of Nicholson's hour having arrived.

With him throughout this dramatic time was Nicholson's 'medieval squire', as Charles Allen refers to Muhammad Hayat Khan. As well as being Nicholson's shadow, he was also, and most certainly not by chance, superintendent or darogah of police in Peshawar. The two men ransacked the postbags searching for evidence of subversion. When they found several such letters, they were taken away to be shown to Edwardes.[71]

Reed and Chamberlain set off for Rawalpindi on 14 May. Reed would set up his new command post and Chamberlain needed sage advice on the column from Lawrence. Edwardes followed the next day, leaving Nicholson in charge of Peshawar. Edwardes was away for what proved a long week, returning on the 21st.

Edwardes telegraphed Nicholson from Rawalpindi to say he had received permission to increase the Multan levies from 1,000 horsemen to 2,000, as well as 2,000 irregular foot soldiers. The proclamation establishing this force and appealing for volunteers went out under the joint names of Edwardes and Nicholson, for as Edwardes conceded, 'the Khans in the Derajut were as much his [Nicholson's] friends as mine'. Even so, recruitment was slow initially. Ever practical, the Pakhtun chiefs were waiting to see how things developed.

On both 15 and 16 May, Nicholson felt obliged to write to his mother to put her mind at rest about what would soon be alarming reports on India appearing in the Irish newspapers:

> I wrote you fully yesterday, via Kurachee, but lest the letter should not reach Bombay in time for the mail of the 28th, I write a few lines via Agra, to say I am quite well, and that the Punjab is perfectly quiet.
>
> I hope this will find you enjoying yourself at some sea-bathing place. There have been disturbances among the native troops in the N.W. Provinces, but they have not extended to the Punjab, and I trust are not likely to do so. Charles also is well ... [72]

With Edwardes away from 17 to 21 May, Nicholson was not one to leave things as they were in Peshawar. He was spoiling for a fight with the locals as his precious Multani horsemen had been 'much taunted in the city'. Nicholson had no doubts about who was at fault. Among his horsemen were men of some rank in their own society. They were not a rabble. He asked Edwardes to find 'a fitting victim' and suggested the newspaper editor. With Edwardes now away, Nicholson quickly had the police arrest the Persian editor of a local newspaper for publishing 'lies' that the Khelat-i-Ghilzai regiment had killed their European officers and that the irregular troops had mutinied. [73]

Late on the evening of 19 May, Nicholson ensured that the Indian guard on the treasury at the Residency was changed to a European one. Early next morning Nicholson had the whole of the treasure, some twenty-four lakhs, moved in one batch and under heavy guard of the 5th Light Cavalry and the Queen's 79th Regiment into the fort, Nicholson wryly noting that a spy he placed in the escort reported that one of the Indian officers had 'talked treason the whole way to the fort'.[74]

Nicholson also telegraphed Edwardes, warning him that treasonable correspondence had been intercepted between troops in Peshawar and an outstation, and urging Sir John Lawrence to agree to a 2,000-strong local levy being raised. He thanked Edwardes for sending him some snuff, though could not refrain from adding, 'I suppose there was no 'Princes mixture'. He also asked for his Omerzye horse, as 'I don't know when the grey will be fit for work again.' After the Mutiny, Edwardes wrote out a captured rebel letter, which stated that the hated new musket cartridges would be handed out at Peshawar on 21 May: 'Here all the Sepoys are at the bidding of Jumunnadan Soobuhdan Buherdoor and Hawildan Major. All are discontent with this business, whether small or great. What more need be written? Do as you think best. High and low send their obeisance, benediction, salutation, and service.' And in another hand on the same letter is added, 'The above is the state of here. In whatever way you can manage it, come in to Peshawur on the 21st instant – Thoroughly understand that point! In fact eat there and drink here!'[75]

Nicholson also had a 'Mahomedan "faqueer"' thrown into jail for carrying in his armpit a cryptic, suspected seditious document written in Persian and for being in possession of forty-six shiny new rupees. What was a religious man doing with such wealth if not inciting trouble? The unfortunate fellow was subsequently put before a commission and then hanged.[76] Dr James Graham in Sailkot, and soon to be the late Dr Graham, formerly of Lisburn, wrote approvingly to his cousin of Nicholson's strong line: 'This decisive mode of treating mutiny is what is wanted. Act now on their fears and trust not on their forbearance.'[77]

Edwardes was back in Peshawar on 21 May. Nicholson had little news to comfort him. Thanks to a spy called Narain, who worked for an assistant commissioner, G.E. Wakefield, a clear enough picture had been gained by Nicholson about what was going on. He even had details of a meeting of representatives of the 24th, 27th and 51st regiments that had been held under a tree on the north side of the cantonment. The comparative numbers of Europeans and Indians were discussed, as was the fact that only the 21st Regiment seemed to hold firm against their schemes.

Edwardes found Nicholson 'immersed in cares and anxieties'. Both Edwardes and Nicholson lay on their beds that night of 21/22 May, fully dressed waiting for news of trouble. About midnight came the intelligence that the Naushera troops were about to rise and that there was to be a rising in

Peshawar the coming day. Though they did not know it at the time, there were mutinies and civilian casualties at Bulandshahr on the 21st and Mainpuri on the 22nd. Edwardes and Nicholson set off together through the dark streets to General Cotton's house. Entering his bedroom, they awoke the sleeping man and told him what they had heard.[78]

The situation was grim indeed for the British. To set off in pursuit of the supposed Naushera mutineers would be to leave their backs exposed to suspect regiments in Peshawar. General Cotton, as much as Nicholson, could see that a precautionary measure was better than this evil when most of the European troops were out of Peshawar. The Indian Peshawar regiments then included: 5th Light Cavalry, 21st Bengal Native Regiment, 24th Bengal Native Infantry, 27th Bengal Native Infantry and 51st Bengal Native Infantry.

These numbered in the region of 3,400 Indian officers and men.[79] It should be noted that these regiments included Nicholson's own 27th Native Infantry Regiment. Some regiments or parts of regiments, such as the 39th, 55th and the 64th, had been sent to outstations in the vain hope that they would remain quiet away from revolutionary influences.

After Edwardes's and Nicholson's sleepless night, the Peshawar suspect regiments were paraded early on the morning of 22 May, with two European regiments, 70th (Surrey) Regiment of Foot and the 87th (Prince of Wales Irish) Foot, and some twelve artillery pieces not far distant. General Cotton and Colonel Edwardes were present at one end of the parade grounds and Colonel Thomas Galloway at the other. Nicholson joined the latter to watch the drama.

The order to pile arms was given and carts moved along the lines picking up the hundreds of rifles and swords. No untoward incidents took place, which was just as well as the massacre that would have resulted from any attempted opposition would have been horrendous.

Only the 21st Native Infantry – said to be still loyal not least because of the quality of its officers who 'were not infected with the disease of "implicit confidence"' – and two regiments of irregular cavalry, the 7th and the 18th, were spared the humiliation of the disarming.[80] The cavalry had the sillidar system whereby the trooper owned his own horse, pony, arms, tent and equipment and was better paid than other soldiers. As such, it was felt they were unlikely to revolt and risk losing what they had.

From the British point of view, it is difficult to deny that disarming worked, grossly unfair as it was to the name and honour of many fine soldiers. The disarming also affected the locals. As Nicholson commented rather sceptically, after the Peshawar disarming of 22 May, 'As we rode back, friends were as thick as summer flies, and levies began from that moment to come in.'[81] This sentiment was repeated by Edwardes in a letter to Harry Lumsden:

> The day before levies were not to be had for love or money. The old wuzeer (Oosman Khan) gravely and sorrowfully opined to Nicholson that this was a crisis in which we must rely upon – whom do you think? – *ourselves!* As we came back from the disarming parade, khans, shahzadahs, haramzadas, mullicks, moollahs, horse and foot swarmed like vermin. They seemed to come out of holes in the ground.[82]

Interestingly, Nicholson was less moralistic about this volte-face than Edwardes, although he remarked of one hill region that had in 1856 given considerable trouble and was now providing recruits in some numbers, 'Miranzai is now as quiet as a Bayswater tea-garden.'[83]

It is wrong to dismiss the appearance of volunteers from the hill tribesmen as a mere cynical piece of opportunism. For a start, it was by no means certain that the British were going to be victorious in the end. Secondly, the decade of British rule on the frontier had built links with various Pakhtun communities. A good many, especially from the south, had fought with Becher, Coke, Coxe, Edwardes, Henderson, James, Ross, Taylor, Nicholson, Lind and Vaughan, and personal knowledge and loyalties began to come into play. Some had received 'a Pension, or a Garden, or perhaps even that climax of good things – a bit of land in perpetuity'.

These levies must be distinguished from the irregular regiments that were raised in the Punjab. Levies were to prove to be invaluable to the British. As well as fighting, if needs be they undertook a host of other duties, such as guarding jails, holding small and isolated forts, picket duty, and guarding public installations and private houses. During the Mutiny, it was estimated that a total of 5,667 such irregular levy troops were raised, 56 per cent being mounted.[84] Edwardes later made an interesting remark: 'I remember no instance of misconduct on their part … They absorbed all the idlers and adventurers of the Peshawur valley … crime was never so rare in the valley as during this crisis.'[85] John Lawrence, however, was very dubious about the 'followers of border Chiefs, without discipline, order, or habits of obedience. Such men would give more trouble than they were worth.' Nicholson disagreed.[86]

Several points need to be made about the practice of disarming regiments, which was repeated many times not only in the Punjab but also along the Ganga basin. First, it very rarely led to violence in the Punjab and nothing like what happened in Benares on 4 June 1857 when a field battery led by Nicholson's fellow countryman William Olpherts, under orders from the notorious General Neill, opened fire on the protesting 37th Bengal Native Infantry.[87] In the Punjab, invariably the sepoys acquiesced. Secondly, as at Peshawar, European officers in Indian infantry regiments were seldom happy with the action; we are told by Kaye, 'it was said that here and there the spurs and swords of English officers fell sympathisingly upon the pile [of discarded weapons]'. Thirdly, disarming created a new problem for the British.

Disarming caused the gravest offence, of course, not least among the Indian troops who were loyal. Among those tending to disloyalty, anger at being outmanoeuvred was added. This had the very real risk of placing waverers firmly in the insurgent camp. The problem for the British was what they did with all these sullen men. To send them home to their villages was to invite many to flock to the rebel standard at Delhi. To keep them in the lines was to invite boredom and ferment further disaffection followed by desertion.

On Nicholson's initiative, new security moves were taken in Peshawar. European families were brought in from any outstations. Public buildings and houses belonging to Europeans were guarded by the 'robber tribes'. The double-storey, solidly built Residency was reinforced and made ready for defence should the need arise. It was stocked with provisions, both military and food. General Cotton and his military headquarters was transferred there, again at Nicholson's suggestion. The Residency was to be the place all European women and children were to make for if a crisis arose, whether the alarm was raised day or night.[88]

At 8.30 on the morning of 22 May, Nicholson telegraphed Captain James, Lawrence's military secretary, 'We have disarmed 3 N.I. and 1 Cavalry Regiment and move out in the evening with European Force against the Mutineers at Noshere.'[89] The situation in Peshawar appeared to have been stabilised by the British, at least for the moment. However, nearby all was not well and attention turned on the unrest in the ranks of the 55th at Naushera (Nowshra), east of Peshawar on the Kabul River, and Mardan, north of Naushera, where the 10th Irregular Cavalry were reported also to be either in revolt or on the verge.

In Peshawar a force had been assembled, not only of European troops (300 in all), but also 250 others made up of a detachment of mounted police, as well as irregular Bengal cavalry and Major John Becher's Multani horsemen, a forerunner of Lieutenant Lind's famous regiment.[90] The commander of the British column was Colonel Chute – the 'Kerry Bull'. But, like an anxious schoolboy begging to go on a day out, Nicholson was allowed to go too, under the euphemism of being the 'political officer' accompanied by his own police sowars. This time Lawrence had no opportunity to object. They moved out of Peshawar at 11 o'clock on the night of 23 May. But Lawrence was by now fully aware of what the British were facing and the day the Peshawar column rode out, he imposed strict censorship on the Indian-language press.

Nicholson was the ideal political officer, the post combining as it did the excitement of action with the essential role of intelligence-gathering, whether through spies, informers or personal reconnaissance. This required a close association with local people, which in turn meant supplying recruits for irregular levies in time of crisis. In *A Year on the Punjab Frontier*, Edwardes commented, 'The army was raised by personal influence; such influence as it becomes every political officer to have in the country under his charge.'[91] As will be seen, Nicholson complained about not having a political officer on his Najafgarh expedition. He also speculated that, should he lead the pursuit column after the fall of Delhi and be unable to find a decent political officer, he would also have to fulfil that function himself.

By 25 May, the British column had reached Maldan to be joined by a second column of five companies of European troops (27th Foot) and a battalion of 200 local Punjab infantry under Major Vaughan, sent across from Rawalpindi.[92] It was Eid, the initial date of the planned Peshawar uprising. Colonel Spottiswoode of the 55th, however, had 'implicit confidence' in his Indian troops.

There was serious trouble at Naushera but not all the Indian troops were prepared to rise. About 120 stood by their officers. There was now, in effect, a standoff. But news of Colonel Chute's approaching column pushed the regiment into open mutiny. Shocked, Colonel Spottiswoode shot himself. Meanwhile, 400 or 500 insurgents from the 55th had marched off with flags flying in the direction of the hill lands of Swat beyond the frontier.[93]

Chute felt that the rebels had too much of a head start into the high hills and jungles enclosing the Soon River valley. Besides, Swat was regarded as trouble and had been so since the early 1850s when 'the Swatees uniformly proved themselves bad neighbours to the British. They seem to have regarded the Plains of Peshawur … as a hunter does his hunting ground.'[94] After several punitive expeditions, in 1852 things had settled down peacefully, at least on the surface. But on 11 May 1857 the Akhund of Swat, Sayyid Akbar Shah, died. Uncertainty and instability led to the emergence of Abdul Ghauffur Khan as the new ruler of Swat. He was pro-Afghan, anti-British and anti-Sikh.

A generation later, Edward Lear wrote a satirical poem called 'The Akond of Swat', basically reflecting on the fact that no one knew anything about him. But there was nothing satirical about the action on 25 May 1857.[95]

Chute had no desire to stir up a hornet's nest. His political officer had fewer qualms, however. With a 'handful of men' mostly police, Lieutenant Lind and some Multanis, with Nicholson on his famous 'big grey' charger, set off in pursuit 'like a cat after scattering mice'. It was a pattern to repeat itself many times in the weeks ahead: largely outnumbered but with no sign of fear and a staunchly loyal cohort of men beside him, Nicholson launched into a frenzied attack. Later he was to admit to Edwardes, 'The 55th fought determined as men who have no chance of escape but by their own exertions always do.' And that was the problem the British faced in the Mutiny; they had trained their men well. As Sir Colin Campbell put it in addressing his men, 'When you meet the enemy, you must remember that he is well armed and well provided with ammunition, and that he can play at long bowls as well as you can.' These were not some rabble but disciplined regimented troops.

The 55th rebels did not find permanent sanctuary in Swat, but were given guides so they could cross the Indus. Few made it to their home villages. In the case of Naushera, Nicholson's pursue-and-destroy mission resulted in 120 insurgent deaths. He claimed that he criss-crossed some 70 miles of terrain in search of his prey. To Edwardes, Nicholson commented, 'I think my police sowars behaved better than any ... I did not get home till 7 pm yesterday, having been exactly 20 hours in the saddle, and in the sun the whole day, so you may fancy I was dead beat, my horse too.' Edwardes told Harry Lumsden that Nicholson himself had killed about a dozen men. One hundred and fifty prisoners were led back to Peshawar in the second week of June.

This military operation in particular confirmed Nicholson's reputation as a fearless and dangerous fighter. It also closed the book for once and for all on Nicholson the administrator. On 3 June, as a subsidiary exercise, Chute and Nicholson, now greatly reinforced, marched to Abasye where a 'noted outlaw' from the hills called Ajoon Khan had arrived, hoping to join with the 55th. On the approach of the British column, he and some rebels fled. A section of the 64th who garrisoned the fort was disarmed.

A footnote needs to be added about the fate of the mutinous 55th Regiment. In late June, Nicholson's friend Major Johnny Becher, the assistant commissioner up at Abbottabad in Hazara, received information that the remnant of the 55th Regiment were making their way north in the hope of reaching Kashmir. They carried with them letters from Abdul Ghauffur Khan 'calling on all good Mussulmans to aid and escort them, and excommunicating and denouncing as unbelievers all who opposed them'. Into the mountainous region they went, along narrow ledges with steep precipices, 'by tracks with scarcely footing for the practiced peasant, through gorges where a few could prevent a host, and over waters where seldom was to be found even the hut of the shepard Goojur'. Watched by spies, it was a journey to nowhere and soon Becher's allies among the hill tribes, encouraged by him, were upon the 'haggard and hungry' Indian troops. As Becher recorded:

> Thus, hunted down to the last like wild beasts, was consummated the miserable fate of the 55th Regiment, and thus they afforded a salutary example to other mutinous regiments, by proving the far reach of our power, and that there was no refuge even beyond our border'[96]

With Becher stopping the passes of Huzara, the rebels were effectively trapped and unable to reach Kashmir where they, no doubt mistakenly, supposed they would gain sanctuary. The unfortunate remnant of the 55th Infantry was taken back to Peshawar where they were summarily charged, found guilty and condemned to death. But none of the senior officers in the Punjab, including Lawrence, Cotton, Edwardes and Nicholson, wanted this to happen. George Lawrence stated the British would not be 'justified in the eyes of the Almighty'. Nicholson wrote to Edwardes:

> spare the Sikhs and the young recruits. Blow away all the rest by all means but spare boys scarcely out of their childhood and men who were really loyal and respectful up to the moment when they allowed themselves to be carried away in a panic of the mass.[97]

In the end, General Cotton imprisoned two-thirds of the captured rebels and confirmed the execution of forty insurgents. The barbarous execution was carried out on the Peshawar parade ground in front of the garrison on 10 June, the day Nicholson arrived back from his expedition 'looking rather the worse for wear'. Two batches of sepoys were 'blown out' using twenty cannon. The grisly spectacle had no deterrent effect on most of the Bengal troops who looked on. It should be noted that this mass execution occurred a good seventeen days before the infamous massacre of European women and children at Satichaura Ghat at Cawnpore, which did so much to stir up a desire for revenge among the British. The executions were also a month after the killing of Europeans and Christian Indians, when Delhi rose in support of the insurrection. There had also been a series of killings of Europeans at stations along the Ganga valley.[98]

Nicholson was not present when the two most notorious massacres took place, that of the 51st, 'one of the finest sepoy corps in the service' (when 659 were killed or executed in late August 1857), and the 26th (when about 237 were executed) on the Ravi river. This is not to try to exonerate Nicholson's part in the tide of retribution, but it is to raise a question as to why he in particular, rather than Colonel Chamberlain or General Cotton, has been singled out by posterity for opprobrium.

A poignant story has survived that the colonel of the 51st tried to save those of his men who were captured and brought in by charging them with the relatively minor offence of 'being absent without leave'. This charge was struck out by General Cotton and replaced with the capital charge of 'desertion'.

The issue of the mass execution of Indian troops who either mutinied or who, after being disarmed, waited in their lines before fleeing only to be cut down in the field or captured and subsequently executed was raised in the British parliament. This prompted Robert Montgomery in the dying days of the Mutiny to reply. He was by then lieutenant governor of the Punjab. When the 26th broke out of their lines and the commanding officer had been killed, the mutineers fled north-west, where they encountered a contingent of Sikh police who defeated them.

Sanctuary was sought on an island on the Ravi river. Here they were captured by the deputy commissioner of Amritsar, a man named Cooper. The next day they were all executed, the only reprimand to Cooper being over the gloating style in which he described his actions and which even the Punjab government found to be inappropriate.[99] It was early that June when Nicholson advised Edwardes to 'Give Montgomery a hint not to publish bad news in his summaries; it travels fast enough without his help.' Saul David describes Montgomery as 'a man of impulse, devoid of caution and circumspection'.[100]

On 9 June, the British field force captured the Ridge overlooking the city of Delhi and the ninety-seven-day standoff between them and the insurgents began. The next day Captain Henry Dermot Daly, from a Galway family, arrived with the Guides on the Ridge after a famous forced march of 580 miles, or fifty regular marches in twenty-one marches from Murdan to Delhi, an extraordinary average of about 27 miles a day. Much has been made by historians about these forced marches, but it is largely forgotten that the rebel Indian armies also followed this practice, indeed frequently outpacing their opponents. On one occasion Nicholson admitted: 'When the 36th and

61st N.I. broke away from Jullundur a few days ago, they marched 80 miles in two days, but this fact was not required to prove to us, that in the matter of forced marches, European Infantry cannot compete with Natives, at this season of the year.'[101]

Normal marches, usually at night when it was cooler, were no great hardship for those who were fit. The men could chat as they trundled along, pipes could be smoked, bands played and songs, such as the 'Jolly Shilling' or the Irish favourite 'The Girl I Left Behind', were sung. Jokes passed up and down the line of march. On some marches five-minute breaks every hour were permitted and about halfway there was the 'coff shop' stop, when the men were served a shot of rum each while the officers had coffee 'as well as other things'.[102] However, one gets the impression that a Nicholson march was a less relaxed affair and that was certainly the case if there was a job to be undertaken at the end of it.

## PROPOSAL TO EVACUATE THE PUNJAB

Nicholson was in Peshawar and witnessed the executions of the remaining sepoys from the 55th. Both the overall shock of the outbreak of the Mutiny and his exertions since then had taken their toll. Writing to Emma, Herbert Edwardes noted his concern:'Nicholson has arrived from camp, looking worn from exposure, and, it seems to me, much greyer than he was; but he says he is well. I am glad to get him for a companion again, if only for a day or two.'[103]

But the British had done an effective job and the reality was that from mid-June 1857, the Punjab was in no serious danger excepting a possible but unlikely Afghan invasion. That is, of course, different from the concept of a united, contented and Punjab loyal to the British. That was a myth, even accepting that the British could rely on locally recruited levies. Much depended upon circumstance and events. Trouble did bubble up now and then in the frontier hill country, but it was quietened without major alarm. Edwardes was probably not too far off the mark when he wrote:

the mischief to be feared from the citizens of Peshawar is more of the pen and the tongue than of the sword, though the town is full of rabble who would plunder and stab freely in the rear of a disaster.

It is therefore surprising that the next development was a proposal by Sir John Lawrence that they evacuate the territory or part of the territory. On 1 June he had written to the governor-general: 'The Chief Commissioner feels assured that with three such officers at Peshawur as Brigadier S. Cotton. Lieut Colonel Edwardes, and Lieut Colonel Nicholson, everything that is possible will be done to maintain order and security.'[104]

Despite such words of reassurance to the supreme government, Sir John was very uneasy about the state of affairs, to the extent of possibly beginning to lose his famous iron nerve – or so it seemed to the cohort of young officers who held the Punjab. Again writing to Emma, Edwardes recounted:

> This has been an eventful day [11 June]. I was awakened in the early morning by a letter from the Chief Commissioner, proposing 'That we should abandon Peshawur and the Trans-Indus; inviting Dos Mujommud Khan down, as a friend, to take Peshawur, and give it to him at the end of the war as a reward for his neutrality. The troops then fall back on Rawul pindee! The Indus to be our future border!'
>
> Unless this had been in his own handwriting, I would not have credited it; so weak, timid, and unreasonable.[105]

The idea was to retreat the 45 miles down to the great fort at Attock on the Indus, so giving up Peshawar and the small but key outpost at Kohat. Lawrence distrusted the new irregular Punjabi forces being raised; he felt the summer weather impacted negatively on the European troops in the Punjab; and he also believed that a retreat to Rawalpindi would mean the army was among a 'friendly population'. And not without wisdom, he stated, 'There is much in prestige up to a certain point, beyond that it is a feeble reed on which to lean.' In actual fact, as Lawrence knew full well, there were upwards of 3,500 European troops in the Punjab, made up of the Queen's 8th (200); 52nd (700); 61st (300); 81st (700); and 24th (800); as well as 800 Bengal Fusiliers.[106] That said, the necessity of getting more European troops down to Delhi was great.

Edwardes immediately told Nicholson and General Cotton. They were as one in their indignation over what was being proposed. Edwardes's reply to Lawrence was polite, firm, logical and resolute. He made the obvious points about the effects of retreat on morale; the cutting of the link through Multan to the sea; and the fact that the Punjab was a safe recruiting ground for fresh troops. He commented to Lawrence, 'Peshawar is the anchor of the Punjab, and if you take it up the whole ship will drift to sea.'[107] And he was correct, for Cotton, Edwardes and Nicholson had turned Peshawar into an impressive armed camp. Here there were three European regiments; twenty-four pieces of field artillery manned by Europeans; three 'loyal' Indian regiments, two Punjabi and one Sikh and Punjabi; as well as 'numerous newly raised Horse and foot levies'. The city's treasury was full. As Nicholson remarked, Peshawar 'is perhaps at this moment our strongest position in the Bengal Presidency'. The triumvirate had no intention of giving it up because the chief commissioner was having a fit of the jitters. The ironic part of this saga of whether or not the British should evacuate was that Nicholson himself had advocated strongly to John Lawrence that British forces in the Punjab should be further consolidated, evacuating various forts, something Lawrence steadfastly refused to do.

In another letter to Sir John, Edwardes asserted that 'the empire's reconquest depends on the Punjab'. Edwardes, who would have resigned his position had an evacuation been ordered, also pointed out that the Indus was a defensible barrier and boundary, 'but the Sulimanee Range is a most complete one'. In Lahore, both Lieutenant James, Lawrence's military secretary, and Robert Montgomery, the judicial commissioner, were opposed to the evacuation. Only Neville Chamberlain appears to have shown any sympathy with Lawrence's suggestion. There was a stalemate and the matter drifted, primarily because of the silence on the suggestion from Calcutta. Only when Lawrence pressed the governor-general did Lord Canning firmly reject the suggestion of retreat across the Indus. His telegram dated 17 June had travelled from Calcutta to Madras, to Bombay and so on up to Rawalpindi, where it eventually arrived more than seven weeks later, on 7 August 1857.[108] This unambiguously read: 'Hold on to Peshâwur to the last.' After Delhi had fallen to the British, Lawrence graciously acknowledged, 'Next to the indomitable valour of European soldiery, the Punjabees, white and black, have done the deed.'[109]

One should not get the wrong impression of Sir John Lawrence from the whole episode of suggesting evacuation of part of the Punjab. Lawrence could be very firm, as the cleverly worded proclamation he issued on 1 June to his rebel army illustrates. Part of this ran:

Sepoys, I warn, and advise you, to prove faithful to your salt, faithful to the Government who have given your forefathers and you service for the last hundred years. Faithful to that Government who both in cantonments and in the field has been careful of your welfare and interests; and who, in your old age, has given you the means of living comfortably in your homes. Those who have studied history know well that no army has ever been more kindly treated than that of India.

If the 'Poorbea' [eastern] Sepoy neglects the present day, it will never return. There is ample force in the Punjab to crush all Mutineers. The Chiefs and people are loyal and obedient, and the latter only long to take your place in the army. All will unite to crush you. Moreover, the Sepoy can have no conception of the power of England. Already from every quarter English soldiers are pouring into India.

You know well enough that the British Government have never interfered with your religion. Those who tell you the contrary, say it for their own base purposes. The Hindoo Temple and the Mahomedan Mosque have both been respected by the English Government. It was but the other day that the Jamma Mosque at Lahore, which had cost lakhs of rupees, and which the Sikhs had converted into a Magazine, was restored to the Mohomedans.[110]

## FLAYING OF MURDERERS

Much has been made in recent years of the letters Nicholson wrote to his mentor Herbert Edwardes in late May and early June 1857 advocating flaying those rebels convicted of murdering women and children.[111] These comments were made during a short period when Nicholson was parted from Edwardes and clearly affected both by the daily rumour as well as by recent military exertion. While Nicholson obviously does not emerge from them in an attractive light, they should still be placed in context. And for the record it also has to be said that Nicholson had no one flayed.

On 28 May 1857 when Edwardes was away from Peshawar, Nicholson had written to him:

> Let us propose a bill for the flaying alive, impalement, or burning of the murderers of the women and children at Delhi. The idea of simply hanging the perpetrators of such atrocities is maddening. I wish I was in that part of the world that I might if necessary take the law into my own hands.

At the same time, and more realistically, he also proposed as a propaganda exercise that they circulate propaganda that the rebels of the 55th Native Infantry who had fled into Swat had been forced to convert to Islam and that their families back home in Bengal were being imprisoned. In fact, the few members of the 'Phantom Regiment' who did emerge from Swat were mainly killed by the British or by villagers.

To Nicholson's earlier rant must be added a new one from Abazie written on 6 June 1857 when he admonished Edwardes: 'Won't you join me in advocating the impalement or burning alive [of the] butchers [of] women and children.' The following day he returned to the subject, declaring to Edwardes, 'If I had them in my power today and knew I was to die tomorrow, I would inflict the most excruciating tortures I could think of on them with a perfectly clear conscience.'[112] Such sentiments were not uncommon and the British government in the queen's annual speech to parliament that August put in what might be read as a carte blanche to the likes of Nicholson: 'Her majesty commands to inform you, that She will omit no measure calculated to quell these grave disorders ...'[113]

So what was wrong with Nicholson? Was he mad, ill or frustrated? On 8 June he wrote in calmer tones to Edwardes, 'I have been horribly idle and dull for the last few days, I am very tired of having so little to occupy me.' The context of the time, boredom, impatience, probably illness and being wound up tight like a spring – all were taking their toll on Nicholson. Maybe the snuff he had asked for recently had also not yet arrived. Given Nicholson's stressed state of mind, even such a relatively trivial annoyance could trigger an outburst. Certainly Captain Hay's denial that Nicholson had handed him some important papers greatly irritated him. He would say rash things that he later regretted, although pride prevented him admitting such in public. When he tried to get European troops in from the hill station of Murree and it was explained to him that they were protecting the local civilian European population, Nicholson pompously exclaimed, 'When an empire is at stake, women and children cease to be of any consideration whatsoever' – an utterance that flatly contradicts many of his more noble actions, let alone his wilder thoughts of vengeful punishment.[114]

On 31 May, Nicholson returned to the subject of flaying and asking Edwardes, 'You do not answer me about a Bill for a new kind of death for the murders and dishonourers of our women. I will propose it alone if you will not help me.' Yet interspersed with all this fervour are personal touches, such as his query if he had left his new gold wrist buttons on his little dressing table in his bedroom back in Peshawar. Indeed, his letters continue to be full of his customary requests for small things: a penknife, shoes, soap, tobacco, beer, candles, soda water and tea.

Charles Allen, in his excellent book *Soldier Sahibs*, points out that Nicholson's comments about flaying were made at a time 'when every post horse from down-country brought fresh news of killings of European men, women and children at one station or another'.[115] It should also not be forgotten that

Nicholson was wont to grumble endlessly in private letters to the few he trusted, frequently against his superiors. The grumbles were magnified by the fact that Nicholson was either unwell at this period or exhausted, or both. It should also be pointed out that he did not pursue the matter beyond private correspondence. He never proposed a 'torture bill'. Nor, indeed, did he practise flaying when he found himself in a situation where he had absolute authority. He was also very cautious, at least at this stage, of executing anyone at all without authority from Lahore. This led to extraordinary, nearly throwaway, lines in his letters, such as: 'I have got a man who taunted my police on the line of march, with siding with Infidels in a religious war – May I hang him? I can have a commission here, if you like.'

Of this episode, in 1939 Hesketh Pearson rather dramatically commented:

His [Nicholson's] letters to Edwardes on the subject [of flaying] reveal the mentality of one whose hatred of evil has festered and become malignant; for the devil is re-created in those who hate him, the reformer's zeal is increased by self-hatred, and Satan is aroused to cast out Satan.[116]

That the torture of flaying entered Nicholson's mind at all was most probably because stories circulated of the torture having been inflicted in not-too-distant times in the Sikh-run Punjab by the notorious governor of Peshawar, the resplendent Italian mercenary Paolo Avitabile, whom Nicholson may well have met. There is no question that Nicholson felt deeply betrayed by the mutineers and determined to extract revenge, but then who did not in that tiny band of beleaguered senior officers, whose position was, to say the least, perilous.

This is not to deny that torture was not a problem in British India of the period, a practice that the authorities were keen to eradicate. In the Madras division (Fort St George) between 1854 and July 1856, 506 officials or their associates were accused of torture. But 80 per cent of these were acquitted.[117] There is no evidence to suggest that Nicholson ever indulged in torture. John Lawrence, much as he looked upon Nicholson as a wayward but honest youth, would not have protected Nicholson had there been so. The example, already discussed, of the hapless Deputy Commissioner Brereton in the Ludhiana district in 1855 is ample evidence that torture was unacceptable to the British hierarchy in India.

But the truth was that the Great Rebellion brought out the worst of human nature on both sides. Two days after Chamberlain relinquished command of the Moveable Column, he wrote the following bitter piece of bravado to his brother Crawford, who was also in the Company's ranks:

Heaven fights on our side, and by November the white Christians will be
overrunning the whole land! The Meerut and Delhi massacres sealed the
conquest of India, and the blood of the wretched sufferers is the leaven
which will in time convert it. Henceforth we shall be able to act boldly,
without danger of our acts being misinterpreted, and the day for fearing to
do right out of respect to impure creeds has passed away for ever.[118]

# 9

# Diary of the Moveable Column

The Chute expeditionary force was out in the field for more than two weeks, mopping up resistance and literally showing the flag. So it was not until the second week of June that it rode back into Peshawar. Things then began to move even faster.

On 8 June 1857 the adjutant general of the Bengal army, the affable Colonel Charles Chester, had been killed at Badli-ki-Serai near Alipur.[1] Chester's death set in motion a chain of officer repositioning. Brigadier General Neville Chamberlain was shifted to become adjutant general. Interestingly, a month later Chamberlain was writing to Nicholson suggesting that they swap positions, a proposal that came to nothing as the Moveable Column was soon to be transferred to Delhi.[2]

According to Sieveking, the last letter Nicholson wrote to his mother at home in Lisburn was dated 12 June. Presumably, this information was gleaned from Theodore Maxwell, Nicholson's nephew who had then possession of the Nicholson papers. If true, it means that Nicholson did not write to his mother for more than three months. Even given the nature of the times, this seems very strange and serves to support the suggestion that certain Nicholson letters were later destroyed, or at the very least simply lost in transit as Nicholson had once feared. The 12 June letter was mundane enough — what one might expect a son to write to a mother in such circumstances:

> I just write a few lines to tell you that we are here, and have made ourselves very secure, by disarming all the disaffected native Regts. Charles is with a wing of his Regt in the neighbourhood of Lahore.
>
> Do not be under any apprehension about either of us. I consider that we are stronger in the Punjab at this moment, than in any other part of the Bengal Presidency. With love to all. Ever dear Mother.[3]

There seems to have been no dispute over Nicholson's selection to lead the Moveable Column. This new appointment carried with it the battlefield rank of brigadier general, a great achievement for an officer whose substantive regimental rank was still captain. With Captain James replacing him as Edwardes's number two, Nicholson left Peshawar at 10 o'clock on the night of 14 June, heading to Rawalpindi to meet Lawrence in accordance with orders received from the chief commissioner by telegram earlier that day. Parting with Edwardes was clearly emotional – and, as fate decreed, the two men would never meet again. To Emma, Edwardes recorded:

> So there goes dear, fine Nicholson – a great loss to me indeed! But a still greater gain to the State, at Delhi or at the head of a Moveable Column at this crisis. God give him health, strength and wisdom and make him useful to his country, and crown his labours with honour. A nobler spirit never went forth to fight his country's battles …

He also confided in Emma about the harsh reality of the British position: 'We have no more reinforcements to send.'

Before departing, Nicholson gave Edwardes to take care of a small desk clock that he clearly valued. Edwardes placed this on his own writing desk, noting to his wife:

> How lonely I shall be among my reminiscences! Your dear face beholding me, and this clock incessantly chattering about 'friendship! friendship!' in the most monotonous and absurdly vacant voice. At the half-hours I observe it yawns; and when it comes to the hour, it says, 'No! No! No! No!' with gravity quite human.[4]

For his part, Edwardes gave his old friend 'my Bunnoo silver drinking-cup (that you remember), because I value it'.[5] He also gave Nicholson a copy of *A Religious Pocket Companion*. This was found by Neville Chamberlain among Nicholson's effects after his death.[6]

Nicholson on his grey charger and with his Pakhtun escort, including Muhammad Hayat Khan,[7] rode through that night. Along the way, they met the buggy that 'Iron John' Lawrence had sent to guide him. The next day Nicholson reached Lahore and received his cherished appointment, command of the Punjab Moveable Column, or Mobile Column as Robert Montgomery always referred to the unit. Montgomery should not be forgotten in this saga.

This fellow Irishman was behind much of the logistics for the column and the movement of the siege train to Delhi. He also offered police patrols, keeping roads open and intimidating villages into shunning insurgency activity. Later in these endeavours, he was greatly assisted by another of the Lawrence brothers, Richard (1817–96) – 'the star that would not shine' – leader of the Kashmiri troop contingent at the siege of Delhi and later commissioner of police in the Punjab.

Nicholson was to keep in regular telegraphic and letter contact with Lawrence during his nearly eight weeks (fifty-four days) in charge of the column, an indication perhaps of the sternness of the words spoken to him by Sir John at that Lahore meeting. That is not to say, however, that Nicholson was subservient. Anything but. As Charles Allen notes, Nicholson sent a letter back to Lawrence after their meeting as he rode to join his new column that came as close to saying 'sorry' as he ever managed: 'I forgot before starting to say one or two things I had omitted saying.' The letter also included the following passage:

> One was to thank you for my appointment. I know you recommended it on *public* grounds but I do not feel the less obliged to you. Another was to tell you I have dismissed old grievances, whether real or imaginary, from my mind, and, as far as I am concerned, bygones are bygones. In return I would ask you not to judge me over-hastily or harshly.[8]

Despite this moment of self-reflection, Nicholson was soon with his column and writing Lawrence a very lengthy and in parts rather foolish letter setting out all his grumbles about the unit. Interestingly, he copied the effusion to Lieutenant Roberts.

Nicholson's advocacy of a centralised strong reserve force and a concentration of all European women and children at Peshawar and Lahore brought a strong rebuke from Lawrence. This was perhaps rather rich given Lawrence had been inclined to vacate the whole of the Punjab. Writing through his military secretary, Sir John made several good points:

> If we abandon our open cantonments, they will be plundered. Plunder leads to disorganisation and to insurrection. If we abandon Murree and Rawulpindi both will probably be plundered, and the perpetrators fearing for the punishment of their crimes, will join against us. The country will gradually become convulsed and this organization will spread on every side.[9]

That said, Nicholson was not completely off the mark, not least that the potentially dangerous Indian regiments left in the Punjab were the 4th, 14th, 33rd, 39th and 46th Native Infantry, as well as the 2nd Irregular Cavalry, the 16th Light Cavalry and a wing of the 9th Light Cavalry.

Having got his long letter off his chest, on 22 June, Nicholson telegraphed Sir John Lawrence, 'Chamberlain started this morning [for Delhi] and I have assumed command of the Column. There is not a reliable cavalry soldier with it, or I believe in this part of the Punjab.' And for good measure, later that day Nicholson followed up with another telegram, 'The moveable Column loses half its value from the want of reliable Cavalry.'[10] The column's lack of sufficient reliable troops lead him to picture the column as 'an English Mastiff let [loose] to intercept the flight of half a dozen jackals'.

Appropriately enough, Nicholson's first full day in command, 23 June, was the centenary of the battle of Plassey, Robert Clive's great victory. Around that time, Dr Graham who also features soon in the Mutiny saga, had written of Nicholson that:

> He has struck awe by his bold and decided steps. The word is said and death surely follows; no idle threats, and if he were put in command of the Moveable Column a just vengeance would have its course and his very name would strike terror wherever he made his appearance.

The new commanding officer of the Moveable Column was a similarly imposing figure. Some weeks later, Nicholson would be described as:

> a man cast in a giant mould, with massive chest and powerful limbs, and an expression ardent and commanding, with a dash of roughness; features of stern beauty; a long black beard and sonorous voice. There was something of immense strength, talent, and resolution in his whole gait and manner, and a power of ruling men on high occasions, that no one could escape noticing at once. His imperial air, which never left him, and which would have been thought arrogance in one less imposing mien, sometimes gave offence to the more unbending of his countrymen, but made him almost worshipped by the pliant Asiatics.[11]

Chamberlain stated that Nicholson's beard was a very dark brown approaching black and that he had a pale face with the features becoming 'more marked in character'. He also said that he held his head high 'and carried it as if he could not see the ground before him. His step was vigorous and firm.'[12]

# NICHOLSON'S ENTOURAGE

Nicholson was accompanied at all times by another giant, his Indian bodyguard, 'a huge Pathan, black-whiskered and moustachioed', who carried a loaded revolver and who slept across the entrance to Nicholson's tent.[13] There can be little doubt that this was Muhammad Hayat Khan. In addition, Nicholson was frequently surrounded by a troop of wild-looking and colourfully dressed men of the hills. He himself often looked for all the world like an Ottoman pasha, a fact that did not endear him any further to the European establishment in the Bengal army. Nor can they have approved much of Nicholson allowing his sowars into the mess where they 'sit down and smoke a cigar, and drink brandy and soda'. 'My enemy's enemy is my friend' was very much Nicholson's order of the day. Cooper recalled how, 'Some of the Afghans who were with the [moveable] column were never weary of declaiming against the cowardice of the Sepoys, who killed women and children. They said, "When we fought against you English we killed men, but we protected your women; *men* do not fight against women, only against men".'[14]

These hill tribesmen should not be confused with the Nikolseinee, or indeed to the Sikh admirers whom Nicholson attacked and who, if Wilberforce is to be believed, were allowed into his tent a dozen at a time to sit on the ground in silence watching Nicholson at work. Disturbance was strictly prohibited and inevitably led to three dozen lashes.[15] The original idea was that the Moveable Column should be composed of two elite European regiments; some European artillery; the Guide Corps, half cavalry and half infantry; 'other Punjabi troops'; and some Gurkhas.[16] Table 2 gives the names of the actual military units associated with the Moveable Column, although this gives a somewhat false impression as sections came and went depending upon circumstance. The column probably averaged no more than 1,200 to 1,500 men at any one time. As well as the field artillery, the two consistent elements of the column were the European 52nd Regiment and Lieutenant Lind's Multani Horse. The former was an 'old' light infantry regiment that had won fame in the Napoleonic wars, but which had had a mediocre existence until the Mutiny. In the summer of 1857, it had about 900 men on active service.

## Table 2: Composition of Moveable Column under Nicholson

(Note: The column was normally constituted by far fewer sections than appears as all those units that at one time or another were attached to it are included)

Period of existence: 13 May to 14 August 1857 (3 months)

*Commanders*
Brigadier General Neville Chamberlain: 13 May to 22 June 1857 (40 days)
Brigadier General John Nicholson: 22 June to 14 August 1857 (54 days)

*Major of Brigade*
Captain Seymour Blane: From 22 June 1857

*Officers included:*
Lieutenant Colonel Dawes
Lieutenant Colonel George Campbell
Major Vigors
Captain Randall: aide-de-camp ('a very steady, intelligent, conscientious fellow')
Captains Bayley, Bourchier, Crosse and Synge
Lieutenant Frederick Roberts
Lieutenant Wilberforce

| Military unit | Approx. Size | Note |
|---|---|---|
| HM 52nd Regiment | *c.* 900 (Arrived from Sialkot on 25 May). By the time the 52nd entered Delhi on 14 August, they were 650 strong. When they finally left Delhi on 5 October 1857, they numbered 173. | Present throughout, commanded by Lieutenant Colonel George Campbell. Present when the column arrived at Delhi. |
| HM 61st Regiment | One wing. | Joined late July. Present when the column arrived at Delhi. |
| 2nd Punjab Cavalry | Detachment. Perhaps as many as 250. | The regiment numbered about 575 men and horses. Arrived shortly after Nicholson took command. About two-thirds were on outpost duty at Delhi. |
| 9th Bengal Light Cavalry | Left wing (from Sialkot on 25 May). | |
| 16th Irregular Cavalry (Sikh) | *c.*133. | Regiment was divided between Hoshiarpur, Rawalpindi and in the commando. |
| 2nd Punjab Infantry | | Present when the column arrived at Delhi. |
| 4th Sikh Infantry | | Present when the column arrived at Delhi. |
| 35th Native Infantry | (From Sialkot on 25 May) | Picked up by Nicholson at Hoshiarpur because of fear of having such a 'disaffected regiment' in his rear. Disarmed by Nicholson. |
| 7th Punjab Police Battalion | | Present when the column arrived at Delhi. |

| Multani Horse (Irregular) | 467/374. | Arrived shortly after Nicholson took command. Many raised by Edwardes from those who had fought with him in the second Anglo-Sikh war of 1848–49. 250 present when the column arrived at Delhi. |
|---|---|---|
| No. 1 Light Field Battery | | Captain George Bourchier in command. |
| No. 17 Light Field Battery | | Lt Col. Dawes in command. Present when the column arrived at Delhi. |
| 1st Bengal Horse Artillery | 3rd troop. 30 Sappers. | Initially Nicholson had 12 pieces of field artillery in total. |

The Multani Horse was recruited mainly from the Muslims of the southern Punjab, 'who never missed a prayer, and many of whom rode with the Koran at their saddle-bow'.[17] It was formed in Peshawar on 24 June 1857 and had an initial roll call of 467 men.[18] James (Jemmy) Burnie Lind had joined the Company's army in 1846, being in the 24th Bengal Native Infantry and subsequently second in command of the 5th Punjab Infantry. In August 1857, Freddie Roberts said he was 'a fine fellow and will distinguish himself'. But a month later Roberts had changed his tune, asserting, 'Lind I left behind at Delhi. He is a fine dashing fellow, but too quick in his temper and not sufficiently thoughtful ever to be a first-rate Officer. His likeness to Lizzie is perfect.'[19]

## REACTION TO NICHOLSON

A major problem facing Nicholson was the fact that he had risen so quickly – from major to acting or brevet lieutenant colonel to brigadier general, the last given to him by the military commander in the Punjab, General Reed. Nicholson was well aware of the situation and wrote to Edwardes on 17 June, 'I fear my nomination will give great offence to the senior Queen's officers, but I shall of course do all in my power to get on well with them.'[20] Most troublesome in this regard was Colonel George Campbell, who had previously objected to Chamberlain being placed over him. For Campbell, it was bad enough being usurped by the diplomatic Neville Chamberlain with his 'courageous and soldier-like demeanour' ensuring that everything had gone on 'smoothly and comfortably', but Nicholson did not know the meaning of the word diplomacy. As Bayley recorded, Nicholson was a 'gallant soldier', making him 'extraordinarily well fitted for the post. His rough manners, and scarcely concealed contempt for European troops and their officers, were an unpleasant change.' As with Chamberlain's command, John Lawrence had to step in to settle matters. Not surprisingly, given the extraordinary circumstances, Lawrence wanted a mixture of ability married to a detailed knowledge of the Punjab. That could be provided only by Company officers, no matter how much their precedence or presence irritated Queen's officers.

That level-headed officer Henry Dermot Daly appears to have assessed the situation correctly when he wrote that Campbell, 'is, I believe, an excellent regimental officer, but there is a vast difference between such a man and one who is able to head and manage a force in the field'.[21] In his memoirs Roberts, who thought Campbell a 'very nice fellow and an excellent officer', notes that Campbell and Nicholson 'became fast friends'. Certainly, later when Nicholson was talking about the necessity of superseding General Wilson as commanding officer at Delhi, it was Campbell's name he put forward as the replacement.[22]

It is interesting to note that the official history of the 52nd Queen's Regiment mentions Nicholson by name only once, although it does quote from a diary that was sympathetic to him. The history otherwise makes much of the fact that the commander of the 52nd twice had to endure being made to serve under an officer with a junior regimental rank – 'a severe instance of submission to discipline under strong sense of injustice!'[23] Europeans looked askance at a commander who preferred the company of Indians to the point of having a personal bodyguard of some 200 irregular Indian rather than European troops when he moved with the column. A month earlier, Nicholson had commented to Edwardes that 'Fatteh Khan with two hundred men would make the Rawalpindi Cantonment as safe as if there was a European Regiment in it.'[24]

But if the official historian wished to airbrush Nicholson from the regimental history, many of the troops in the 52nd felt otherwise. Indeed, one lieutenant, Reginald Wilberforce, a nephew of the celebrated anti-slavery bishop, devoted a great part of his in his 1894 book *An Unrecorded Chapter of the Indian Mutiny* to the glorification of Nicholson, and did more than either Kaye or Trotter as biographers to bolster the Nicholson derring-do myth. Many of the oft-repeated stories about Nicholson's heroic deeds are contained in Wilberforce's book.[25]

The second and more serious problem facing Nicholson was that he believed that his column was like 'a lion surrounded by a pack of dogs'. This was because a number of Indian regiments in the Punjab were fully under arms and if not mutinous had the potential to become so, according to his spy network. Matters were complicated by commanding officers who were, not unnaturally, hostile to their regiments being effectively abolished. No such qualms inhibited Nicholson, but he still had a dilemma. The lion might 'by a suddenly spring kill one or two [dogs]; but then the rest would be off'.

To assist his scheming, Nicholson first insisted that the column move with as few encumbrances as possible. This was unusual for an army in India on the march. Normally, along with the troops went the 'mess, band, library, canteen, and officers' private property'; a large number of oxen, camels and elephants; and virtually a secondary army of camp followers. With the disarming of several cavalry regiments, there was now an additional supply of confiscated horses. Volunteers from European regiments were given horses and cobbled together into the 5th Light Cavalry. General Cotton tried using elephants with small carts from the Engineers' department to transport European troops, but the elephants did not prove very successful. The 'Land Transport Train', an idea of Lieutenant Brownlow from the ordnance commissariat, did succeed. This consisted of converted ammunition wagons drawn by oxen or horses. It was claimed to be capable (presumably with teams of fresh animals) of covering 40 miles during the cool of the night. Each wagon carried sixteen men with their equipment and personal effects in long boxes that also served as benches. It was a system that appealed to Nicholson and one he used, though it has to be said, only a proportion of his army could be transported in this manner. According to Roberts, Nicholson also used the smaller two-wheeled carts for transporting European troops.

## THE COLUMN DAY BY DAY

*Saturday 20 June 1857*
Nicholson joined the Moveable Column and took command.

*Tuesday 23 / Wednesday 24 June 1857*
Jalandhar. The Indian garrison had mutinied in early June and fled, leaving the town defenceless. The raja of Kapurthala had taken control of the fortress with the permission of the local British commissioner, Major Edward Lake. As was so often the case, the raja was loyal enough to the British, but many of his followers were sceptical of Britain's chances. There was therefore an air of defiance about the town. Nicholson's arrival with the Moveable Column gave Lake an opportunity to 'show the flag' and a durbar was held, which Nicholson attended. As the ceremony ended, Nicholson moved to

the door of the chamber while the guests were leaving, blocking the exit of one of the raja's relatives and generals, Mehtab Sing. Nicholson permitted the other visitors to leave and then admonished the general for still wearing his shoes, this being perceived as a sign of disrespect. Speaking in Hindi, Nicholson intoned:

> There is no possible excuse for such as act of gross impertinence. Mehtab Sing knows perfectly well that he would not venture to step on his own father's carpet save barefooted, and he has only committed this breach of etiquette to-day because he thinks we are not in a position to resent the insult, and that he can treat us as he would not have dared to do a month ago.[26]

The hapless officer had to remove his shoes and leave, so that all those outside could witness his 'discomfort'. Unlike so many Nicholson stories, which have a fantastical feel about them, this one of in-your-face assertion of authority has the ring of truth about it. So, indeed does Roberts's postscript that some years later the same raja told Roberts that the raja's circle 'often chaff him [General Mehtab Sing] about the little affair, and tell him that he richly deserved the treatment he received from the great Nicholson *Sahib*'.

While this show of one-upmanship was going on, in Lahore Sir John Lawrence was issuing a series of edicts restricting the sale of lead, saltpetre, sulphur and percussion caps.[27] Prisons were also cleared of the sick and infirm and those whose sentences were nearly up and officials were advised to use fines and flogging rather than imprisonment when handing down sentence. This helped release pressure on the jails for an influx of insurgents.

### Wednesday 24/Thursday 25 June 1857

During the night of 24/25 June Nicholson moved his force from Phagwara to 'the strong little fort' of Phillaur on the north bank of the Sutlej River, having let it be known that he would move eastward toward Delhi. Here there had been a sizeable munitions dump that supplied the British at Delhi with much of what they required to conduct the siege. The fort was then under reconstruction under the supervision of Lieutenant Oliphant. By the end of July the earth works and repair of the walls was complete and the 'fort bristled with twenty heavy guns in position, including howitzers, in addition to nine guns at various angles'.[28]

On arriving at Phillaur on 24 June, where the European 8th Regiment was in possession of the fort, Nicholson repeated the same trick that he and

Edwardes had performed at Peshawar a month before. Two suspect regiments, the 33rd and 35th, were disarmed without incident as each arrived at the town. First came the 35th Native Infantry, which was actually in the Moveable Column under Major Younghusband. His reaction when told his regiment was to be disarmed was a relieved, 'Thank God'. He also remarked that of his men, 'Their general temper exhibited a determined passive indifference.' Two hours later, when the 33rd appeared with some 874 men, thirteen Indian officers, fourteen European officers and two European NCOs, the same manoeuvre was carried out, also successfully and without violence.

European troops and artillery were opposite the regiments as the disarming took place, with some European troops feigning casualness, lying in a relaxed way on the ground. And as at Peshawar, artillery pieces were ready for the bloodbath should the sepoys resist. Nicholson was seen leaning over one of these guns quietly waiting for trouble.

A poignant scene played out just after the 33rd arrived. Its old grey-haired Colonel Sandeman rode up to Nicholson and requested a day's halt as his men had made a double march to catch up with Nicholson so they could go down to Delhi with him. Nicholson's response was to say, 'Colonel Sandeman, I regret extremely to say that I must request you to return to your regiment, and order them to lay down their arms.' Years later, Bayley recalled the colonel's reaction:

> The old man started as if he had been shot, and I thought he would have fallen off his horse. He gave one long look at the brigadier, and then turning round, went slowly back to his men, who at once laid down their arms, and were marched off the ground.[29]

An old Sikh colonel near at hand was less sentimental, stating simply, 'You have drawn the fangs of 1500 snakes.' It was symbolic of the end of the old order. Of the seventy-three regiments that mutinied, only four of their colonels were later given new commands.[30]

After the disarming, Nicholson addressed the sepoys and told them that desertion would be punished by death. For eight unfortunates who subsequently did make a bolt for it, a speedy trial led to just that. He said that if they remained quiet and did not desert 'no harm would befall them; but that he had guards on the all the bridges and fords'. All this news soon circulated widely in the Punjab; enhancing Nicholson's standing while generally helping to raise faltering British morale.

The disarmings were, nevertheless, in contradiction of Sir John Lawrence's telegraphed instructions. 'I shall lose the command of the column for this,'

Nicholson confided in Captain Blane when the process was completed. The reprimand, however, when it arrived was very restrained:

> I wish to hear of what is done and the grounds of it – a few words will suffice – But it looks foolish being in charge of the Punjab and telling Gnt [Government] that this and that has been done and not being able to add a line as to the reason.[31]

Yet ten days later, Lawrence had to clarify the requirement, 'I am perfectly satisfied with your note of the 5th. Pray don't think I want to bother you I cannot, nor do expect, that after knocking about perhaps all day in the sun, you should write long yarns.' He pleaded for only a couple of lines, 'What I want is to know what is done and the reason.'[32]

While at Phillaur, Nicholson added some gunners from the British garrison to his own column without asking permission from General Gowan, who was in command of the fortress. This caused a great storm, but by now Nicholson had no masters and even 'Iron John' Lawrence could bring himself to deliver only a mild rebuke:

> I gather that you again vexed him [General Gowan] by taking Arty men out of Pillour without his leave. I fear you are incorrigible, so I shall leave you to your fate. But depend on it you would get on equally well, and much more smoothly, if you worked with men rather than by ignoring them.[33]

Roberts and Nicholson parted at the Sutlej river. One account has Roberts being requested by the authorities in Delhi, but in his letter home written from the Ridge at Delhi on 29 June, Roberts merely says that he felt it a pity to go back to Lahore with the column and asked to be released to travel by mail cart to Delhi. They were certainly looking for gunners at Delhi. To Roberts's decision to go Nicholson replied, 'Well, Roberts your loss I can't replace, both personally and publicly I regret your going, but, at the same time you have more chance of getting on before Delhi.'[34] He also asked Roberts to find him a replacement staff officer as he did not know 'a single [junior] officer with the column'. Nicholson had approved of young Roberts, praising the lieutenant in his letters to Edwardes on several occasions. On 30 May, for example, Nicholson wrote, 'Please put down the name of Lt Roberts of the 87th as a candidate for an Adjty or 2nd in command in any newly raised Irgr [Irregular] corps.' And on 4 June Nicholson observed, 'Under a good C.O. Lt R will soon get the requisite knowledge and experience to fit him for command.'

That evening in Lahore, John Lawrence wrote to his wayward commander, 'I was glad to receive your last note and to find that you had given up all old matters.' Lawrence went on to say that the Moveable Column:

> does not require more Europeans, it wants some good native troops – We are sending you two companies of Henderson's, 250 test'd footmen, and 400 Multanee horse. The 2 Cos, and the Multantee horse ought to make you very strong in a pursuit … do you want more foot levies – I telegraphed and asked you this, but you do not seem to have got the message.[35]

### Saturday 27/Sunday 28 June 1857
On the march. It took two full days for the column to cross the River Beas in boats, the old bridge of boats having been carried away by the fast-rising river. Parting with Captain Farrington, the local political officer, Nicholson said, 'You'll soon see me back again.'

### Tuesday 30 June 1857
Phagwara.

### Wednesday 1 July 1857
Jalandhar.

### Thursday 2 July 1857
Khartarpur.

### Friday 3 July 1857
Gorana. In the British camp outside Delhi, it was reported that this day saw the beginning of the annual monsoon when 'rain descended in sheets of water for many hours'.[36]

### Saturday 4 July 1857
Crossing the Beas River. Rayya. Although Nicholson would not hear the news for a month, this was the day his mentor Henry Lawrence died of wounds sustained at the siege of Lucknow.

### Sunday 5 July 1857
Jundiala. General Bernard died at Delhi and General Reed succeeded to command, although the effort of running the Delhi operation fell on Neville Chamberlain's shoulders.

Nicholson and his column arrived at Amritsar and the great fort of Gobindgarh, where the column stayed four days. That day he telegraphed Lawrence asking for 500 or 600 new levies to be sent to him.[37]

Nicholson received an envoy from the emir in Kabul, Dost Mahommed, sent to assure the British of Afghanistan's loyalty to them. The young administrator, Frederic Cooper (1827–69), who published this incident a year later astutely observed, 'The fact of Dost sending the message to Nicholson instead of to Sir John Lawrence, the Lieut.-Governor of the Punjab, shows how much Nicholson was thought of, even by those who were not under English rule.'

Nicholson was now permanently in the field and sleeping usually in a hot tent. He was kept abreast of developments by receiving notes and telegrams. For example, on 5 July Herbert Edwardes had commented in such a note, 'John L. [Lawrence] still goes on with that retirement from the Trans-Indus, and I don't know when he may say "March!"'[38] Edwardes offered to sell Nicholson's Bucherah horse, which he left in Peshawar. News is given of Edwardes's wife Emma, who was staying in Edinburgh for some time to consult a doctor. Edwardes observed to Nicholson about friends back home in Britain and Ireland, 'What a state they must all be in now.'[39] Emma even wrote to Nicholson's mother in Lisburn and received a reply, 'Just like Nicholson's mother.' An invitation to Ireland was declined by Emma on grounds of ill health. However, the old and the young woman became regular correspondents, and after Nicholson's victory at Najafgarh it was through Emma that Clara received news of the official despatch in which John was honourably mentioned.

In these notes, part semi-official and part personal, the evangelical Edwardes offered Nicholson solace in religion, though by then the subject of religion barely appears in Nicholson's own letters:

> Your and J.L.s accounts of affairs at Delhi are very bad; and look almost as
> if we were to drink this cup to the dregs. But God can help us if He wills,
> and I trust and believe it is not His will that these conspicuously before
> the world the Xtian cause up? – fail, and be trampled on by Hindoos and
> Muhommudans … I am very glad you are going to Delhi, as it is the place
> of struggle; and I feel sure that no reinforcement will be so welcome, or so
> effectual, as your presence in Council and the field.

Cooper's book, *The Crisis in the Punjab*, while containing gloating reference to the mass executions of soldiers in the 26th Native Regiment on 31 July, is an interesting source document. One such snippet is that Nicholson had given the order that any Indian who passed a European had to dismount and salaam. Cooper then recounted how the Moveable Column's orderly officer had ridden ahead of the column the night before in order to set up camp in Amritsar. In threatening terms, the young officer demanded this salaam of the regal figure on an approaching elephant. He duly complied. Next morning the subaltern was summoned to Nicholson's tent:

> The General was sitting, writing at his table; near him stood a native magnificently dressed, with a clear olive complexion, black beard and whiskers. Nicholson said: 'You met an elephant on the road this morning, and made the rider get down and salaam to you; why did you do it?'
>
> 'Your order, Sir, that no natives should pass a white man riding, without dismounting and salaaming.' Nicholson turned to his companion and said something in a language unintelligible to the young officer, and then turning to him, said, 'You owe your life to this gentleman, for his attendant would have shot you, but he prevented him.' The stranger said something in the same unintelligible language to Nicholson, who then said, 'You can go, but before you do so, I may tell you what he has just said to me: "No wonder you English conquer India when mere boys obey orders as this one did."'[40]

### Monday 6 July 1857

Nicholson had news of 400 Multan Horse on the way to join him. As ever pushing the limits, Nicholson requested 500 more foot levies.

### Wednesday 8 July 1857

It was now high summer and extremely hot. The in-tent temperature in the column's camp that Wednesday was 114°F (45°C).

That day Nicholson disarmed the 59th Native Infantry, in much the same fashion as had been his practice. Such an action had been suggested to him by Lawrence two weeks earlier. In fact, there was no evidence that the 59th was suspect and had remained loyal while defending the fort when there were only a handful of European officers. But now the Queen's 81st Regiment was in occupation and it was considered too much of a risk to leave the 59th to the rear of the column.

### Thursday 9 July 1857

At 4 a.m., 42 miles away to the north at Sialkot the Muslim-dominated 9th Bengal Light Cavalry (right wing) and the predominantly Hindu 46th Native Infantry mutinied, the former carried by zeal while the latter were downright casual in their hesitancy, 'being inclined to be loyal to their officers, if not their Colours'; Colonel Campbell commanded the former and Colonel Farquharson the latter. The 46th actually offered Farquharson 2,000 rupees a month to lead them in revolt.

The decision of the mutineers to evacuate Sialkot a mere twelve hours after the revolt had commenced was probably related, at least in part, to the knowledge that Nicholson was in the neighbourhood of Amritsar. Their problem was that they had to slip past him if they wished to escape and make it south-east to Delhi. They therefore made all possible speed for the Ravi river, which they crossed successfully 9 miles from Gurdaspur.

The news about what was happening at Sialkot reached Lahore quite rapidly, thanks to a drummer boy called McDougal who dashed off early in the morning of the 9th on a 'bazar tat' (pony) with a message requesting help from Assistant Commissioner Iain Mahon that read: 'The Troops here are in open mutiny: jail broken – Brigadier wounded. Bishop killed. Many have escaped to the Fort. Bring the Movable Column at once if possible. 6½ a.m. July 9.'[41]

Reports of unrest at Jhelum also came in that day. The news of the rising at Sialkot appears to have reached Nicholson from Lahore by two sources, both in the early morning of Friday, 10 July: by telegraph and through a note received via the mailcart by Arthur Austin Roberts, the commissioner for Lahore, and passed on to Nicholson. According to one source, the telegram had arrived the day before, but the telegraphist had been drunk.[42] If that was the case, his punishment must have been severe. Roberts wrote:

> It is I am afraid all over with them at Sealkot. The 9th Cavalry were up and Montgomery of the 9th has just galloped in quite done up … Montgomery requests me to say that he hopes you will disarm your cavalry at once. Your signaller is not awake. We have been at him for the last half hour.

Roberts also attached the note from Sialkot from Iain Mahon.[43]

In scenes reminiscent of Delhi two months earlier, the Indian cavalry had ridden through the station killing any European man or Indian loyalist they encountered.[44] It was not the worst killings of civilians in the Great Rebellion, as out of a European population of about seventy-five, about ten people were killed by the insurgents but these included one woman and her child. The settlement was thoroughly plundered, one commentator stating that 'no city was ever more completely sacked than the station of Sealkote'. This was primarily because nearby villagers flooded into the town and took what they could grab and carry off. The fort remained in British hands, where those

Europeans who survived and their servants who stayed with them found sanctuary under the protection of a few European troops, the Indian foot police and about 300 Sikh irregulars.

One of the notable victims of the Sialkot killings was a man from Lisburn, Dr James Graham, the local superintending surgeon. Ironically, Graham had mixed views on Nicholson. On the day before he was shot, Graham wrote, 'Nicholson and his Moveable Column will make a desperate effort to cut these rascals up. Mercy is not a word to be found in his vocabulary.' Nor was it in the minds of Graham's assassins.[45]

On hearing that there was trouble and not wishing to frighten his daughter, Dr Graham had allowed her time to dress and prepare herself at her own pace. But as a result, their buggy was intercepted and Dr Graham was shot dead.[46] With great presence of mind, his daughter Sarah snatched the reins and, supporting her dying father, steered the buggy and stampeding horse out of immediate danger. Later, thanks to the efforts of Indian helpers, she and others made it safely that evening to the fort.

As a footnote to the Sialkot saga, after Nicholson had cleared the region of mutineers, the British began to consolidate their position. They threatened local village headmen that they would be hanged if looted material from the Sialkot cantonment was not returned. Pragmatically, the headmen acquiesced. As a result, a long bizarre caravan of men and animals was seen approaching the town. It was laden down with 'tents, chairs, tables, trunks, doors and window-blinds; some carried books, clothing and bedding; others were the bearers of teapots, dishes, silk dresses, mill-stones, bureaus, pictures, and all imaginable house-hold articles'.

### Friday 10 July 1857

The left wing of the 9th Cavalry formed part of Nicholson's Moveable Column, having marched from Sialkot with the 52nd European infantry regiment and the 35th Native Infantry to join the column only six weeks earlier. On Friday, 10 July, just a day after the Sialkot mutiny, Nicholson ordered Captain Bayley to disarm the left wing of the 9th Bengal Light Cavalry, which was achieved without incident. Eighteen years later, Bayley found in an old desk the receipt he had been given when he turned over the weaponry of the 9th to the fort at Govindghur.

This disarming usefully resulted in an excess of horses, gleaned from officers of Indian regiments that had mutinied. This greatly assisted Nicholson with his policy of rapid movement for the whole column. So did the large number of carts, ekkas and bylees for the transport of European troops, which the district officers at Amritsar and Lahore were able to commandeer on the tarred Grand Trunk Road and send to Nicholson.

That day a proclamation set out substantial rewards for the capture and conviction of rebels: 30 rupees, or 50 rupees if the captured soldier had a firearm belonging to the state.[47]

### Night of Friday 10 and Saturday 11 July 1857

On the evening of 10 July, the Moveable Column raised camp and began the massive 42-mile (68km) march to Gurdaspur. According to another of Wilberforce's tales, at dinner that evening Nicholson remained quiet until suddenly he announced, 'Gentlemen, I do not want you to hurry your dinner, but the column marches in half-an-hour.'[48]

This was to prove to be one of Nicholson's epic forced marches. Through the night the long column, with its multitude of small vehicles and carts, perhaps 200 in total carrying members of the 52nd Regiment, snaked its way north accompanied by Captain Bourchier and his nine field guns. The horses of the disarmed 9th Cavalry had been allocated to the Sikh contingent. Even with such assistance, a great many of the men had to walk, carrying their muskets and a pack that included sixty rounds of ammunition.[49]

Next morning, at the village of Batala, the column halted briefly and bread, rum and 'an abundance of milk' were served to the men. Here the column was joined by Commissioner Roberts and his assistant commissioner, Captain Perkins. In the heat of the day, between 10 and 12, there was a stop under a 'gigantic tree', probably a banyan. After some time Nicholson was seen on his horse waiting in the middle of the road for the resumption of the march.

The vanguard reached Gurdaspur about 2 o'clock on the Saturday afternoon; the artillery rode in at about 3 p.m. and it was about 6 p.m. when the rearguard arrived in camp.[50] But the march had been at a cost of quite a few men who had fallen from sunstroke (*coup de soleil*) and a lack of water. It was said that there was not even water available to put in the commissariat rum, 'a most horrible spirit'. Three horses were in such a terrible state after the ordeal that they had to be shot. And then fate was cruel: as the column began to pitch camp, a great thunderstorm broke and the ground was deluged with rain.

That evening while walking through the camp of the 52nd, crowded with local villagers selling milk, fruit, eggs and vegetables, Nicholson spotted disguised among them two sepoys from the 46th whom he had arrested.[51]

The enemy were 12 miles away and Nicholson feared they might try to retreat, so word was sent out that the column might have to march at midnight.

Fortunately for the exhausted soldiers, this did not transpire and they slept through undisturbed until the morning.

### Sunday 12 July 1857: The First Battle of Trimmu Ghat

Sunday was 12 July, an auspicious day for an Ulsterman to fight a battle. Leaving a guard at Gurdaspur, Nicholson led the column in the 'broiling-hot' down to Trimmu Ghat, near the Ravi River, where the Sialkot and Jhelum insurgents had combined to face their nemesis. At about 1 p.m., groups of the insurgent wing of the 9th Cavalry in their grey jackets were spotted. When Captain Bourchier expressed concern that Indian drivers of his artillery pieces might desert, his farrier sergeant replied, 'If they only attempt to run, sir, we'll cut all their heads off.' But they did not run, then or later during the war.

It was said that the mutineers numbered some 800 infantry and 300 cavalry, 'all being in British uniforms and with their colours'. The Queen's 52nd, on the other hand, had had its uniforms all dyed grey khaki and it is said that the rebels at first thought these were members of the Amritsar Police Battalion.

The battle started in an untidy manner for the British. Captain Bourchier's artillery rode across a bridge over a stream and began to form up. In front of them were two police troops of 'Cutcherry Hussars', for whom the 52nd had utter contempt: 'a lot of "tag, rag, and bobtail", caught in the neighbourhood of Umritzur, shoved into antiquated uniforms, mounted, and told off for the protection of the civil authorities there.' Tension between them and the European regiment was never very far from the surface. The British rear was defended by a small number of Sikh police.

No sooner were the British guns deployed than the insurgents' 9th Cavalry, 'gnashing their teeth … with intoxicating drugs', were down among them and passing through the guns, their infantry approaching dangerously close. Nicholson's police line scattered. As Bourchier later wrote, this 'made things at first look very ugly'.

But the 52nd, with their Enfield rifle-muskets and bayonets fixed, were streaming across the bridge and fanning out on either flank of the field guns and between the guns, which fired mainly grapeshot. The 52nd were well officered and the advanced insurgent cavalry were rapidly shot down. Within twenty minutes the insurgent fire 'was subdued'. Ten minutes later the insurgents were in retreat, albeit in an orderly and military fashion, down the road to the Ravi River, which lay to their rear, pursued by Sikh levies on horseback under the command of Lieutenant Boswell. But the column's horses were as exhausted as the infantry. As Nicholson had no professional cavalry, the surviving insurgents reached the river. Many waded, with the water above their waists, across to a large long island in the middle of the river.

The official history criticises 'the officer commanding' (Nicholson) for the positioning of the troops on the banks of the Ravi River that day. That the battle was a victory for the 52nd and its first pitched battle victory in forty years seems to have passed over the writer in his desire to play down Nicholson's victory. The battle was, however, a close enough encounter and the insurgent 46th Native Infantry gave a good account of itself, initially breaking the British irregular cavalry and approaching dangerously close to their guns, finally being driven back by the bayonets of the 52nd. The inclination of Nicholson's police to pull back was later criticised.

Short of cavalry and with his forces exhausted, Nicholson had little choice but to retreat back to Gurdaspur. He left a body of men under Lieutenant Boswell to guard the ford, which they achieved successfully when the mutineers tried to recapture the crossing later that day after the main British force had left.

The British lost five killed and about fifty wounded. The injured included Colonel Campbell, who had been struck a glancing blow on the collarbone by a musket ball. Estimates of the enemy's death toll vary but seem to have been about 200 killed, though Captain Bouchier put the figure at between 300 and 400. Nicholson conceded to Chamberlain that the insurgents had fought well. Speaking of his attack, he commented, 'for above 10 minutes they stood up very well indeed against the great odds opposed to them'. Wilberforce claims that a strike from Nicholson's sword 'clove' an insurgent's head in two.

### Monday 13 July 1857

The following day was quiet enough. Various items of loot had been recovered from the retreating insurgent army. These included 'ladies' lace collars, Bibles, eau de cologne, lockets with hair, and an overland letter'. Other accounts mention carriages, furniture and property taken from Sialkot. Renewed tensions erupted between the Sikhs and the Europeans about these spoils of war.

Back in Lahore, news of Nicholson's initial victory caused a stir. His telegram had been modest, although sent to five different military stations. It set out what he had accomplished so far, spurring John Lawrence to write to Neville Chamberlain that evening, 'Nicholson will I am sure give a good account the Sealkote Muntineers. But for the want of faithful Cavalry he had done so ere this. He has given them one good thrashing already.'

*Tuesday 14 July 1857*

Nicholson was back at the Ravi River, where he heard of 300 insurgents well ensconced on the island and with a piece of artillery. As the water level was rising, Nicholson had to arrange for two boats to be brought to the river, which took a good day to arrange.

To reinforce the small force left behind by Nicholson on the left bank to guard the ford on 12 July, a camp was established opposite the island occupied by the insurgents.

*Thursday 16 July 1857: The Second Battle of Trimmu Ghat*

Nicholson did not rush back to Trimmu Ghat to finish the job he had begun on the Sunday. He allowed three full days to pass before acting. This was in part because his men were searching for serviceable boats. The swollen river ran north-east to south-west. The current around the elongated island was faster on the side away from the British position than the side with a ford where the British infantry was positioned. Just upstream, the British artillery was positioned to mislead the insurgents that they would attack there.

Before dawn on 16th, the assault party led by Nicholson crossed over unnoticed onto the jungle-covered island. Should more firepower be required, two elephants were on standby to wade across with dismantled field guns.

After the assault party had crossed, the British artillery upstream opened up and began shelling the insurgents' main position. The British formed a skirmishing line and with bayonets fixed succeeded in penetrating a fair way up the island before being detected. The insurgents' one artillery piece was the old gun that they had brought from Sialkot. This had merely fired the town's daily morning and evening gun but now it was in full field use. The Indian gunners held their position bravely but, overrun by the British infantry, they died at their posts fighting with their *tulwars* to the end. Only two gunners tried to make a run for it and they were 'accounted for' by Nicholson himself. Wilberforce claimed that Nicholson chased on horseback an insurgent gunner running from his post, 'overtook him, and rising in his stirrups dealt him such a mighty blow that he actually severed the man in two!' Wilberforce also related how Nicholson had joined the 52nd as they advanced along the island 'and as he rode [Nicholson] told me a story of how he had killed a tiger on horseback with his sword', then adds in a rare moment of caution, 'I think he said on that island, but I may be mistaken.'[52]

The British swept up the island, through a village that the insurgents had used as a base, and to the end of the island, killing any enemies they encountered.

Not surprisingly, 'a miscellaneous mob of sepoys, villagers, and camp followers' fled before the British advance to the upper end of the island, many of them being bayoneted. Some jumped into the fast-flowing Ravi River but either drowned, or were bayoneted at the water's edge or shot from the bank.

Nicholson's victory was complete. J.W. Kaye, the later historian of the Mutiny, writing in 1859 as secretary in the Political and Secret Department of the India Office, astutely observed that rivers act as non-conductors of political electricity.[53] So it proved for the Sialkot rebels, for across the river they found no sanctuary and the local villagers, who had no wish for a war on their land, drove the unfortunates back into the river, or rounded up many desperate sepoys and turned them over to the British for summary execution.[54] The Goordaspoor and Kangra police were also active in rounding up fleeing rebels.[55]

Some insurgents did manage to reach the territory of Gulab Singh, only to be either turned over to the British by the Jammu leader or rounded up by Lieutenant McMahan, whom Nicholson sent in their pursuit. A wide range of accounts exist as to what happened to the prisoners. One was that Nicholson interviewed each prisoner in turn and asked him if he was a sepoy. If the reply was yes, the hapless rebel was summarily executed. According to Edwardes, Nicholson carried out the executions according to martial law.[56] A less dramatic version states that Lieutenant McMahon and Captain Adams tried the prisoners. Some were banished, but most were executed, many being blown from cannon.[57] 'Clouds of vultures' now infested what had been the battlefield.

Yet another version of this story was related by Captain Bayley and is worth relating in full as a reflection of the sordid aftermath of such a battle:

the dispersed sepoys being continually brought in by the Sikh levies, in parties of ten or twelve, were summarily executed. I witnessed the arrival of one gang of ten. Nicholson was called out of the Dâk Bungalow, and the Sikh corporal in charge gave him a paper, which he looked at, and then counted the prisoners. Going down the line he asked each in turn what he was? Each answered 'Sapahi' [cavalryman]. 'Take them away half a koss [measurement of distance], and shoot them,' said he, and went indoors. Some of our men went to see the first execution, and came back very angry; saying that instead of shooting them, the Sikhs had slowly cut two or three up with their tulwars, asking between each slash, whether 'that was as pleasant as cutting up unarmed sahibs and mem-sahibs (ladies)'. But this having been brought to the notice of the brigadier [Nicholson], was at once put a stop to. An angry telegram came from Calcutta, forbidding the execution of the mutineers without trial: but Nicholson answered, that he had no officers to spare for court martial; that the prisoners had all admitted that they were sepoys; and he added, it was his intention to shoot all that he caught. This was apparently satisfactory, as no further telegrams on the subject were received.[58]

This would seem to confirm that while Nicholson did execute prisoners without formal trial during the Mutiny, his actions were not in defiance of his superiors. On a different level, it is also interesting to note that at the height of the Mutiny, while Nicholson was only a few miles from a battlefield, he was connected by telegraph to his superiors, albeit by a very circuitous route. The connection must have been to Lahore, however, rather than Calcutta as Bayley claimed.

Many hundreds of Europeans, perhaps as many as 1,000, died as a consequence of the Sialkot and Jhelum mutinies. But another facet of the Mutiny was now emerging. On 20 August William Graham, writing to his cousin James, observed, 'We must have revenge and of no ordinary description.' In fact, he would seem to have been achieving that already for he had joined Nicholson's Moveable Column. The psychology of revenge was now well and truly established. But it would be multiplied many fold, for on the same day as Nicholson's victory at Trimmu Ghat, Henry Havelock reached Cawnpore with its charnel house and its well of horrors.

*Friday 17 July 1857*
Camp at Goordasore.

*Saturday 18 July 1857*
On the Delhi Ridge, General Reed was invalided out as commander and replaced by General Wilson.

Between 18 and 24 July, Nicholson was away from camp for four days as he was at military headquarters in Lahore consulting with Sir John Lawrence and senior military commanders. We know that Nicholson was quick to get replacements for the horses he had lost, no doubt by fair or foul tactics. His precious Multani Horse had lost sixty-four animals, twenty-two being killed in action, the remaining injured. The casualty ratio of both men and horses killed and injured had been 1:2.2.

As well as killing prisoners, other reports of Nicholson's alleged tactics were circulating. In his diary, Lieutenant Edward Ommaney, a military engineer, made the following entry for Tuesday 21 July:

Out for my walk this morning with the Major. Saw Nicholson pass on his way to Lahore, he shows himself to be a great brute. I think for instance he thrashed a cook boy for getting in his way on the line of march (he has a regular man a very muscular one for this duty) the boy complained he was brought up again and died from the effects of the 2nd thrashing.

A man of the 2nd Irregulars who showed the Seelkot the ford, had his 2 hands cut off. a Bayonet run through his body and then hung; batches of prisoners with their hands tied were taken into jungle and the Sikhs let at them. Such cruelties must tell against us in the long run, because these men have done the same by us and God knows what barbarities have been committed upon the sons and daughters of England, still because they do it is no reason we should emulate them. Kill them by all means by hanging or shooting the really guilty incl every man belonging to Regts who have mutinied and were present at the time, and also those men living around the spot where any European has met his death.[59]

The claim of the thrashing may be true, though the episodes of the floggings were clearly not witnessed by Ommaney, but came to him second-hand. Flogging was part of daily army life. This was the case even in the Queen's army, as distinct from the Company's armies. In 1858, for example, as many as 9,338 lashes were inflicted on soldiers stationed in the British Isles alone, the usual sentence being fifty lashes per punishment.[60] It should also be noted that, although corporal punishment in the Indian police had been abolished under Lord Bentinck's governor-generalship, it was reinstated some fifteen years later by Lord Hardinge.[61] It must also be added that Ommaney himself was not beyond inflicting a 'thrashing'.

That Nicholson's name struck terror into the hearts of many is beyond question, as is the fact that he was not popular with many officers, who regarded him as aloof, haughty and arrogant, 'the Autocrat of all the Russias', as some called him. It is the contrast between this attitude and that towards those he befriended that is one of the most intriguing features of the Nicholson saga. The story was recounted of how when the column was in the region of the Beas, a European officer seeing one of 'Nicholson's men' looking exhausted on duty at the river bank offered the man a drink of spirits from his flask. The man declined even when pressed on the grounds that when he returned to camp Nicholson would 'beat me severely'.[62]

How many of these stories were the product of reputation and how much fact is impossible to judge absolutely. There was much talk but very little first-hand proof, and the same writer who recounted the Beas River episode admitted that 'it is impossible to avoid sometimes repeating false reports'. This, combined with the hostility against Nicholson among Europeans in the Bengal army, makes the quest for even the approximate truth much more difficult to discern. Modern attitudes to empire are another factor that must be added to the issue of trying to determine how culpable Nicholson was of being brutal beyond what was even the norm then. In 1852, he had written to Henry Lawrence:

> I hope all this does not read very bloodthirsty – I do not believe that I am cruel, and there are many cases in which I think great allowance should be made for a savage who sheds blood in a moment of passion, or under the influence of strongly existed feelings, but for a professional cold blooded murder, I can feel no sympathy and most of our Bannoochee murders belong to that class.[63]

The hostility towards Nicholson may very well have been motivated by his shy and awkward manner, but also in part both by the inevitable jealousy that his meteoric rise engendered among fellow officers and by the fact that his 'eccentric and peculiar' behaviour may have been perceived as being symptomatic of his being homosexual, at least in inclination. But Nicholson did have some friends in high places. James Graham observed on 8 July, 'Some references have been made to Hd qrs regards Chamberlain and Nicholson's appointment,' complaining of the supercession. The answer was, 'If you have any objection to serve under them, you may take leave of absence for an indefinite period.'[64]

On 18 July, John Lawrence was to write a despatch to Calcutta recounting Nicholson's successes surrounding the Sialkot mutiny and the subsequent pursuit and destruction of the insurgent forces.[65] However, Lawrence did not write to congratulate Nicholson himself for the rather petulant reason that Nicholson had not written to Lawrence telling him at first-hand about the victory. This caused great offence to the hyper-sensitive Nicholson. Indeed, as will be seen, the matter became the subject of a sharp exchange between Edwardes and John Lawrence after Nicholson's death. Writing to Nicholson some ten days after the Sialkot victory, Edwardes was sympathetic towards Nicholson but also added an astute and telling comment:

> John L not thanking you is past all understanding ... that absence of *impulse-to-applaud* which makes him so difficult to serve with sustained zeal and happiness. In his own mind I am sure he said 'Well done Nicholson! – Just

like Nicholson!' – but there is an ungenerous hesitation to out with it – a fear
of committing himself to an opinion. It is apparently a theory in his scheme
of administration, that praise is not good for men – that it puffs them up and
makes them careless.[66]

Despite such human misunderstandings, it was now clear that Nicholson was
the big hope for British success at Delhi and that was where he and his troops
should be.

*Tuesday 21 July 1857*
Nicholson at Buttala. At Delhi, 130 Indian troops deserted the British camp
on the Ridge to join the insurgents in the city, a stark reminder to the British
of their precarious position. The point also must be made, however, that the
insurgents were losing troops who slipped away out of the city and set off for
their villages.[67]

*Wednesday 22 July 1857*
Column at Amritsar while Nicholson was still at Lahore. Far away in London,
the Court of Directors of the East India Company, unaware of Sir Henry
Lawrence's death, appointed him as governor-general in waiting should
anything happen to Lord Canning, the existing governor-general.[68]

*Thursday 23 July 1857*
Nicholson said goodbye to Sir John Lawrence. They were not to meet again.

*Friday 24 July 1857*
Nicholson re-joined the column at Rayya.

*Saturday 25 July 1857*
As Captain Farrington had predicted, the column again crossed the fast-flowing
Beas river, this time by the restored bridge of boats. The entire regiment, the
baggage train and the camels crossed the rickety structure in single file. The
elephants sensibly took to the river and waded across. Lastly, came the Indian
women camp followers in the ekkas, an elegant cart with a shade awning
drawn by a pony. Halfway across the bridge of boats gave way and the carts,
or at least some of them, were carried downstream. Fortunately, they were
swept onto the river bank without anyone being drowned. The column now
consisted of the 52nd, Dawes's troop of artillery, Bourchier's battery, a wing of
the Amritsar police and 240 ever-faithful Multani horsemen.[69]

Nicholson wrote to Captain John Younghusband, captain of police at Kangra, requesting troops. This hilly region was under the firm control of Nicholson's old associate Major Reynell Taylor. Nicholson asked Taylor's police chief to send him four companies of police, which he would like to be 'Dewa Sing's, Kahh Sing's, Sune Sings 7 No. 7'; an indication of Nicholson's thorough knowledge of the Punjab forces. He agreed with Younghusband that 'men do not act nearly so well when mixed up together as when with their own company'. As a postscript Nicholson added, 'I wish you were coming with us.'[70]

The distressed state of General Wilson's mind is well illustrated by the series of telegrams and notes he sent Nicholson from 25 July onwards regarding the column's approach to Delhi. At first, he advised a slow pace as he had no wish for the column's men and horses to be 'harassed by fatiguing marches'. A week later he was urging Nicholson to 'push forward with the utmost expedition in your power'. There was also a discussion on whether the 52nd should be split and one section go ahead to Delhi. Debate continued, depending on now threatened Wilson considered the British position was on the Ridge.

### Sunday 26 and Monday 27 July 1857

Gorana. Crossed the Beas River. At Kartarpur, between the Beas River and Jalandhar, Nicholson started interfering with General Wilson at Delhi. He telegraphed Wilson correcting him for saying he did not want artillery, by which Nicholson meant field artillery as distinct from heavy siege artillery. Nicholson made the point that after Delhi had fallen, such moveable guns would be needed as half a dozen brigades would be sent out in different directions.[71] Lawrence, however, would have none of this, 'as regards the Artillery,' he responded, 'I cannot agree to more than 12 guns going to Delhi.'[72] Meanwhile, that Monday Edwardes wrote tongue-in-cheek to Captain Harry Dermot Daly, 'And our Fancy Man, Nicholson, has gone down from this side [to Delhi] with his shirt sleeves up.'[73]

### Tuesday 28 July 1857

From camp at Phagwara, Nicholson telegraphed Lawrence, stating that his Multani Horse and police battalion were badly off for medical assistance and requesting that one of the four doctors at Sialkot be sent to the column. The oft-quoted story is told of a member of the column passing through Jalandhar, saying to a friend, 'Jack, the General's here,' and pointing to six men hanging from gallows and several bullock-carts filled with insurgents awaiting a similar fate.[74]

*Wednesday 29 July 1857*
Crossed the Lattay, Phillaur.

*Thursday 30 July–Saturday 1 August 1857*
Ludhiana. At this time, Nicholson recorded that the Moveable Column consisted of the 52nd Queen's Regiment, Dawe's Troop, Captain Bourchier's artillery battery and a wing of the Amritsar Police battery. A few days earlier Wilson had suggested that the 52nd should come on to Delhi, being replaced in the column by the Bombay Fusiliers. This did not materialise, but there was soon to be a colourful addition for the Moveable Column; more hillmen were not far distant.

Nicholson found the Ludhiana camping ground was under flood water and the men had to seek what shelter they could. It was here that Nicholson discharged eighty-three of the Multani horse as being unfit. Their numbers appear to have been filled rapidly for they were up to strength a couple of weeks later. It was here also that the column was joined by a wing of the European 61st Regiment. The exact location of enemy forces in the region was unclear to Nicholson as he was receiving differing reports from Lawrence and from General Lake – 'This conflicting intelligence is puzzling'.[75]

On 30 July the 26th Native Infantry had mutinied at Lahore and made its escape under cover of a dust storm.

All was not well in the city of Ludhiana, where people were supplying the insurgent forces with food and shelter. After an encounter in front of the city gate, some of these people fled into the maze of houses outside the city wall. The deputy commissioner of the region, G.H.M. Ricketts reported:

> As these houses were obnoxious in a military point of view, and the spirit of their inmates was hostile also, I obtained General Nicholson's permission to level all within 300 yards, and I did so, banishing the unhoused Goojurs to seek a residence in their own lands, separate from the city by a deep nullah.[76]

Charles Nicholson and his 2nd Punjab Cavalry were in the town and helped 'sweep the inhabitants back to their houses'. Outside the town, Charles's men rounded up eight insurgents. In this tense atmosphere, John Nicholson decided to leave 100 Multani Horse at Ludhiana and also to send out Lieutenant Lind with 100 more Multani Horse to scout around. Nicholson quite frequently used these smaller flying columns as part of his intelligence gathering, an exercise that was quite the match for William Hodson's famous network of spies.

*Friday 31 July 1857*

Beyond Ludhiana lay the great Sutlej River, which the column began the laborious task of crossing. Heavy rains resulted in the river floodplain becoming a swamp. First the cavalry, the field guns and the commissariat were crossed, but then the rain increased and the river came down in force, delaying matters. It took the best part of a day for the 52nd Regiment to cross, but many of its vehicles had for the moment to be left on the northern, or right-hand bank with what there was in the way of replacements being commandeered on the far side.

*Saturday 1 August 1857*

The rains continued the next day.

It is said that the two to three-day delay cost the column dear, for sickness spread, rapidly incapacitating officers and men. And as they moved along, we are told, rats driven from their burrows by flooding 'trotted along with the column like so many small terriers'.

On discovering the 26th had not come his way, Nicholson telegraphed Lawrence, 'Very well. I have recalled the Sowars. I hope the parties who misinformed you as to the route taken by the 26th will receive their deserts [sic].' And to Lind out in the field, Nicholson scribbled a note:

> Come back by the Trunk road as fast as you conveniently can – Order the Red purgree men to reconaise [reconnoitre] wherever they may be, till they receive further orders
>
> It seems that Sir John was off the scent of the 26th N.I. for a good hours, and that they really seem North … Give your men a 'Currie Bhana' at Govt expense to recruit themselves with.[77]

The news of Nicholson's approach created two very different types of excitement and tension in the two opposing camps at Delhi. One report from behind Delhi city wall as Nicholson approached was 'that 25,000 European troops were coming towards Delhi'.[78] With such stories circulating, a last great attempt was made on the night of 1/2 August by the insurgents, who came out of the city 'in great force' and attempted to break through Wilson's front-line defences. This failed.

*Sunday 2 August 1857*

Luskree Serai. Nicholson telegraphed Lawrence, 'I hope the mutineers force on the Rhotuck road will remain till I get into their neighbourhood'. That day Wilson wrote to Nicholson asking him to come ahead of the column to Delhi to consult with him.

In the city of Delhi gambling was banned.

### Monday 3 August 1857

Bara. Leaving Ludhiana, the column was now well supplied with bullock gharries to transport the troops.

General Wilson informed Nicholson by express mail that the enemy at Delhi was trying to establish themselves in force in his rear.

### Tuesday 4 August 1857

Rajpura. Forced march. At Delhi, the news of General Havelock's entry into Cawnpore reached the British camp.[79]

### Wednesday 5 August 1857

Ambala. Forced march, meeting another British unit on the road. Lieutenant Julius Medley, an engineer, recorded that Nicholson had 'a small force, but whose avenging march under their stern leader, had been like the track of the destroying angel through the land'.

### Thursday 6 August 1857

During this brief stop at Ambala, Lieutenant Medley had occasion to visit Nicholson in his tent. He recorded:

> Imagine a man 6 feet 2 inches high, and powerfully made in proportion, with a massive-looking head and face, short, curly grey hair, and long black beard – the expression stern and quick, according well to the deep voice and abrupt speech, full of animation, and a very pleasant smile.
>
> The whole face and figure showed a man of iron constitution, indomitable energy and resolve, great self-reliance, and born to command; and I could quite understand the extraordinary influence he possessed over all who came in contact with him, in spite of a *hauteur* of manner and a certain want of tact, which often gave offence to men who did not know the sterling qualities of his character.[80]

It was on that day Nicholson set off for Delhi by mailcart, the column moving on to Shahbad.

With the Moveable Column approaching the British camp outside Delhi, Sir John Lawrence accurately summed up the risky position in which the British were exposed in the Punjab: 'But, though the country is friendly we have a long border to guard, and, above all, upwards of 20,000 Hindustani Soldiers to guard. The majority of these men are desperate.' That was on 5 August, the day Sir John heard of the death at Lucknow of his brother Henry on 4 July. Edwardes's comment on hearing the news was, 'It is like a good King dying.' The next day he added: 'I have already raised 10 new Regiments of Punjaub Infantry, and am still going on. I sent all my old Regiments down to Delhi, so far as I can spare them, and hold the country with new ones.'[81]

### Friday 7 August 1857

Column reached Pipli. Nicholson arrived at the British position on the Ridge. He was pleased at the nature of the British position, overlooking the city and with 'strong buildings on it in front, and the river and canal protecting our flanks and rear'. As for the attitude of the British camp towards him, there was a stark difference between Nicholson's detractors and the bulk of the force. His fellow Irishman, Captain Henry Daly of the Corps of Guides, observed, 'His merits were recognized throughout the camp. Between the 6th and 7th [August] he rose higher and higher in the minds of all.'

At 4 o'clock on the afternoon of 7th the great magazine within Delhi blew up, killing hundreds of workers and causing a fire that lasted for two days.[82]

### Saturday 8 August 1857

The column was at Karnal. It was either this night or the next that another legendary incident – of the cooks and the soup – was said to have occurred, if it occurred. As the source was Lieutenant Wilberforce, it should be treated with caution, not least because that night Nicholson was in the British camp at Delhi. That said, Wilberforce recounted the anecdote as follows:

One night we were all waiting for our dinner and none appeared, messengers were sent to the cooking tent, but only brought back word that dinner was coming, till about half an hour after the appointed time, Nicholson, who always dined with us, came on the scene, with 'I am sorry, Gentlemen, to have kept you waiting for your dinner, but I have been hanging your cooks!'

We soon learnt the story. One of the cook boys, whose conscience revolted at wholesale murder, went to Nicholson and told him that the soup was poisoned with aconite. Nicholson kept the boy safe until just before dinner was to be served, when he sent for and arrested the cooks. The soup was brought in with the cooks. Nicholson told one of the cooks to eat some; the cook protested, on the ground of caste. Nicholson knew that a Mussulman had no caste, and peremptorily ordered the cook to swallow some, telling him at the same time that he, Nicholson, knew it was poisoned; of course the cook denied this. Nicholson then had a small monkey brought in, and some soup poured down its throat. In a few minutes the truth of the cook boy's story was seen – the little monkey was dying of poison. Sentence of death was at once passed, and a few minutes afterwards our regimental cooks were ornamenting a neighbouring tree.[83]

### Sunday 9 August 1857
Column at Paniput. Meanwhile in Delhi, Nicholson was inspecting the British gun positions.

### Monday 10 and Tuesday 11 August 1857 (Three Marches from Delhi)
Column at Larsauli, a village held for the British by the raja of Jind, who had established a line of defence along the road.

Perhaps more plausible than the soup saga was Wilberforce's account how on the evening of 10 August an officer's bulldog, called Billy, captured a thief, naked and oiled all over. Having slipped past the sentries and camp guards, the thief had, as it turned out, entered the tent in which the dog was sleeping. Though slightly wounded by the intruder's knife, the dog held his grip until help arrived. The fate of the hapless villain is not related.

Nicholson re-joined the column at Larsauli on the 11th. The column was also joined that day by Captain Green's Punjab Regiment.

Telegrams and notes passed in and out of the British camp letting Nicholson and other British commanders know what was happening. Some of these were significant but some verged on the bizarre. Nicholson became obsessed with the issue of light artillery and the need for as many field guns as possible to be brought into the British camp at Delhi. However, others thought otherwise. First Nicholson was ordered to send one of his two batteries back to Jalandhar. John Lawrence quickly denied knowledge. This order was then reversed. Another issue playing itself out was General Wilson's attitude to Nicholson. The latter's habit of working independently frightened Wilson, who had only been in charge for three weeks. Although Nicholson was difficult to deal with, not surprisingly, Wilson wanted him around when it appeared that the British position on the Ridge was at risk. It was a tension that was to continue until the assault on the city. Nevertheless, well before Nicholson arrived on the Ridge the sense already existed that it was Nicholson and Nicholson alone who would save the day.

*Wednesday 12 August 1857*

Column reaches Rhae. One account states it was here that Nicholson re-joined his column.

In the distance could be heard the sounds of the British guns firing on the walls of Delhi. In the early hours of that morning, Brigadier Showers and a column captured the strategic former residency of Ludlow Castle and the Kudsia Bagh [garden] outside the city wall near to the Kashmir Gate, a job that Nicholson had hoped his column would achieve when it arrived.

A telegraph received in the Foreign Office in London on 25 September read: 'The latest dates from Delhi the 12th August, when that city was still in possession of the rebels; but an attack was expected to be made shortly, as General Nicholson was within a day's march with considerable reinforcements.'[84]

*Thursday 13 August 1857*

Column at Alipur, 10 miles from Delhi. The Flagstaff Tower on the British Ridge outside Delhi could be seen with field glasses.[85]

From then on the march to the British camp was through a no-man's-land. Captain Boucher commented, 'death in every shape greeted our approach; even the trees, hacked about for the camels' food, had a most desolate appearance, throwing their naked boughs towards heaven as if invoking pity for themselves or punishment on their destroyers.' And all around was a swamp.

The column moved forward with great caution, but rumours of an insurgent attack did not materialise.

*Friday 14 August 1857*

On 19 July, Nicholson's friend Johnny Becher had written to him, 'Yours has been the brightest exploits we have had.' There is no doubt that Nicholson had brought hope to the British camp and with that the prospect of success. Indeed, his approach most probably was the key to an attempt by the rebel leadership to enter into what the British dismissed as 'hollow' negotiations.[86] Now, on 14 August, the Moveable Column arrived in the British camp outside Delhi. Hervey Greathed wrote to his wife that day:

> It was a fine sight this morning to see Nicholson's column march in. There were great greetings among both officers and men, and they received a hearty welcome … They [52nd Regiment] were followed by a splendid regiment of Seikhs, the biggest men I have seen for a long time; they also had a band. The column was played in by the 8th. Altogether it was a cheery

sight, and would have struck gloom among the Pandees, if they could have seen it. The battery is commanded by Bouchier.[87]

Captain Trotter estimated the force that Nicholson brought in at about 3,000 men. As well as the troops there were field guns, some siege guns, military stores and ordnance. Nicholson also brought in seven lakhs of treasure, or 700,000 rupees (typically, Wilberforce exaggerates this to nine lakhs). In the fifty-four days that Nicholson had been in command, the column had covered 508 miles (813km) in thirty-six marches. If one leaves aside two extended forced marches of 42 and 38 miles each, that averages a fairly steady 12 miles per march.[88] It also needs to be mentioned that various other remnants from regiments, about some 1,200 men, came into the British camp not far behind the Moveable Column, so greatly increasing the size of Wilson's force before Delhi.

But there was the time bomb of sickness among the British troops outside Delhi. Fever had for many decades been a problem for the British, with a death rate of some 69 per 1,000 being the average mortality rate in European regiments in India. Now things were even worse. Take, for instance, the 52nd. When Nicholson led the unit into camp, it was 680 strong with only six sick. Exactly one month later, illness had reduced its ranks to 240 active men.[89]

And there was another concern. On 15 August, Sir John Lawrence sent Nicholson a letter quoting the governor-general and making it clear, 'no reinforcements can be expected from below for many a day – I should say not before troops arrive in numbers from England'.[90] Edwardes had advised delaying the assault on Delhi until British reinforcements arrived. Between 1 July and 4 August, the British had engaged an armada of fifty-four troop ships ranging from the 640-ton *Adelaide* to the 2,700-ton *Golden Fleece* to sail to India. This contained 400 officers and 18,000 troops, mainly destined to land at Calcutta, with a few sent to Madras and Karachi.[91] The British advance would be up the Ganga River Valley and that meant via Cawnpore and Lucknow. This would take months. The British outside Delhi were alone.

# 10

# Siege of Delhi

In the minds of both the British high command and the insurgents, the future in India hinged on the success or failure of taking Delhi. The insurgents saw this as the key to ridding themselves of the imperial power. But the British felt the fate of their whole empire was bound up in the outcome. As Nicholson was by now the British military's star turn, the psychological as well as the military advantage of having him at Delhi was more important to the British than what he could achieve dashing around the northern Punjab putting out mutinous fires.

General Wilson was a cautious man. He was also not in good health. He was the third British commander before the walls of Delhi. Sir Henry Bernard had died of cholera on 5 July. Then General Reed had been invalided out less than two weeks later on 17 July. The strain had meant that Reed was not sleeping well, which was not helped by pain in his legs and feet.[1] The hopes of British success now rested on the shoulders of Wilson. He and Nicholson made an odd combination – in a spectrum of extremes, the two neatly sat on either end. Nicholson's reputation and physical stature were also such that his influence far outweighed the impact on decision-making of men older, more experienced and of senior rank. To Wilson's credit, he recognised the extraordinary soldier he had in Nicholson and was, if anything, more tolerant of the quiet but volatile giant than were either of Henry or John Lawrence, who both professed a deep affection for him. Nicholson at first found Wilson to be an intelligent man, but easily swayed by too many advisers. Later, Nicholson's attitude would become more negative.

Wilson cannot have been oblivious to the feeling of the younger officer, and yet Wilson had himself bought into the Nicholson legend. On 5 August, Wilson wrote to his wife from the Ridge that 2,000 British soldiers could not just hop over the wall and massacre 30,000 to 40,000 rebels in the city 'as easy as toasting cheese'. He praised the British in having 'kept the fellows at bay so long', a not unreasonable boast. And then, significantly, he added, 'I shall be more than satisfied if I can hold my position until Nicholson joins.'[2] That happened on Friday, 14 August, with 1,000 European and 1,000 Indian troops, along with 200 Multani horsemen and six field guns, arriving at the Ridge.

The aura of a saviour had been gathering around Nicholson – but hero worship in the face of British success had turned the stomach of many of his fellow officers, including his number two in the former Moveable Column. A week before Nicholson first arrived at Delhi, the Muslim holy day of Eid had seen a concerted and bloody attempt by the insurgents to break the British line of defence on the Ridge. Its failure reversed the position at Delhi. It was now the British who were doing the besieging.

No sooner was Nicholson in camp than Wilson was having problems, as he confided to his wife Ellen:

> I have been much bothered to-day from two Queen's officers, Colonels Dennis and Campbell of the 52nd both Senior to Nicholson and unwilling to serve under him. The former also Senior to Showers [a friend of Nicholson's], and claiming a brigade Command. It is hard upon them to serve under Nicholson who is only a lt colonel, but as I tell them he has been appointed a Brig'r Gen'l by the Govr' Gen'l right or wrong and I can't interfere with his orders, even if I wished to. I have made a kind of compromise with them, putting them on the same roster as Brigadiers, so that they will not clash by having to take duties under Nicholson, but I believe Dennis will leave the Camp. I gave him leave to do so and he seemed inclined to avail himself of it.[3]

It was by such mealie-mouthed methods that Wilson kept the peace in the British camp in its hour of crisis. Dennis did not leave the camp but, as it emerged many years later, he was not slow to spread gossip about Nicholson. Ironically, at one stage Nicholson said that if Wilson were removed he would be prepared to serve under Campbell as the commander of the Ridge force, 'so none can ever accuse me of personal motives'.[4]

Jealousy among some European officers at Nicholson's meteoric rise was common knowledge. Writing to his sister Anne back in Lisburn, James Graham observed, 'Col Nicholson has arrived at Delhi and commands a brigade. His being put over the heads of so many of his seniors has I hear given great annoyance, but in these days the right man is sought for the right place.'[5]

# PREPARING FOR THE BATTLE OF NAJAFGARH

One of the secrets of being a long-term success as a commanding general is preparation and Wilson was correct to wait until the heavy siege guns in the British military stations at Ferozepur and Phillaur trundled their way down in an 80-mile cavalcade to the imperial insurgent capital. Ferozepur was 280 miles from Delhi and Phillaur 220 miles. The Grand Trunk road was completed, including bridges, as far as Karnal, 78 miles from Delhi. The road from Karnal to Ambala was being constructed, but beyond Ambala lay a great challenge for the siege train, as there were no bridges over streams or rivers.[6] The British badly needed these large siege guns because they were still using mainly 18-pounders and were outgunned by the insurgents' 24- and 32-pounders, as well as by the insurgents' 13in mortars.[7]

The war of spies meant the occupants of Delhi soon got wind of what was afoot and, quite sensibly sent out a strong force to intercept and destroy the leviathan. Indeed, when the insurgent army left the city on 24 August, the British on the Ridge were able to watch its exodus through their field glasses. It consisted of the Nimach Brigade under General Sudhari Singh and Brigade Major Hira Singh, and the Bareilly Brigade under the imposing General Bakht Khan.[8]

Sensibly, early next morning Wilson sent Nicholson and a new Moveable Column of some 2,000 men to seek out the mutineer army and destroy it. The strategy aimed to preserve the siege train and also protect the British rear, keeping open their fragile supply line.[9] Accounts written afterwards focused largely on the 61st Regiment and the 1st Fusiliers but, in fact, 60 per cent of the column was composed of Indian troops:

    16 Horse artillery guns
    1 squadron of 9th Lancers
    80 Punjab cavalry
    100 Guides cavalry
    200 Multani cavalry
    420 Her Majesty's 61st Regiment
    380 1st Fusiliers
    400 1st Punjab Infantry
    400 2nd Punjab Infantry
    30 sappers[10]

## NO TURNING BACK

It was not the first time Nicholson had ventured out of the British camp with a column, but the earlier sortie had been stymied by the heavy monsoon rains. This time, however, Nicholson was not to be turned despite 'long and heavy rain'. To intercept the enemy, he had to move particularly fast for the conditions. Instead of obeying Wilson's orders, Nicholson took the advice of Theo Metcalfe and was guided by a hand-drawn sketch map made for him by the injured Freddy Roberts. Nicholson left the Grand Trunk road and cut off into the countryside across what he described as 'a tolerably deep and broad ford'. This in turn meant negotiating two large swamp lands that intervened. It was a dramatic and perilous journey with the horses and the unfortunate cavalry having to wade through muddy water, 'a perfect morass', which varied in depth up to a metre or more, 'a journey by water rather than by land'. The infantry waded waist-deep through the water with their ammunition pouches on their heads. At one point an artillery officer recalled, the water was over the horses' backs. He looked ahead and saw 'Nicholson's great form riding steadily on, as if nothing was the matter, and so he felt sure all was right'.[11]

Nicholson's officers on this expedition included his brother Charles; Lieutenant Gabbett; Lieutenant Geneste with his sappers; Lieutenant Sandford; Captain Low, Nicholson's ADC; Captain Sarel of the 9th Lancers; Captain Trench; Lieutenant Charles Griffiths; and Lieutenant William Lumsden, brother of the more famous Harry Lumsden of the Guides. The horse artillery was under Major Tombs, of whom it was said that he 'had as little idea of an obstacle being insurmountable as the General [Nicholson] himself'.[12] There was also Major Jacobs of 1st Bengal Fusiliers and Colonel Rainer of 61st Foot.

About 4 p.m. on 25 August 1857, twelve hours after the column left the Ridge camp at Delhi, Nicholson caught up with his prey near the village of Najafgarh. This is some 20 miles to the west of Delhi, in the area where the Indira Gandhi international and the Delhi domestic airports are today. The insurgent force was led by General Sudhari Singh and Brigade Major Hira Singh and the brigade, which had arrived at Delhi on 26 July. All had not been well among the insurgents, who had been poorly supplied and grumbled about not being paid.[13] Now they had extended their force along a line stretching some 2 miles fortified by thirteen guns, some of them from the Red Fort at Delhi and bearing the imperial insignia. Four artillery pieces were located at an old travellers' rest hut or serai, and the other nine between the serai and the bridge. Estimates of the size of the insurgent force went as high as 9,000 men, although Nicholson put it at between 3,000 and 4,000. In Delhi city the rumour was that 20,000 villagers had risen up and been defeated by Nicholson's small army.[14]

## RALLYING THE TROOPS

Nicholson gathered the assault troops around him. Two versions of what he said survived, although it is equally possible that each speech was delivered to a different regiment. Both were typically Nicholson, short and essentially saying do not waste ammunition until we are upon the enemy. A soldier in the 61st Regiment recorded the following as Nicholson's words:

> Now, 61st, I have but few words to say. You all know what Sir Colin Campbell said to you at Chillianwallah; and you must also have heard that he used a similar expression at the battle of Alma, that is 'Hold your fire till within twenty or thirty yards of that battery, and then, my boys, we will make short work of it'.

The other speech ran:

> Remember men, the experience which others have gained. Take for your example the 93rd, and other regiments in the Crimea, who spurned to waste ammunition while at a distance from the enemy. Reserve your fire for a close range, and victory must be ours.

Charles Allen recounts that as the speech reached this climax an insurgent came forward and challenged Nicholson to a duel, whereupon Muhammad Hayat Khan 'fell upon the man with a blow from his tulwar that killed him instantly'.[15]

After a brief bombardment from the British field guns, with bayonets fixed Nicholson led his infantry across a deep ford on a branch of the Najafgarh jheel. His horse was struck and Nicholson continued with his men on foot. It was now about 5 p.m. To his left was the serai, to his right, the village of Najafgarh. The enemy were to his left and in front of him, where their line extended from the town to a bridge across the Najafgarh canal. Nicholson was hampered by a lack of intelligence. So, as was his way in such situations, he reconnoitred himself.

Nicholson later wrote, 'after the Arty had fired a few rounds, I advanced and charged with the Infy.' Wheeling to his left, he overran the serai, capturing the four enemy guns. He then allowed his own fourteen artillery pieces to let off some rounds, before advancing, leading his men from the front. He broke the enemy line, turning to his left as he did so and working down towards the canal. William Lumsden and the 1st Punjab Infantry could then sweep straight down the enemy line, capturing the village of Najafgarh.

With Nicholson in the advance were the 2nd Punjab Infantry and two European regiments, the 1st Fusiliers and the 61st Regiment. In support were a body of reserve infantry kept back from the three regiments, as well as the 2nd Punjab Cavalry under Charles Nicholson and a body of Multani horsemen. These reserves and baggage guards numbered no more than 300 men. The infantry advance was supported by a cavalry squadron of 9th Lancers and the Guides Corps. In his advance to the canal, Nicholson's force was able to capture the remaining nine enemy guns.

## THE COST OF BATTLE

It was a short battle, but a group of insurgents still occupied the village of Nugli, to the right of the road leading from Najafgarh to the bridge. Nicholson ordered Lumsden to clear the village. This, however, proved a tough task and Nicholson had to send the 61st to reinforce the Punjabis. The result was that Lieutenant Lumsden and the 18-year-old Lieutenant Elkington were killed, Lieutenant Gabbett died of wounds soon after the battle, as did eleven other Punjabis and five men of the 61st before the village fell to the British.

Nicholson wrote promptly to Lieutenant Gabbett's mother saying that had he survived he would have recommended the young officer for the Victoria Cross.[16] But it took a week for Nicholson to bring himself to write to Harry Lumsden telling him of his brother William's death. Indeed, Edwardes was considering undertaking the unpleasant task. But once Nicholson had sat down and picked up his pen, he wrote what was a good letter of its kind, so much so that Peter Lumsden in his biography of Harry Lumsden, *Lumsden of the Guides*, included a facsimile of the letter as well as a full transcript in the text:

It is with great grief I have to communicate news which will be a sore trial to you and Peter. You will not have been wholly unprepared for it, for you know that hard fighting has been going on here for some time.

Your poor brother was killed at the head of his regiment in action on 25th. He died nobly doing his duty, and sincerely regretted by the whole army. His last words, as he fell dying to the ground, were ones of encouragement to his men and officers.

He was in command of the corps at the item, Coke having been wounded and Travers killed in previous actions.

We shall assault [Delhi] before the 10th most probably, and I hope that his and other losses will be amply avenged. Give my love to Peter. You have my sympathy with you more than I can express. Ever, dear Joe.[17]

British casualties were twenty-five killed and seventy wounded. Lieutenant Griffiths put the enemy casualties at about five times that number.[18] That night of 25/26 August the British troops went without food or grog as the wagon train could not cross the ford to reach them. Nicholson spent the night at the bridge with the 1st Fusiliers, the 2nd Punjab Infantry, a detachment of artillery and the Lancers. Nicholson's eight-page account continued, 'I had the bridge mined and blown up by the sappers, and all the wagons and tumbrels which I had not the means of bringing away were also blown up by Major Tombs.'[19] However, the spoils of war included a buggy believed to have belonged to General Bakht Khan and a male peacock with 'an immense tail', the latter being purloined by a horse man who rode along with the hapless bird under his arm.[20]

The next day shortly after daybreak, Nicholson turned for home and led his exhausted but buoyant column back behind British lines, arriving before sundown. They received a great welcome from the army on the Ridge, with two military bands playing them into camp. One officer recorded, 'our fellows were stuffed with plunder, and in great delight.' In the British camp, there was a chatty letter awaiting Nicholson written by John Lawrence on the day of the battle. It lacked the tension of earlier notes and also shared with Nicholson some views of what was necessary in the future. Part of it ran:

If Delhy falls wh I hope and trust it will, I do not think it should be left with less than 3000 men of whom 1100 should be European. I should place them all in the Police and turn out all the people now in it …

I think it will be very good plan to proclaim martial law Genl Wilson ought at once to act and propose it to Colum [Sir Colin Campbell, the commander-in-chief]. It would be inappropriate for me to interfere in this and other matters – I should do more good than harm – I quite agree with you that we should reward the Leihh Chiefs handsomely, but Gnt [Government] would not brook my acting off my own bat.

I think that Genl Wilson ought not to delay a day in pursuing the defeated enemy. He will do more by thus acting during the first week than in a month afterwards.[21]

Najafgarh was a noted victory and, in a sense, is Nicholson's great battle victory. Nicholson's task, however, was greatly assisted by two key factors. The insurgent troops had been poorly fed before this battle. Also, rivalry and division between the two insurgent commanders led to one of them, General Bakht Khan with the Bareilly division, holding his forces back. As such, the enemy force Nicholson encountered, the Nimach Brigade, was much less than it should have been. Captain Bouchier of the artillery had known Khan before the Great Rebellion, as Bakht Khan had for decades been a *subedar* also in the Bengal artillery. He said of him:

> Bukht Khan, like Nana, was always very fond of English society. At one time, when studying Persian, he used to come twice a day to my house to read and talk with me. He was a most intelligent character, but a more dreadful hypocrite never stepped on earth.[22]

The British victory was complete and the road between Ferozepur and Delhi was open for the siege train of eighteen heavy 'guns, howitzers and mortar carts' pulled by elephants to complete its laborious twenty-three-day journey, arriving from 4 September onwards. It was accompanied by some 800 bullock wagons of ordnance; 'shot, shell and ammunition' enough, it was said, 'to grind Delhi to powder'.[23] Not far behind the train came Richard Lawrence in command of a force from Jammu as well as Wilde's Rifles.

The question remains: why did Nicholson not go after the Bareilly brigade, which was only a few miles off? His own explanation was that he did not have 'a decent political officer with me to get me a little information'. This is probably true. Whatever Nicholson's faults, he was not reticent about taking the fight to the enemy. But there was another factor. General Wilson had pressed Nicholson to return to camp as soon as possible because his own force on the Ridge at Delhi had been under attack.[24]

## NICHOLSON'S PROSPECTS

The victory at Najafgarh further enhanced Nicholson's reputation for being the field commander of the moment. The remnant of the sepoy army retired back to Delhi, itself suffering from desertion on the way. According to the great spy-master William Hodson, in Delhi itself, the news of the defeat caused dismay, increasing desertions from the imperial capital. While Nicholson had been out gathering glory, a concerted attack was made on the Ridge by the insurgents inside the town, who believed that the British had denuded its force for the expedition. This raid failed miserably. As one commentator who had observed the assault noted:

> The fugitives on their return declared they had been fighting the whole army, so an attack was at once made on our camp by the other divisions, expecting to find it unguarded, but they fought off on seeing the unwelcome faces of the rifles and Ghoorkas grinning over the breast-works.[25]

This account James Graham sent to his sister Anne in Lisburn with instructions to send a copy to Clare Nicholson as well as to the two local newspapers, adding, 'I hope it will have a better fate than the last paper I sent about him.'

Not surprisingly, by now many mutineers were tired of the struggle and slipped away, quietly returning to their villages. Later they, quite sensibly, claimed to have been there throughout the Mutiny.[26]

General Wilson was delighted and in his mind, and in private correspondence with his wife, he determined now to attempt an assault on the city once the siege train had arrived. Recounting Nicholson's exploit to his wife, Wilson concluded, 'I look upon it as one of the most heroic instances of pluck and endurance on record, and [it] does great credit as well to Nicholson as [to] the gallant fellows under him.'[27] And publicly, Wilson did not hold back in his praise, noting on 30 August, 'To Brigadier General Nicholson's judgement, energy, and determination I attribute mainly the glorious result of the expedition.' Writing personally to Nicholson on 26 August, General Wilson enthused how the expedition, 'with such weather and over such country – must have been incredible ... Again I congratulate you and thank you'.[28]

John Lawrence was unrestrained in his own enthusiastic response to the news of Nicholson's victory at Najafgarh:

> I wish I had the power of knighting you on the spot. It should be done. I hope you destroyed no end of villainous Pandees! ... Don't assault until you have given the mutineers all the powder and shot wh. the siege train can spare and then go in, and God be with you all.

Two days later Lawrence wrote, telling Nicholson that he had written to General Wilson urging him to assault the city 'after the siege train has done its work'.[29]

Lawrence followed up on 6 September with an apparently incongruous proposal given the life-and-death situation at Delhi, although intended as recognition of Nicholson's achievements. He recommended Nicholson as commissioner of the southern Punjab district of Leiah (Layyah). This position had become vacant following the death of Lieutenant Colonel Ross. But he added, 'I hope Genl Wilson will give you the command of the pursuing force. I trust you will be in Delhi when this reaches you. I trust you will escape the dangers of the assault and gain increased honour.' Nicholson accepted the Leiah commissionership on 8 September.[30] Because Nicholson was in the field with his troops, Lawrence placed Major C. Browne as the interim acting commissioner.

One can see why Lawrence selected this sparsely populated area for Nicholson as many of Nicholson's most devoted admirers came from there. It is, however, doubtful if Nicholson would have been satisfied with such a modest trophy had he survived the Mutiny. Besides, five days earlier, General Wilson had told Nicholson that he intended nominating him to be military governor of Delhi once it was captured. Nicholson had the good grace to record, 'for this I am much obliged'. Then on 7 September, John Lawrence wrote to Commissioner H.H. Greathed, 'I think on reflection that Nicholson would be a better man for the pursuit than for Delhi. If Government want to follow and cut up the insurgents, he has not his equal in the force.' A week later William Muir in the Intelligence Department asserted that Nicholson would lead the new Moveable Column.[31]

Alexander Taylor commented a few days after Nicholson's death, though as yet unaware his friend had finally succumbed to the bullet wound, 'If Nicholson lives retribution will out – He knows all about it – so does Daly.'[32] Lieutenant Wilberforce asserted that Nicholson would have been commander of the force sent to relieve Agra. After this he would have proceeded down the Grand Trunk road to link up with General Colin Campbell, the newly arrived commander-in-chief. Taylor quotes Nicholson as saying, 'I am certain that old ___ ['Creeping'?] Colin will put me under arrest before I have been twenty-four hours with him.'[33]

William Hodson, of Hodson's Horse, added a footnote to the proposed column of revenge. On 13 September, Hodson learnt that Nicholson had requested Hodson should be part of the pursuit party once the city fell. As Hodson found Delhi to be a 'dreadfully unhealthy' place, he jumped at this idea, no doubt also encouraged by the prospect. He wrote, 'when Nicholson urged my going on with him I was only too ready to second the motion, for I am able to work and to fight, and I must do so as long as I can.'[34]

Edwardes was delighted to hear about the future military governorship, writing to Nicholson, 'I believe it will yet call to your fortune to take Delhi, and I hope it may with all my heart.'[35] When Nicholson's friend, Captain Daly, congratulated him about the Leiah appointment, he told Nicholson that he would not take the commissionership as they would make him a general with his own division. To this Nicholson 'laughed haughtily' and said, 'A General! You don't think I'd like to be a general of division, do you? Look at them! Look at the Generals!' Nicholson had a point.

Down at Agra, William Muir, head of the Intelligence Department, wrote to General Havelock: 'Yesterday's news of Nicholson's victory over the Barerlly Brigade has put us all here in good heart. Even those who disapproved and prophesied evil things, begin now to look for an easy and final success against the city.'[36]

## QUESTIONS OF LOYALTY

Nicholson was never slow to give either Lawrence brother advice. Regarding the issue of winning back the loyalty of mutineers, the Punjabi authorities were restricted by a Calcutta proclamation excluding pardon. A point overlooked by his later detractors is that Nicholson would have none of this. He was against a pardon for the leading corps in the uprising and for those who had murdered their officers. But Nicholson was in favour of bringing back into the fold the rest, in particular the cavalry who had generally been more reluctant to commit to revolt and in any case had a natural disdain for the infantry. He also recommended that the prohibition on issuing pardons be ignored as 'the state of affairs is different now to what it was when the order was issued'.[37]

This attitude somewhat muddies the waters for Nicholson's detractors. As a relevant aside, the point needs to be made that it has been erroneously believed that Nicholson was involved in quelling fresh trouble back in Peshawar. General Cotton gave orders to Captain Bartlett and his newly raised 18th Punjab Infantry to search for arms in the living quarters and the lines of the restless 51st Regiment at Peshawar. Needless to say, arms and ammunition were discovered and skirmishing broke out on 27 August between the sepoys and the Punjabi troops. As a result, most of the 51st fled the town and headed for the Khyber Pass where a 'religious enthusiast called Synd Ameer' was preparing to ferment unrest against the British. One of the worst bloodbaths of the Mutiny ensued. Many sepoys were killed in the hills by the pursuing troops. Others were captured, returned to Peshawar and shot. About 570 men of the 51st were killed, nearly 80 per cent of the regiment. Contrary to popular belief, Nicholson had nothing to do with this affair. He was at the time back on the Ridge outside Delhi. On 1 September Edwardes wrote to Nicholson, 'a pursuit took place up to near Jamrood – Before evening 400 were killed and in 36 hours 700 were put to death.'[38]

In the same letter Edwardes ruminated about the Mughal king in Delhi:

I want you to tell me what is the impression in yr camp about the King of Delhi? – from Mr. Greenshed's letters to J.L. [John Lawrence] lead me to think the King negotiated with our people. Now anyone who knows natives ought to understand the value of a leg in each boat, and I do hope that whenever Delhi is taken, no maudlin sentiment will save the king and every one of the Shahzaduks from instant death.

Edwardes then went on to attack Sir Colin Campbell as a 'worn out general'.

On 28 August, Charles Nicholson wrote home to his mother with all the news of John's exploits. It was a much more informative and chatty letter than John Nicholson would have written:

We don't get many letters as you may suppose in the present state of the country, but I think that we shall capture Delhi before a month is gone and that our communications will be re-established. John as you will see in the papers has been made a Brig Genl. This more than sustained his former reputation. He [was] first in command of the Punjab Moveable Column defeated th Sealkot Mutineers and in 2 engagements and destroyed them. Since his arrival at Delhi he defeated on the 25th Inst a very large body of the insurgents capturing their guns and Camp and utterly routing them. I would dearest mother rather have saved you from the anxiety of knowing the danger to which he is exposed had it been possible to do so, but as in his position that is out of the question … For the rest [?] he is looking better vein better spirit than I have seen him for years. The weather has been unusually cool and neither of us has suffered from exposure.[39]

This was all very true and among the British force Nicholson's presence was a reassurance to frightened men. In a letter to his mother back home in Waterford, Roberts asserted that:

Nicholson is really the only Commander we have here, now that Chamberlain is laid up, and, in my opinion, he is superior to him. Such a sensible man in every sense of the word. He is very kind to me, and, as you see Mother dear, a true friend to me.[40]

Outwardly, Nicholson showed no change of character. He was friendly and warm to those he liked, quiet and cautious towards those he either disliked or did not know. But, in truth, he was a stranger in the British camp. His brother Charles was around, but many of those whose company Nicholson himself enjoyed were either elsewhere, wounded or sick on the Ridge. On the wounded roster were various Nicholson associates:

Captain Harry Daly, 1st Bombay Fusiliers and officiating commandant of the Guide Corps, severely wounded 19 June 1857.

Nicholson's now re-established friend, Brigadier General Neville Chamberlain, officiating adjutant general of the Army, shot in the left shoulder on 14 July 1857, when the British suffered about 200 casualties in a skirmish. Boils on Chamberlain's shoulder added to his pain.

The young Lieutenant Freddie Roberts, officiating deputy assistant quartermaster general, slightly wounded on 14 July 1857. Off the sick list on 25 August.

Brigadier John Coke (1806–97), commanding 1st Punjab Infantry, which had arrived ahead of the Moveable Column on 2 July, severely wounded on 12 August 1857.

Brigadier St G.D. Showers, commanding 1st Infantry Brigade, severely wounded on 12 August 1857.

## THE LONG WAIT

No doubt with a conscience about the former coolness between the two, Nicholson paid much attention to the recuperating Chamberlain, visiting him daily and having him taken in a *doolie* (covered stretcher) to view from a safe distance the siege guns in operation. Nicholson said that no wounded man had any business to go under fire. Chamberlain noted of Nicholson's attention that 'no woman could have shown more consideration'.[41] A few days earlier Edwardes, still holding the frontier at Peshawar, had written to Nicholson, 'give my love to Chamberlain. I am glad you are both together there, and wish I was with you.'[42]

Later Chamberlain recalled how Charles Nicholson used to call in as if by accident when he knew John was around. He recorded the rather gauche Ulster way the brothers greeted each other: 'Hilloa, John! Are *you* there?' To which Nicholson would reply, 'Ah, Charles! Come in!' Beyond that there appears not to have been much outward affection between the brothers, yet as

Chamberlain observed, 'They were shy of giving way to any expression of it; but you saw it in their behaviour to one another.'

The officers' mess was one institution Nicholson could hardly ignore, but he was notorious for being out of place there. Unless someone he trusted was present, he chose to eat alone and speak to no one. The ever-gossipy Hervey Greathed in a letter from the British camp outside Delhi recorded:

> General Nicholson was at dinner [8 August 1857]. He is a fine, imposing-looking man, who never speaks if he can help it, which is a great gift for a public man. But if we all had been as solemn and as taciturn during the last two months, I do not think we should have survived. Our genial, jolly mess-dinners have kept up our spirits. [43]

In the three weeks between the victory at Najafgarh and the British assault on Delhi, Nicholson was like a caged tiger. He paced. He was a frequent visitor to the breastworks, the artillery batteries and the outposts. Appearing like a ghost from nowhere, wearing no insignia of his rank, he chatted quietly to the men on that forward watch, and then slipped away again. It is well recorded that Commissioner George Barnes, probably in league with Captain Hodson, ran a network of his own spies into the walled city, but Nicholson also had his spies. Bayley records:

> The inhabitants of the Punjab believed that he [Nicholson] was in league with the Evil One, and knew what was going on everywhere, and even what was passing in their minds, and, in consequence, every one who received intelligence of anything worth knowing, at once begged, borrowed, or stole a horse, and rode off to tell it to Nicholson. [44]

Now, while waiting before the walls of Delhi, Nicholson also had his spies within the city. [45] Some reports from such informers have survived in the India Office papers. Reading them, it is clear that they were of dubious value. As one spy conceded about a particular case, 'in consequence of the want of unity of counsels among them, no dependence can be placed upon their words'.

Bayley recalled that one morning he was in the Subzee Mundee, a suburb outside the walls that the British had largely flattened, when an Afghani man and a woman who was apparently his wife, an Anglo-Indian, were brought to him, having apparently escaped out of the city over the walls. At that moment, Nicholson arrived and started interrogating the man in his native tongue. He told Bayley that he knew the place the man came from and he knew his father and his brother and thought him a spy. Suspected spies were routinely executed by the officers commanding the pickets.[46]

In this instance, though, the pair were not summarily executed. They were brought into Nicholson's camp in the hope that 'one of my fellows will be sure to know him'. The woman was looked after by the wife of one of Nicholson's staff.[47] Versions of this story were repeated by Griffiths and by Wilberforce in their books, so clearly there is some truth in the saga of a European or an Anglo-Indian woman called Seeson or Leeson, the wife of the Delhi postmaster, being rescued from Delhi by an Afghan, or by two Afghans as another version went. Nicholson saved the Afghans from execution on the understanding that the two become his spies, conditions they accepted with some alacrity.[48] The woman was sent to Ambala, where she arrived safely.[49]

Stories also circulated that Nicholson actually went into the city of Delhi, moving at night and without disguise along the walls between the Lahore Gate and the Kashmir Gate. He was not spotted by any sepoy guard, but was recognised by some Sikh artillery gunners, who 'prostrated themselves in reverence when they saw the giant figure of the man they believed to be their Incarnate God'.

Given Nicholson's rash character, he might well have entered the city just out of bravado if nothing else. One can, however, be fairly certain that he inspected the breaches made by the British artillery in the city walls to ascertain whether they could be stormed by his troops.[50] The story about the Sikhs might not be as far-fetched as it sounds. We know the British believed they might be turned and indeed tried to turn them, but without success.[51]

An anomaly existed concerning Nicholson's position during the period in the British camp on the Ridge. Once when passing some soldiers, one said to his companion, 'Jack, here's the General, present arms.' Nicholson gave the salute but said, 'Thank you, but I am not *General*, only Captain Nicholson.' His brigadier generalship had gone with the command of the military column and only later when he was placed in command of a brigade did the title technically return.

## TENSION AND TREPIDATION

This situation did, however, give Nicholson a considerable amount of freedom to go where he liked, when he liked and to mix with those he wished. He became increasingly close to the two key engineers involved in placing of the siege guns and ensuring that embasements were created sufficiently large for a military column to scramble over them into the city. These were the

31-year-old Captain Alexander Taylor and his superior, the legendary Colonel Richard Baird Smith. The biographer of the latter said that Smith gained great support from Nicholson, 'as that noble officer's views were the same as his own'.

This was undoubtedly true, not least because of the frustration caused each by General Wilson and his indecisiveness. What Colonel Richard Baird Smith wrote on the eve of the assault on Delhi could as easily have come from the pen of Nicholson: 'All goes well, except that I am satisfied Wilson has gone off his head.' And five years later Baird Smith's secretary, Henry Martin, who was with him at Delhi, recalled in a letter to Baird Smith's widow, 'Well do I know what a trying time Delhi was to him until he had Genl. Nicholson to endorse his views, and the vigour of both was allowed full play.'[52] But Baird Smith was not a well man. He had been wounded in the knee on 12 August, which seemed to be healing well until 23 August, when he became lame. Generally, too, Baird Smith was in a poor state. As he commented himself: 'An attack of camp scurvy had filled my mouth with sores, shaken every joint in my body, and covered me all over with livid spots, so I was marvellously unlovely to look upon.'[53]

It was clear that Taylor would have to fill in great part the role Baird Smith had been playing. Nicholson had been the person who had recommended to John Lawrence that Lieutenant Alex Taylor be brought to Delhi from his job as executive chief of roads. So, borrowing a sword from Sam Black, Taylor had set off from Lahore to Delhi, where he had arrived on 27 June.

It was said that Nicholson was the only senior officer who was not an engineer who bothered to survey the front line. Just before the assault on Delhi, Nicholson was in Chamberlain's tent and suddenly exclaimed, 'Well, if I live through this, I will let the world know who took Delhi; – that Alexander Taylor did it.' In fact, Taylor did well for himself and ended up a general, with a knighthood and president of the famous Royal Engineering College at Cooper's Hill at Windsor near London.[54] This college also trained foresters for the Indian empire.

On the Ridge, Nicholson was surrounded by Europeans again, albeit mostly dressed in khaki rather than the red or summer white Company tunics. As had happened in the past, having to mix with large numbers of Europeans made him lonely, defensive and rather morbid. The one European Nicholson wanted by his side, Lieutenant Roberts, was denied him by John Lawrence on the grounds that he could not spare him from the Lahore division where he had eventually ended up. But also, Lawrence conceded, 'I have no authority to supersede Greathed and by trying to do so once only raised a nest of hornets about my ears to no purpose.'[55]

That impending death was a real prospect facing him was clearly in Nicholson's mind. A 'poor orderly' of Nicholson's called Saadut Khan died of cholera on the Ridge. Nicholson wrote to Herbert Edwardes back in Peshawar saying that Khan had a mother, brother and possibly a wife in the Eusufzye country. He asked that should he not survive, 'will you kindly provide for the brother, and give the woman a couple of hundred rupees out of my estate.' And in reply to a rambling pious letter that ran to eight foolscap pages from Edwardes about the death of their mentor Sir Henry Lawrence, Nicholson let down his guard:

> If it please Providence that I live through this business, you must get me alongside of you again, and be my guide and help in endeavouring to follow his [Henry Lawrence's] example, for I am so weak and unstable that I shall never do any good of myself.[56]

# Assault on Delhi

In 1857 Delhi was 'one of the largest, most beautiful, and certainly the richest city in Hindostan', wrote Lieutenant John Griffiths of the 61st Regiment.[1] At that time Delhi was surrounded by a wall that the British had helped to fortify. It was 7 miles long, with ten gates and a water bastion. A census carried out in Delhi in 1846 estimated, from a total population of about 138,000 people, 52 per cent were Hindu, 48 per cent Muslim and about 0.2 per cent Christian. By 1857 the city's population had risen to about 150,000, the wider district of 488 square miles having a population of 245,133; when Hindus constituted 59 per cent of the population and Muslims 41 per cent.[2] Delhi had approximately 10,000 shops, 260 mosques, 188 temples and one church. There were 25,000 houses, 196 schools and 678 wells.[3] About 40,000 insurgent troops were present at the time of the siege.[4] This was the city the British were about to capture and loot. During this process, nearly the entire civilian population fled to the countryside or to one of the thirteen satellite villages. Ironically, the place inside the walls where the British would break through had been an area of European residence and nearby, also inside the walls, was the Anglican St James' church.

The pressures and tensions behind the high city walls when the insurgents were in control have been well documented by Mahmood Farooqui, who translated from Urdu and Persian a large selection of documents in these languages that fell into British hands. After an initial period of looting and lawlessness, a form of stability was re-established. But the influx of many thousands more mutineers into the city created new difficulties and rivalries. Plundering continued, despite a proclamation that any soldier found doing so would be shot. There was also another factor as Brigade Major, and British informer, Gauri Shankar pointed out in a letter dated 6 July: 'The mujahideed are very popular in the city. The maulvis give speeches in all the mosques and exhort people to do jihad against the Christians. The mujahideen are pouring in from all directions.'[5]

Of course, the British were also not beyond stirring the pot. Greathed recalls that on 23 August, 'The account of the Cawnpore tragedy was read out after mess last night: it made one's blood boil again.'[6]

In the city of Delhi, inevitably, traditional cultural values came to the fore during the siege. The killing of a cow now carried the penalty of death by being blown from a cannon, as did spying and looting. Gambling was banned. And to help fund the hungry insurgent army, shopkeepers were ordered to hand over three months' rent. On the other hand, matters in the city were not continuously or universally anarchic and 'a functioning bureaucracy was vigilantly maintained'. Farooqui makes the good point that there was no civil rebellion in Delhi and that 'most citizens remained indifferent or even hostile' to the largely billeted and not always well-controlled soldiers.[7] Tensions within the insurgent army, between military leaders and the royal court, and between civilians and soldiers, all intensified by the hostile and vengeful British army camped a few miles off did not lead to any sense of normality. The main stabilising influence appears to have been the police, who had been under the control of the British magistracy prior to the Great Rebellion.[8]

On 5 August Herbert Edwardes had written to Nicholson from Peshawar: 'A city may either be yielded without a contest, or disputed most savage street by street and you sh [should have] enough men for either event, and for pursuit afterwards.'[9]

Savage fighting was indeed now the order of the day. The 'enough men' was a moot point. But along with such sage advice, Edwardes could be quite bizarre, urging Nicholson: 'If you have it in your power to protect old Sudda Sookh's house in Delhi, on the day of the storm, and afterwards, I know you would be glad to do it.'[10]

That letter, the last Nicholson would receive from Edwardes before the assault, ended poignantly enough, 'I am looking most anxiously for the attack on Delhi, for I fear it will be no child's play if there is no breach made. God shield you my dear friend.'

An account of the extent of Nicholson's control at this time is given in a letter written by William Graham of Lisburn, who was in the besieging British army outside Delhi:

We have two of our advance batteries open and the old Moree Bastion we have knocked to bits, but they show wonderful pluck and still fight their guns in it. I hear it is a Seikh who commands it, and he must be a very fine fellow. I hear from one of Nicholson's friends that he is in communication with the above party, and I think the Seikhs who are inside once the attack is made are ready to hold any part of the city for us we like to name. I can't vouch for the truth of this, but report says so … Ni[cho]lson issued an order the other day entreating our Europeans when they get in not to forget they [there] are Christians [in Delhi], and spare women and children, but no quarter to any one else.[11]

## NICHOLSON AND THE ENGINEERS

The same day that Graham wrote this, Nicholson was writing to John Lawrence:

> The game is completely in our hands, we only want the player to move the pieces. Fortunately, after making all kinds of objections and obstructions, and even threatening more than once to withdraw the guns and abandon the attempt, Wilson has made everything over to the engineers, and they alone will deserve the credit for taking Delhi. Had Wilson carried out his threat of withdrawing the guns, I was quite prepared to appeal to the army to set him aside, and elect a successor.[12]

So it was that Baird Smith and then Alex Taylor came into his own. And Nicholson spent most of his day with Taylor, but kept in regular touch with Baird Smith, even during the actual assault. It was dangerous work being a gunner so close to the city walls. Casualties in the batteries from 7 to 14 September were 327 killed or wounded. Nor was it safe for Nicholson and Taylor as they constantly scouted the ground in the days before the assault. Many years later, the then General Fisher recalled those difficult times when he was a young man on the Ridge:

> I recollect watching Alex Taylor and Nicholson from Reid's look-out on the top of Hindu Rao's House; both were on horseback, examining sites for the advanced Batteries, after the Siege Train had arrived; and very perilous work it was, for no sooner were they discovered by the enemy's sentries than they had to ride through a storm of bullets for the nearest cover.[13]

Taylor was only slightly younger than Nicholson, yet the road builder was certainly the less dominant. Bosworth Smith asserted that, 'Nicholson himself, the bravest of the brave and rashest of the rash, used, in his devotion to Taylor, to be nervously, nay, amusingly anxious, lest he should expose himself to unnecessary danger.' Taylor's daughter later wrote that the pair would sit behind a rock or a ruin with bullets whistling overhead as they drank claret and discussed 'freewill, predestination, election, salvation, grace'. When Nicholson was killed, Alex Taylor wrote to a friend:

> latterly he used to come to my most difficult posts, and spend the greater part of the day with me. He used to talk of home, and religion, and many other things in a very open and simple way while resting from actual work, and, although we differed often enough, I could not but be greatly struck by his honest and very truthful character.

The engineers had been busy with preparations for the assault, preparing and storing a vast quantity of siege materials, including:

10,000 fascines (bundles of brushwood)
10,000 gabions (large defence blocks or cages filled with rock)
100,000 sandbags
Field magazines
Scaling ladders
Spare platforms

They also prepared the sites for the gun emplacements, cutting down trees and bushes around the site and clearing any obstacle obstructing the line of fire, though there was still a lot of dense cover from the orange gardens between the customs house and the walls. As well as the professional gunners, Roberts states that assistance was also given by soldiers from the carabineers and the 9th Lancers (the Delhi spearmen). On 6 September, ten heavy guns were established within 600 yards of the city walls. These opened their barrage next day, 7 September. That same day batteries were erected even closer to the walls, at 150 yards. By the morning of 11 September, all fifty-six of the British heavy guns and mortars were in place and 'in full play', pounding 'the doomed city'.[14] In private Lawrence conceded to Bartle Frere, chief commissioner of Sindh and advisor to John Lawrence, that 'we should have it [Delhi] [already], did Nicholson command!'[15]

The defenders could see the artillery build up and were experiencing its effect. On 8 September, the insurgent commander-in-chief told his officers to prepare to move to this part of the wall 'along with guns so that they can decimate the kafirs who are in the range of shots. It is desirable that the infantry troops should appear there and give battle.' Then, two days later, Subedar

(Lieutenant) Ananti Mishr, writing from the Lahore Gate, warned, 'The goras (Europeans) are concentrating on the Kashmiri Gate front. I hope that arrangements would be made for the defence of Kashmiri Gate. Everything here is all right.' At the same time, an offer of a reward of 100 rupees to any insurgent soldier who brought in the head of a British captain, colonel or general or 50 rupees for the 'head of any other gora' does not seem to have produced any results.[16] The firing of 32lb rockets into the British camp on the Ridge was more effective than bounty-hunting offers.

The extent of the Indian defences for the area that the British were eventually to attack can be clearly judged by the 244 artillery pieces that were captured by the British during the assault. In the insurgents' magazine, 203 were found, with a further forty-one captured on the streets or on the walls. Of those forty-one, 76 per cent or thirty-one were in the region of the Water, Kashmir and Moree Gates, with thirteen alone at the Kashmir gate where the British assault commenced.[17]

The dénouement was now not far off. Only after four drafts of a Project of Attack, written by Taylor and refined by Baird Smith, did General Wilson consent. According to Taylor, on 4 September, 'Nicholson has just read it, and I think it suits him to a "T".' So it was that on Saturday, 12 September 1857, things at last began to happen. At 11 a.m., the senior officers on the Ridge were summoned to General Wilson's tent to receive their orders for the all too long-awaited assault on the old imperial city. Nicholson, true to form, did not appear but was instead at the bottom of the hill beside the 'great breaching battery within one hundred and sixty yards of the water bastion'. Wilson does not seem to have been put out. Perhaps it was easier for him not to have the man whom many considered the real commander present.

Besides, it was already decided that Nicholson, now as commander of the 4th Infantry Brigade, would lead the assault on the city. He would take personal command of one of the columns that would scale the 16ft-deep ditch, which was at least as broad as it was deep, and then the battered walls between the Water Bastion and the Kashmir Gate. As Table 3 illustrates, there were to be five columns. Two months earlier Wilson had told Nicholson that he needed 4,500 men to storm Delhi. This was indeed about the size of the force that would go over the city wall. There had already been a proposal to storm the city on 2 July, but General Bernard, Wilson's predecessor, had withheld his consent and was supported by Neville Chamberlain.[18] Given the nature of the assault on the walls and the victory to be achieved once inside the city, though, the army Nicholson led was a very small force for the task.

*Table 3: Storming of Delhi: 14 September 1857*

| Column | Commander | Regiments in column | Approx. size of column | Where assaulted |
|---|---|---|---|---|
|  | Lt Col Jones | 60th Rifles | 200 | Skirmishing. |
| 1st | Major General Nicholson | - 75th Regt (300)<br>- 1st European Bengal Fusiliers (250)<br>- Punjab Infantry (Green's Rifles) 450 | 1,000 | Breach to the riverside of the Kashmir Gate. |
| 2nd | Brigadier W. Jones | - HM 8th (the King's) Regt. (250)<br>- 2nd Europeans Bengal Fusiliers (250)<br>- 4th Sikhs (350) | 850 | Breach nearest the Water Bastion beside the river. |
| 3rd | Colonel Campbell | - 52nd Regt.(200)<br>- Gurkhas (Kumaon Batt.) (250)<br>- 1st Punjab Infantry (Coke's Rifles, under Lt. Charles Nicholson) (500) | 950 | Kashmir Gate after it had been blown. |
| 4th | Major Charles Reid | - 60th Rifles (part)<br>- Gurkhas (Sirmur Batt.)<br>- Detachments from European regts<br>- Kashmir contingent | 1,850 | To attack the fortified suburbs of Kishanganj. Kissengunge and Paharipur. To enter Delhi via the Lahore Gate and rendezvous with columns 1 and 2. |
| 5th Reserve | Brigadier Longfield (HM 8th Regt) | - 61st Regt. (250)<br>- HM 60th Rifles<br>- Baluch Batt. (300)<br>- 4th Punjab Infantry (450)<br>- Jind troops | c. 1,500 | To cover the advance of Nicholson's column and act as a reserve. |
| Cavalry Brigade | Colonel Grant | - 9th Lancers<br>- Sikh Cavalry<br>- Punjab Cavalry (sections)<br>- Horse Artillery (some) |  | On the right of No. 1 Advanced Battery, facing the Mori Gate, within range of Kishanganj. |

Their purpose was to protect the storming parties' flank, monitor the enemy's movements and guard the British camp from surprise attack.

Even at this stage, not everyone seems to have agreed that Nicholson was the perfect choice to lead the assault. Interestingly, Captain Bouchier commented about Nicholson and command in his narrative of the siege, 'It seems a pity that a man with such administrative capacity was allowed to do what fifty others would have done equally well, and whose loss would have been less of a national calamity.'[19]

# COUNTDOWN TO THE ASSAULT

That Saturday evening Nicholson clung to Chamberlain, accompanying him on his routine inspection of the British camp along the Ridge as far as Hindu Rao's house, where as usual Nicholson had to shout up to Major Charles Reid in his lookout that his Gurkha sentry would not let him up the ladder: 'he always stops me.' Maybe that was because Reid did not much like Nicholson: 'I thought I had never seen a man I disliked so much at first sight. His haughty manner and peculiar sneer I could not stand.'[20] When Reid intimated this to Baird Smith, the latter responded, 'Yes, but that wears off. You'll like him better when you have seen more of him.' And according to Trotter, that is exactly what happened. It was at Hindu Rao's house on 9 September that both Reid and Nicholson were nearly killed when a shell burst above them, sending shrapnel all around. After visiting Reid, that Saturday evening, Nicholson insisted that Chamberlain dine with him in his tent.

On the morning of Sunday 13 September, Nicholson was back at Hindu Rao's house once more, speaking excitedly about next day's assault. After Reid's column had captured the suburbs to the west, Nicholson said he would personally open the Kabul Gate for Reid 'from the inside'.

Throughout the day, Nicholson on several occasions rode over to Chamberlain's tent to pressurise him to go to General Wilson with various proposals. It would seem that Nicholson had absolutely no illusions about the chasm that persisted between himself and his commanding officer. According to Captain Daly, all the officers present when Wilson announced that Nicholson would lead the assault were pleased to hear the news. There is no reason to doubt Harry Daly's perception of the situation. He commanded the elite and very effective cavalry Guides Corps. Though he was very much a product of empire, Daly's family owned the estate of Daly's Grove in County Galway, the big house 'dropped down at the edge of a marsh'.[21] If anyone understood both Nicholson's background and his impact on others, it was this quiet and respected Irish officer.

At 3 p.m. Nicholson summoned his adjutants to his tent for a council of war. Very tight security was enforced with no one allowed near the general's tent during the meeting. Nicholson made it clear what would happen if senior officers were killed, leaving no doubt in everyone's mind that casualties were going to be very high. Detailed orders to the commanders' senior officers would be distributed to them only early the following morning. According to Wilberforce, who was not present at the briefing, next day when the British were into the city they found an army notebook with details of the assault.

This story, however, would be more credible were the source more reliable. Besides, the insurgents would have been incredibly remiss had they not realised that the long-awaited assault was now pending.

A short but telling pen sketch of Nicholson in his tent during the briefing that Sunday afternoon before the assault was written twelve years later by the then Lieutenant Richard Barter, adjutant of the 75th Gordon Highlanders:

> He seemed to be about forty [he was 35] years of age or it may be younger with brown hair and beard and rather bald; he was tall, over six feet, and stout built without being fat. On a table before him was a map of the city and he stood up, his right foot on his chair, and explained what we were expected to do in a clear and lucid manner.[22]

This is probably an accurate description, down to his standing with a foot on the chair. The only reliable image we have of Nicholson is the daguerreotype photograph taken when on furlough leave in Britain in 1850. The much-reproduced painting of Nicholson standing with his hands on the hilt of his sword was painted after his death. As discussed elsewhere, the other picture of Nicholson with a goatee beard maybe a sketch of Charles Nicholson.[23] Two photographs very probably of Nicholson were recently discovered and are reproduced in this book.

The council of war broke up at 4.30 p.m. and Nicholson went down to see his friends in the batteries, entering Number 2 with a hearty greeting: 'I must shake hands with you fellows; you have done your best to make my work easy to-morrow.'[24] That evening Nicholson was back with Chamberlain, but by 8 o'clock, declining Chamberlain's offer of dinner, Nicholson was now highly restless and anxious to move back to his own quarters to brief his officers again and sort out last-minute details.

It is doubtful that Nicholson slept much that night. In fact, Lieutenant Roberts said there was not that much sleep in camp that night. Men prepared their kit and in particular padded protection to wrap around hats as heads would be exposed as the ladders were climbed. Lieutenant Barter said the same:

> I dropped off now and then but never for long and whenever I awoke I could see that there was a light in more than one of the officers' tents and talking was going on in a low tone amongst the men, the snapping of a lock or springing of a ramrod sounding far in the still air telling of preparation for the approaching strife.[25]

But even those who did sleep had a short night. At 2 a.m., the troops were assembled. In the cold air before sunrise, orders were read out to them. The gunners' mess was a hive of activity with men reading their orders and 'poring over a large map of Delhi on which our various routes were marked, buckling on revolvers, filling haversacks with flasks and bread, and snatching a few mouthfuls of supper by candle-light'. Each private carried 200 rounds of ammunition. It was made clear to the men that very heavy casualties were expected:

> Any officer or man who might be wounded was to be left where he fell: no one was to step from the ranks to help him as we had no men to spare; if the assault were successful he'd be taken up by the doolies and carried to the rear or to wherever he could best receive medical assistance; if we failed, wounded and sound should be prepared to bear the worse. There was to be no plundering, but all prize taken was to be put into a common stock for fair division after all was over. No prisoners were to be made, as we had no one to guard them, and care was to be taken that no women or children were injured.

It is said to the last the men answered, 'No fear sir.'[26] Lieutenant Griffiths recalled what happened next:

> The troops fell in on their respective lines, and assembling at the slope of the ridge, the four columns of attack marched in silence to the Flagstaff Tower. Thence, picking up the men on picket, who were all withdrawn from the outlying posts, the force moved by the road to the neighbourhood of Ludlow Castle, and close to No. 2 Advanced Battery. Our movements were entirely concealed from the enemy; the darkness which prevailed, and the ample cover from trees, gardens, and houses, masking the march of the columns, while the breaching batteries, which kept up their fire all night long, still continued the bombardment; nor did they cease till the actual moment when the columns were set in motion and took their way to the city.[27]

Ludlow Castle was the nearest British-occupied building to the walls and was used as a military hospital during the assault. It was here that John and Charles Nicholson met that early morning, shaking hands and then parting, each to face his fate. Charles was now acting commander of Coke's Rifles, all the principal officers having been either killed or wounded. Also beside Nicholson in the gloom before dawn was Alex Taylor.

The day before the British assault on the Kashmir Gate and surrounding wall, the following order was issued under the seal of the imperial privy council to the kotwal or officer in charge of that part of the defences: 'You are directed to issue a general proclamation that whoever in the city is a soldier or is armed should assemble at Kashmiri Gate at night and should stay there as long as the fighting continues.'[28]

## ENTERING THE WALLED CITY

Nicholson's No. 1 Column was in the centre of four columns; Colonel Campbell's No. 3 Column was to his right; Brigadier Jones' No. 2 Column was to his left; and Brigadier Longfield's No. 5 Column was immediately behind Nicholson's. In front of this formation were three breaching gun batteries and behind Nicholson was a heavy mortar battery of cannon. The engineering officers in Nicholson's column were Captain Taylor, Lieutenant Bingham, Lieutenant Lang, Lieutenant Medley and Ensign Chalmers.[29]

Far to the west (right) was Colonel Reid's No. 4 Column, which was meant to attack the fortified suburbs of Kishanganj, Kissengunge and Paharipur then enter Delhi via the Lahore Gate to rendezvous with columns 1 and 2. The failure of this column to achieve this ambitious goal stymied the plan and greatly prolonged the battle to seize the city. But it is questionable whether this had in any case been the optimal plan to adopt. Once inside the walls between the Water Bastion and the Kashmir Gate there was a relatively open sweep of land stretching deep into the city. Had the British occupied and consolidated themselves in this area, bringing in field artillery, they might well have done better than they did, instead being pinned down along the perimeter of the wall for a day.

Accounts differ as to what was the signal for attack. One was that Nicholson walked over to the No. 2 Column and laying his hand on Lieutenant Colonel Jones's shoulder, asked him if he was ready. When Jones said yes, Nicholson then ordered the 60th Rifles to advance, which they did, firing at the defenders on the wall, so giving covering fire for the ladder men to get forward. Most accounts, however, give the signal to advance as the blowing of the Kashmir Gate, which occurred at 5.45 a.m., and was immediately followed by a bugler sounding the advance and the regimental call of the 52nd.[30] This explosion was set by two sapper officers and five sergeants. Only two men survived this hazardous task because once the British bombardment ceased in order to allow the three columns to advance 'the walls were lined with the enemy in shoals who kept up an incessant fire and brought up light guns on platforms on the breach'. Wilberforce says that as Nicholson passed the 52nd Regiment in No. 2 Column as they awaited the assault he said, 'Good-bye! I wish I was going with you.' In the hours that followed, the 52nd lost one in every two men who took part in the assault. Captain Bouchier says that he shook hands with Nicholson as the commander 'passed on the road leading to the Cashmere Gate'.

Nicholson's No. 1 Column had first advanced to Ludlow Castle. One witness said that Nicholson 'looked quiet and anxious'. They were briefly joined by General Wilson who also was, not surprisingly, 'evidently full of anxiety'. At the Castle those on horses dismounted. The ladder men came to the front with the officers and No. 1 Column moved left at a quick march into the Kudsia/Koosya Bagh. Jones's No. 2 Column moved into the custom house garden, and Campbell's No.3 Column moved onto the road leading to the Kashmir Gate. There were now only about 200 yards between the British force and the towering city wall.

The British advance was met with a hail of musket shot from the walls. We know that some of the insurgent defenders were from the 9th Native Infantry and the Kashmir Gate itself was defended by Doorga Singh's company. Stories of a European man fighting alongside the insurgents in the vicinity circulated. Other such reports were not infrequent elsewhere in the war zone. In the Delhi case, this was said to have been an artillery sergeant major who commanded the artillery against the British. Certainly, there was nothing unique about Europeans fighting in Indian-led armies.[31]

The fire from the defenders around the Kashmir Gate was so intense that for a period of some ten minutes the ladder men could not get into the 16 to 20ft deep ditch before the wall. It was at this glacis that much damage was done rather than in the actual 25ft-wide ditch itself, or climbing up through the rubble of the breach made by the siege cannon.[32] Three times the ladder party was 'swept away' in 'a perfect hailstorm of bullets' before men were able to start climbing up the far side of the ditch. The scene was truly desperate and the casualty rate very high. One soldier's contemporary account of Nicholson's advancing force vividly brings this home:

> The brutes fought till we regularly cut and hacked our way through them with sword and baynot. Unfortunately the first thing my sword struck in was the body of a colour sergeant of mine just along side of me on the next ladder who was shot and fell on my sword. But the next moment it was shivering through a pandy and then another. All order and formation was

over and we cut and hacked wherever we could. I never throught of drawing my pistol but poked, thrust and hacked till my arm was tired.

By this time we had not a firm footing inside the Quadrangle and sent out a skirmishing party to avoid a new approach and allow a formation. We formed a column and went round the walls to the right. We took with our Colours (of 75th Queens, 2nd Fusiliers and 4th Sikhs) gate after gate and barricade and house after house, the natives defending every place inch by inch till we reached the 5th gate viz – the Cabul Gate. It was a tough fight there and they had numbers and guns [light cannon] against our few remaining men with muskets … we had nothing to eat or drink all day and were awfully done, my sole consolation, a soda water bottle of weak brandy and water hanging to my side had been shot through and the liquor wasted.[33]

Two accounts exist as to Nicholson's role in the assault. One has it that initially Nicholson was with the 1st European Bengal Fusiliers, what would eventually become the Munster Fusiliers. But there was a delay at the ditch as many of the ladder men had been shot and new ladder men had to come up. It was not getting down into the ditch which was the problem as most slid down, but getting up the far side. Impatient as ever, Nicholson ran along the base of the city wall to join the 75th, which was nearby on his left, and crossed the breach into the city with them. Alex Taylor regarded this as a mercy as otherwise Nicholson would have been first man over the top with the 1st Fusiliers and almost certainly shot then. Although Roberts asserted that Nicholson was the first to ascend the breach in the curtain, this is probably not correct as the first wave must have been shot down. That said, however, Nicholson cannot have been far behind.

Another variation on this saga was that while awaiting the order to attack, Nicholson was informed, possibly by Wilson, that he was to command both No. 1 Column and No. 2. Certainly, the plan was for them to unite once inside the wall. On hearing that he had a dual column command, Nicholson left Taylor in charge of No. 1 Column and went over to speak to Brigadier General Jones. Having spoken to Jones, Nicholson placed himself at the head of a wing of No. 1 Column so that when the advance was sounded Taylor, Nicholson and Jones were leading men over the breach.[34] Both accounts are not incompatible, but clearly detail is missing.

The plan had been that once over the two breaches, Nicholson was to turn right and to push as far as the Ajmir Gate by way of the road that skirted the inside of the city wall, taking also the broad ledge on top of the wall. The Ajmir Gate was a considerable way around the city wall. However, the last reliable report of the chaos inside the walls once the British were over the breaches sees

Nicholson and Alex Taylor running towards Skinner's House and not right and along the city wall as had been the plan.

Some idea about the scale of the carnage can be grasped from the figures reflected in table 4. Between 30 May and 20 September, there had been 3,837 British casualties, an average of thirty-four a day. On the day of the initial assault on Delhi, there was well over 100 times the average casualty rate, or 38 per cent of all casualties for that four-month period.

*Table 4: British Casualties at Delhi, 30 May to 20 September 1857*

| Dates | Number of days | Number of Casualties | Average per day |
|---|---|---|---|
| 30 May to 8 September | 102 | 2,163 | 21 |
| 9 to 13 September | 5 | 327 | 65 |
| 14 September | 1 | 1,170 | 1,170 |
| 15 to 20 September | 6 | 177 | 30 |
| Total | 114 | 3,837 | 34 |

## INSIDE THE WALLS

What exactly Nicholson did and where he was before being shot is uncertain. Having rallied a large number of men over the breach in the wall, he reassembled them in the open square, the main Guard, beyond the Kashmir Gate on the city side. Columns No. 1 and No. 2 now appeared to have been united – as much as the chaotic situation would allow. Nicholson then, as planned, turned to the right and tried to make his way along the inner side of the city gate at the foot of the wall towards the Moree Gate. This advance initially failed. But soon Brigadier Jones was clearing the top of the wall right the way up to the Kabul Gate. Sir Hope Grant, the cavalry officer, recorded that he saw Brigadier Nicholson on top of the Mori Bastion leading his brigade: 'He called out to me that the fighting was going well for us in the town, and that he was on his way to attack the Lahore gate and bastion, about 500 yards farther on.'[35]

But serious trouble lay ahead. In no small part, this was due to the failure of No. 4 Column to gain entrance into the city, meaning that a pincer movement by British troops along the walls could not be achieved.

The green flag that had been Nicholson's personal standard and which was to have been carried by 'one of his Afghan followers' was not seen again. It is not known whether this flag was a hankering back to Ireland or of local Punjab or, more likely, Afghan significance. Only a few days earlier Edwardes had told Nicholson about a green flag seen flying in the Khyber Pass, which might have put the idea into Nicholson's head.[36]

Nicholson and Taylor met near Skinner's House and discussed how best to consolidate a defence of that area. The two men parted, as it was to turn out, forever. 'I am sorry not to have you with me,' were apparently Nicholson's last words to his friend.

Nicholson then appears to have driven forward with his own enthusiasm and pushed into the city with a small force around him, sword in right hand and revolver in left, as portrayed in the Lisburn statue. Taylor's daughter suggested years later that he had taken a right turn at some stage coming up Canal Street or Kabul Road in order to re-join his troops on the wall around Kabul Street. That is certainly possible, but others at the time speculated that Nicholson pressed even deeper into the city.

Because of their home town link of Lisburn, the Graham brothers, James and William, kept a special eye on Nicholson during the Mutiny. According to William Graham, writing a fortnight later, Nicholson and the band of fighters around him did indeed penetrate very deep into the city – as far as the great mosque, the Jumna Musjid. This seems extraordinary. But Nicholson was not beyond the extraordinary.

After entering the city, most of the British force milled around before advancing in a fairly disorganised manner along the Rampart Road under the city wall. Brigadier Jones followed at his own pace. Other troops remained for the moment in the area around the Kashmir Gate, but did not follow their orders:

> Isolated groups of men, European and native, led sometimes by officers, and often without any leaders, roamed through the narrow streets, entering houses from which the fire was more than severe, putting to death without mercy all who were found inside.[37]

Campbell in No. 3 Column, which included the 52nd, succeeded in reaching Begum's Bagh and indeed as far as the closed gates of the great mosque. Graham believed the failure of the Column No. 4 to break into the city meant Nicholson and his men had to retreat back across the great boulevard, the Chandni Chowk, which led straight down to the main entrance of the imperial palace. On the other hand, if Nicholson did not set off for the great mosque, where was he before he suddenly reappeared in the region of the Kabul Gate several hours later? He may have joined up with some members of No. 3 Column, possibly members of the 52nd, and pushed deep into the city.

The 52nd was back at the ruined Anglican St James' church near the Kashmir
Gate at about 11.30 a.m., which would dovetail approximately with the time
Nicholson reappeared in the accounts of the drive along the lane under the
city wall where he was soon to meet his fate. The other factor was the need
for Nicholson to consolidate a base and headquarters within the northern city.
That must have taken time.

Meanwhile, the telegraph wire from the British camp was busy. Even that
very morning, Edwardes in Peshawar received the message, 'Delhi assaulted,
and fighting still going on! The attack successful.' Certainly, the breach was
successful but many days of gruelling fighting still lay ahead of the invading
force. No sooner had a group of British troops passed the ends of some of
the buildings adjoining the lane and the city wall than insurgents reappeared,
ensuring that the next body of British troops passing had to fight their
way through again. On the Ridge, news from the city was hard to get but
Chamberlain was in some form of communication as his men cleared the
Moree Gate, the first major hurdle after the Kashmir Gate. A short distance
along from the Moree Gate, the city wall turned at a bastion. Ahead lay the
Kabul Gate and further beyond the Lahore Gate. Still further was Nicholson's
ultimate goal, the Ajmir Gate. Jones had managed to get his men to storm and
take the Kabul Bastion, where the flag of No. 2 Column was raised.

The Kabul Gate was an obvious and sensible place to stop and consolidate,
but Nicholson would not listen to reason and determined to press on. His next
object was to get to the Lahore Gate, open it and allow Reid's column to enter.
But beyond the wall, Brigadier James Hope Grant's cavalry, including many
of Nicholson's mounted hill fighters, were suffering from the insurgent guns
on the western walls. Reid and his No. 4 Column was being pressed hard and
having to retreat.[38]

Two hours after the breach was forced, Nicholson re-emerged on the
Rampart Road. On the right towered the city wall, with deep indentations
or recesses about 4 or 5ft in depth, tall enough for several men to shelter in
if necessary. Opposite the wall were some 'mud huts' and farther along some
houses with flat roofs and parapets. But none of these had windows looking out
onto the lane in which 'scarce 4 men could stand abreast'. About 60 yards down
this death trap, the lane bent around to the left following the wall. An insurgent
brass artillery gun was at the bend and 100 yards further on was a field gun.
Behind the field guns were large sheets of metal acting as bulletproof screens
for the insurgent troops. And high up on the wall was the Burn Bastion, with
yet more enemy field guns as well as insurgent sharp-shooters. Then on the
rooftops were insurgents throwing stones and round shot by hand.[39]

The plan was that as the Fusiliers stormed the lane, above on the top of the city wall the 75th would sweep the 'ramparts and carry the position above'. But this did not happen, so the lane was under fire from insurgent forces from ahead and above. Twice the Fusiliers stormed up the alleyway and captured the brass gun, the first time having to retreat because the fury of grapeshot, musket balls, rifle bullets and even stones was so great. According to Captain Brookes of the 75th Regiment, two hours of repeated attempts were made to force the passageway. One soldier, Lieutenant Butler actually succeeded in passing the second gun and reached the metal sheets, but then retired to re-join the men. The chance came again from the British mainly 1st European Bengal Fusiliers. Led by Major G.O. Jacobs, they again captured the brass gun (which Captain Greville of the 1st Fusiliers spiked) and again made for the second gun, only to be met with deadly fire. The carnage was great. Seven officers fell, dead or mortally wounded: first Major Jacobs, and later Butler, Caulfield, Greville, Speke (brother of the famous African explorer), Wemyss and Woodcock all fell.[40] They fell back a second time. As Lieutenant Griffiths remarked, there 'is nothing so destructive of the morale and discipline of soldiers as street-fighting'.

Some time earlier, Sir John Lawrence had written, 'Old Nick is such a forward fellow, and is only too likely to get knocked over.'[41] Now was that time. After the second failed attempt to storm the alleyway and the wavering troops had again pulled back, they heard the 'stentorian voice' of John Nicholson already making his way down the laneway, 'his sword waving over his head, a very impersonification of the heroic in war', and turning to encourage them to follow. Several officers, including Captain Graydon, were immediately behind him but the men had hesitated. And it was as Nicholson's turned to shout at these exhausted troops that a musket ball struck him in the back under the right armpit. This was possibly shot by an insurgent sniper from the Burn Bastion.[42] One source states, 'The ball had penetrated and broken a rib – the fractured rib wounding the pleura and opening the cavity of the chest.'[43]

It is amazing given Nicholson's recklessness that he had not been picked off long before. Indeed, the point has to be made that this urban fighting was not familiar to Nicholson. He was a horse-and-sabre man, who fought in the open and close to his enemy. The only other experience he had had of urban warfare was at Ghazni in Afghanistan, which had been a brief action. Delhi was quite different. Once the British were over the walls, they found the enemy was seldom close at hand. A sabre against sniper and artillery fire at 100 yards was of little use. It was this new age of warfare that killed Nicholson.

# The Lion of the Punjab Falls

The intense confusion of a major battle scene means that the sequence of events after Nicholson was shot remains puzzling to this day. Complicating the situation, several officers of the 1st Fusiliers were also shot down at about the same time as Nicholson. At some point, when is not sure, the command of the assault army passed to Brigadier Jones.

As Nicholson fell, he was caught by a sergeant, who lowered him to the ground inside one of the recesses of the city wall. It was said that one fusilier told Nicholson he was shot, to which Nicholson replied irritably, 'Yes, yes.' Another, and less likely, version has Nicholson being laid under a tree. Most versions say that Nicholson allowed no one to move him. Captain Graydon immediately dashed across the lane to assist and gave Nicholson a swig of brandy. Graydon's concern was that the enemy would come up the lane and Nicholson fall into their hands. But ever stubborn, Nicholson repeatedly refused to be moved, saying he would die there.

So Graydon set off in the direction of the Kabul Gate to fetch help, leaving Nicholson in the care of his 'faithful servant'. Meeting an officer and a clump of men, he told them of Nicholson's injury before continuing until he encountered Lieutenant Le Poer Trench of the 35th Native Infantry, Nicholson's aide-de-camp and another Anglo-Irish officer in Nicholson's circle. That the aide-de-camp was not with the general shows what a state of confusion reigned.

Nicholson continued to be difficult, and refused to be moved by 'the men who would not follow me'. One version of events has him saying, 'The men that would not follow me shall not lift me from the ground,' and he called to his native 'orderlies' to carry him into camp.[1]

There then seems now to have been a hiatus with no one knowing what to do until Captain Hay appeared on the scene. Hay was from the 60th Native Infantry and was clearly trusted by the wounded and sulking Nicholson, even though the two had some time previously had an altercation. This had involved Hay denying that Nicholson had given him in June some papers relating to the 10th Irregular Cavalry. But now the sight of a Native Infantry company officer settled matters in Nicholson's mind: 'I will make up my difference with you, Hay. I will let you take me back.' At this point there appeared on the scene two other men whom Nicholson trusted, Muhammad Hayat Khan and Eusuf Khan. The two Indians raised their commander to his feet and the three began the slow walk to the Kabul Gate, 'with tears streaming from their eyes'. Here Nicholson requested to be put in the shade. Whether this is true or not is uncertain. If it is, why did Hayat Khan not stick like a leech to his fallen hero, and what happened to him when Nicholson was being carried back to camp? It is more likely that the unnamed sergeant who had stayed with Nicholson since he fell brought him back to the relative safety of the Kabul Gate. Nicholson asked to see Graydon, who came over to find Nicholson suffering greatly. He gave him a little more brandy.

All that is known for certain is that at the Kabul Gate Nicholson was placed in a *doolie* and four bearers carried him off to the field hospital at Ludlow Castle. They seem to have just emerged from the city via the Kashmir Gate when the bearers put down their charge and went off to join in the looting that was now under way, indicating that one of these clearly could not have been Hayat Khan. It seems shocking that a badly wounded commanding field officer should have been treated like this. Unfortunately, it is clear that the officers in the alleyway were still so engrossed in the firefight swirling around them that they did not check whether their commander had been effectively evacuated to the field hospital.

Then, by an extraordinary coincidence, the wounded and abandoned Nicholson was found by young Freddie Roberts, who had been recently redeployed to General Wilson's staff. Roberts wrote to his mother on 16 September, 'At last we are inside this wretched city … the first day all was confusion, soldiers lost their Regiments in the streets … Such a scene of desolation as the whole place is – the Church is a ruin, and all the European houses and our men now sack and destroy all the Native ones.'[2]

News coming into Skinner's House was so bad that Wilson sent Roberts out to try and get an accurate picture of what was going on, especially to the No. 4 Column outside the walls:

> while riding through the Kashmir gate I observed by the side of the road a doolie, without bearers, and with evidently a wounded man inside. I dismounted to see if I could be of any use to the occupant, when I found to my grief and consternation, that it was John Nicholson, with death written

on his face. He told me that the bearers had put the doolie down and gone off to plunder; that he was in great pain, and wished to be taken to the hospital. He was lying on his back, no wound was visible, and but for the pallor of his face, always colourless, there was no sign of the agony he must have been enduring. On my expressing a hope that he was not seriously wounded, he said: 'I am dying; there is no chance for me.'

Having with difficulty collected four men, I put them in charge of a sergeant of the 61st Foot. Taking down his name, I told him who the wounded officer was, and ordered him to go directly to the field hospital.

This was the last I saw of Nicholson. I found time to ride several times to the hospital to inquire after him, but I was never allowed to see him again.[3]

So eventually John Nicholson was carried to Ludlow Castle, probably late on the Monday afternoon.

He was not the only Nicholson at the field hospital. Charles Nicholson had also proved himself a hero and a victim that day. The young lieutenant leading his own unit had received shrapnel wounds that left his right arm hanging by his side. There was nothing the army surgeon, Dr H. Buckle, could do but to amputate it immediately.

Buckle also saw John Nicholson when he reached the field hospital. John Nicholson asked for some lemonade, which was given to him. Buckle went on:

He was then quite quiet, and as collected and composed as usual, but very low – almost pulseless. What struck me was his face – it was always one of power – but then, in its calm pale state, it was quite beautiful.[4]

At the military tent hospital, Nicholson was given close attention by two doctors, Hare and Broome. To these hardened battlefield surgeons, the case was quite clearly hopeless. He was bled on several occasions, which cannot have helped a man who had lost so much blood from the large wound of a musket shot. His blood pressure remained alarmingly low, even when he appeared to be reviving. Dr O'Callaghan, from the artillery, also turned up and looked at Nicholson, confirming the grim prognosis. In a touching scene, it is said that the fellow Irishman took 'Nicholson's hand in both his own, pressed it, and left the tent unable to control his feelings'.

Buckle had Charles's *doolie* brought out and placed beside his brother's for a while before they were sent into camp, John to the tent of his friend Harry Daly. One account by a soldier called Jim in the 52nd who was also wounded in the field hospital, should probably to be taken with caution. He claimed that

Nicholson let it be known that any man who had served under him might come and say farewell:

> Many wounded soldiers availed themselves of the opportunity to look upon the prostrate figure of him, who, with them, had shared the hardships and toils in the Punjaub. They took the general's hand, he spoke a kindly word to them, and then they said farewell. In two days from his last request, he died as he lived, a valiant soldier.[5]

Lieutenant Montgomery of the Guides was on duty and helped lift the brigadier general out of the *doolie* onto a bed. Nicholson was in 'fearful agony, and the blood was flowing down his side. He was shot through the body'. In a touching attempt to make his senior officer more comfortable, Montgomery bathed the wounded soldier's forehead with the Victorian standby of eau de cologne. Montgomery later wrote:

> I could have followed him anywhere, so brave, cool, and self-possessed, and so energetic you would have thought he was made of iron. The shot that killed him was worth more to the Pandy than all the rest put together.[6]

That evening at 8 o'clock Chamberlain saw Nicholson and said he was lying on a charpoy bed and breathing very heavily, 'only able to jerk out his words in syllables at long intervals and with pain'. Large doses of morphine inevitably led to drowsiness, but he had enough of his wits about him to speak of Herbert Edwardes and to ask Chamberlain the obvious questions: what the doctors were really saying about his condition, and how much of the town was in British hands and what they were going to do next? Chamberlain looked in again at about 11 that night and found Nicholson complaining of being chilly, probably due to shock. He covered him with a light Rampore blanket.[7]

A footnote needs to be added to this battle scene. Some accounts have a subsequent assault down the lane taking place and succeeding, but if this is true the position was not held and the force retreated back to the Kabul Gate, where about 200 men held the precarious position through the night, 100 on the gate itself and two groups of fifty each on the rooftops 'of the highest houses down the street', the enemy regularly attacking 'with about 3,000 men and 2 light guns'.[8] That these exhausted men held the gate until reinforcements arrived was extraordinary.

Back near the Kashmir Gate at Skinner's House, the British headquarters had been established with 'a goodly tiffin spread out on tables under a shamiana on the chabootra'. But inside in a long room, General Wilson paced up and down agonising over the ever-mounting casualty figures.[9]

## WAS NICHOLSON MURDERED?

So-called 'friendly fire' became a recognised cause of British casualties in the most recent British foray into Afghanistan in the early twenty-first century. Nearly a century earlier, on 10 February 1917, *The Times* newspaper carried the following extraordinary allegation:

A LINK WITH THE MUTINY
THE TRUE STORY OF NICHOLSON'S DEATH
The death has occurred in Kensington, at the age of 82, of Mrs. Dennis, widow of the General Dennis who was the first Commandant at Delhi after the fall.

'Her Physician' writes:-

As hostess she had entertained John Nicholson, Hodgson [Hodson], of the famous Horse, Sir Henry Lawrence, and others of note in that stirring time. At the age of 18, herself a widow already, she married Colonel Dennis, who took her to India. He became General Dennis, and as such served on the Ridge at Delhi. She recalled Lord Roberts as a very young man, and admitted that his version of Nicholson's death was promulgated by Sir John Lawrence, as he then was.

In the ferment in which India was at that time the truth would have had a very sinister influence on native troops on the edge of disaffection. General Dennis and those on the staff on the Ridge knew that Nicholson was shot by one of his own men, whom the day before he had degraded to the ranks from the position of havildar for some neglect of the rigid discipline enacted by him. The man was arrested and executed the following day. She was frankly frightened of Nicholson when he came to her house, and as frankly charmed by the condescension and courtesy of Hodgson. I think that in her has passed the last hostess to these famous men.[10]

Immediately, there is some confusion about which Dennis or Denniss is intended. Lieutenant Colonel George Gladwin Denniss (1821–62) was neither a general nor commandant of the city of Delhi when it fell, but was in the

1st Bengal Fusiliers, Herbert Edwardes's old regiment. According to Roberts, Denniss was in charge of the Moveable Column in the few days between Chamberlain leaving and Nicholson taking up the command. Lieutenant Roberts did not think much of Denniss, writing in his memoir:

> I reported myself to Denniss, who, though an officer of many years' service, had never before held a command, not even that of a regiment; poor man! Was considerably taken aback when he heard that he must be in charge of the column for some days. He practically left everything to me – a somewhat trying position for almost the youngest officer in the force. It was under these circumstances I found what an able man Colonel Campbell really was. He correctly gauged Denniss's fitness, or rather unfitness, for command, and appreciating the awkwardness of my position, advised me so wisely that I had no difficulty in carrying on the work.[11]

But there must be a confusion here as the colonel in the 52nd Infantry was John Leslie Dennis (not Denniss), who most certainly had seen action. He was with the 52nd under Nicholson but when the city was stormed General Wilson left him in charge of the British camp on the Ridge. Here he remained on 14 and 15 September before entering the city to take command of the 52nd on 16 September. [12] John Leslie Dennis did become a general.

George Gladwin Denniss was the son and a grandson of senior military officers, his father being a colonial in the Bengal Artillery and his grandfather a colonel in the 43rd Light Infantry. The family was of Anglo-Irish stock. George Gladwin Denniss had joined the 1st Fusiliers in 1840, just after Nicholson had entered the Company's service. In 1849 he had a regimental rank of captain and was seconded as second-in-command of the 4th Punjab Infantry. But he could not have been in Delhi on 14 September when the city was assaulted because he left the British camp on 5 September and on 15 September was writing to his wife Eleanor back in England from the hill station of Dagshai, 155 miles north of Delhi.[13] Matters are not made any easier by the fact that the name Denniss is sometimes spelt Dennis in records.

In the 1917 newspaper report the deceased Mrs Dennis is given as aged 82. That would take her back to being born about 1835. The report states that she was married aged 18. We know that Colonel George Cladwin Denniss married Eleanor Talbot in October 1846 (in India, not in England as the report indicates), apparently making her only 11 years old at the time.

As to Nicholson being shot by one of his own soldiers, the likelihood is against the story being true rather than in support of it. The tale was certainly third- and possibly fourth-hand. The notion that the culprit was arrested, taken back to camp, tried and executed next day just does not ring true given the chaotic situation inside the city on 14 September, as indeed is well illustrated by the manner in which the wounded Nicholson was treated. Had the incident occurred at all, it is more likely that the culprit would have been shot out of hand by his associates. No reference has been unearthed to any such incident or to a court martial in official or in private papers. But most telling of all, no contemporary account exists to corroborate the story and nothing has been found either before 1917 or since to substantiate the allegation.

There was no shortage of soldiers close to Nicholson when he was shot. It would have been impossible to cover the matter up. In private correspondence, Chamberlain, Roberts, Wilson, Edwardes, John Lawrence and Charles Nicholson are all silent on any such incident. There was in any case a 'no prisoners' policy in operation – which meant on the ground, summary executions were the order of the day. But as the former Indian journalist George Birdwood noted in *The Times* a couple of days after the 1917 report appeared, 'had Nicholson been shot by one of his men we should all have heard of it'.[14]

Assuming that the doctor who leaked the juicy saga to *The Times* was telling the truth in reporting what he had heard, and the chances are that he was, then the focus must rest on Mrs Denniss. Lieutenant Colonel George Gladwin Denniss died aged 40 at Burdwan in Bengal in March 1862, predeceasing her by forty-nine years.[15] She had admitted to her doctor that she was afraid of Nicholson and therefore was no doubt jealous of his being immortalised as a British military hero, an attitude that might have been fostered as her husband brooded over his lack of success in his brief days commanding the Moveable Column before Nicholson took charge. Mrs Denniss was, of course, not alone in being afraid of Nicholson.

It is also uncertain when she might have played hostess to Henry Lawrence, Nicholson, Hodson and Roberts. Henry Lawrence was never on the Ridge during hostilities and Nicholson was there for only a month. There is no record of such social niceties among 'cakies' on the Ridge, when a sizeable proportion of the garrison were dying of cholera and the air was thick with flies. And prior to the Great Rebellion, such figures mentioned by her were scattered across the Punjab.

Not surprisingly, when this story appeared in *The Times* in 1917, it was roundly condemned by indignant old soldiers who had fought at Delhi and known Nicholson. It was denounced as 'absolute rubbish' for example, by Colonel Kendal 'Paddy' Coghill, then lieutenant and adjutant of the 2nd European Bengal Fusiliers, who had been with Nicholson and Brigadier

Jones that fateful morning, and indeed was one of the first British soldiers along with Nicholson to reach the top of the breach and enter the city.[16]

## A LINGERING DEATH

Despite the musket ball still inside him, Nicholson held on to life longer than one might expect. It was a testament to both his great physical strength as well as his psychological tenacity that he survived for ten days. Chamberlain quite clearly acted with great humanity in dealing with the dying Nicholson, visiting him whenever he could.

That Tuesday, the 15th, Chamberlain again visited Nicholson and found him in better shape, breathing more easily. Something of Nicholson's *méchant* sparkle had also returned. On Chamberlain telling his friend that 'a certain officer' (Wilson) was considering withdrawing the troops from the bitter street fighting within the city, Nicholson was quoted by Chamberlain as having said, 'Thank God I have strength yet to shoot him, if necessary.'[17]

Later this comment became common knowledge. As with so much Nicholson said, this repartee has been taken too seriously and out of context. One of Nicholson's contemporaries in the Anglo-Sikh wars, on the frontier and at Delhi, was Henry Norman, later a field marshal. In 1883 Norman dismissed Nicholson's comment on the grounds that 'Nicholson disliked Wilson' and also criticised 'the officer who told Nicholson' (Chamberlain) that Wilson was thinking of withdrawing from Delhi after the assault had begun. Colonel Vibart correctly observed that Nicholson's attitude to Wilson was understandable enough as Wilson 'had no steadfastness and determination'. He also recognised that, as with much Nicholson blurted out, regarding his remark that he would shoot Wilson if he withdrew need not be taken *au pied de la lettre*.[18] As the days progressed, Chamberlain's attitude was not that much different from the one that Nicholson had held, telling Edwardes that, 'I look forward to going back to the frontier.'[19]

Ironically, Wilson's attitude towards Nicholson was very different. To his wife he confided, 'Brigadier General Nicholson is a very great loss to me. I have no one who can supply his place. I am very much afraid we shall lose him.'[20] And Wilson had good reason to worry. On the 15th he wrote to his wife that the assault had not gone so well:

> The Europeans with the column with me got hold of lots of beer in the shops, and made themselves helpless. I had not a Queen's officer under me

worth a pin, or who can preserve any sort of discipline except Jones of the 60th Rifles, in fact the men are so badly officered that they will and can do nothing tomorrow.[21]

The next day Wilson's morale was no better: 'Our Force is too weak for street fighting.' He was not far off the mark.

It was some time during these two days in Daly's tent that an episode that was to become part of Nicholson folklore occurred. The novelist Flora Steel in her hopelessly partisan Mutiny novel, *On the Face of the Waters*, had Hodson telling Nicholson about the capture of the last Mughal king on the 21st. This must be artistic licence at best as by then Nicholson was no longer under canvas. Nonetheless, the story goes that when in the tent the endless chatter and racket created by his Multani troopers outside annoyed the injured man so much that he fired a pistol shot through the tent wall to silence them. Steel was probably correct, though, about the delighted reaction this incident had on the bearded hillmen: 'Since as they retired further off, they agreed that *Nikkalseyn* was *Nikkalseyn* still; and surely death dare not claim one so full of life?'[22] Another version of this, probably true, story has one soldier outside the tent saying, '*Wah, wah, Generale Sahib ke hookhum hai.*' ('Oh, oh, there is the general's order.')

On Wednesday the 16th, Chamberlain was temporarily in charge of the British assault as General Wilson's nerves were at breaking point and he was avoiding his staff. Before riding over to Skinner's House, Chamberlain had Nicholson moved to a nearby small bungalow that had been partially destroyed by an enemy shell. This house in the old cantonment had once been inhabited by some regimental sergeants. Its position gave Nicholson the benefit of a breeze, making him much more comfortable, as he told Chamberlain. Nicholson also dictated a rather touching note to Herbert Edwardes:

Tell him I should have been a better man if I had continued to live with him, and our heavy public duties had not prevented my seeing more of him privately. I was always the better for a residence with him and his wife, however short. Give my love to them both.

News of the British assault against the walled city was spread by telegraph. Up in Peshawar, the telegrams began to arrive for Edwardes:

*14 September*
Delhi assaulted, and fighting still going on! The attack successful!

*15 September*

Yesterday at 7p.m. we had from the Cashmere to the Cabul Gate. Fighting inside still very severe. Many officers killed and wounded. Both the Nicholsons severely. The latter [Charles] has lost an arm.

*16 September*

John Nicholson is *badly* wounded.

*16 September*

Poor John Nicholson is worse, and there is little or no hope now. He has directed a few kind words to be sent to you. I fear a letter from Peshawur may not reach in time. Send me any message you wish given to him. He talks MUCH of you BOTH.

Messages passed in transit, for that Wednesday Edwardes wrote a four-page message to his dying friend. John Lawrence, though as ever truthful, had not offered much hope by telegraphing to Peshawar that he feared Nicholson was badly wounded. To the governor-general, Lawrence was more gracious:

> I am to add that our loss appears to have been very severe. Among many brave and good soldiers, there is not one who in merit by general consent can surpass Brigadier General John Nicholson – He was an officer equal to any emergency. His loss comes particularly at a time like this, is greatly to be deplored.[23]

In a letter to Nicholson, Edwardes told him he had written to Emma and told her to let Nicholson's mother know what had happened: 'I told her to say that I looked on these wounds as the saving of both your lives; and to comfort your mother as much as possible.' He wondered which had lost the arm, adding, 'It is a tremendous loss to a soldier; – though there is not a true woman in England, Ireland or Scotland who will not love either of you the better for the empty sleeve.'

From the Thursday to the following Tuesday (17–22 September) Nicholson's condition fluctuated. The army surgeon principally responsible for Nicholson's care was William Fullarton Mactier (1822–1915). He summoned another doctor, Dr Campbell Mackinnon of the Horse Artillery, who was a friend of Chamberlain. On 17 September, Mactier noted:

> The Brigadier is certainly better. He is free from cough or pain in the chest, and his breathing is much easier than it was. The only bad symptom is the pulse which keeps very high. His wound is one of such a serious nature that notwithstanding the improvement which has taken place we cannot be

sanguine as to the ultimate result ... fragments of the fractured rib have wounded the Pleura, and opened the cavity of the chest. [24]

Edwardes's last letter to Nicholson is dated Friday, 18 September. It is only a page and the handwriting is uneven. It ends, 'If you should need a sea voyage we will go home again together. God bless you ever dear N.' And then, as if to break his grief, Edwardes adds the mundane PS: 'All here much as usual – anxious – but never going far wrong. How's yr brother?' [25]

By Saturday, Wilson had given up hope for Nicholson's recovery. He was clearly very distressed by this. That Saturday was also the day that the Burn Bastion, which had been Nicholson's nemesis, at last fell to British troops.

Elsewhere in the British camp, others were saddened by news of the fallen soldier. William Graham noted to his cousin on Sunday, 'Nicholson is dying. I cannot tell you what a fellow he is. His loss like Mackeson's and Sir H Lawrence's is a dreadful calamity, especially in such times. His poor mother I pity for, well may she be proud of such a son.' [26] A Major McNabb intoned in a letter, '... the brave, the terrible Nicholson is down ... much feared by all classes of evil doer from Queen's officers on leave in Cashmere, to the horse stealers and midnight murderers of the Peshr valley.' [27]

On Tuesday the 22nd, William Hodson captured the old Mughal king and then shot dead two of his sons who were with him. For this cold-blooded deed, Hodson received a warm note of commendation from Robert Montgomery, but many on the British side were shocked. That same afternoon Dr Mactier confided in Chamberlain that there was 'little or no hope' for Nicholson. That did not stop Nicholson dictating to Mactier a letter for Sir John Lawrence setting out the reasons why General Wilson should be removed and Chamberlain put in his place.

Throughout his ten-day ordeal, Nicholson never complained about the pain and discomfort. It was like when he was a child and the gunpowder exploded in his face – he lay and awaited his fate, more animal than human.

On Tuesday he became weaker and weaker, though if roused with 'smelling salts and stimulant', he could talk quite lucidly. Nicholson realised that he was going to die, though said that this world had no interest to him. He told Chamberlain that he regretted not having made a will. In fact, as has been seen, Nicholson had made a will at Peshawar in August 1848, the beneficiary being his mother. [28] If Nicholson planned a new will, it would have been interesting to see who would have benefited from his modest estate. The implication is that Clara Nicholson would not have fared so well, while Edwardes and possibly Chamberlain and several Indians would have benefited.

In Chamberlain's lengthy account of Nicholson's last days, two interlinked aspects strike one very forcibly. The first is that Clara is mentioned on only one occasion. In the afternoon before he died, Nicholson asked Chamberlain to send another message from him to Edwardes. This ran, 'Say that at this moment a good fairy were to give me a wish, my wish would be to have him here next to my mother.' And a few minutes later, having brought his mother to mind, he added, 'Tell ... mother that I do not think we shall be unhappy in the next world. God has visited her with a great affliction, but tell her she must not give way to grief.' The second striking factor is the lack of more direct religious comment. This was also noticed by the ever-observant Colonel Daly. And after Nicholson's death Edwardes commented:

> I long to get Chamberlain's account of his last days, and to know whether our dear friend was blest at last by the grace of God to see things free from doubt, and happy in his resting on his Saviour ... Nicholson was the soul of truth. If he doubted, it was sincerely.[29]

Later that Tuesday evening, Nicholson said he was too weak to dictate his will and that he would do so the next morning. But John Nicholson became weaker and weaker, and the following morning 'his soul passed away to another and a better world'. According to Jemmy Lind, who had kept Nicholson company whenever he could during the previous ten days:

> He suffered much from his wound, but latterly was not in much pain. It pleased god to take him from us yesterday morning. Poor Nicholson turned once on his side, and died without a sigh.

It was Wednesday, 23 September 1857 at 10.30 a.m.[30]

That same morning, too late, Herbert Edwardes sent the following telegram:

> Give John Nicholson our love in Time and Eternity; and read him thirty first verse of 16th chap: Acts, and 9th v: 10th Romans. God ever bless him. I do not cease to hope and pray for him as a dear brother.[31]

Edwardes later made no pretence of hiding his feelings in his official report about Peshawar during the Mutiny: 'On the 23rd that hope was extinguished; and with a grief unfeigned and deep, and stern, and worthy of the man, the news was whispered, "Nicholson is dead".'[32]

And to Nicholson's friend Harry Lumsden, Edwardes commented, 'We shall never shake his hand again. You can understand all I feel about it. Henry Lawrence and John N. were the father and brother of my public life.'[33]

Alexander Taylor, the engineer who had worked so closely with Nicholson in the days before the assault, simply commented, 'I feel his loss more than I could have believed possible.'[34] Later some recalled Nicholson's comment, 'If I live through this the world shall know that Alex Taylor took Delhi.'[35]

An internet blog entitled 'Victorian blogs of John Nicholson' has Nicholson dying in the arms of Hayat Khan. There is no evidence for this, although it is probable that Khan cannot have been far distant. Charles Allen states that Khan tended his master throughout his final ordeal, 'washed him, gave him water, and saw to it that he was not troubled by unwanted visitors'.[36]

## THE AFTERSHOCK

The fall of Delhi was reported in the Irish newspapers by 27 October. That day James Hogg wrote to his sister Clara Nicholson:

> We have received our telegraphic message from Bombay announcing the fall of Delhi and I grieve to say that John is in the list of wounded. The list of 'wounded' is given generally, but nothing is added separately in each case whether slight or severe … In the same list of wounded, is the name of 'Lt Nicholson, Scotch regiment'. The addition induces a hope that it may not be Charles, but I am complelled [sic] to add my fear that poor Charles is also among those wounded.

A week later a message concerning the casualties at Delhi was brought to Hogg. It included the comment: 'Brigadier Nicholson very severely [wounded], and his Brother 31st N.I.' To raise Clara's spirits, Hogg pointed out that at least the name after Nicholson had the addition of 'dangerously wounded'.

News of Nicholson's death took a long time to reach Ireland and Britain. Even the *Bombay Times* carried the death of 'gallant General Nicholson' only on 17 October, a full twenty-seven days after the event. The *Pottinger* sailed from Bombay on 18 October, reaching Egypt on 2 November, from where the telegraph took over. The news reached the British Foreign Office in London on 11 November 1857.[37] Dublin's *Freeman's Journal* recorded the death of 'our countryman' on 12 November, following up the next day with a piece on Nicholson and General Neill taken from *The Times*. Clara sent her brother in

London either the original or a copy of the 1851 photograph of John. Hogg had it copied and forwarded to *The Times* and to the *Illustrated London News*.

## THE FUNERAL, OBSEQUIES AND MEMORIALS

In India the burden of Nicholson's death lay on Chamberlain's shoulders. Given the fact that a major battle had just been fought nearby, matters by necessity had to be simple. He left a touching picture of a visit by the Indian officers of the Multani Horse to pay their respects to the dead body of Nicholson. This must have been later on the day he died:

> The Sirdars of the Mooltanee Horse, and some other natives, were admitted to see him after death, and their honest praise could hardly find utterance for the tears they shed as they looked on their late master.
>
> The servants and orderlies also who were in attendance on him, when the fact flashed across their minds that he had left this world for ever, broke out into lamentations, and much as all natives feared to displease him, there could be no question but that he commanded their respect to an extent almost equal to love.[38]

John Nicholson's funeral was not a grand affair. That in itself is interesting. Lieutenant Wilberforce had a tendency to exaggerate so greatly did he admire Nicholson, but his account of the 'mutiny' of the 52nd over Nicholson's funeral rings true. After parade on the evening that Nicholson died, a private in the regiment stepped forward and politely asked Colonel Campbell if the regiment was 'going to go to the General's funeral to-morrow'. 'Certainly not,' was the reply. To this, the old soldier stood his ground and replied, 'I joined the regiment before you did, and you know the character I have had while in the regiment. I mean no disrespect, sir, but *we are going*.' The colonel flushed and threatened to use force if such an attempt was made to attend the funeral. Again the private spoke, 'And what force will you get, sir? The regiment [52nd] will march through all other regiments that are here.' This last phrase Wilberforce surmised must have pleased the colonel, who did not answer and turned away.

Soon after sunrise on the morning after he died, Thursday the 24th, John Nicholson's body was placed in a simple coffin and taken on a working gun carriage to a new cemetery only several hundred yards from his greatest victory near the Kashmir Gate and near the great gun-breaching batteries at Ludlow Castle. There was no great attendance from the highest ranks,

Chamberlain being the most senior officer present. There were no muffled
drums, no band and no gun salute. But the remnant of the 52nd was present.
An odd assortment stood over the open grave as Rev. Rotton read the service:
'officers and men, some with sunburnt faces, some bleached white by fever
and sickness, their plain *kharkee* uniforms contrasting with the picturesque
dresses of Pathans and Afghans, and others of his Mooltanee Horse.'

Charles Saunders, the commissioner of Delhi, was present. So was Lieutenant
Lind with two of his officers, Nowrung Khan and Atta Mahommud. Lind
commented that these two men 'wept with me, and we felt we had lost one
of our dearest friends on earth'.[39] As the coffin was lowered, it is said that the
deep emotions of the wild hillmen gave way and, 'Throwing themselves on
the ground, they sobbed and wept as if their very hearts were breaking.' As
Wilberforce commented:

> for them Nicholson was everything. For him they had left their frontier
> homes. For him they had forsaken their beloved hills to come down to the
> detested plains; they acknowledged none but him, they served none but him,
> they obeyed none but him.

This was not a patriotic matter, nor an issue of cause, but a personal
attachment to those very characteristics denounced by his critics: Nicholson's
fundamentalist approach to life and the over-simplified, yet honest enough
manner in which he dealt with people.

That morning, away at the far southern side of the city, a British column
rode out. It passed the numerous dead bodies, the scavenging dogs and the
vultures. It was an appropriately macabre setting for the launch of the British
revenge column.

Writing to Edwardes, Chamberlain told him that he had taken as 'my relics
of our dear and noble minded friend' a prayer book with an inscription in it to
Nicholson in Emma Edwardes's handwriting and a photograph of Nicholson,
Chamberlain and Edwardes together. Chamberlain also took quite a few
locks of Nicholson's hair – perhaps rather too many for decorum, though
emotions were generally running high. There were locks for various members
of the Nicholson family, for various friends, no doubt for himself, for Herbert
Edwardes and for Emma Edwardes. Chamberlain promised to send Edwardes
Nicholson's little pewter snuff box.[40] Many of these mementos must still be in
private possession. The National Army Museum in Chelsea has various items
including a Nicholson travelling bureau and a writing box. Quite correctly,
Chamberlain thought that Nicholson would have 'abhorred the idea of a sale

by public auction' of his clothes, and he suggested to Edwardes that instead they be given to help the boys in the Lawrence Asylum school.

Just over two weeks after his elder brother died, Charles Nicholson wrote in an unsteady hand from his camp hospital bed in Delhi to his sister Mary that their brother 'died easily and happily, having won for himself a reputation 2nd to none in India'.[41]

It was a time for writing letters, though for some it was easier than others. Neville Chamberlain was clearly deeply affected by Nicholson's death. He organised the funeral and we know that he went through Nicholson's papers after the death. But it was not until 25 October, a full month after his death, that Chamberlain could bring himself to write to Peshawar and Herbert Edwardes about 'our dear friend'. This very long and agonising letter has left us the fullest account of Nicholson's last days. Chamberlain asked Edwardes to extract parts of this letter for 'our good friend Becher'.[42] Sir Robert Montgomery also wrote to Edwardes expressing regret that Edwardes had now lost his two best friends, 'the two great men', Henry Lawrence and John Nicholson.

Meanwhile in Peshawar, Herbert Edwardes was devastated by Nicholson's death, telling Charles in a letter written on 9 October, 'I have felt the loss of your brother as if he had been my own, and shall continue to do so all my life.' Edwardes sent Charles some new clothes and a:

fur chagah [choga] wh will be as comfort to you as a dressing gown – yr brother's dressing case given him by Lady Hogg, yr dear mother's picture – and some books – also a little French carriage clock of wh John was very fond, and wh he left under my care the last thing when he was going away – wh I thought wd be a nice thing for yr mother's own writing table.[43]

One hopes that Nicholson's little clock still survives and is the one safely preserved in the National Army Museum, where it continues to 'yawn' on the half hour.

Nicholson's estate does not seem to have been complicated. His major asset was his Company commission or papers. His cash amounted to 29,500 rupees and his debt to 2,705 rupees, a quarter of which was Nicholson's share in a 17th regimental bond. His mother was the main beneficiary, receiving all the financial assets as well as his Bible (presumably that given to Nicholson by Mary) and his furs and pashmina. Whether or not his Uncle Richardson received Nicholson's promised writing desk is not known, though Charles was bound to receive 'my horses gun, pistols, books and all other property to keep or dispose of'. John was also due some of the Delhi prize money, but only in

February 1862 did this materialise. Charles Nicholson gained seven and a half shares of the loot, and John Nicholson's estate fifty-one share –, a welcome bonus for Clara Nicholson, who appears to have been living then with the Maxwells in the very pleasant High Roding Rectory near Dunmow in Essex.[44]

Charles Nicholson did not receive the mandatory letter of condolence from the chief commissioner until 12 November, by which time he was greatly recovered and making preparations to return home to Lisburn, via the Bombay route. In typical John Lawrence style, the letter was stilted and awkward and spoke in pompous terms of 'your noble brother' and of his death being 'a national misfortune' – in his despatch to the governor-general, Lawrence similarly used the phase 'public misfortune'. Yet on 26 September, Lawrence had clearly been distressed when writing to Chamberlain, 'Pray write and tell me how he died. Did he get my telegraphic message/I fear not. He was a glorious soldier. It is long before we shall look on his like again.'[45]

On 3 December 1857, Lawrence sent Charles copies of extracts from seven despatches that Lawrence had written to the governor-general ('the Supreme Government') between 1 June and 2 October 1857.[46] Some of the letters of condolences were genuine and some cardboard. The governor-general spoke of Nicholson as a 'very meritorious officer'. Back in Peshawar, though, the 65-year-old Sydney Cotton was elegant in praise of the young officer who had worked under him:

Bold, resolute, and determined, this daring soldier and inestimable man fell mortally wounded when gallantly heading a column of attack at the assault of Delhi on the 14th instant. In him England has lost one of her noblest sons, the Army one of its brightest ornaments, and a large circle of acquaintances a friend warm-hearted, generous, and true. All will now bewail his irreparable loss.[47]

Edwardes's distress was so great at Nicholson's death that he foolishly wrote to John Lawrence accusing him of not doing justice to Nicholson while he had been alive. Lawrence stoutly denied this:

Nicholson had many and great qualities. He had also some defects, which time would have lessened, perhaps removed. Respecting Nicholson as I did I could not encourage him in his faults. I may therefore have appeared cold and niggard in my estimation of him. As regards the Trimmas Ghât affair, he never wrote me even a line after his success. And altho' in my report of it to Govt, which if he had lived he would have seen, with their reply, I gave him full credit. I did not think it was necessary at the time to thank him for that which he would not even take the trouble to report.[48]

Sir John Kaye wrote in 1868 that once the news of Nicholson's death was known, 'there rose a voice of wail from one end of India to the other'. There is no doubt that the death of Nicholson was a blow to the British. But this was counterbalanced by the fact that the fall of Delhi heralded the turn in the fortunes of war outwardly in their favour, though there were clear signs by then of the insurgents' resolve disintegrating.

In the future, the legend of Nicholson as a Victorian and Edwardian boys' hero would be created. At the time, he was genuinely mourned by those who were close to him and those who recognised that, accepting his faults, he was a different and remarkable man. For Britain, he was a remote figure, one among several soldiers who had fallen gallantly. In that sense, Nicholson was the fallen hero of the moment, with British papers referring to him as the 'lion of the Punjab' and the 'iron officer of the Punjab'.

Sir Robert Montgomery commented that Nicholson 'left a name which will never be forgotten in the Punjab'. To an extent, this was true well into the twentieth century. At the time of Nicholson's death beyond his small and highly educated circle of friends in India, those who most genuinely mourned him were not British but ordinary Indians, in particular the Indian troops who served under him. Nicholson's name features on the Mutiny memorial on the Delhi Ridge. In the immediate years following his death, a memorial plaque was erected in the Anglican church in Bannu. An elaborate frieze depicting the capture of Delhi was placed in the cathedral in Lisburn. Most impressive was a blue-grey limestone 230ft-high stone obelisk, designed by Nicholson's friend Alex Taylor, and erected in 1868 on the crest of the Margalla Pass, situated today between the old and the new Grand Trunk Road.

Following his death, the memory of Nicholson was to be become a contested domain, appropriated by two very different camps. From the 1890s through to the end of empire, Nicholson came to embody the great masculine British soldier hero. Statues to him were erected in Delhi in 1906 and later in Lisburn in 1922.[49] Children's books appeared featuring Nicholson. Ballads were written in his honour. Kipling mentions Nicholson in his classic *Kim*. Hagiographic lives of Nicholson were written. Posthumous portraits were painted. And in more modern times, Nicholson has received the opprobrium of anti-empire writers.

## THE FATE OF THOSE LEFT BEHIND

There remains one question to be answered: what was the fate of the other actors in this saga? As far as the family was concerned, Clara Nicholson received an annual pension of £500, dying on 17 February 1874 aged 88. She outlived all her children except Mary, who died in 1889, aged 67. Lily died in 1861 and Charles, who married an American called Elizabeth Gillilan, but was weakened by an injury to a lung at Delhi, died on 18 December 1862 during the journey upcountry to take command of the Gurkha Regiment. Like his brother John, Charles was only 34 years old when he died.

Then there were the Nikolseinee. Cholmeley asserted that the sect's two headmen committed suicide. A generation later, Sieveking asserted, 'several of the members asked to be instructed in Christianity, saying that if they ever wished to see him again, they must worship Nicholson's God.' That is possible in a few cases, but more likely they returned to the life they had come from. This is not to say that Nicholson was forgotten.

At Christmas 1880, General John William Younghusband gave his sister a scrapbook, complete with intricate watercolour drawings he had made, photographs and comments. One of the comments relates to Nicholson:

> Some of his [Nicholson's] old soldiers have been known to visit the cemetery at Delhi, and place a <u>chiragh</u> (oil lamp) at the head of his tomb. For some years after Nicholson's death the guards of the Sikh Regt stationed at Delhi, when going past the cemetery near the cashmere gate, always saluted by carrying arms when passing his grave; and to within the last few years many of his men came long distances to visit the spot and make their Salaams to it.[50]

And what of those hill horsemen, the Multani Horse? As a unit, they survived their master by some two years, being broken up on 1 November 1859, ninety-seven being 'entertained' in the Pathan Cavalry Regiment, ninety-five transferred to the Multani Cavalry Regiment and ninety-five transferred to near home with the Dera Ismail Khan Police. The balance of 143 men – a third of the 426-strong regiment – was discharged.

After Nicholson's death, Jemmy Lind had continued in command, being based at Kohtuk for some time. The Multani Horse were with General Penny's column for a while before ending up at Moradabad. From there, they were at various times at Mohumdi, Shahjehanpur, Agra, Allyghur and Lahore, before being stationed at Meean Meer. They had seen action with Nicholson's column, and then later at Delhi, Narnool, Kuteraoli, Barrielly, Phillieet, Bumaye and

Moohumdi, the last action being about 1 July 1858. After this date, there were no battle casualties.[51] But there had been those who had left the British lines in the immediate wake of John Nicholson's death. Lieutenant Charles Griffiths of the 61st Regiment recorded an incident he experienced two days after Nicholson's death:

> On the 25th [September 1857] I mounted guard with fifty men at the Lahore Gate. The orders were 'on no account to allow soldiers, either European or native, nor camp-followers without passes, to enter or leave the city.' My post was constantly at the gate, where I examined passes; and while thus occupied some thirty troopers of the Mooltani Horse – wild, truculent-looking fellows, armed to the teeth – rode up demanding entrance. I explained to them what my orders were, and refused admission. Whereupon they commenced talking among themselves, and presently had the audacity to move towards the sentries with the intention of forcing their way. I was exasperated beyond measure, and turned out the guard, at the same time telling the Mooltanis that, if they did not at once retire, I would fire upon them without more ado. They then at once changed their threatening attitude, contented themselves with swearing at the *Gore log* [whiteman], and rode away, saying that now Nicholson was dead no one cared for them, and they would return to their homes.[52]

# Notes

## PREFACE

1 Sieveking, *A Turning Point in the Mutiny*, pp.159–160.

2 Dalrymple, *Return of a King*, p.438.

3 Wilberforce, *An Unrecorded Chapter of the Indian Mutiny*, p.71n.

4 Harrison (ed.) and Fraser, *The Graham Indian Mutiny Papers*, p.lix.

5 Dalrymple, *The Last Mughal: The Fall of Delhi, 1857*, pp.xxv, 196–197, 199, 306–307 and 572.

6 Cholmeley, *John Nicholson*, p.86.

7 BL, India Office papers, Mss Eur E 211/8, Nicholson to Henry Lawrence, 5 September 1852.

8 BL, India Office papers, Mss Eur E 211/3, Nicholson to Edwardes, 18 December 1855.

## CHAPTER 1

1 BL, India Office papers, Mss Eur F 171/101/1, John Nicholson to Clara Nicholson, Lecroll, Benares, 13 October 1839. The letters in this file have been transcribed by Evelyn Thomas.

2 Trotter, *The Life of John Nicholson, Soldier and Administrator: Based on Private and Hitherto Unpublished Documents*, p.20.

3 Rankin, *The Linen Houses of the Lagan Valley: The Story of their Families*, section 4. See also Crawford, 'Ulster landowners and the linen industry' in Ward and Wilson (eds), *Land and Industry*, p.118.

4 Cohen, 'Rural paths of capitalist development: Class formation, paternalism and gender in County Down's linen industry', in Proudfoot (ed.), *Down. History and Society: Interdisciplinary Essays on the History of an Irish County*, pp.570 and 585.

5 In March 1859 Charles Nicholson, back in Ireland from India, revisited Stramore and found it and its garden neglected but the farm well looked-after. See BL, India Office papers, Mss Eur F 171/5, Charles Nicholson to Clara Nicholson, 9 March [1859].

6    *Irish Times*, 2 March 1922.

7    Buckland, *Dictionary of Indian Biography*, p.204. Hogg was member of
     Parliament for the Yorkshire constituency of Beverley (1835–47) and for the
     east Devon constituency of Honiton (1847–1857). The latter seat he lost by
     two votes the year of the Indian Mutiny.

8    In 2011 Number 3 Vergemont Terrace was offered for sale at nearly €6 million.

9    BL, India Office papers, Mss Cadet papers (1838/1839), L/MIL/9/190, f.272.

10   Leslie, *Clergy of Connor*, p.587.

11   BL, India Office papers, Mss Eur F 171/7, L.J. Trotter to Rev. E. Maxwell,
     17 August 1897; and NAI, T/15392, Land Cases Reserved.

12   Dalrymple, p.xxv, in his *The Last Mughal*, also gives Nicholson's birth year as 1821.

13   *Belfast Daily Mercury*, 14 November 1857.

14   Dean and Leslie (compilers), *Succession Lists of the Diocese of Dromore*, Belfast,
     1933, reproduced in 1996 by the Ulster Historical Foundation under the title
     *Clergy of Down and Dromore*.

15   George Bellett was to hold a variety of parishes. Having completed his
     apprenticeship in Magherahamlet, a parish now grouped with Annahilt, he
     was a prebendary of the parish of Dromore (1821–27); and successively rector
     of Arundel in Somerset (1821–27); Ballymoden in Cork (1827); Bridgnorth
     in Shropshire (1835–79); and finally Whitbourne in Herefordshire (1870–86).
     Bellett was 34 when he married well, to Elizabeth Denny, who was the
     daughter of the owner of Tralee Castle and the local MP.

15   [Bellett], *Memoir of the Rev. George Bellett, M.A.*, London, 1889, pp.14 and 42–43.

16   Trollope, *Britannia's Daughters: Women of the British Empire*, p.133.

17   *The Parliamentary Gazetteer of Ireland*, p.416.

18   Lisburn continued to have a reputation as being a 'narrow and bigoted' town
     right into the twentieth century. In August 1920 many Catholics were burned
     out of their homes and business premises in the town following sectarian
     attacks brought on by the murder by the IRA of a policeman, District
     Inspector Swanzy. See Mackey, *Lisburn: The Town and its People, 1873–1973*,
     pp.16–17 and 88–93.

19   Erskine, *Essay on Faith*, 1822; letter quoted in BL, India Office papers, Mss Eur
     F 171/95, Thomas typescript.

20   Bowen, *The Protestant Crusade*, pp.61–62.

21   Leslie and Swanzy, *Biographical Succession Lists of the Diocese of Down*, pp.156–
     158.

22   Lunney, 'John Gifford Bellett', *Dictionary of Irish Biography*, pp.431–432.

23   Carmody, *Lisburn Cathedral*, p.140.

24   See Evelyn Thomas' notes in BL, India Office papers, Mss Eur F 171/101/1.

25   Gurrin, *A Century of Struggle in Delgany and Kilcoole*, p.21.

26   Wright, *A Guide to the County of Wicklow*, pp.40–44.

27   Lewis, *A Topographical Dictionary of Ireland*, vol. 2, p.435.

28 Leslie (compiled) and Wallace (revised and edited), *Clergy of Dublin and Glendalough: Biographical Succession Lists*, pp.485 and 683.

29 *Irish Times*, 5 April 1922.

30 A poorly-reproduced photograph of Holywell is to be found in Derek Paine's *A Pictorial History of Kilcoole, Newcastle, Newtownmountkennedy, Glen o' the Downs, Delgany, Greystones, 1860–1985: A Collection of Old Photographs*, p.125. Holywell is clearly marked on the 1838–39 Irish Ordnance Survey map of Delgany/Kilcoole.

31 As early as 1868, Sir John Kaye described Nicholson as precocious, a view he must have gleaned from Clara Nicholson.

32 Cholmeley, *John Nicholson: The Lion of the Punjaub*, pp.4–5; and Kaye, *Lives of Indian Officers*, vol. 2, p.417.

33 Gillman, *The Best of Boys*, p.253.

34 BL, India Office papers, Mss Eur F 171, Thomas typescript, letter from James Nicholson to Mary Nicholson, 27 August 1838, p.36.

35 Moravian Church papers, Gracehill, Hesketh Pearson to John K. Berry, 21 June 1955.

36 BL, India Office papers, Mss Eur 171/95/1, Bellett to Clara Nicholson, November 1832, Thomas typescript, p.26.

37 Moravian school register, Gracehill, County Antrim.

38 BL, India office papers, Mss Eur F 171, Thomas typescript, p.35.

39 BL, India Office papers, Mss Eur F 171/1, Clara Nicholson to Nicholson, 2 April 1837, and Mss Eur F 171/95/1, Thomas typescript, p.25.

40 Trotter, *Nicholson*, p.26.

41 Pearson, *The Hero of Delhi*, p.11.

42 BL, India Office papers, Mss Eur F 171, Thomas typescript.

43 BL, India Office papers, Mss L/MIL (/190, Cadet papers (1838/1839), John Nicholson.

44 BL, India Office papers, Mss Eur F 171/95/2, Thomas typescript.

45 Forrest, *Life of Field Marshal Sir Neville Chamberlain*, p.179.

46 Trotter, *The Life of John Nicholson*, p.9.

47 BL, Indian Office papers, EIC military record, John Nicholson, ff.117 and 385.

48 Pearson, *The Hero of Delhi*, p.12.

49 Kaye, *Lives of Indian Officers*, vol. 2, p.420.

50 BL, India Office papers, Mss Eur F 171/7, Lionel Trotter to Edward Maxwell, 25 April 1896.

51 BL, India Office papers, Mss Eur F 171/5, Charles Nicholson to Clara Nicholson, 16 March 1852.

52 BL, India Office papers, Mss Eur F 171/101/1, John Nicholson to Clara Nicholson, Ferozepore, 3 March 1840.

53 Trotter, *The Life of John Nicholson*, p.12–14.

54 BL, India Office papers, Mss Eur F 171/101/1, John Nicholson to J.W. Hogg,

55 Upper Grosvenor Street, London, Ferozepore, 6 April 1840; and Sieveking, *A Turning Point in the Indian Mutiny*, pp.173–174.

# CHAPTER 2

1   Forbes, *The Afghan Wars*, p.40.

2   Sieveking, *A Turning Point in the Indian Mutiny*, p.169.

3   A griff or griffon was army slang for a young subaltern not long out from Britain.

4   BL, India Office papers, Mss Eur F 171/5, Charles Nicholson to Clara Nicholson, Algiers, 20 January 1862.

5   BL, India Office papers, Mss Eur F 171/2, Nicholson to Mary Nicholson, 26 March 1841.

6   Captain, later Major, Hector Straith was an instructor in artillery and fortifications at the East India Company's Addiscombe Military College near Croydon in Surrey. His book, first published in 1833, went into at least seven editions and was used as a standard training manual.

7   Sieveking, *A Turning Point in the Indian Mutiny*, p.157. It appears that the original of this letter was lost.

8   BL, India Office papers, Mss Eur F 171/2, Nicholson to Mary Nicholson, 26 March 1841.

9   'Native States' (Despatch from Brigadier Shelton to Major-General Elphinstone), *Asiatic Journal and Military Registery*, June 1841, pp.82–84.

10  Allen, *Soldier Sahibs*, p.39.

11  BL, India Office papers, Mss Eur F 171.101/1, Nicholson to Mary Nicholson, 26 March 1841.

12  Forrest, *Chamberlain*, p.67.

13  Forrest, *Chamberlain*, p.178.

14  Kaye, *Lives of Indian Officers*, p.421n.

15  BL, India Office papers, Mss Eur F 171.101/1, Nicholson to Mary Nicholson, 26 March 1841.

16  Forbes, *The Afghan Wars*, p.110.

17  Kaye, *Lives of Indian Officers*, p.422.

18  Trotter, *The Life of John Nicholson*, pp.26–27.

19  Forbes, *The Afghan Wars*, p.142.

20  Haigh and Turner, 'Nickalsain', p.40.

21  Lawrence, *Reminiscences of Forty-three Years in India*, pp.183 and 213.

22  Allen, *Soldier Sahibs*, p.45.

23  Trotter, *The Life of John Nicholson*, pp.29.

24  BL, India Office papers, Mss Eur F 171/101/1, Nicholson to Clara Nicholson, 18 April 1843.

25  Broadfoot, 'The Defence of Jalalabad', *English Historical Review*, vol. 29, no. 8, 1893, pp.93–98.

26  Forbes, *The Afghan Wars*, pp.134 and 139.

27  Haigh and Turner, 'Nickalsain', p.40.

28  Kaye, *Lives of Indian Officers*, p.424.

29   Lawrence, *Reminiscences of Forty-three Years in India*, p.213.

30   Forbes, *The Afghan Wars*, p.148.

31   PRONI, Pottinger papers, D 1584/1/2, Eldred Pottinger to his mother, 4 November 1842.

32   Lawrence, *Reminiscences of Forty-three Years in India*, pp.216–217.

33   Lawrence, *Reminiscences of Forty-three Years in India*, p.218.

34   Forbes, *The Afghan Wars*, pp.152–155; Lawrence, *Reminiscences of Forty-three Years in India*, pp.220–221; and Kaye, *Sepoy War*, vol. 2, p.427.

35   Haigh and Turner, 'Nickalsain', p.51.

36   Hourican, 'Eldred Pottinger', *Dictionary of Irish Biography*, vol. 8, pp.244–245.

37   Allen, *Soldier Sahibs*, p.50; and Haigh and Turner, 'Nickalsain', p.54.

38   NAM, Dennys papers, 'Some reminiscences of my life' (typescript), pp.28–29.

39   BL, India Office papers, Mss Eur F 171/101/1, Nicholson to Clara Nicholson, 6 November 1842, quoted in Kaye, *Lives of Indian Officers*, pp.425–426.

40   BL, India Office papers, Mss Eur F 171/101/1 and F 171/2, Nicholson to Clara Nicholson, 8 November 1842.

41   BL, India Office papers, Mss Eur F 171/101/1 and F 171/2, Nicholson to Clara Nicholson, 18 April 1843, quoted in part in Sieveking, *A Turning Point in the Indian Mutiny*, pp.179–180.

42   BL, India Office papers, Mss Eur F 171/101/1, Nicholson to Mary Hogg, 8 May 1843.

43   PRONI, Pottinger papers, D 1584/1/4, Lieutenant Webb (38th Madras Native Infantry) to Eldred Pottinger, 19 December 1842.

# CHAPTER 3

1   *East India Register for 1844*, p.72.

2   Haigh and Turner, 'Nickalsain', p.65.

3   Roberts, *Letters Written During the Indian Mutiny*, p.53.

4   BL, India Office papers, Mss Eur F 171/101/1, Nicholson to Clara Nicholson, 7 August 1843.

5   *East-India Register and Army List, 1850*, pp.122 and 171.

6   Kaye, *Lives of Indian Officers*, vol. 2, p.427n.

7   BL, India Office papers, Mss Eur F 171/ 101/2, notes by Evelyn Thomas on Bible lent to her by Miss Seymour.

8   Taylor, *Sir Alex Taylor*, pp.41 and 44.

9   Allen, *Soldier Sahibs*, p.62.

10   Cholmeley, *John Nicholson*, pp.24–25.

11   Bayley, *Reminiscences*, p.160.

12   BL, India Office papers, Mss Eur F 171/102.

13   Kaye, *Lives of Indian Officers*, vol. 2, p.428.

14   BL, India Office papers, Mss Eur F 171/9.

15   Moreman, 'Edwardes', *Oxford Dictionary of National Biography*, vol. 17, pp.903–906.

16 PRONI, Lawrence and Steele papers, D1271, ff.87–88.

17 Lumsden, *Lumsden of the Guides*, p.25.

18 Lumsden, *Lumsden of the Guides*, p.36.

19 Allen, *Soldier Sahibs*, pp.83 and 86.

20 BL, India Office papers, Mss Eur F 171/101/1 and F 171/2, Nicholson to Charles Nicholson, 23 November 1846. See also NAM, Cocks papers, 6412-8, Nicholson to Cocks, 2 August 1848.

21 Lee, *Brothers in the Raj*, p.144.

22 BL, India Office papers, Mss Eur F 171/102, Nicholson to Lawrence, 7 March 1847.

23 Kaye, *Lives of Indian Officers*, vol.2, p.431.

24 Lawrence, *Lawrence of Lucknow: A Biography*, part 3.

25 BL, India Office papers, Mss Eur F 171/102, Nicholson to Henry Lawrence, 7 June 1847.

26 Haigh and Turner, *'Nickalsain'*, p.82.

27 Lee, *Brothers in the Raj*, p.198.

28 BL, India Office papers, Mss Eur E 211/3, Nicholson to Edwardes, 20 September 1847.

29 BPP, Punjab Government Records: Lahore Political Division, 1847–1849, vol. 6, pp.303–305.

30 BL, India Office papers, Mss Eur F 171/102, Nicholson to unspecified/John Lawrence and Frederick Currie, 23 February; 1, 4, 5, 7, 8, 16, 28 and 29 March; and 10 April 1848.

31 NAM, Cocks papers, Nicholson to Cocks, 17 May 1848.

32 NAM, Cocks papers, Nicholson to Cocks, 2 June 1848.

33 NAM, Cocks papers, Nicholson to Cocks, 26 June 1848.

34 Allen, *Soldier Sahibs*, p.159.

35 NAM, Cocks papers, Nicholson to Cocks, 13 June 1848.

36 NAM, Cocks papers, Nicholson to Cocks, 1 May 1848.

37 NAM, Cocks papers, Nicholson to Cocks, 20 September 1848.

38 Haigh and Turner, *'Nickalsain'*, pp.139–146.

39 BL, India Office papers, Mss Eur E 211/8, Nicholson to Henry Nicholson, 5 September 1852.

40 NAM, Cocks papers, Nicholson to Cocks, 27 June 1848.

41 NAM, Cocks papers, Nicholson to Cocks, 28 May and 6 August 1848.

42 Parnau, 'The *Delhi Urdu Akhbari*', *Urdu Studies*, 2003, pp.105–131.

43 NAM, Cocks papers, Nicholson to Cocks, 28 June and 15 July 1848.

44 Haigh and Turner, *'Nickalsain'*, p.95.

45 NAM, Cocks papers, Nicholson to Cocks, 5 July 1848.

46 Lawrence, *Reminiscences of Forty-three Years in India*, p.244.

47 NAM, Cocks papers, Nicholson to Cocks, 17 and 22 May 1848.

# CHAPTER 4

1   Sir John Kaye and Captain Trotter give slightly different versions, but the spirit of the comment is the same.

2   Allen, *Soldier Sahibs*, p.36.

3   Haigh and Turner, *'Nickalsain'*, pp.108–110.

4   BL, India Office papers, Mss Eur E 211/8, Nicholson to Henry Lawrence, 1 February 1849.

5   BL, India Office papers, Mss Eur E 211/3, Nicholson to Edwardes, 18 December [1848]; and Eur 171/7, L.J. Trotter to Rev. E. Maxwell, 24 May 1896.

6   Trotter, *The Life of John Nicholson*, pp.89–90.

7   Kaye, *Lives of Indian Officers*, vol. 2, p.437; and BL, India Office papers, Mss Eur E 211/3, Nicholson to Edwardes, 27 September 1848.

8   Allen, *Soldier Sahibs*, p.337.

9   BL, India Office papers, Mss Eur E 211/3, Nicholson to Clara Nicholson, 27 September 1848.

10  NAM, Cocks papers, Nicholson to Cocks, 10 December 1848.

11  Malleson, *Decisive Battles of India*, p.363.

12  NAM, Cocks papers, 6412-8, Nicholson to Cocks, 19 November and 8 December [1848].

13  Forrest, *Chamberlain*, p.201.

14  Haigh and Turner, *'Nickalsain'*, pp.127–129.

15  BL, India Office papers, Mss Eur F 171/102, Nicholson to Secretary to the Board of Administration, Lahore, 25 December 1851.

16  *The Times*, 5 January 1849.

17  BL, India Office papers, Punjab Government transcripts, F/171/102, Robkaree dated 22 November 1848.

18  BL, India Office papers, Mss Eur F 171/102, incomplete document unsigned to Nicholson, 22 November 1848.

19  Haigh and Turner, *'Nickalsain'*, pp.133–134.

20  BL, India Office papers, A45, Charles Herbert to John Nicholson, 3 December 1848.

21  BL, India Office papers, A45, Herbert to Reynell, 11 December 1848.

22  NAM, Cocks papers, Nicholson to Cocks, 9 December 1848.

23  Edwardes, *Sir Herbert B. Edwardes*, vol. 1, p.132.

24  NAM, Cocks papers, Nicholson to Cocks, 29, 30 and 31 January 1849.

25  BL, India Office papers, Mss Eur E 211/8, Nicholson to Lawrence, 5 February [1849].

26  'Brig.-Gen. Nicholson's flying column in the Punjaub', *United Services Magazine*, vol. 13, April 1896, p.75.

27  BL, India Office papers, A45, James Abbott to Reynell Taylor, 5 February 1849.

28  NAM, Cocks papers, Nicholson to Cocks, 1 February 1849.

29  BL, India Office papers, Mss Eur E 211/8, Nicholson to Henry Lawrence, 5 February [1849].

30  BL, India Office papers, Eur E 211/8, Nicholson to Henry Lawrence, 17 February [1849].

31  Allen, *Soldier Sahibs*, pp.74–75.

32  BL, India Office papers, F 171/101/6.

33  BL, India Office papers, MIL 10/48, EIC military records, John Nicholson, f.385.

34  BL, India Office papers, Mss Eur E 211/8, Nicholson to Henry Lawrence, 24 February [1849].

35  BL, India Office papers, Mss Eur E 211/8, Nicholson to Henry Lawrence, 24 February [1849].

36  BL, India Office papers, Mss Eur E 211/8, Nicholson to Edwardes, 27 and 28 February [1849].

37  Haigh and Turner, 'Nickalsain', p.153.

38  Allen, *Soldier Sahibs*, p.9.

39  Allen, *Soldier Sahibs*, pp.225–226.

40  BL, India Office papers, Mss Eur F 171/102, Robert Montgomery to R.Temple, 16 May 1855.

41  BL, India Office papers, Mss Eur E 211/8, Nicholson to Henry Lawrence, 6 March [1849].

42  BL, India Office papers, Mss Eur E 211/8, Nicholson to Henry Lawrence, 8 April [1849].

43  BL, India Office papers, Mss Eur E 211/8, Nicholson to Henry Lawrence, 7 March [1849].

44  BL, India Office papers, Mss Eur E, 211/8, Nicholson to Henry Lawrence, 13 March [1849].

45  Haigh and Turner, 'Nickalsain', p.157; and Trotter, *The Life of John Nicholson*, pp.119–120.

46  BL, India Office papers, Mss Eur E 211/8, Nicholson to Henry Lawrence, 19 March [1849].

47  BL, India Office papers, Mss Eur E 211/8, Nicholson to Henry Lawrence, 29 March [1849].

48  BL: India Office papers, MIL 10/48, f.385, EIC military records.

49  For George Lawrence further urging Nicholson to be indiscreet with his masters, see BL, India Office papers, Mss Eur E 211/8, Nicholson to Henry Lawrence, 26 April [1849].

50  BL, India Office papers, Mss Eur E 211/14, Nicholson to Henry Lawrence, 11 April [1849].

51  BL, India Office papers, EIC military records, John Nicholson, f.385; and BL, India and Bengal despatches, Mss Eur E 4/808, vol. 61, 4 April to 18 July 1849, no. 7 of 1849, 20 June 1849, f.836.

52  BL, India Office papers, Mss Eur E 211/8, Nicholson to Henry Lawrence, 14 April [1849].

53    Trotter, *Life of John Nicholson*, p.122.

54    Edwardes, *A Year on the Punjab Frontier, in 1848–49*, vol. 1, p.209.

55    BL, India Office papers, Mss Eur F 171/102, accounts, August 1848.

56    BL, India Office papers, Mss Eur E 211/8, Nicholson to Henry Lawrence, 24 March [1849].

57    BL, India Office papers, Mss Eur E 211/8, Nicholson to Henry Lawrence, 10 April [1849].

58    Sieveking, *A Turning Point in the Indian Mutiny*, pp.199–200.

59    Sieveking, *A Turning Point in the Indian Mutiny*, p.199.

60    BL, India Office papers, Mss Eur F 171/102, Nicholson to Henry Lawrence, 1 March 1848.

61    *Hansard* (House of Lords), 24 April 1849.

62    BL, India Office papers, Mss Eur E 211/8, Nicholson to Henry Lawrence, 4 March 1849.

63    BL, India Office papers, Mss Eur F 171/4, William Nicholson to Clara Nicholson, 21 December 1848.

64    F. Clark, *The East-India Regiment and Army List, 1848*, p.67 and *1850*, p.118.

65    BL, India Office papers, Mss Eur E 211/11, Charles Nicholson to John Nicholson, 1 July [1849].

66    BL, India Office papers, Mss Eur F 171/7, L.J. Trotter to Rev. Edward Maxwell, 4 May 1896. Sir John Kaye also asserted that William Nicholson had died by falling down a 'steep declivity' while 'in a state of somnambulancy'. See Kaye, *Lives of Indian officers*, vol. 2, p.442.

67    BL, India Office papers, Mss Eur F 171/6, Charles Nicholson to Mary Maxwell, 8 September 1849.

68    BL, India Office papers, Mss Eur E 211/8, Nicholson to Henry Lawrence, 2 April [1849].

69    Rt Hon. Lord Radcliffe, GBE, *Sir Henry Lawrence*, Londonderry, 1957, pp.4–5. The author attended the same school from 1957 to 1968, when one of the four houses was called Lawrence (house colour blue) and another Montgomery (green). It was also during these years that the statue of John Lawrence was brought from Lahore and placed in the school grounds. Other versions of this story are contained in Montgomery, *Monty's Grandfather*, p.3; and Lawrence, *Lawrence of Lucknow*, pp.202–203.

70    BL, India and Bengal Despatches, Mss Eur E 4/801, 1 August to 31 October 1849, vol. 62, no. 34 of 1849, ff.1251–1257.

# CHAPTER 5

1   Quoted in *The Times*, 21 February 1850.

2   For a link between Guyon and Stratford Canning, see NA, FO 78/816, Guyon to Stratford Canning, 13 April 1850.

3   Lajos Lukács, *Magyar politikai emigráció 1849–1867*, Budapest, 1984, pp.32, 36, 38 and 66.

4   BL, India Office papers, Mss Eur E 211/8, Honoria Lawrence to Nicholson, September 1850.

5   Kaye, *Lives of Indian Officers*, vol. 2, p.444.

6   Kaye, *Lives of Indian Officers*, vol. 2, p.445.

7   Personal correspondence: Dr Csaba Lévai, University of Debrecen, Hungary, to Donal McCracken, 3 March 2011.

8   BL, India Office papers, Mss Eur F 171/2, Nicholson to Clara Nicholson, 20 March 1850.

9   Sieveking, *A Turning Point in the Indian Mutiny*, pp.196–197.

10  Haigh and Turner, 'Nickalsain', p.181.

11  *Blackwell's Edinburgh Review*, February 1898, p.215.

12  BL, India Office papers, Mss Eur F 171/7, Trotter to Maxwell, 7 January 1897.

13  *Hansard*, House of Lords, 24 April 1849.

14  Edwardes and Merivale, *Life of Sir Henry Lawrence*, p.515.

15  BL, India Office papers, Mss Eur F 171/7, Trotter to Maxwell, 11 November 1896; and *The Times*, 25 April 1850.

16  *Belfast News-Letter*, 28 May 1850.

17  Forrest, *Chamberlain*, p.457.

18  Roberts, *Letters Written During the Indian Mutiny*, p.119.

19  Leslie and Wallace, *Clergy of Dublin and Glendalough*, pp.1150–1151.

20  *Blackwell's Edinburgh Review*, February 1898, pp.215–216.

21  BL, India Office papers, Mss Eur E 211/8, Honoria Lawrence to Nicholson, 11 September 1850.

22  *The Times*, 10 June 1850.

23  Edwardes to Mr Libby, 11 September 1850, property of the author.

24  *The Times*, 15 June 1850; and J.M. Bourne, 'The East India Company's Military Seminary, Addiscombe, 1809–1858', *Journal of the Society for Army Historical Research*, 1979, vol. 57, pp.206–222.

25  Haigh and Turner, 'Nickalsain', p.186.

26  BL, India Office papers, Mss Eur F 171/101/1 and F 171/2, Nicholson to Edward Maxwell, 28 October 1850.

27  Haigh and Turner, 'Nickalsain', p.187.

28  BL, India Office papers, Mss Eur F 171/7, Trotter to Maxwell, 7 January 1897; and Haigh and Turner, 'Nickalsain', p.187.

29  BL, India and Bengal despatches, Mss Eur E 4/808, despatch no. 13 of 1851, 5 February 1851.

30 BL, India Office papers, Mss Eur E 211/3, Edwardes to Nicholson, 13 February 1851.

31 Edwardes, *A Year on the Punjab Frontier, in 1848–49*, p.xii and map opposite p.3.

32 Edwardes, *A Year on the Punjab Frontier, in 1848–49*, vol. 1, pp.17 and 214, and vol. 2, pp.721–722.

33 India Office papers, Mss Eur 211/3, Edwardes to Nicholson, 28 February [1851].

34 BL, India and Bengal despatches, Mss Eur E 4/809, 2 April to 28 May 1851, vol. 70, f.414.

35 BL, India and Bengal despatches, Mss Eur E 4/812, 3 September to 29 October 1851, vol. 73, 10 September 1851, f.351.

36 BL, India Office papers, Mss Eur E 211/3 Nicholson to Edwardes, 8 March [1851]. His mother wrote in the year 1850, but it must be 1851 as Nicholson was in Constantinople in early March 1850. That Clara Nicholson had access to her son's correspondence with Edwardes is interesting. It must at some time after John's death been lent or given to her.

37 Haigh and Turner, 'Nickalsain', pp.185 and 190.

38 Haigh and Turner, 'Nickalsain', p.190.

39 BL, India Office papers, Mss Eur F 171/101/1, notes by Evelyn Thomas, *c.* 1939.

40 BL, India Office papers, Mss Eur F 171/101/2, Evelyn Thomas's notes on Nicholson photographs lent to her by Miss Seymour.

41 NAM, 1999-09-42-1, General Sir Sam Browne album. General Sir Peter Lumsden also had a Nicholson autograph in his scrapbook.

42 Forrest, *Chamberlain*, p.304.

43 BL, India Office papers, Mss Eur F 171/5, Charles Nicholson to Clara Nicholson, 29 November 1850.

44 BL, India Office papers, Mss Eur E 211/3, Nicholson to Edwardes, 1 September 1855.

45 BL, India Office papers, Mss Eur E 211/3 Nicholson to Charles Nicholson, 23 March 1851.

46 BL, India Office papers, Mss Eur E 211/3, Nicholson to Charles Nicholson, 20 August 1851; and *Illustrated London News*, 9 August 1851.

47 *Irish Times*, 7 March 1922.

48 BL, EIC military records, John Nicholson, f.385.

49 Forrest, *Chamberlain*, p.182.

## CHAPTER 6

1 BL, India Office papers, Mss Eur F 171/7, Trotter to Maxwell, 7 January 1897; and Forrest, *Chamberlain*, p.305.

2 BL, India Office papers, Mss Eur F 171/101/6, Sir James Hogg to Sir Henry Lawrence, 8 February 1853.

3    Bayley, *Reminiscences of School and Army Life, 1839 to 1859*, p.169.

4    Sieveking, pp.170–171; Trotter, *Life of John Nicholson*, p.126.

5    *The Poetical Works of Thomas Moore*, p.363.

6    BL, India Office papers, Mss Eur E 211/3, Nicholson to Edwardes, 28 September 1853; and Roberts, *Forty-one Years in India*, pp.21 and 41.

7    Taylor, *Sir Alex Taylor*, pp.144–145.

8    Lawrence, *Lawrence of Lucknow*, p.167.

9    Buckland, *Dictionary of Indian Biography*, p.32.

10   Carne and Tapp were collectors of the salt tax who were murdered in 1852.

11   BL, India Office papers, Mss Eur E 211/7, Becher to Edwardes, 5 December 1858.

12   Edwardes, *A Year on the Punjab Frontier, in 1848–49*.

13   BL, India Office papers, Mss Eur E 211/3, Nicholson to Edwardes, 21 January 1856.

14   BL, India Office papers, Mss Eur F 171/102, Nicholson to deputy secretary, Board of Administration, Lahore, 28 September 1849.

15   BL, India Office papers, Mss Eur F 171/102, 5 October 1849.

16   BL, India Office papers, Mss Eur F 171/102, Nicholson to Major D. Ross, 21 June 1853.

17   BL, India Office papers, Mss Eur F 171/102, Nicholson to R. Temple, 17 March 1856.

18   BL, India Office papers, Mss Eur F 171/102, Nicholson to the secretary of the Board of Administration, Lahore, 25 December and 26 December 1851.

19   Haigh and Turner, 'Nickalsain', p.201.

20   Thorburn, *Bannú: Or our Afghan Frontier*, p.54.

21   Forbes, *The Afghan Wars*, p.55

22   Malleson, *Decisive Battles of India*, p.22.

23   BPP, East India (Area, Population, etc.), pp.2–3; and BPP, Selections from the records of the government of India (Foreign Department.) ..., p.27.

24   Thorburn, *Bannú: Or our Afghan Frontier*, chapter 3.

25   BPP, Selections from the records of the government of India. (Foreign Department.) ....

26   BL, India Office papers, Mss Eur E 211/8, Nicholson to Henry Lawrence, 19 July 1852.

27   BL, India Office papers, Mss Eur F 171/5, Charles Nicholson to Clara Nicholson, 13 February 1852.

28   BPP, Selections from the records of the government of India. (Foreign Department.) ..., postscript.

29   BL, India Office papers, Mss Eur F 171/5, Charles Nicholson to Clara Nicholson, 14 May 1852.

30   BL, India Office papers, Mss Eur F 171/5, Charles Nicholson to Clara Nicholson, 5 June 1853.

31    BL, India Office papers, Mss Eur F 171/2, Nicholson to Lily Nicholson,
      6 March 1855; and Mss Eur F 171/101/2, 4 February 1856.

32    BL, India Office papers, Mss Eur F 171/5, Charles Nicholson to Clara
      Nicholson, 14 May 1852.

33    BPP, Selections from the records of the government of India (Foreign
      Department.) ..., p.14.

34    BPP, Selections from the records of the government of India. (Foreign
      Department.) ..., p.53.

35    BPP, Selections from the records of the government of India. (Foreign
      Department.) ..., p.54.

36    Haigh and Turner, 'Nickalsain', p.221.

37    Details of these expeditions extracted from BPP, Punjab etc. ....

38    Haigh and Turner, 'Nickalsain', p.199.

39    BPP, Selections from the records of the government of India. (Foreign
      Department.) ..., p.32.

40    Cholmeley, John Nicholson: The Lion of the Punjaub, p.28.

41    Haigh and Turner, 'Nickalsain', pp.202–206.

42    Haigh and Turner, 'Nickalsain', pp.202–204.

43    BL, India Office papers, Mss Eur E 211/8, Younghusband to Henry Lawrence,
      25 December 1852.

44    BL, India Office papers, Mss Eur E 211/8, Nicholson to Henry Lawrence,
      19 July 1852.

45    BL, India Office papers, Mss Eur E 211/8, Nicholson to Henry Lawrence,
      5 September 1852.

46    BL, India Office papers, Mss Eur E 211/8, Nicholson to Henry Lawrence,
      26 July 1852.

47    BL, India Office Papers, Mss Eur F 171/102, Nicholson to Major D. Ross,
      11 February 1853.

48    BL, India Office papers, Mss Eur F 171/102, F.R. Pollock to Nicholson,
      1 November 1855.

49    BL, India Office papers, Mss Eur F 171/102, Nicholson to Chamberlain,
      19 September 1852.

50    BL, India and Bengal despatches, Mss Eur E 4/814, vol. 75, 4 February to
      31 March 1852, 2 March 1852, f.723.

51    BL, India Office papers, Mss Eur F 171/101/6, Nicholson to Honoria
      Lawrence, 16 November 1852.

52    Kaye, The Sepoy Mutiny, vol. 2, p.472.

53    Edwardes and Merivale, Life of Sir Henry Lawrence, pp.490–491.

54    Allen, Soldier Sahibs, p.205.

55    Haigh and Turner, 'Nickalsain', p.220.

56    BL, India Office papers, Mss Eur E 211/8, Nicholson to Henry Nicholson,
      21 September [1853].

57   Kaye, *Lives of Indian Officers*, vol. 2, p.449.

58   BL, India Office papers, Mss Eur F 171/101/1 and F 171/2, Nicholson to Clara Nicholson, 13 April 1854.

59   Sieveking, *A Turning Point in the Indian Mutiny*, pp.216–217.

60   Clark, *The East-India Register and Army List, 1855*, p.132.

61   Haigh and Turner, 'Nickalsain', p.226.

62   A reference to William Howard of Naworth Castle in Cumberland, who appeared as 'Belted Will' in Sir Walter Scott's 1805 narrative verse 'Lay of the last minstrel'.

63   Forrest, *Chamberlain*, p.307.

64   BL, India Office papers, Mss Eur E 211/3, Nicholson to Edwardes, 18 December 1855.

65   BL, India Office papers, Mss Eur F 171/101/3, Nicholson to Edwardes, 28 April 1857.

66   Lee, *Brothers in the Raj*, p.145.

67   'A soldier of the frontier: Coke of Coke's Rifles', *Blackwood's Edinburgh Review*, 1898, p.775.

68   BL, India Office papers, Mss Eur E 211/3, Nicholson to Edwardes, 7 January 1856.

69   Kaye, *Lives of Indian Officers*, vol. 2, p.456.

70   Edwardes, *Memorials of the Life and Letters of Major-General Sir Herbert B. Edwardes*, vol. 2, p.77.

71   BL, India Office papers, Mss Eur E 211/3, Nicholson to Edwardes, 7 January 1856.

72   BL, India Office papers, Mss Eur E 211/3, Nicholson to Edwardes, 23 October 1855 and 21 January 1856.

73   This story was related by Thorburn in his *Bannú: Or our Afghan Frontier*, pp.53–54.

74   Cholmeley, *John Nicholson: The Lion of the Punjaub*, pp.28–30.

75   Thorburn, Report of the first regular land revenue settlement of the Bannu district, p.25.

76   Thorburn, *Bannú: Or our Afghan Frontier*, pp.55 and 111; and Thorburn, *Report of the First Regular Land Revenue Settlement of the Bannu District*, pp.25–27 and 160–162.

77   BL, India Office papers, Mss Eur F 171/102, Nicholson to R. Temple, 5 July 1855 and R. Temple to Secretary to Government (Calcutta).

78   PRONI, Graham papers, D812/14/152, W.S. Graham to Daniel Cullimore, 27 September 1857, quoted in Harrison, *The Graham Indian Mutiny Papers*, p.81.

# CHAPTER 7

1 BL, India Office papers, Mss Eur E 211/3, Nicholson to Edwardes, 1 September 1855.

2 BL, India Office papers, Mss Eur E 211/3, Nicholson to Edwardes, 25 February 1856.

3 BL, India Office papers, Mss Eur F 171/102, Nicholson to R. Temple, 9 May 1856.

4 For websites relating to colocynth see: www.herbs2000.com/homeopathy/colocynthis.htm accessed 18 April 2014; and www.vithoulkas.com/en/books-study/online-materia-medica/2620.html Accessed 18 April 2014.

5 BL, India Office papers, Mss Eur E 211/3, R. Temple to Nicholson, 2 July 1856 and G.F. Edmonstone to Nicholson, 18 June 1856.

6 Trotter, *The Life of John Nicholson*, p.188.

7 www.seth-smith.org.uk/familytree/trees/urmstonbrabazon.html Accessed 20 September 2015.

8 BL, India Office papers, Mss Eur E 211/3, Nicholson to Edwardes, 9 July 1856.

9 Roberts, *Forty-one Years in India*, pp.38–39.

10 Haigh and Turner, 'Nickalsain', p.232.

11 BL, India Office papers, Mss Eur F 171/102, Nicholson to R. Temple, 20 July 1856.

12 BL, India Office papers, Mss Eur F 171/2, 31 August 1856.

13 BL, India Office papers, Mss Eur E 211/3, Nicholson to Edwardes, 6 August 1856.

14 Correspondence relating to the incident is to be found in and attached to the following: BL, India Office papers, Mss Eur F 171/102, Nicholson to R. Temple, 10 September 1856.

15 BL, India Office papers, Mss Eur E 211/3, Nicholson to Edwardes, 6 August 1856.

16 BL, India Office papers, Mss Eur E 211/3, Nicholson to Emma Edwardes, 7 October 1856.

17 Lee, *Brothers in the Raj*, p.321.

18 BL, India Office papers, Mss Eur E 211/3, Nicholson to Edwardes, 2 October 1856.

19 BL, India Office papers, Mss Eur E 211/3, Nicholson to Edwardes, 13 and 19 November 1856.

20 BL, India Office papers, Mss Eur F 171/101/3, Nicholson to Edwardes, 21 June 1854.

21 BL, India Office papers, Mss Eur E 211/3, Nicholson to Edwardes, 9 March 1857.

22 BL, India Office papers, Mss Eur E 211/3, Nicholson to Edwardes, 23 April 1857.

23 BL, India Office papers, Mss Eur F 171/1, Clara Nicholson to Nicholson, 17 April 1857; and BL, India Office papers, Mss Eur F 171/2, Nicholson to Lily Nicholson, 4 February 1856. See also Walker, *Parliamentary Election Results in Ireland, 1801–1922*, p.91.

24 BL, India Office papers, Eur 171/1, Mary Nicholson to John Nicholson, 17 April 1857.

# CHAPTER 8

1 BPP, Army (India), HC 514, 2pp.
2 BPP, Peel Commission, 1859, p.299.
3 BPP, Papers relating to East India affairs (Madras Army), HC 95; and BPP, Papers relating to East India affairs, Mutiny at Vellore, HC 194.
4 NAM, Cocks papers, 6412-8, Nicholson to Cocks, 26 May 1848.
5 BPP, East India, Papers relating to the resignation by General Sir Charles Napier, HC 80, p.19.
6 *General Charles Napier*, pp.23 and 26.
7 David, *The Indian Mutiny*, p.19.
8 The new rifle had a range more than three times its predecessor and could be fired much more rapidly.
9 BPP, East Indies (Punjab), HC 238, p.95.
10 BPP, Army in India (Number of Officers), HC 509, pp.3–4.
11 Muir, *Records of the Intelligence Department*, p.112.
12 BPP, East Indies (Punjab), HC 238, p.5.
13 Singh, 'Re-assessing writings on the rebellion: Savarkar to Surendra Nath Sen', in Sabyasachi Bhattacharya (ed.), *Rethinking 1857*, p.50.
14 BPP, Peel Commission, appendix 1, p.6.
15 The traditional British assertion regarding the 'loyalty' of the Sikh population has been questioned. See Boparai, *Revolt of 1857 in Punjab and Role of the Sikhs*.
16 BPP, Military map of India, n.d. *c*. 1878.
17 Edwardes, *A Year on the Punjab Frontier, in 1848–49*, vol. 1, p.203.
18 BPP, East India (Castes of Hindoos), HC 129, p.14.
19 Chattopadhyay, 'Panic Sunday in Calcutta: 14 June 1857'; and Syiemlieh, 'Historiography of literature and sources on the uprising of 1857 in North East India', both in Bhattacharya (ed.), *Rethinking 1857*, pp.165–179 and 217.
20 Choudhury, '"1857" and the communication crisis', in Bhattacharya (ed.), *Rethinking 1857*, pp.261–265.
21 Roberts, *Letters Written During the Indian Mutiny*, p.1.
22 Farooqui, Besieged, p.xxi.
23 BPP, East India (Punjab), HC 212, p.24.
24 BPP, East India (Punjab), HC 212, pp.21–22.
25 BPP, East Indies (Punjab), HC 238, p.92.

26    BPP, East Indies (Punjab), HC 238, 1859, pp.5 and 51.

27    BPP, India Office … HC.

28    Forbes-Mitchell, *Reminiscences of the Great Mutiny*, p.26.

29    Montgomery, *Monty's Grandfather*, pp.73–74.

30    Roberts, *Letters Written During the Indian Mutiny*, p.75.

31    Muir, *Records of the Intelligence Department*, p.268.

32    BPP, East India (Punjab), HC 212, p.5.

33    Griffiths, *A Narrative of the Siege of Delhi*, p.22.

34    Bouchier, *Eight Months' Campaign*, p.39.

35    NAM, Roberts papers, 8310-155-1/3, 14 and 22 May 1857.

36    BPP, East Indies (Punjab), HC 212, p.39.

37    David, *The Indian Mutiny*, p.233.

38    BPP, East India (Indian Law Commission), 'On the Articles of War for East India Company's native troops', pp.331–606; BPP, Appendix to papers relative to the mutinies in the East Indies, pp.185 and 370; and Chattopadhyay, 'Panic Sunday in Calcutta: 14 June 1857', in Bhattacharya (ed.), *Rethinking 1857*, p.176.

39    BPP, East Indies (Punjab), HC 212, p.8.

40    BL, India Office papers, Mss Eur E 211/15, Edwardes' memorandum on the Mutiny in the Punjab, 2 March 1858, paragraph 66.

41    NA, PRO 30/29/23/10, Abstracts of secret letters, received December 14, 1857, from the governor-general in Council.

42    Montgomery, *Monty's Grandfather*, pp.73–74.

43    BPP, East Indies (Punjab), HC 212, pp.28–29.

44    BPP, East Indies (Punjab), HC 212, p.44.

45    Cadell, 'Irish soldiers in India', p.79; and Bartlett, 'Irish soldiers in India, 1750–1947', pp.15–16.

46    Information extrapolated from BPP, East India (Punjab), HC 212; and BPP, East India (Mutiny) HC 133.

47    BPP, East Indies (Punjab), HC 212, p.33.

48    David, *The Indian Mutiny*, p.137.

49    Sieveking, *A Turning Point in the Mutiny*, p.207.

50    BL, India Office papers, Eur 171/5, Charles Nicholson to Mary Maxwell, 10 May 1857; and BL, India Office papers, Eur 171/5, Clara Nicholson to Charles Nicholson, 17 June 1857.

51    Bourchier, *Eight Months' Campaign*, p.2.

52    Cooper, *The Crisis in the Punjab*, p.91.

53    Farooqui, *Besieged*, p.272 (document 16,16).

54    Even Forrest's sympathetic biographer concedes that Chamberlain was 'a stern disciplinarian, swift to punish the wrongdoer'. See Forrest, *Chamberlain*, p.viii.

55    Allen, *Soldier Sahibs*, pp.63–65.

56    Taylor, *Sir Alex Taylor*, vol. 2, p.67.

57    Lawrence, *Reminiscences of Forty-three Years in India*, pp.295–296.

58   Montgomery, *Monty's Grandfather*, p.88; and Farooqui, *Besieged*, p.xxii.

59   Roberts, *Letters Written During the Indian Mutiny*, p.30.

60   BL, India Office papers, Mss Eur C 203, John Lawrence to Neville Chamberlain, 29 May 1857.

61   BPP, Appendix to papers relative to the mutinies in the East Indies, HC, 1857, p.365.

62   BL, India Office, Mss Eur E 211/9, 5 August 1857.

63   BL, India Office papers, Mss Eur E 211/9, 5 August 1857.

64   BL, India Office papers, Mss Eur F 171/5, John Nicholson to Clara Nicholson, 10 May 1857.

65   Roberts, *Forty-one Years in India*, vol. 1, pp.59–60.

66   Roberts, *Letters Written During the Indian Mutiny*, p.2.

67   Buckland, *Dictionary of Indian Biography*, p.354.

68   BL, India Office papers, Mss E 211/15, Edwardes' memorandum on the Mutiny in the Punjab, 2 March 1858, paragraph 24.

69   Roberts, *Forty-one Years in India*, vol. 1, pp.66–73.

70   Kaye, *Lives of Indian Officers*, vol. 2, p.457.

71   Haigh and Turner, 'Nickalsain', p.260.

72   Sieveking, *A Turning Point in the Mutiny*, pp.205–206.

73   Haigh and Turner, 'Nickalsain', p.267.

74   BPP, East Indies (Punjab), HC 238, p.133.

75   BL, India Office papers, Mss E 211/15, Edwardes' memorandum on the Mutiny in the Punjab, 2 March 1858, paragraph 41.

76   Kaye, *Lives of Indian Officers*, vol. 2, pp.458–459.

77   Harrison, *The Graham Indian Mutiny Papers*, p.22.

78   Cotton, *Nine Years on the North-West Frontier of India*, pp.164–165.

79   BPP, East Indies (Punjab), HC 212, pp.50–5.

80   Haigh and Turner, 'Nickalsain', p.271.

81   BPP, East Indies (Punjab), HC 238, p.65.

82   Lumsden, *Lumsden of the Guides*, p.183.

83   Trotter, *The Life of John Nicholson*, p.213.

84   BL, India Office papers, Mss Eur E 211/15, Edwardes' memorandum on the Mutiny in the Punjab, 2 March 1858.

85   BL, India Office papers, Mss Eur E 211/15, Edwardes' memorandum on the Mutiny in the Punjab, 2 March 1858, paragraphs 148 and 149.

86   Muir, *Records of the Intelligence Department*, p.270.

87   Moreman, 'Sir William Olpherts', *Oxford Dictionary of National Biography*, vol. 41, p.787.

88   BL, India Office papers, Mss Eur E 211/15, Edwardes' memorandum on the Mutiny in the Punjab, 2 March 1858, paragraph 31.

89   BL, India Office papers, 'Mutiny telegrams', Mss Eur F 171/102, Nicholson to James, 22 May 1857.

90  There were 53,000 police in the Punjab of whom 30,000 were rural, but 13,000, or a quarter, were military police. There were also 9,000 civil police and 1,200 city police.

91  Edwardes, *A Year on the Punjab Frontier, in 1848–49*, vol. 1, p.271.

92  Haigh and Turner, 'Nickalsain', pp.271–274.

93  David, *The Indian Mutiny*, p.144.

94  BPP, Selections from the records of the government of India. (Foreign Department.) …, pp.8 and 12.

95  BPP, East Indies (Punjab), HC 238, p.70.

96  BPP, East Indies (Punjab), HC 238, pp.120 and 139.

97  Haigh and Turner, 'Nickalsain', p.278.

98  David, *The Indian Mutiny*, chapter 11.

99  BPP, East India (26th Native Infantry), pp.1–4; and BL, India Office papers, Mss Eur E 211/11, John Lawrence to Nicholson, 2 August 1857.

100  David, *The Indian Mutiny*, p.xxi.

101  BL, India Office papers, 'Mutiny telegrams', Mss Eur F 171/102, Nicholson to Lawrence, 21 June 1857.

102  Wilberforce, *An Unrecorded Chapter of the Indian Mutiny*, pp.80–81.

103  Edwardes, *Memorials of the Life and Letters of Major-General Sir Herbert B. Edwardes*, vol. 2, p.3.

104  BL, India Office papers, Mss Eur E 211/12, Extract from despatch dated 1 June 1857.

105  Edwardes, *Memorials of the Life and Letters of Major-General Sir Herbert B. Edwardes*, vol. 2, p.4.

106  BL, India Office papers, Mss Eur E 211/10, John Lawrence to Nicholson, 7 July 1857.

107  Haigh and Turner, 'Nickalsain', p.284.

108  Montgomery, *Monty's Grandfather*, p.77.

109  Edwardes, *Memorials of the Life and Letters of Major-General Sir Herbert B. Edwardes*, vol. 2, p.24.

110  Cooper, *The Crisis in the Punjab*, pp.26–27.

111  Allen, *Soldier Sahibs*, pp.279–280; Dalrymple, *The Last Mughal*, pp.197–198; and Silvestri, *Ireland and India: Nationalism, empire and memory*, p.79.

112  BL, India Office papers, Mss Eur F 171/101/4, Nicholson to Edwardes, 28 May and 6 June 1857.

113  NA: PRO 30/29/23/10, The speech of the lords commissioners to both houses of Parliament, on Friday, August 28, 1857

114  *Blackwell's Magazine*, 1898, p.222.

115  Allen, *Soldier Sahibs*, p.279.

116  Pearson, *The Hero of Delhi*, pp.182–183.

117  BPP, East India (torture), p.49.

118  Forrest, *Chamberlain*, p.338.

# CHAPTER 9

1    David, *The Indian Mutiny*, pp.152 and 158.

2    BL, India Office papers, Mss Eur E 211/11, Chamberlain to Nicholson, 19 July 1857.

3    BL, India Office papers, Mss Eur F 171/101/1, John Nicholson to Clare Nicholson, 12 June 1857. On the back of the letter Clara Nicholson has written, 'John's last June 1857'.

4    This 'yawning clock' may well be the one now housed in the National Army Museum in Chelsea, London.

5    Edwardes, *Memorials of the Life and Letters of Major-General Sir Herbert B. Edwardes*, vol. 2, p.19.

6    BL, Mss Eur E 211/7, Chamberlain to Edwardes, 2 October 1857.

7    Allen, *Soldier Sahibs*, pp.286–287.

8    Allen, *Soldier Sahibs*, p.287.

9    Nicholson letter, dated 21 June, and Lawrence's reply, dated 30 June 1857 are contained in BL, India Office papers, Mss Eur F 171/120. See also BL, India Office papers, Mss Eur E 211/10, Lt Col. Macpherson to Major General Gowan, 30 June 1857.

10   BL, India Office papers, 'Mutiny telegrams', Mss Eur F 171/120, Nicholson to Lawrence, 22 May 1857.

11   *History of the Siege of Delhi, by an Officer who Served There*; and Kaye, *Lives of Indian officers*, p.466n.

12   Trotter, *The Life of John Nicholson*, p.179.

13   Wilberforce, *An Unrecorded Chapter of the Indian Mutiny*, p.26.

14   Cooper, *The Crisis in the Punjab*, p.47.

15   Griffiths, *A Narrative of the Siege of Delhi*, p.30.

16   Forrest, *Chamberlain*, p.331.

17   BPP, East Indies (Punjab), HC 238, p.68.

18   BPP, East India (Native Cavalry), HC, pp.162–165.

19   Roberts, *Letters Written During the Indian Mutiny*, pp.47 and 76.

20   BL, India Office papers, Mss Eur F 171/101/4, Nicholson to Edwardes, 17 June 1857.

21   Daly, *Memoirs of General Sir Henry Dermot Daly*, p.168.

22   Roberts, *Forty-one Years in India*, vol. 1, p.215.

23   W.S. Moorsom, *Historical Record of the Fifty-Second (Oxfordshire Light Infantry) from the Year 1755 to the Year 1858*.

24   India Office papers, Mss Eur F 171/10, 'Mutiny telegrams', Nicholson to Edwardes, 20 May 1857.

25   Wilberforce (pp.98–99) does give a list of places and dates for the Moveable Column, but this is out by several days in some instances.

26   Roberts, *Forty-one Years in India*, vol. 1, pp.134–137.

27    BPP, East Indies (Punjab), HC 238, p.38.

28    Cooper, *The Crisis in the Punjab*, p.65.

29    Bayley, *Reminiscences*, p.171.

30    Roberts, *Forty-one Years in India*, vol. 1, p.437.

31    BL, India Office papers, Mss Eur E 211/10, John Lawrence to Nicholson, 26 June 1857.

32    BL, India Office papers, Mss Eur E 211/10, John Lawrence to Nicholson, 7 July 1857; and Kaye, *A History of the Sepoy War in India*, vol. 2, p.647.

33    BL, India Office papers, Mss Eur F 171/101/4, John Lawrence to Nicholson, 4 August 1857.

34    Roberts, *Letters Written During the Indian Mutiny*, p.18.

35    BL, India Office papers, Mss Eur E 211/10, John Lawrence to Nicholson, 25 June 1857.

36    Griffiths, *Narrative of the Siege of Delhi*, p.73.

37    BL, India Office papers, Mss Eur F 171/10, 'Mutiny telegrams', Nicholson to Lawrence, 5 July 1857.

38    BL, India Office papers, Mss Eur E.211/9, Edwardes to Nicholson, 5 July 1857.

39    BL, India Office papers, Mss Eur E 211/9, Edwardes to Nicholson, 5 July 1857.

40    Cooper, *The Crisis in the Punjab*, pp.43–47.

41    Trotter, *The Life of John Nicholson*, p.238. There are minor discrepancies in Trotter's transcribing of this message.

42    BPP, East Indies (Punjab), HC 238, p.41.

43    BL, India Office papers, Mss Eur E 211/11, A.A. Roberts to Nicholson, 9 July 1857; and BL, India Office papers, Mss Eur E 211/11, Nicholson to Chamberlain, 19 July 1857.

44    Rich, *The Mutiny in Sialkot*, p.19.

45    PRONI, Graham papers, James Graham to his cousin James Graham, 8 July 1857, D 812/10/B/35, quoted in Harrison, *The Graham Indian Mutiny papers*, p.42.

46    Harrison, *The Graham Indian Mutiny papers*, introduction. Confusingly, there were in fact two Dr Grahams in Sialkot, both of whom were shot, in separate vehicles, while trying to reach safety. See also *The Times*, 31 August 1857.

47    BPP, Appendix A to further papers (No. 5) relative to the mutinies in the East Indies. (Inclosures in no. 1.), HP, p.321.

48    Wilberforce, *An Unrecorded Chapter of the Indian Mutiny*, p.49.

49    Bourchier, *Eight Months' Campaign*, p.14.

50    Bayley, *Reminiscences*, p.174; and BL, India Office papers, Mss Eur E 211/11, Nicholson to Chamberlain, 19 July 1857.

51    Trotter, *The Life of John Nicholson*, p.243.

52    Wilberforce, *An Unrecorded Chapter of the Indian Mutiny*, pp.69 and 71.

53    BPP, East India (Punjab), HC 212, p.6.

54    Bouchier, *Eight Months' Campaign*, pp.20–22.

55 BPP, East India (Punjab), HC 212, p.20.

56 BPP, East Indies (Punjab), HC 238, p.41.

57 Rich, *The Mutiny in Sialkot*, pp.69–70.

58 Bayley, *Reminiscences*, pp.179–180.

59 National Army Museum, Ommaney papers, 21 July 1857, ff.90–91.

60 BPP, Flogging (Army and Militia), p.5.

61 BPP, Peel Commission, p.xix.

62 Bayley, *Reminiscences*, p.170.

63 BL, India Office papers, Mss Eur E 211/8, John Nicholson to Henry Nicholson, 5 September 1852.

64 PRONI, Graham papers, B36, 8 July 1857.

65 BL, India Office papers, Mss Eur E 211/12, Extract of despatch dated 18 July 1857.

66 BL, India Office papers, Mss Eur E 211/9, Edwardes to Nicholson, 5 August 1857.

67 Farooqui, *Besieged*, pp.xxii, xxiv, xxv and xxvi.

68 David, *The Indian Mutiny*, p.277n.

69 Trotter, *The Life of John Nicholson*, p.252.

70 See Evelyn Thomas's notes in BL, Mss Eur F 171/101/1.

71 BL, India Office papers, Mss Eur F 171/102, 'Mutiny telegrams', Nicholson to Lawrence (reporting his telegram to Wilson), 26 July 1857.

72 BL, India Office papers, Mss Eur E 211/10, John Lawrence to Nicholson, 28 July 1957.

73 Daly, *Memoirs of General Sir Henry Dermot Daly*, p.164.

74 Wilberforce, *An Unrecorded Chapter of the Indian Mutiny*, p.39.

75 BL, India Office papers, 'Mutiny telegrams', Mss Eur F 171/102, Nicholson to Lawrence, 1 August 1857; and BPP, East Indies (Punjab), HC 238, p.104.

76 BPP, East Indies (Punjab), HC 238, p.113.

77 BL, Hardicke papers, Add. 46, 917, Nicholson to Lind, 1 August 1857, f.64.

78 BL, India Office papers, Mss Eur E 211/11, Report for period 6–10 August 1857 by Foorab Ali.

79 Trotter, *Hodson of Hodson's Horse*, p.179.

80 Medley, *A Year's Campaigning in India*, pp.38–39.

81 Muir, *Records of the Intelligence Department*, pp.268–269.

82 Farooqui, *Besieged*, pp.412 and 433n.

83 Wilberforce, *An Unrecorded Chapter of the Indian Mutiny*, pp.87–89.

84 *Annual Register*, 1857, p.182.

85 Nicholson's field glasses are now an exhibit in the Red Fort, Delhi.

86 BPP, Further papers (No. 4) relative to the mutinies in the East Indies, HP, p.115; see also Farooqui, *Besieged*, p.xxvi.

87 Greathed, *Letters Written During the Siege of Delhi*, p.193.

88 Extrapolated from Wilberforce, *An Unrecorded Chapter of the Indian Mutiny*, p.99.

89   Moorsom, *Historical Record*, p.379.

90   BL, India Office papers, Mss Eur E 211/10, John Lawrence to Nicholson, 15 August 1857.

91   NA, PRO 30/29/23/10, List of ships and screw-steamers engaged for the conveyance of troops to India.

## CHAPTER 10

1   NAM, Wilson papers, 6807-483, Wilson to Ellen Wilson, 5 September 1857, f.77.

2   NAM, Wilson papers, 6807-483, Wilson to Ellen Wilson, 5 August 1857, ff.59-60.

3   NAM, Wilson papers, 6807-483, Wilson to Ellen Wilson, 14 August 1857, f.65.

4   Trotter, *The Life of John Nicholson*, p.283.

5   PRONI, Graham papers, D812/14/149, James Graham to Anne Graham, 25 August 1857.

6   Vibart, *Richard Baird Smith*, p.14.

7   Griffiths, *A Narrative of the Siege of Delhi*, p.83.

8   Dalrymple, *The Last Mughal*, p.xx.

9   NAM, Wilson papers, 6807-483, Wilson to Ellen Wilson, 25 August 1857, f.71.

10   BL, India Office papers, Mss Eur E 211/11, Nicholson to Major Ewart, n.d.

11   Edwardes, *Memorials of the Life and Letters of Major-General Sir Herbert B. Edwardes*, vol. 2, p.46.

12   Bouchier, *Eight Months' Campaign*, p.41.

13   Farooqui, *Besieged*, p.137.

14   NAM, Wilson papers, 6807-483, Wilson to Ellen Wilson, 29 August 1857, f.74.

15   Allen, *Soldier Sahibs*, p.309.

16   Griffiths, *Narrative of the Siege of Delhi*, p.127.

17   Harry Lumsden was known to his closest friends as Joe. For the Nicholson letter, see BL, India Office papers, Nicholson to H.B. Lumsden, Before Delhi, 1 September 1857, reproduced in Lumsden and Elsmie, *Lumsden of the Guides*, p.212.

18   Griffiths, *A Narrative of the Siege of Delhi*, p.128.

19   BL, India Office papers, Mss Eur E 211/11, Nicholson to Major Ewert, n.d. See also *Friend of India*, 14 January 1858; and NAM, Wilson papers, 6807-483, Wilson to Ellen Wilson, 27 August 1857, f.73.

20   Greathed, *Letters Written During the Siege of Delhi*, pp.226–227.

21   BL, India Office papers, Mss Eur E 211/10, 24 August 1857.

22   Bouchier, *Eight Months' Campaign*, p.44n.

23   Vibart, *Richard Baird Smith*, p.55. Griffiths (p.135) gives the number of heavy guns and mortars as twenty-six.

24   For an account of the battle of Najafgarh, see Kaye, *Lives of Indian Officers*, vol. 2, appendices, pp.498–502; BL, India Office papers, Mss Eur E 211/11, Wilson to Nicholson, 25 August [1857]; and India Office papers, Mss Eur E 211/11, Nicholson to Chamberlain, n.d. See also Trotter, *The Life of John Nicholson*, p.269.

25    Harrison, *The Graham Indian Mutiny Papers*, pp.78–79.

26    Large number of leave passes were produced by sepoys after the Mutiny had been crushed as proof that they had not been involved in the insurrection.

27    NAM, Wilson papers, 6807-483, 27 August 1857, f.73.

28    Supplement to the *London Gazette*, 15 December 1857, p.4434; and BL, India Office papers, Mss Eur E 211/11, Wilson to Nicholson, 26 August [1857].

29    BL, India Office papers, Mss Eur E 211/10, 27 and 29 August 1857.

30    BL, India Office papers, Mss Eur F 171/102, 'Mutiny telegrams', Nicholson to Lawrence, 8 September 1857; and Mss Eur E 211/12, despatch dated 9 September 1857.

31    Muir, *Records of the Intelligence Department*, pp.183 and 271.

32    NAM, Taylor papers, 7605-21-18, 27 September 1857.

33    Wilberforce, *An Unrecorded Chapter of the Indian Mutiny*, pp.204–205.

34    Trotter, *Hodson of Hodson's Horse*, p.193.

35    BL, MSS Eur E 211/9, 1 September 1857.

36    Muir, *Records of the Intelligence Department*, p.153.

37    Kaye, *Lives of Indian Officers*, vol. 2, p.470.

38    BL, India Office papers, Mss Eur E 211/9, Edwardes to Nicholson, 1 September 1857.

39    BL, India Office papers, Mss Eur F 171/5, Charles Nicholson to Clara Nicholson, 28 August 1857.

40    Roberts, *Letters Written During the Indian Mutiny*, p.50.

41    Kaye, *Lives of Indian Officers*, vol. 2, p.478.

42    BL, India Office papers, Mss Eur E 211/9, Edwardes to Nicholson, 20 August 1857.

43    Greathed, *Letters Written During the Siege of Delhi*, p.179.

44    Bayley, *Reminiscences*, pp.169–170.

45    PRONI, Graham papers, B44, September 1857.

46    Griffiths, *Narrative of the Siege of Delhi*, p.70.

47    Bayley, *Reminiscences*, pp.191–192.

48    Wilberforce, *An Unrecorded Chapter of the Indian Mutiny*, pp.121–122; and Griffiths, *A Narrative of the Siege of Delhi*, pp.120–121.

49    David, *The Indian Mutiny*, p.287.

50    Wilberforce, *An Unrecorded chapter of the Indian Mutiny*, p.209.

51    Trotter, *The Life of John Nicholson*, p.273.

52    Vibart, *Richard Baird Smith*, pp.82, 130 and 148.

53    Taylor, *Sir Alex Taylor*, p.251.

54    Buckland, *Dictionary of Indian Biography*, p.416.

55    BL, India Office papers, Mss Eur F 171/101/4 and E 211/10, John Lawrence to Nicholson, 5 September 1857.

56    BL, India Office papers, Mss Eur E 211/9, Edwardes to Nicholson, 20 August 1857.

# CHAPTER 11

1   Griffiths, *A Narrative of the Siege of Delhi*, p.64.

2   Saul David (*The Indian Mutiny*, p.xxiii) gives the population at 100,000.

3   *Annual Register*, p.183; and BPP, East India (Area, Population, etc.), pp.6–7.

4   Griffiths, *Narrative of the Siege of Delhi*, p.141.

5   Farooqui, *Besieged Voices from Delhi 1857*, p.78 (document 60, 309) and 257 (document 18, 1).

6   Greathed, *Letters Written During the Siege of Delhi*, p.217.

7   Farooqui, *Besieged*, pp.xix–xxvii; xxix, 19–22, 155–158, 166, 201 and 254.

8   Farooqui, *Besieged*, pp.221 and 413.

9   BL, India Office papers, Mss Eur E. 211/9, Edwardes to Nicholson, 5 August 1857.

10   BL, India Office papers, Mss Eur E 211/9, Edwardes to Nicholson, 9 September 1857.

11   PRONI, Graham papers, D 812/10/B/44, William Graham to James Graham, 11 September 1857. Also in Harrison and Fraser, *The Graham Indian Mutiny Papers*, p.48.

12   Vibart, *Richard Baird Smith*, p.53.

13   Taylor, *Sir Alex Taylor*, 1.315n.

14   NAM, W.C. Justice papers, 6909-4, 30 September 1857; and Griffiths, *Narrative of the Siege of Delhi*, p.147.

15   Taylor, *Sir Alex Taylor*, 1.284.

16   Farooqui, *Besieged*, pp.50 and 60–61 (documents 73,158; 92, 77; and 57,483).

17   Muir, *Records of the Intelligence Department*, p.186.

18   BL, India Office papers, Mss Eur E 211/11, General Wilson to Nicholson, 19 July 1857.

19   Bouchier, *Eight Months' Campaign*, p.60.

20   Quoted in Dalrymple, *The Last Mughal*, p.307.

21   Buckland, *Dictionary of Indian Biography*, p.108 and Murphy, 'Sir Henry Dermot Daly', *Dictionary of Irish Biography*, vol. 3, p.23

22   Hibbert, *The Siege of Delhi*, p.47.

23   The picture is identified as Charles Nicholson in Sieveking's 1910 book *A Turning Point in the Mutiny*. The pictures of the Nicholsons were lent by John Nicholson's nephew, Dr Theodore Maxwell. Copies of these pictures may be found in the India Office section of the British Library. The National Portrait Gallery in London lists the sketch as being of John Nicholson.

24   Roberts, *Forty-one Years in India*, vol. 1, p.221; and Taylor, *Sir Alex Taylor*, vol. 1. p.322.

25   Hibbert, *The Siege of Delhi*, p.48.

26   Roberts, *Forty-one Years in India*, vol. 1, p.224.

27   Griffiths, *A Narrative of the Siege of Delhi*, pp.155–156.

28 Farooqui, *Besieged*, pp.xxvi and p.49 (document 111d 171). Lieutenant Roberts' father back in Ireland also knew the British were coming as his son had let him know in a letter dated 13 August, a month before the assault.

29 Supplement to the *London Gazette*, 15 December 1857, p.4449.

30 NAM, Coghill papers, 6609-139, Coghill to Joss, 22 September 1857; and Taylor, *Sir Alex Taylor*, 2.16.

31 Forbes-Mitchell, *Reminiscences of the Great Mutiny*, 'Europeans among the rebels', appendix B; and Gough, *Under Deadly Fire*, pp.48–49.

32 Malleson, *The Indian Mutiny of 1857*, p.298.

33 NAM, Coghill papers, Coghill to Joss, 22 September 1857. For another account of the column's assault, see Medley, *A Year's Campaigning in India*, pp.101–112.

34 Taylor, *Sir Alex Taylor*, vol. 2, 36.

35 Trotter, *Hodson of Hodson's Horse*, p.195.

36 BL, India Office papers, Mss Eur E 211/9, Edwardes to Nicholson, 9 September 1857.

37 Griffiths, *Narrative of the Siege of Delhi*, p.160–161.

38 Allen, *Soldier Sahibs*, p.322.

39 See, for example, NAM, Roberts papers, 8310-155-12, Roberts to his mother, 26 September 1857.

40 Malleson, *The Indian Mutiny of 1857*, pp.302–303.

41 Taylor, *General Sir Alex Taylor*.

42 Dalrymple, *The Last Mughal*, p.353.

43 Edwardes, *Memorials of the Life and Letters of Major-General Sir Herbert B. Edwardes*, vol. 2, p.57n.

# CHAPTER 12

1 Edwardes, *Memorials of the Life and Letters of Major-General Sir Herbert B. Edwardes*, vol. 2, p.57n.

2 NAM, Roberts papers, 8310-155-11, Frederick Roberts to his mother, 16 September 1857. For Neville Chamberlain's second-hand account of Nicholson being shot, see Forrest, *Chamberlain*, pp.363–365.

3 Roberts, *Forty-one Years in India*, vol. 1, p.236.

4 BL, India Office papers, Mss Eur E 211/7, J.R. Becher to Edwardes, 28 October 1857; quoted in Kaye, *Lives of Indian Officers*, vol. 2, p.483.

5 'Brig.-Gen. Nicholson's flying column in the Punjaub', *United Services Magazine*, vol. 13, April 1896, p.80.

6 Edwardes, *Memorials of the Life and Letters of Major-General Sir Herbert B. Edwardes*, vol. 2, pp.62–63; and Trotter, *The Life of John Nicholson*, p.297.

7 Forrest, *Chamberlain*, p.365.

8 NAM, Coghill papers, 22 September 1857.

9 Hibbert, *The Siege of Delhi*, p.57.

10   *The Times*, 10 February 1917.

11   Roberts, *Forty-one Years in India*, vol. 1, pp.133–134.

12   Supplement to the *London Gazette* of Tuesday, 15 December, number 22073, 1857, p.4444.

13   Personal correspondence: Peter Chantler to Donal McCracken, 22 January 2014. Dagshai was where many of the Irish soldiers who mutinied in 1920 were to be imprisoned.

14   *The Times*, 12 February 1917.

15   *The Gentleman's Magazine*, ser. 3, vol. 12, (1862), p.790.

16   Colonel H.G. Hart, *The New Annual Army List and Militia List for 1868*, London, John Murray, p.159; and *The Times*, 20 February 1917.

17   BL, India Office papers, Mss Eur E 211/7, 25 October 1857.

18   Vibart, *Richard Baird Smith*, p.164.

19   BL, India Office papers, Mss Eur E 211/7, Chamberlain to Edwardes, 2 October 1857 and 31 October 1857.

20   NAM, Wilson papers, 6807-483, Wilson to Ellen Wilson, 19 September 1857, ff.84–85.

21   NAM, Wilson papers, 6807-483, Wilson to Ellen Wilson, 15 September 1858.

22   Steel, *On the Face of the Waters*, p.411.

23   BL, India Office papers, Mss Eur E 211/12, despatch dated 15 September 1857.

24   BL, India Office papers, Mss Eur F 171/101/4, transcript of Dr Mactier's report, 17 September 1857.

25   BL, India Office papers, Mss Eur E 211/9, Edwardes to Nicholson, 18 September 1857.

26   PRONI, Graham papers, William Graham to James Graham, 20 September 1857, D812/10/B/45, reproduced in Harrison, *The Graham Indian Mutiny papers*, p.49.

27   BL, India office papers, Mss Eur F 171/101/4, 20 September 1857.

28   BL, India Office papers, Mss Eur F 171/9.

29   Edwardes, *Memorials of the Life and Letters of Major-General Sir Herbert B. Edwardes*, vol. 2, pp.50–51.

30   Captain Trotter gives the time of death as 9.30 a.m.

31   BL, India Office papers, Mss E 211/14, copy of Edwardes's telegram, 23 September 1857.

32   BPP, East Indies (Punjab), HC 238, p.79.

33   Lumsden, *Lumsden of the Guides*, p.217.

34   NAM, Taylor papers, 7605-21-18.

35   *The Times*, 7 June 1957.

36   www.johnnicholsongreatmutiny.wordpress.com, accessed 22 February 2014); and Allen, *Soldier Sahibs*, p.326.

37   *Annual Register*, 1857.

38    BL, India Office papers, Mss Eur E 211/7, Becker to Edwardes, 12 December
      1857, quoted in Kaye, *Lives of Indian officers*, vol. 2, pp.483–484 and Edwardes,
      *Memorials of the life and letters of Major-General Sir Herbert B. Edwardes*, vol. 2,
      p.63.

39    Edwardes, *Memorials of the Life and Letters of Major-General Sir Herbert B.
      Edwardes*, vol. 2, p.52.

40    BL India Office papers, Mss Eur E 211/7, Chamberlain to Edwardes,
      31 October 1857.

41    BL, India Office papers, Mss Eur F 171/5, Charles Nicholson to Mary
      Maxwell, 9 October 1857.

42    Colonel John R. Becher, C.B.

43    BL, India Office papers, Mss Eur E 211/9, Edwardes to Charles Nicholson,
      9 October 1857.

44    BL, India Office papers, Mss Eur F 171/5, Charles Nicholson to Clara
      Nicholson, 2 February 1862.

45    BL, Mss Eur C 203, John Lawrence to Neville Henderson, 26 September 1857.

46    BL India Office papers, Mss Eur E 211/12, despatch number 3176, sent by
      Lt Col Macpherson, 3 December 1857.

47    These memorials are quoted in Keye's *Lives of Indian Officers*, vol. 2, pp.486–
      491.

48    BL, India Office papers, Mss Eur E 211/7, John Lawrence to Edwardes,
      12 October 1857 (copy).

48    The Delhi statue of Nicholson was by Sir Thomas Brock RA (1847–1922), and
      the Lisburn statue by F.W. Pomeroy. Since 1960, the Delhi statue has stood in
      the grounds of the Royal School, Dungannon. The Lisburn statue surprisingly
      survived a bomb that exploded nearby during the troubles of the 1970s.

50    BL India Office papers, Mss Eur F 197/37, Younghusband scrapbook, f.6.

51    BPP, East India (Native Cavalry), HC, pp.162–165.

52    Griffiths, *A Narrative of the Siege of Delhi*, pp.209–210.

# Select Bibliography

## NOTE ON THE NICHOLSON PAPERS

In October 1857 Colonel Herbert Edwardes, wrote to John Nicholson's brother Charles:

> A great number of private letters and demi-official etc; all bearing on dear John's career are here [at Peshawar] collected, and I am going to send them down to you, as you ought to dispose of them, and perhaps will like to keep and examine them at leisure. I picked out all in the handwriting of Sir Henry and Lady Lawrence, because we are collecting their letters for a Biography.

This was the first sorting. A fire in the home of Nicholson's biographer Sir John Kaye destroyed some letters, and we shall never know what documents were condemned to the fire grate in Lisburn by Nicholson's mother in her quest to immortalise her son as a hero. Over the decades, the letters would pass through at least six sets of hands before most of them – or the remnants, we do not know – arrived in the India Office Library in London and are now in the British Library. These papers are contained under two broad classifications: Thomas papers (European manuscripts F 171) and the Edwardes papers (European manuscripts E 211). Mention also needs to be made of the Nicholson letters that are housed in the National Army Museum in London.

One biography of Nicholson that was not written, but which if it had materialised would have been worth all contemporary accounts put together, was proposed by Nicholson's friend James Abbott (1807–96), sometime deputy commissioner of Hazara. In an irascible postscript in a letter to Sir Herbert Edwardes written from Bannu on 6 January 1856, Nicholson comments, 'Little Abbott has cut me, (and I am really very sorry for it) because I would not allow him to write a book about me' (Mss Eur E 211/3).

# MANUSCRIPT MATERIAL

*British Library (BL): Asian and African Studies*
Abbott papers
Chamberlain papers
East India Company Cadet papers (1838–39)
Edwardes papers
Herbert papers
Lawrence papers
Montgomery papers
Thomas papers (Nicholson family papers)
East India Company Cadet papers
A lock of John Nicholson's hair can be found in European manuscripts A142.

*Moravian Church, Gracehill, County Antrim, Northern Ireland*
Letters, enrolment registers and scrap books

*National Army Museum*, London (NAM)
Cocks papers [Arthur H. Cocks (1819–81), containing forty-eight Nicholson letters dating from the second Anglo-Sikh War. Reference: 6412-6418]
Coghill papers
Dennys papers
Justice papers
Lind papers
Ommaney papers
Roberts papers
Taylor papers
Wilson papers

*National Library of Ireland*
Roberts' letter, 1897, ms 41,844

*Public Record of Northern Ireland* (PRONI)
Graham papers
Pottinger papers

*Representative Church Body, Dublin*
Parish records

*Material in India and Pakistan*

There are various document and reports in the archives in New Delhi and Lahore that relate to Nicholson in his capacity as a government official. Many of these were printed and may be found scattered among Punjab Blue Books and published series. Other Nicholson communications were transcribed in the 1940s on the authority of the Keeper of Records of the Punjab government. The India Office papers kept by the British Library in London have copies of a collection of Nicholson documents and memorabilia in Delhi under the classification: Eur Mss 171/105 (Thomas papers).

It is hoped that with the emergence of various documents in vernacular languages relating to the Great Rebellion, and in particular to the British spy network operating within the walled city, that new material will eventually due emerge relating to contemporary Indian insurgent attitudes to Nicholson, the narrative a step further.

# BRITISH PARLIAMENTARY PAPERS AND INDIAN GOVERNMENT RECORDS [BPP]

Account of the total annual expense of military force under each presidency in each year from 1850–51, according to the annual military statements received from India (Mr Henry Baillie) 201-XII, 15 July 1858.

Appendix A to further papers (No. 5) relative to the mutinies in the East Indies. (Inclosures in no. 1.). Houses of Parliament, 1857.

Appendix to papers relative to the mutinies in the East Indies. (Inclosures in nos. 7 to 19). Houses of Parliament, 1857.

Army (India). A return 'of the Number of Divisional and Brigade Commands of the Army under the Presidencies in India; distinguishing the Number of Commands held by Her Majesty's Officers, and those held by Company's Officers.' House of Commons 514, London, 12 August 1854, 2pp.

Army in India (Number of Officers). House of Commons 509, London, 19 June 1871.

East India (26th Native Infantry). Copy of a letter from Sir R. Montgomery to Lord Stanley, of the 29th of April 1859, and of a statement of facts connected with the execution of the 26th Native Infantry, forwarded therewith. House of Commons 125 – Sess. 2, 4pp.

East India (Area, Population, etc.). A return 'of the area and population of each district of each presidency of India, from the latest inquiries; comprising, also, the area and estimated population of native states'. House of Commons 215, 28 July 1857, Sess. 2, 16pp.

East India (Castes of Hindoos). HC 129, 5 February 1858, 15pp.

East India (Indian Law Commission). Copies of the special reports of the Indian Law Commissioners. 14. House of Commons, 26 January 1847.

East India (Mutiny). Return of the name or number of each regiment and regular and irregular corps in India which has mutinied, or manifested a disposition to mutiny, since 1 January 1857; of the number of officers and men present with each regiment and corps at the outbreak of the mutiny; of the date of the first intimation received by any officer of the regiment or corps being disposed to mutiny; and the date when information thereof was received by the Governor-General of India or the governor of Bombay; etc. House of Commons (133), 15 March 1859, 71pp.

East India (Native Cavalry). A 'Return of the number of regular and irregular regiments of native cavalry in India which have been employed upon Field Service from April 1857 to December 1859, stating their respective fixed establishment of men and horses; the number of men and horses present for duty on the 1st and 15th day of each month in each regiment; the number of horses and men sick present; and of absentees from head-quarters at the same dates, stating causes of absence.' India Office, 18 February 1861. House of Commons, 22 February 1861.

East India (Punjab). Return to an address of the Honourable The House of Commons, dated 4 March 1859; for, A 'Copy of general report on the administration of the Punjab territories, for the years 1856–7 and 1857–8'. India Office, 212, 11 April 1859, 48pp.

East India. Papers relating to the resignation by General Sir Charles Napier, G.C.B., of the office of commander-in-chief in India. House of Commons 80, London, 2 March 1854.

East Indies (Punjab). Papers relating to the mutiny in the Punjab, in 1857. House of Commons 238, 15 April 1859.

East India (Wars on or beyond the borders of British India). Return setting out (1) Wars and military operations on or beyond the borders of British India in which the government of India has engaged since 1849, in chronological order; (2) the causes of such wars or operations; (3) the locality in which troops operated; (4) the results obtained;(5) the numbers approximately of troops employed; (6) the cost of such wars or operations where shown separately in the accounts of the government of India; and (7) the amount of any contributions towards such cost from the British treasury. (Mr. John Morley.). House of Commons 13, 31 January 1900.

Flogging (Army and Militia). Return of the number of persons flogged in the Army and Militia of Great Britain and Ireland in the year 1858, specifying the offence, the regiments, the place of station, the time, the sentence, and the number of lashes inflicted on each person (in continuation of Parliamentary Paper, No. 519, of session 1855–58). House of Commons 47, 3 February 1860.

Further papers relative to the mutinies in the East Indies. Houses of Parliament, 1857.

Further papers (No. 4) relative to the mutinies in the East Indies. Houses of Parliament, 1857.

Further papers (No. 7) (in continuation of No. 5) relative to the mutinies in the East Indies. Houses of Parliament, 1857.

India Office. A copy of the memorandum laid before the court of directors of the East India Company upon railways in India, sanctioned and projected, with map. House of Commons, 1857.

Military map of India: The headquarters of all the commands are named, with the number of British and native troops attached to the whole command. East India (Progress and condition), n.d. c. 1878.

Papers relating to East India affairs (Madras Army). House of Commons 95, London, 1810, 39pp.

Papers relating to East India affairs, Mutiny at Vellore. House of Commons 194, London, 1813, 103pp.

[Peel Commission]. Report of the commissioners appointed to inquire into the organisation of the Indian army; together with the minutes of evidence and appendix. Presented to both Houses of Parliament by command of Her Majesty. [2515], London, HMSO, 1859.

Punjab, etc. Return to an address of the House of Lords, dated 28 July 1873, for return of the services in the field of the army on the Punjab Frontier from 1849 to 1863, for which medals were granted; showing the strength of the force employed, the name of the officer who commanded, the number of casualties, upon each occasion separately: And for similar return respecting the Bazotee expedition of February 1869. (The Lord Somerhill) (272) 1 August 1873, 3pp.

Punjab Government Records: Lahore Political Division 1847–1849, vol. vi, Allahahabad, c. 1915, diaries 7 and 8.

Selections from the records of the government of India (Foreign Department). Published by authority. No. XII. Report showing the relations of the British government with the tribes, independent and dependent, on the North-West Frontier of the Punjab, from the annexation in 1849 to the close of 1855. District Memorandum. Derah Ishmael Khan. Thos. Jones, *Calcutta Gazette* Office. 1856. [Contains a memorandum from Major Reynell G. Taylor to Major J. Nicholson on Derah Ishmael Khan, with appendix and postscript, pp. 67–176.]

## NEWSPAPER AND MAGAZINE REPORTS RELATING TO JOHN NICHOLSON

*Belfast Daily Mercury*, 14 November 1857.

*Belfast Newsletter*, 28 May 1850; 23 September 1857.

*Blackwood's Edinburgh Magazine*, February 1898.

*Bombay Times*, 17 October 1857.

*Freeman's Journal*, 27 October 1857.

*Friend of India*, 14 January 1858.

*Illustrated London News*, 9 August 1851; 10 May 1862; 31 October 1857; 12 and 21 November 1857; and 5 December 1857.

*Indian Public Opinion* (supplement), 19 April 1867.

*Irish Times*, 2 September 1905; 6 March 1909; 20 December 1911; 4 January 1913; 19 December 1914; 27 February 1922; 2, 7 and 10 March 1922; 5 April 1922; 26 September 1929; and 25 March and 11 July 1960.

*The Times*, 27 October and 3 November 1848; 5 January and 18 April 1849; 21 February, 25 April, 10 June and 14 June 1850; 7 June, 29 and 31 August, 12 November, 13 October, 26 November and 28 November 1857; 16 April 1859; 7 August 1902; 13 February 1904; 9 April 1906; 6 January 1909; 24 May 1911; 10 July 1913; 10, 12 and 20 February 1917; and 7 June 1957.

*Northern Whig*, 26 March 1906.

*Weekly Irish Times*, 18 September 1903; 4 January 1913.

## CONTEMPORARY AND NEAR CONTEMPORARY WORKS

Anonymous, 'A soldier of the frontier: Coke of Coke's Rifles', *Blackwood's Edinburgh Review*, June 1898, pp.765–778.

Anonymous, 'A wounded soldier' [Brig. Gen. Nicholson's Flying Column in the Punjab], *United Service Magazine*, vol. 13, April 1896, pp.74–82.

Anonymous [Jim], 'Brig.-Gen. Nicholson's flying column in the Punjaub. By a wounded soldier', *United Service Magazine*, vol. 13, April 1896, pp.74–82.

Anonymous, 'John Nicholson of Delhi', *Blackwood Edinburgh Review*, February 1898, pp.207–223.

Anonymous [Montgomery, Robert], *The Crisis in the Punjab, from the 10th of May Until the Fall of Delhi by a Punjab Employee. For the Benefit of the 'Lawrence Asylum'*, Lahore, 1858. Pamphlet, copy in BL, India Office papers, Montgomery papers, D 1019.

Anonymous, *The Story of the Indian Mutiny (1857–58)*, Edinburgh, W.P. Nimmo, Hay and Mitchell, 1896.

*Annual Register*, London, 1857.

Bayley, John Arthur, *Reminiscences of School and Army Life, 1839 to 1859*: 'The following reminiscences were originally intended solely for the amusement of the writer's nephew and nieces. They are now printed for the use of such of his friends as may care to read them.' Privately printed, April 1875.

[Bellett] *Memoir of the Rev. George Bellett, M.A.*, 'formerly incumbent of S. Leonard's, Bridgenorth, late rector of Whitbourne, Herefordshire. Autobiography and continuation by his daughter. With an introduction by the Rev. Samuel Bentley', London, 1889.

Bourchier, Colonel George, *Eight Months' Campaign Against the Bengal Sepoy Army, During the Mutiny of 1857*, London, Smith, Elder, 1858.

Broadfoot, W., 'The defence of Jalalabad', *English Historical Review*, vol. 29, number 8, 1893, pp.93–98.

Buckland, C.E., *Dictionary of Indian Biography*, London, Swan Sonnenschein, 1906.

Buist, George, 'Papers relating to the Punjab. 1847–1849', *Calcutta Review*, 12.23, 1849, pp.238–296.

Cave-Browne, Rev. J., *The Punjab and Delhi in 1857 Being a Narrative of the Measures by which the Punjab was Saved and Delhi Recovered During the Indian Mutiny*, Edinburgh and London, William Blackwood, 1861, 2 vols.

Cholmeley, R.E., *John Nicholson: The Lion of the Punjaub*, The World's Heroes series, London, Andrew Melrose, n.d., *c.* 1908.

Clark, F., *The East-India Regiment and Army List*, London, William H. Allen, 1840s and 1850s.

(Cooper, Frederic Henry), *The Crisis in the Punjab, from the 10th of May until the Fall of Delhi, by a Punjab Employee for the Benefit of the Lawrence Asylum*, London, Smith, Elder, 1858.

Cotton, Lieut.-General Sir Sydney, *Nine Years on the North-West Frontier of India from 1854 to 1863*, London, Richard Bentley, 1868.

Daly, Major H. *Memoirs of General Sir Henry Dermot Daly*, GCB, CIE *Sometime Commander of Central India Horse, Political Assistant for Western Malwa, etc, etc*, London, John Murray, 1905.


(Edwardes, Emma) *Memorials of the Life and Letters of Major-General Sir Herbert B. Edwardes by his Wife*, London, Kegan Paul, Trench, 1886, 2 vols, .

Edwardes, Herbert, *A Year on the Punjab Frontier, in 1848–49*, London, Richard Bentley, 1851.

Edwardes, Sir Herbert, and Merivale, Herman, *Life of Sir Henry Lawrence*, London, Smith, Elder, 1873.

Edwards, W. (ed.), *Reminiscences of Forty-three Years in India by Sir George Lawrence, KCSI, CB Including the Cabul Disasters, Captivities in Afghanistan and the Punjab, and a Narrative of the Mutinies in Rajputana*, London, John Murray, 1874.

Erskine, Thomas, *Essay on Faith*, London, Waugh and Innes, 1822.

Forbes, Archibald, *The Afghan Wars: 1839–42 and 1878–80*, 2nd ed., London, Seeley, 1892.

Forbes-Mitchell, William, *Reminiscences of the Great Mutiny 1857–59*, London, Macmillan, 1904.

Forrest, G.W., *Life of Field Marshal Sir Neville Chamberlain G.C.B., G.C.S.I.*, Edinburgh and London, William Blackwood, 1909.

Gough, Hugh, *Under Deadly Fire: The First Hand Experiences of a Young Officer of the 3rd Bengal Native Cavalry and Hodson's Horse During the Indian Mutiny, 1857*, reprinted by Leonaur, 2011.

Greathed, *Letters Written During the Siege of Delhi*, London, Longman, Brown, Green, Longmans and Roberts, 1858.

Griffiths, Charles John (ed. Henry John Yonge), *A Narrative of the Siege of Delhi with an Account of the Mutiny at Ferozepore in 1857*, London, John Murray, 1910.

Hart, Colonel H.G., *The New Annual Army List and Militia List for 1868*, London, John Murray.

Hunter, W.W., *The Indian Empire: Its History, People and Products*, London, Trübner, 1882.

Kaye FRS, John William, *A History of the Sepoy War in India*, London, W.H. Allen, 1876, 2 vols.

Kaye, John William, 'General John Nicholson', in *Lives of Indian Officers, Illustrative of the History of the Civil and Military service of India*, London, A. Strahan and Bell & Daldy, 1867, p.417–491. With Nicholson letter dated 28 August 1857 concerning the battle of Nujufgurh, pp.498–500; and Chaplain's narrative of the siege of Delhi, pp.500–502.

Kaye, John William, 'Our Indian heroes: VIII – Brigadier-General Nicholson', *Good Words: An Illustrated Monthly Magazine*, part VIII, 1 August 1865, pp.621–632.

Lewis, Samuel, *A Topographical Dictionary of Ireland*, London, S. Lewis, 1846, 2 vols .

Lumsden and Elsmie, *Lumsden of the Guides: A Sketch of the Life of Lieut.-Gen. Sir Harry Burnett Lumsden, K.C.S.I., C.B., with Selections from his Correspondence and Occasional Papers*, London, John Murray, 1899.

Malleson, G.B., *Decisive Battles of India: From 1746 to 1849 Inclusive*, London, W.H. Allen, 1883.

Malleson CSI, Colonel G.B., *The Indian Mutiny of 1857*, 2nd ed., London, Seeley, 1891.

Martin, Montgomery, *The Indian Empire*, vol. 2, London Printing and Publishing Company, 1861.

Medley, Julius George, *A Year's Campaigning in India: From March, 1857, to March, 1858*, London, W. Thacker, 1858.

Moorsom, W.S., *Historical Record of the Fifty-Second (Oxfordshire Light Infantry) from the Year 1755 to the Year 1858*, 2nd ed., London, Richard Bentley, 1860.

Muir, Sir William, *Records of the Intelligence Department of the Government of the North-West Provinces of India During the Mutiny of 1857, Including Correspondence with the supreme Government, Delhi, Cawnpore, and Other Places*, vol. 2, Edinburgh, T. & T. Clark, 1902.

Murray, Hugh, *History of British India Continued to the Year 1856*, London, T. Nelson, 1860.

Nolan PhD, LLD, E.H., *The Illustrated History of the British Empire in India and the East from the Earliest Times to the Suppression of the Sepoy Mutiny in 1859*, London, James S. Virtue, *c.* 1860, 2 vols.

*Punjab Government Records: Lahore Political Division, 1847–1849*, vol. 6, Allahabad, *c.* 1915, diaries 7 and 8.

Raike, Charles, *Notes on the Revolt in the North-Western Provinces of India*, London, Longmans, Brown, Green, Longmans and Roberts, 1858.

Rich, Captain Gregory, *The Mutiny in Sialkot: With a Brief Description of the Cantonment from 1852 to 1857*, privately printed, 1925.

Roberts, Fred, *Letters Written during the Indian Mutiny … with a Preface by his Daughter Countess Roberts*, London, Macmillan, 1924.

Roberts of Kandahar, Field Marshal Lord, *Forty-One Years in India from Subaltern to Commander-in-Chief*, London, Richard Bentley, 1897, 2 vols.

Shelton, 'Native States' (despatch from Brigadier Shelton to Major-General Elphinstone), *Asiatic Journal and Military Registery*, June 1841, pp.82–84.

Showers, Charles Lionel, *A Missing Chapter of the Indian Mutiny*, London, Longman, Green, 1888.

Sieveking, I. Giberne, *A Turning Point in the Indian Mutiny*, London, David Nutt, 1910.

Steel, Flora Annie, *On the Face of the Waters*, London, William Heinemann, 1897.

*The Parliamentary Gazetteer of Ireland, 1844–45*, Dublin, London and Edinburgh, 1846, 3 vols.

Taylor, A. Cameron, *General Sir Alex Taylor GCB, RE: His Times, his Friends, and his Work*, London, Williams and Norgate, 1913, 2 vols.

Thorburn, Septimus Smet, *Bannú Or our Afghan Frontier*, London, Trübner, 1876.

Thorburn, S.S., *Report on the First Regular Land Settlement of the Bannu District in the Derajat Division of the Punjab*, Lahore, Central Jail Press, 1879.

Trotter, Captain Lionel J., *The Life of Hodson of Hodson's Horse*, London, J.M. Dent, 1910 ed.

Trotter, Captain Lionel J., *The Life of John Nicholson, Soldier and Administrator: Based on Private and Hitherto Unpublished Documents*, John Murray, London, 1897.

Vibart, Col H.M., *Richard Baird Smith: The Leader of the Delhi Heroes in 1857. Private Correspondence of the Commanding Engineer During the Siege, and Other Interesting Letters Hitherto Unpublished*, Westminster, Archibald Constable, 1897.

Webb, Alfred, *A Compendium of Irish Biography*, Dublin, M.H. Gill, 1878.

Wilberforce, Reginald Garton, *An Unrecorded Chapter of the Indian Mutiny; by the Personal Reminiscences of Reginald G. Wilberforce, Late 52nd Light Infantry. Compiled from a Diary and Letters Written on the Spot*, London, John Murray, 1894.

*Wilson's Dublin Directory*, 1823, 1824, 1827 and 1828.

Wright, Rev. G.N., *A Guide to the County of Wicklow.* Illustrated by engravings, after the designs of George Petrie, Esq. and a large map of the county, from an original survey, London, Baldwin, Cradock and Joy.

Yonge, Henry John (ed.), *A Narrative of the Siege of Delhi with an Account of the Mutiny at Ferozepore in 1857 by Charles John Griffiths Late Captain 61st Regiment*, London, John Murray, 1910.

Younghusband, Francis (paintings by E. Molyneaux), *Kashmir*, London, Adam and Charles Black, 1909.

## FICTIONAL WORK FEATURING JOHN NICHOLSON

Forrest, B.E., *Eight Days*: *A Tale of the Indian Mutiny*, London, Edinburgh and New York, Thomas Nelson, n.d.

Gray, Ernest, *Nikkal Seyn: A Tale of John Nicholson, Hero of Delhi, Saviour of India*, London and Glasgow, Collins, 1947.

Kipling, Rudyard, *Kim*, New York, Doubleday, 1901.

Leasor, James, *Follow the Drum*, London, Heinemann, 1972.

Miles, Alfred H., *52 Stories of the Indian Mutiny, and the Men Who Saved India*, London, Hutchinson, *c.* 1895.

Newbold, Sir Henry, *Admirals All, and Other Verses*, New York, John Lane, 1898.

Steel, Flora Annie, *On the Face of the Waters*, London, William Heinemann, 1897.

Wood, J. Claverdon, *When Nicholson Kept the Border: A Tale of the Mutiny Days*, London, 'The *Boy's Own* paper' Office, n.d., *c.* 1920.

## DETAILED STUDIES

Allen, Charles, *Soldier Sahibs: The Men who Made the North-West Frontier*, London, 2000.

Anonymous, 'Lawrence statue now back at Foyle', *Londonderry Sentinel*, 5 March 1963.

Barter, Richard, *The Siege of Delhi: Mutiny Memories of an Old Officer*, London, Folio Society, 1984.

Bartlett, Thomas, 'Irish soldiers in India, 1750–1947', in Michael Holmes and Denis Holmes (eds), *Ireland and India: Connections, Comparisons, Contrasts*, Dublin, Folens, 1997, pp.12–28.

[Bellett] *Memoir of the Rev. George Bellett, MA, Formerly Incumbent of S. Leonard's, Bridgenorth, Late Rector of Whitbourne, Herefordshire.* Autobiography and continuation by his daughter. With an introduction by the Rev. Samuel Bentley, M.A., London, 1889.

Bhattacharya, Sabyasachi (ed.), *Rethinking 1857*, New Delhi, Orient Black Swan, 2007.

Bishop, Anthony, 'John Nicholson in the Indian Mutiny', *Irish Sword*, vol. 8, no. 33, 1968, pp.277–287.

Boparai, Hari Singh, *Revolt of 1857 in Punjab and Role of the Sikhs*, Delhi, Gyan Sagar Publications, 2000.

Bourne, J.M., 'The East India Company's Military Seminary, Addiscombe, 1809–1858', *Journal of the Society for Army Historical Research*, 1979, vol. 57, pp.206–222.

Bowen, Desmond, *The Protestant Crusade in Ireland, 1800–70*, Gill and Macmillan, Dublin, 1978.

Cadell, Sir Patrick, 'Irish soldiers in India', *Irish Sword*, vol. 1, no. 2, 1949–1953, pp.75–79.

Carmody, W.P., *Lisburn Cathedral and its Past Rectors*, Belfast, 1926.

Chattopadhyay, Basudeb, 'Panic Sunday in Calcutta: 14 June 1857', in Sabyasachi Bhattacharya (ed.), *Rethinking 1857*, New Delhi, Orient Black Swan, 2007.

Choudhury, Deep Kanta Lahiri, '"1857" and the communication crisis', in Sabyasachi Bhattacharya (ed.), *Rethinking 1857*, New Delhi, Orient Black Swan, 2007, pp.261–282.

Clark, F., *The East-India Register and Army List, 1850*, London, Wm. H. Allen. 1850.

*Clergy of Down and Dromore* (Part I: Fred Rankin. Part II: J.B. Leslie and Henry B. Swanzy), Belfast, Ulster Historical Foundation, 1996.

Cohen, Marilyn, 'Rural paths of capitalist development: Class formation, paternalism and gender in County Down's linen industry', in Lindsay

Proudfoot (ed.), *Down. History and Society: Interdisciplinary Essays on the History of an Irish County*, Dublin, Geography Publications, 1997.

Cook, S.B., *Imperial Affinities: Nineteenth Century Analogies and Exchanges Between India and Ireland*, Sage, London, 1993.

Cook, Scott B., 'The Irish Raj: Social origins and careers of Irishmen in the Indian civil service, 1855–1914', in *Journal of Social History*, vol. 20, no. 3, 1987, pp.507–529.

Crawford, W., 'Ulster landowners and the linen industry' in J. Ward and R. Wilson (eds), *Land and Industry in the Industrial Revolution*, Newton Abbott, David and Charles, 1971.

Dalrymple, William, *The Last Mughal: The Fall of Delhi, 1857*, London, Bloomsbury, 2009.

David, Saul, *The Indian Mutiny 1857*, London, Penguin, 2003.

Dean, J.B., and Leslie, H.B. (compilers), *Succession Lists of the Diocese of Dromore, Belfast, 1933*, reproduced in 1996 by the Ulster Historical Foundation under the title *Clergy of Down and Dromore*.

Farooqui, Mahmood (compiled and translated), *Besieged Voices from Delhi 1857*, with notes on the Mutiny Papers and governance in Delhi 1857 by the translator, New Delhi, Penguin Viking, 2010.

Ferguson, W.S., 'An illustrious Derryman. Sir Robert Montgomery, 1809–87; Indian administrator', *Derry Standard*, 24 May 1960 and 5 July 1960.

Flannery, Judith, *Christ Church Delgany, 1789–1990: Between the Mountains and the Sea*, Delgany, 1990.

Gillman, Claire, *The Best of Boys: Helping your Sons Keep their Teenage Years*, London, Pan, 2003.

Griffiths, Charles John (ed. Henry John Yonge), *A Narrative of the Siege of Delhi with an Account of the Mutiny at Ferozepore in 1857*, London, John Murray, 1910.

Gurrin, Brian, *A Century of Struggle in Delgany and Kilcoole: An Exploration of the Social Implication of Population Change in North-East Wicklow*, Dublin and Portland, Irish Academic Press, 2000.

Haigh, R.H., and Turner, P.W., *'Nickalsain' (The Life and Times of John Nicholson, Brigadier-General in the Army of the Honourable East India Company, 1822–1857)*, Military Affairs/Aerospace Historian Publishing, Kansas State University, 1980.

Harrison, A.T. (ed.), and Fraser, T.G. (historical essay), *The Graham Indian Mutiny papers*, Belfast, PRONI, 1980.

Hibbert, Christopher, *The Siege of Delhi: Mutiny Memories of an Old Officer by Richard Barter Late of the 75th Gordon Highlanders and the 15th Ludhiana Sikhs*, London, Folio Society, 1984.

Jeffery, Keith (ed.), *An Irish Empire? Aspects of Ireland and the British Empire*, Manchester University Press, 1996.

Kapur, Narinder, *The Irish Raj: Illustrated Stories about Irish in India and Indians in Ireland*, Greystone Press, Antrim, 1997.

Kenny, Kevin (ed.), *Ireland and the British Empire*, Oxford University Press, 2004.

Lawrence, John (ed. Audrey Woodiwiss), *Lawrence of Lucknow: A Story of Love*, London, Hodder and Stoughton, 1990.

Leasor, James, *The Red Fort: An Account of the Siege of Delhi*, London, W. Laurie, 1956.

Lee, Harold, *Brothers in the Raj: The Lives of John and Henry Lawrence*, Oxford University Press, 2002.

Leslie, J.B., *Clergy of Connor from Patrician Times to the Present Day*, Belfast, Ulster Historical Foundation, 1993.

Leslie, J.B., and Wallace, W.J.R., *Clergy of Dublin and Glendalough*, Belfast, Ulster Historical Foundation, 2001.

Lukács, Lajos, *Magyar Politikai Emigráció 1849–1867*, Budapest, Kossuth, 1984.

Mackey, Brian, *Lisburn: The Town and its People, 1873–1973*, Belfast, Blackstaff Press, 2000.

Montgomery, Brian, *Monty's Grandfather: Sir Robert Montgomery GCSI, KCB, LLD 1809–87, A Life's Service for the Raj*, Poole, Blandford Press, 1984.

O'leary, Patrick, *Servants of the Empire: The Irish in Punjab, 1881–1921*, Manchester University Press, 2011.

Paine, Derek, *A Pictorial History of Kilcoole, Newcastle, Newtownmountkennedy, Glen o' the Downs, Delgany, Greystones, 1860–1985: A Collection of Old Photographs*, Blackrock, Martello Press, 1996.

Pearson, Hesketh, *Hesketh Pearson by Himself*, London, Harper and Row, 1965.

Pearson, Hesketh, *The Hero of Delhi: A Life of John Nicholson, Saviour of India and a History of his Wars*, London, Collins, 1939; and Penguin, West Drayton, 1948 ed.

Pernau, Margrit, 'The Delhi Urdu Akhbar: Between Persian, Akhbarat and English newspapers', *The Annual of Urdu Studies*, 2003, pp. 105–131.

Proudfoot, Lindsay (ed.), *Down. History and Society: Interdisciplinary Essays on the History of an Irish County*, Dublin, Geography Publications, 1997.

Radcliffe, Rt Hon. Lord, *Sir Henry Lawrence; Centenary Address Delivered in the Common Hall of Magee University College Londonderry, 8 November 1957*, published by Foyle College Old Boys' Association.

Rankin, Kathleen, *The Linen Houses of the Lagan Valley: The Story of their Families*, Belfast, Ulster Historical Foundation, 2002.

Sen, Surendra Nath, *Eighteen Fifty-Seven*, Delhi, Government of India, 1857.

Silvestri, Michael, *Ireland and India: Nationalism, Empire and Memory*, Basingstoke, Palgrave Macmillan, 2009.

Singh, P.R., 'Re-assessing writings on the rebellion: Savarkar to Surendra Nath Sen', in Sabyasachi Bhattacharya (ed.), *Rethinking 1857*, New Delhi, Orient Black Swan, 2007, pp.44–57.

Syiemlieh, David R., 'Historiography of literature and sources on the uprising of 1857 in North East India', in Sabyasachi Bhattacharya, (ed.), *Rethinking 1857*, New Delhi, Orient Black Swan, 2007, pp.210–218.

Terrell, Richard (ed.), *John Chalmers: Letters from the Indian Mutiny, 1857–1859*, Norwich, Michael Russell, 1992.

*The Poetical Works of Thomas Moore*, London, Frederick Warrne, n.d.

Trollope, Joanna, *Britannia's Daughters: Women of the British Empire*, London, Random House, 2006.

## ENTRIES IN THE *DICTIONARY OF IRISH BIOGRAPHY*, ROYAL IRISH ACADEMY AND CAMBRIDGE UNIVERSITY PRESS, 2009

Bellett, John Gifford (1794?x1797?–1864): Linde Lunney, pp.431–432.

Daly, Sir Henry Dermot (1853–1935): David Murphy, vol. 3, p.23.

Nicholson, John (1822–1857): David Murphy, vol. 6, pp.915–917.

Pottinger, Eldred (1811–1843): Bridget Hourican, vol. 8, pp.244–245.

Ross, Sir John (1853–1935): William Murphy, vol. 8, pp.616–617.

## ENTRIES IN THE *OXFORD DICTIONARY OF NATIONAL BIOGRAPHY*, OXFORD UNIVERSITY PRESS, 2004

Broadfoot, George (1807–1845): A.J. Arbuthnot, revised by Roger T. Stearn.

Chamberlain, Sir Neville Bowles (1807–1845): E.M. Lloyd, revised by James Lunt.

Cocks, Arthur Herbert (1819–1881): H.M. Stephens, revised by Katherine Prior.

Cotton, Sir Sydney John (1792–1874): H.M. Chichester, revised by James Lunt.

Edwardes, Sir Herbert Benjamin Edwardes (1819–1868): T.R. Moreman.

Hogg, James Macnaghten McGarel (1823–1890): John Davis.

Hogg, Sir James Weir (1790–1876): G.F.R. Barker, revised by Katherine Prior.

Nicholson, John (1822–1857): R.H. Vetch, revised by Ainslie T. Emtree.

Olpherts, Sir William (1822–1902): T.R. Moreman.

## WEBSITES

historyview.blogspot.com/2008/12/brigadier-and-brigadier-general-john.html – Accessed 22 July 2009.

www.reuters.com/assets/print?aid=USBRE9980BD20131009 – Accessed 6 January 2014.

www.johnnicholsongreatmutiny.wordpress.com Accessed 22 February 2014.

en.wikipedia.org/wiki/John_Nicholson_%28East_India_Company_officer%29 – Accessed 1 March 2014.

imagesonline.uk/?service=page&action=show_home_page&language=en – Accessed 1 November 2014.

www.herbs2000.com/homeopathy/colocynthis.htm – Accessed 18 April 2014.

www.vithoulkas.com/en/books-study/online-materia-medica/2620.html [International Academy of Classical Homeopathy] – Accessed 18 April 2014.

en.wikipedia.org/wiki/Muhammad_Hayat_Khan – Accessed 22 July 2015.

www.seth-smith.org.uk/familytree/trees/urmstonbrabazon.html – Accessed 20 September 2015.

# Index